COMEDY
New Perspectives

Published twice a year, Spring and Winter, New York Literary Forum acknowledges the support
of the Division of Humanities and the Arts, Hunter College, C.U.N.Y., and its dean Gerald Freund.
Single volume, $7.50; subscription (two volumes), $13.00; libraries, $9.50 per volume; discounts
for course adoption upon request. Outside the United States, add $2.00 per volume except in Canada
add $1.00 only per volume. Prices subject to change.
Send orders and changes of address to: New York Literary Forum
                                          P.O. Box 262
                                          Lenox Hill Station
                                          New York, N.Y. 10021
To submit a manuscript, send the original and one copy together with a self-addressed, stamped
envelope to Professor Jeanine P. Plottel, General Editor, at above address. Manuscript should follow
the MLA Style Sheet.

COMEDY
New Perspectives

EDITED BY
MAURICE CHARNEY

VOLUME 1

NEW YORK LITERARY FORUM

NEW YORK • SPRING 1978

Library of Congress Cataloging in Publication Data
Main entry under title:

Comedy.

    (New York literary forum; v. 1   ISSN 0149-1040)
    Bibliography: p.
    Includes index.
    1. Comedy—Addresses, essays, lectures.
2. Comic, The—Addresses, essays, lectures.
I. Charney, Maurice. II. Series.
PN1922.C58   809.2'52   77-18626
ISBN 0-931196-00-0

# CONTENTS

Editor's Preface

JEANINE PARISIER PLOTTEL

New York Literary Forum was founded to study, elucidate, and inter-
pret important subjects worthy of investigation; to assert the value of
diversity and plurality of approaches; and to reflect the main currents
of literature without regard to methodological and geographical limitations. The locus of its title—*New York*—suggests not only many
cultures, languages, idioms, and styles but also a modern venture supported by some of the city's international scholars, critics, and teachers
of literature, and encouraged by the Hunter College Division of Humanities and the Arts. *Literary Forum* implies an appropriate structure
where the many voices and tones of modern critical inquiry, here and
abroad, meet to order, direct, and shape texts.

The inaugural issue, *Comedy: New Perspectives,* is a model for
future issues. The specific topic with which it deals was developed and
prepared by a foremost expert, Maurice Charney, Distinguished Professor at Rutgers University, whose latest book, *Comedy High and Low:
An Introduction to the Experience of Comedy,* is being published by
Oxford University Press. The aim is to bring together the best papers
about comedy so as to present an important book in which a significant
constant of our culture is analyzed, reviewed, and explored. The practice of including original texts and documents such as Norman Shapiro's translation of Georges Feydeau's play *Hortense a dit: "Je m'en
fous!"* (the first time this play has appeared in English) will be a regular
feature of future issues. Our readers can also look forward to parodies,
poetry, long reviews, translations, unpublished letters, texts by young
writers, among other special features.

Forthcoming volumes of *New York Literary Forum* include issues
on *Intertextuality* (how texts allude to other texts), *André Malraux:
Metamorphosis and Imagination,* and *The Occult in Language and
Literature.* Featured will be some of the most modern analyses published anywhere to date. While the list of authors reads like a
veritable *Who's Who* of contemporary criticism, it also will include
the best papers of young scholars: Juan V. Agudiez, George Bauer,
Michel Beaujour, Haskell Block, Germaine Brée, LeRoy C. Breunig,

Pierre Bockel, Jean Carduner, Philippe Carrard, Mary Ann Caws, Hanna Charney, Maurice Charney, Tom Conley, Martine de Courcel, Françoise Dorenlot, Jean-Marie Drot, Claudia Gosselin, Susan Handelman, James R. Hewitt, Renée Hubert, Bettina Knapp, Charles Krance, Reinhard Kuhn, Walter Langlois, Gérard Le Coat, Marie-Rose Logan, Henri Peyre, Hermine Riffaterre, Michael Riffaterre, Rizel Sigele, Albert Sonnenfeld, Bryan Thompson, Micheline Tison-Braun, Kurt Weinberg.

These outstanding authors, together with an index, notes, and bibliography which will appear in each volume, make *New York Literary Forum* an indispensable reference for teachers, scholars, students, and librarians. Finally, the multiplicity of points of view, the examination of theory together with practice, the one illustrating the other, will afford an opportunity to scrutinize the scholarly scene of the late seventies as it develops and shapes Anglo-American and continental criticism of the coming decade.

Introduction

MAURICE CHARNEY

The "new perspectives" promised in our title are not meant as an idle puff for novel fulfillments beyond the capacity of a mere editor. It is difficult to write about comedy without saying something new. The subject has not been formalized, or perhaps even rigidified, as has the study of tragedy, which proceeds from Aristotle's *Poetics* and the abundant commentaries thereon. The theory of comedy has no classic text, not even Bergson's imaginative essay on laughter or Freud's troubled speculations in *Jokes and Their Relation to the Unconscious*. The contributors to this volume felt especially pleased to be asked to write on comedy—pleased and perhaps a little guilty to be allowed such a rich self-indulgence. It is difficult to break the hidden link between producing comedy and writing about comedy.

Our volume is divided into six distinct parts, although there is a good deal of potential overlapping between theory and practice; and the literary examples are generally meant to support some special view of comedy. In Part 1, the writers chiefly address themselves to the blackness of comedy, its connections with anxiety and fear-producing situations. John O'Connor's essay derives from Aristotle's dictum that comedy is a species of the ugly or grotesque, and chivalric laughter in late medieval and Renaissance romances reminds us of our own "sick" jokes. Tyranny of the most overwhelming and hopeless kind tends to rely on a deeply irrational (and therefore comic) metaphysics, as Daniel Gerould so strongly demonstrates. Although pursuing other specific points, the essays of Mathew Winston and Morton Gurewitch offer copious examples to support this close tie between comedy and anxiety. For the Jacobean period in England, Malcolm Kiniry underscores the amoral realism of comedy, stripped of any comforting demonstration of economic or moral lessons.

Part 2 is more specifically focussed on comic theory. Anne Paolucci shows that Hegel had a significant theory of comedy (as well as of tragedy), and the essays of Herbert Levowitz and Margaret Ganz make abundant use of psychoanalytic theory. Laughter has its own psychodynamics that help us accommodate ourselves to bitter truths. Margaret Ganz's group of Don Juan playwrights avoids tragedy by various techniques of devaluation.

Shakespeare has the distinction of having a section to himself, Part 3, in which the tragic-comic issues of *Twelfth Night* are debated. Ralph Berry's "autumnal" *Twelfth Night* of the contemporary theater is set against a festive *Twelfth Night* conceived on different principles by Maurice Charney. Charles Frey also emphasizes comic values in his piece on *As You Like It*. In both of these plays, much depends on the reader or audience's assumptions about what to expect from comedy.

A mixed group of contemporary authors is the subject of Part 4: Stoppard, Behrman, Southern, and Hoffenberg. Coppélia Kahn makes the essential link between Stoppard's *Travesties* and Wilde's *Importance of Being Earnest* and tries to explicate the larger significance of parodic art. Cyrus Hoy deftly places S. N. Behrman as a comic dramatist; this essay should rekindle interest in Behrman's very considerable achievement in the American theater. *Candy* doesn't fit comfortably with "high" literature, but William Walling makes a case for its cultural appropriateness in relation to the literature and politics of its time.

Comic Nostalgia, in Part 5, indulges in a bit of nostalgia of its own. By invoking the lost world of the silents, B. H. Fussell reminds us that "a pratfall can be a beautiful thing"—an incontrovertible and irresistable proposition, no doubt, as is the wistful, pastoral world of radio comedy of the thirties that is conjured up by Don Wiener. In the best sense of the term, we may include the superb journalist, A. J. Liebling, in this domain of "pop" culture. Elmer Blistein's short piece revives our delight in this splendidly intelligent bon vivant.

Part 6: Texts and Documents is really an appendix to the critical essays in the previous five sections, and *New York Literary Forum* intends to print texts and documents as a regular feature of its volumes. No apologies need be offered for Feydeau's very late, very mad, and very aggressively lubricious farce, *Hortense Said, "No Skin Off My Ass!"* which is here translated into English for the first time by Norman R. Shapiro, who has already established himself as the leading translator of Feydeau. Without this invaluable text, how could we ever realize how much we had been deprived of by not having this play available in English!

Readers are invited to indulge themselves in the diversity of points of view expressed in the essays that follow. We have cultivated a healthy, if not actually luxuriant, pluralism at the expense of any single methodological commitment. The one unifying mystery is the nature of comedy itself with the ingenious laughter that seems to validate the comic experience.

PART 1

ASSUMPTIONS OF
COMEDY:
TYRANNY, BLACKNESS,
IRONY, DEFORMITY,
AND
SOCIAL UTILITY

Tyranny and Comedy

DANIEL GEROULD

Comedy thrives on tyranny. Here is a proposition that can lead in a number of different directions. As a matter of theater history, we know that farces and light comedies have flourished on the stage under totalitarian regimes and brutal military occupations. Comedy, in such a context, is nothing more than a shallow escape or, perhaps, a tool of manipulation on the part of the authorities. If, on the other hand, we examine the psychology of the innumerable jokes directed at dictators by the victims suffering unjustly at their hands, even in the depths of secret prisons and concentration camps, the comic spirit under tyranny emerges as a positive force, necessary for survival and, indeed, liberating and heroic. Systematic repression induces laughter as a healthy outburst. And provided we define tyranny in the broadest sense, it is surprising how many of the traditional targets of comedy, since its earliest days, have been tyrants. Consider, for example, the *senex* of Roman drama, the pedants and doctors of commedia dell'arte, and all the despotic parents and jealous husbands peopling the stage since the time of Molière and the English Restoration dramatists.

Comedy characteristically relishes and ridicules tyrants.

Among possible approaches to the topic, I have chosen to single out one striking phenomenon: the comic portrayal in drama of the all-powerful political tyrant wielding the apparatus of mass oppression and ruthlessly crushing the human rights of others on a vast scale. By using such a peculiarly modern and troublesome test case for standard comic theory, I should like to push back certain supposedly fixed boundaries of comedy and to reformulate some of its laws.[1] Can savage tyranny, with its reign of terror and death, be treated as comical? Can even the indiscriminate victimization of the guiltless be laughable?

Traditional theories say no. According to Plato in the *Philebus*, the object of ridicule must not have the power to harm, or else fear will prevent laughter.[2] In "Notes on the Comic," W. H. Auden finds that Hitler is no fit subject for humor, declaring that we cannot consider comic what we hate.[3] On these grounds, the comic despot who is both hateful and powerful becomes an impossibility. And yet the evidence will show that in actual fact the loathsome dictator is by his very nature grotesquely ludicrous, and the terrible plight of the tyrannized may well be equally preposterous. The arbitrary exercise of absolute power by a deranged tyrant can be a source of comic pleasure to an audience—and comic, not in spite of the arbitrariness, but precisely because of it. The ridiculous and the terrifying coalesce.

In an unusual transformation of an older comic pattern, the clever rogue swindling his gullible victims becomes the twentieth-century tyrant using the totalitarian state to defraud his citizens of their freedom. The modern era of tyrannies (which, according to the French historian Elie Halévy, began in August 1914, when the coercive state first gained total control over man's daily life and thought)[4] has made it possible for the traditional comic relationship of duper and duped to exist on a new scale and in a new dimension—those of the nation and of public life—which had previously been reserved for serious drama. Comic scoundrels like Volpone and Mosca now become heads of state and usurp dictatorial powers; their foolish prey is the masses of people who, out of stupidity and servility, actively collaborate in their own enslavement. The frequent blows and beatings of ancient farce grow magnified and multiplied into large-scale torture and killing.

During the period between world wars in which Hitler, Mussolini, and Stalin rose to power and turned Europe into a madhouse, a handful of farsighted playwrights, obsessed with a similar vision and themselves witnesses and victims of dictatorship, dramatized the absurd spectacle of tyranny in a number of intensely theatrical works for the stage. Among the most brilliant of these plays about comic tyrants are *Gyubal Wahazar* (1921) and *The Cuttlefish* (1922) by the Polish avant-gardist Stanisław Ignacy Witkiewicz; Jules Romains's *Dr. Knock* (1923); Ernst Toller's *Wotan Unbound* (1923); *Angelica* (1928/29) by the Italian exile Leo Ferrero; *The Naked King* (1933), *The Shadow* (1940), and *The Dragon* (1941) by the Russian children's author Yevgeni Shvarts; and Bertolt Brecht's *The Resistible Rise of Arturo Ui* (1941). Here are the principal examples upon which to base any theories concerning comedy and political tyranny.[5]

But it is a mistake to think that the subject is an exclusively twentieth-century one.[6] The Renaissance, another spectacular era of tyrannies, was also productive of comic dictators, as witness Herod the Great, an ever-popular figure of ridicule and loathing since the late Middle Ages, and Shakespeare's Richard III, the prototype for subsequent upstart rogues cheating and killing their way to the top of the political ladder. Writing in 1523 of the German princes of his day, Martin Luther commented that God Almighty must have driven such rulers mad, observing that tyrants "are usually the greatest fools or the worst scoundrels in the world"[7]—a view shared by all the playwrights here under consideration. Already in Luther's formulation we can start to perceive one of the prime reasons why tyranny naturally lends itself to the comic sense of existence: buffoons, swindlers, and demented charlatans, no matter what the scope of their folly and vice, cannot be treated seriously or accorded tragic dignity.

In nineteenth-century czarist Russia, where stagnant institutional despotism prevailed, the small cogs in the machinery of tyranny—themselves both the victims and perpetrators of the oppressive system—become richly comic figures in the works of Nikolai Gogol and Alexander Sukhovo-Kobylin. Fear of sudden arrest and imprisonment, confession to uncommitted crimes, universal mistrust and suspicion in the face of swarms of spies and informers, and gradually deepening terror are all transformed, through the comic vision of these Russian masters, into the preposterous events of a farcical nightmare. In France, at the end of the century, Alfred Jarry's *Ubu Roi* made it possible for audiences to enjoy the excesses and outrages of arbitrary power and even to identify with the moronic barbarian who commits such atrocities with slobbish zest.

Herod, Shakespeare, the Russians, and Jarry provide antecedents to the comic portrayal of the dictator in the Hitler years. Since then, in contemporary theater, we have become familiarized with the comic dimensions of tyranny as reflected by the bizarre shifts in power between Pozzo and Lucky in *Waiting for Godot* and the thundering herds of conformists in *Rhinoceros,* as well as in dozens of other works. As a recognizable theme in dramatic literature, comic despots and despotism are well established, even classic, and I have briefly sketched the scope and ancestry of the topic. Now it is time to enunciate laws and working principles governing the comic treatment of tyranny.

Metamorphosis is the modus operandi of dictatorship: human nature and human society are remade. Tyranny systematically transforms its subjects into automatons; the tyrant himself is an immense

Figure 1. *Gyubal Wahazar,* from a production at the Teatr Narodowy, Warsaw, March 1968, which was stopped by the censor after the final dress rehearsal. "Dr. Rypmann, the Albanian ambassador goes to the yellow chamber," the tyrant roars, frothing at the mouth. "Get a room ready for special tortures. . . . Arrest everyone." (Photo: W. Prazuch)

puppet. Here Henri Bergson's basic postulate—that laughter results when the mechanical is encrusted on the living—finds a perfect illustration, but the process of mechanization is carried out on such a vast scale as to be both ludicrous and terrifying. Instead of one rigid eccentric quarantined by laughter in the midst of a healthy, living society, as envisaged by the French philosopher, the comedy of tyranny presents a single all-powerful maniac who forces the entire world to conform to his monstrous notions. The Bergsonian "transformation of a person into a thing" applies to everyone in the realm, for the dictator regards human beings solely as objects.

In Witkiewicz's *Gyubal Wahazar, or Along the Cliffs of the Absurd*—"A Non-Euclidean Drama in Four Acts"[8]—the absolute dictator, Wahazar, is transforming all the women in the sixth-dimensional continuum over which he rules either into Mechanical Mothers or androgynous Masculettes (see Figure 1). Although he beats and abuses his subjects with savage glee, his Onlyness—as Wahazar is called—considers himself a martyr and benefactor to mankind, regimenting human beings only in order to restore them to the homogeneous happiness of the primitive tribe and of the anthill and wasp's nest.[9] At the same time, the dictator's private scientist, the sinister Dr. Rypmann, is conducting strange experiments involving "the fission of psychic atoms" and will soon be able to fabricate new Wahazars out of hyenas, jackals, or even bedbugs. Thus his Onlyness, who has imagined that he is the sole deity, can be mechanically reproduced. In fact, his subjects refer to Wahazar as an old puppet, and large Gyubal dolls have started to appear on the market, while in Albania lesser tyrants are already imitating his Onlyness.[10] When Wahazar is finally assassinated by Morbidetto, head of the secret police, the tyrant's glands are cut out and transplanted still warm into a senile old man who then becomes Wahazar II.[11]

Comic proliferation and reduplication overtake not only the tyrant's automated subjects but also the tyrant. The metamorphosis into brutes and beasts, traditional to comedy, itself undergoes a transformation in the machine age; as science and technology become the tools of the tyrant, a system of mechanical indoctrination can forge herds of identical, docile fools ready to be manipulated like marionettes.

Jules Romains's *Dr. Knock* likewise is a drama of tyranny that explores the remarkable power of pseudoscience allied to technology in bringing the masses into total submission. Ostensibly a satire on medicine—a traditional subject for French farce since the Middle Ages—Romains's comedy shows a small-time con man availing himself of all the modern techniques of mass production and advertising in order to create an infallible propaganda machine and achieve absolute power over others. Although it still has one foot firmly planted in the festive world of old-fashioned farce, *Dr. Knock* is perhaps the most prophetic of all plays about the growth and operation of the totalitarian corporate state because it reveals the tyrant's extraordinary ability to galvanize and transform the community by giving the people a purpose in life, no matter how bogus that purpose may be.

Using only the simplest materials and devices of farce, Romains has written a universal parable about tyranny, without secret police, killing, or any sort of violence. Yet by the end of this seemingly light-hearted comedy, the free, open, nineteenth-century countryside and village of Acts I and II have become transformed into the white, sterile, regimented world of totalitarian dictatorship that anticipates the anti-utopias of Zamyatin's *We* and Huxley's *Brave New World*. Through Dr. Knock's hypnotic genius, everyone in the small town has been made to imagine that he is sick and has been transofrmed into a patient and then put to bed in the local hotel, now metamorphosed into a hospital. The subjective mania of Molière's "le malade imaginaire" has been artificially imposed on an entire population for manipulative purposes, thereby satisfying the deepest needs of both the tyrant and the tyrannized. Rendered mentally ill, a human society becomes refashioned as a smoothly functioning machine.

The final revelation of the nature of the new community—the "redeemed society" in Northrop Frye's Mythos of Spring[12]—comes at the very end of the play after night has fallen. Instead of the usual hymeneal celebration preparatory to the consummation of the marriage that serves as the traditional denouement of comedy, the collective rectal temperature-taking at precisely 10 P.M. by all of Dr. Knock's several hundred patients becomes the appropriate ritual in honor of the new "medical existence"—a perfect image of the synthetic, asexual, and technologically efficient civilization ushered in by totalitarianism.[13]

In another parable play that demonstrates exactly how the dictator comes to power, Brecht's *The Resistible Rise of Arturo Ui,* blind greed, masked as capitalist ideology, is revealed as the motive force driving human beings to submit to tyranny. The tyrant is exposed as a simple bandit whose field of operations has been extended to the public arena. In discussing his own "great historical gangster play," Brecht stresses that comedy is the most effective way to destroy the dangerous respect commonly felt for great tyrants.

> The petty rogue whom the rulers permit to become a rogue on the grand scale can occupy a special position in roguery, but not in our attitude to history. Anyway there is truth in the principle that comedy is less likely than tragedy to fail to take human suffering seriously enough.[14]

In other words, comedy—rather than tragedy or melodrama, both of which magnify evil and render it exceptional—is the best antidote to the tyrant's pretenses to grandeur because the comic spirit revels in universal pettiness and vulgar complicity, reducing the mighty dictator to a properly banal, everyday plane. "It is this reverence for killers that has to be done away with," Brecht writes; "whatever applies to small situations must be made to apply to big ones."[15] Through the device of microscopic reduction, Brecht in *Arturo Ui* shrinks Hitler and Nazism to a bloodthirsty Chicago gangster and a protection racket called the Cauliflower Trust, just as Romains in *Dr. Knock* even more drastically contracts the figure of the modern demagogue to a farcical quack doctor in a tiny provincial village. On these reduced stages, we can perceive step by step, as in the numbered pictures of a cartoon, how Knock and Ui gradually seize possession of a community and gain complete control of the minds and bodies of its inhabitants through the spreading of terror.

While maintaining exactly the same equation between small and large that Brecht demands, Jarry in *Ubu Roi* works by expansion rather than contraction. Père Ubu is blown up out of all proportion and assumes a rank perfectly unbefitting to his character (see Figure 2). In Jarry's monstrous farce we are shown how a crude nobody—the personification of bourgeois stupidity and mediocrity—can become a great actor on the world-historical stage, on which, in the company of kings and emperors, he commands armies and determines the destiny of nations by robbing, plundering, and slaughtering along with the best of them. All of human history is a bloody farce. Ubu's elevation to the realm of a Shakespearian monarch proves that anyone—a hyena, a jackal, or even a bedbug—can become transformed into a powerful dictator.

As a moralist, Brecht would have us believe that the tyrant-rogue is discredited through the process of comic deflation. Certainly, through inflation, Père Ubu, the contemptible clown with unlimited power, the gigantic guignolesque marionette with base appetites, elicits our sympathy and gives us comic pleasure when he abuses others as well as when he himself is abused. In *Le Symbolisme au théâtre,* Jacques Robichez suggests that Ubu appeals to all that is most trivial and gross within us: "he demands the complicity of our least avowable instincts."[16]

In "Thoughts on Dictatorship," Leo Ferrero, who fled from Mussolini's Italy to France in 1928, comes to similar conclusions about the rise of fascism, finding the reverence for tyrants to lie deep in human nature:

> The popularity of dictators and our admiration for them can be explained by the life of the instinct, by our love for ourselves. We identify with them . . . The dictator is only the projection on another person of the desire to find ourselves in an imaginary situation where this frenetic love of

True portrait of Monsieur Ubu

Figure 2. Ubu, in one of Jarry's drawings, appears at one and the same time bellicose and dim-witted, sinister and absurd. As portrayed by Jarry, Ubu—it has been said—represents a composite portrait of Himmler, Goering, and Hitler.

self could be satisfied.[17]

In Ferrero's satirical drama, *Angelica,* the inhabitants of the Fascist City of Masks are all the old commedia dell'arte characters who seek new roles under the totalitarian regime; Arlequin, Scaramouche, Pantalon, Pulcinella, and Tartaglia eventually find positions of security, wealth, and power through successful accommodation to dictatorship. Only the hero and heroine appear to stand apart from this world of corruption, for they are Orlando and Angelica, the chivalrous knight and his lady from Ariosto's heroic Renaissance epic. But love and honor can no longer survive in a modern dictatorship, and no one—especially not the beautiful Angelica—can tolerate Orlando's gauche and naive insistence on fighting for freedom.

In the commedia world of masks, the populace grows accustomed to tyranny and learns to live comfortably in slavery, resisting and resenting any attempts to restore its lost liberty. The tyrant Regent—an elegantly dressed poet and playwright with sense of style and theatrical spectacle—is about to violate liberty in the person of Angelica on the eve of her marriage, according to the ancient *droit du seigneur.* The people approve of the Regent's staging of the event as he approaches on a purple carpet, illumined by colored spotlights and flaming torches; and Angelica—the perfidious ideal of freedom—actually wishes to be raped. Although Orlando succeeds in provoking a revolution and temporarily brings back a republican form of government, the Regent, as he is being deposed, explains to the noble-minded hero that the fundamental stupidity, pettiness, and envy of the commedia citizens make them willing to follow any imposing strong man. Democracy proves to be chaos, tyranny is soon restored, and Orlando is betrayed and shot by Angelica. Describing what life is like under the Regent's dictatorship, one of the masks declares:

> There are no laws any more. It is the regime of the arbitrary.
> Spies, police, agents, traitors abound.

Such a quintessential perception corresponds to John Locke's concise definition: "Wherever law ends, tyranny begins."[18] And herein lies the crucial issue—under dictatorship the comic results from the very fact that all normal laws are suspended and the arbitrary reigns. As in the wildest farce, every restraint is gone. The famous scene in Jarry's play in which Ubu takes the Nobles, Magistrates, and Financiers and one after the other dispatches them "down the trap door" shows how total capriciousness combined with absolute power can create comedy.[19] Senseless cruelty and pandemic injustice, in becoming the norm, become preposterous; if whole classes of people can be arrested and liquidated for no reason, the world is a madhouse. Ubu's disembraining machine is used on friend and foe alike. We are in the realm of pure nonsense.

In *The Other Kingdom,* a study of life in the concentration camps, that ultimate form of tyranny, the French author David Rousset sees Ubu as the reigning spirit and god of the camps and speaks of "the fascinating discovery of humor, not so much as a projection of the personality, but as an objective pattern of the universe."

> Ubu and Kafka cease to be literary fantasies and become component elements of the living world. The discovery of this humor enabled many of us to survive.[20]

TERROR AND COMEDY

The arbitrary arrest of a single individual in an essentially ordered and just world is an outrage, arousing feelings of pity and indignation. If, however, millions of people are unjustly arrested—as happened under Stalin—and then those who arrested them are themselves arrested by agents who will later be arrested, the arbitrariness becomes all-inclusive, self-propelling, and grotesquely laughable. In this absurd and frightening realm of the totally arbitrary, there is neither freedom nor necessity, and thus tragedy is an impossibility. Any realistic portrayal of such a world in drama is ruled out because life under tyranny lacks known probabilities and produces no sense of reality; and it is for these reasons that the playwrights under consideration go for their models to farce and to fable.

Tyrannical power is so arbitrary in its sudden shifts that those who arrogantly wield it at one moment are unexpectedly struck down by it at the next. The tyrant invariably rewards his own loyal henchmen by killing them; Ui has his lieutenant Ernesto Roma (Ernst Röhm) gunned down, and Gyubal Wahazar personally shoots Baron Oskar von den Binden-Gnumben, his commander of the guard, who has just dutifully beaten a crowd of defenseless prisoners. From such turns of the wheel of blind fortune, represented by the dictator's capricious will, a bizarre sort of justice may even be seen to emerge in the form of a crude punitive nemesis that levels all to the same base destiny. Regardless of deserts, everyone goes "down the trap door." Even the tyrant himself is subject to the vicissitudes of arbitrary power and feels constantly threatened by the terrors of arrest, imprisonment, and execution. Pursuing the insane logic of his own absolute authority, Wahazar declares: "I can condemn myself to death if I feel like it—if I become convinced that I'm wrong." After putting all his followers—including the secret police chief—in an underground dungeon, his Onlyness unexpectedly finds that he has been imprisoned along with them by some mysterious higher power of arbitrariness. Witkiewicz's THEY—those higher, faceless oppressors who control all our destinies, even those of dictators—are utterly inscrutable and unpredictable.

The anonymous, institutional tyranny of the state and its organs represents a subject for comedy of even greater scope than the tyranny of the individual. Particular despots may come and go, but the despotic state continues triumphant. In czarist Russia, for example, tyranny was deeply entrenched, and its inflexible bureaucracy and ubiquitous police agents gave rise to a rich literature of comic dread in the face of arbitrary power.

Fear of arrest by the authorities for crimes real or imaginary haunts the imaginations of Gogol's abject, petty-minded cheats and swindlers. In his great comic novel, *Dead Souls,* the enigmatic hero, Chichikov, travels about Russia buying up "dead souls" (serfs who are no longer living but still remain on the tax lists), causing the officials he meets to wonder "whether he was the sort of man who was to be seized and detained as an undesirable character, or whether he was the sort of person who might seize and detain them all himself as undesirable characters."[21] This ambiguous state of apprehension and uncertainty is the inevitable result of the ever-changing winds of arbitrariness in the unstable world of tyranny. In *The Inspector General,* Gogol's masterpiece for the stage, Khlestakov, the penniless clerk from St. Petersburg, waits fearfully in his provincial hotel room, expecting to be arrested for debts by the town officials, while at the same time the corrupt town officials gather nervously at the Mayor's, expecting to be arrested by Khlestakov—whom they imagine to be the dreaded inspector general. At the end of the play, the "real" inspector general—that higher power of absolute authority always waiting in the wings—is announced, literally petrifying in a frozen tableau all the petty tyrants for what is the most spectacular *coup de théâtre* in Russian drama.

Gogol's successor in the art of grotesque comedy, Sukhovo-Kobylin, brought to perfection the comic terrors of police interrogation in *The Death of Tarelkin,* which the author—who spent seven nightmarish years in and out of Russian courts and jails on charges of murdering his mistress—calls a "comedy-farce." Here the itch to arrest and the conviction that everyone is a traitor engaged in heinous conspiracies reach such colossal proportions that the madness threatens to engulf all of Russia. The last half of Sukhovo-Kobylin's comedy-farce takes place in a gloomy, dimly lit police station, where loutish rogues in police uniforms conduct their investigations with the aid of broomsticks and a specially devised human beating machine constructed out of their moronic subordinates. Guilt by association is the fundamental principle of justice, innocent landowners and merchants are sent off to "the secret chamber," and terrified victims name as their accomplices "all Petersburg and all Moscow" and readily confess to being vampires and werewolves who have sucked the blood of their neighbors. The interrogators and torturers grow so enchanted with their work that they declare:

Everything belongs to us now. We'll demand all of Russia!
... There aren't any people here—just monsters ... All they
deserve is Siberia and chains ... That's why we have to establish a rule of subjecting every one to arrest! ... The machinery
will operate by itself.[22]

In *The Death of Tarelkin* the reign of institutional terror is presented by means of the techniques of nineteenth-century comedy-
vaudeville, which Sukhovo-Kobylin knew and admired from his visits
to Paris.[23] "Because of its humorous character," the author explains in
a note, "the play should be performed in a lively, gay, loud manner—
avec entrain."[24] The Russian equivalent of Père Ubu's disembraining
machine and trapdoor for disposing of unwanted social classes, Sukhovo-Kobylin's police-station state functions automatically, generating its own savage energy.

HUMAN NATURE AND TYRANNY

A later Soviet satirist in the same tradition, Yevgeni Shvarts (who
survived all the Stalin years by writing children's literature) had an
excellent vantage point from which to observe how the machinery of
tyranny operates and maintains itself in power; and the worst traits
of human nature, which are brought out by dictatorship, become the
subject of his mockery in a series of brilliantly allusive fairy-tale plays.
Shvarts's parables can apply to any totalitarian regime, but for reasons
of prudence in the USSR it has usually been argued that they are directed only against fascism; for example, in *The Naked King*, the
tyrant's anti-Semitism, book burning, and threats of sterilization may
be seen as direct references to Nazi Germany, but of course the absurd
cult of personality, the intellectual dishonesty, and the servile, creaking
bureaucracy that characterize the court all strike closer to home (see
Figure 3).[25] Written in the style of a slapstick comedy and music-hall
revue, *The Naked King* renders hilarious the stupidity and cruelty of a
highly personalized dictatorship and suggests that it can be destroyed
quickly once the truth about the king's nakedness is publicly acknowledged.
  Unfortunately, human beings prefer lies, and the stubborn persis-
tence of tyranny becomes the theme of Shvarts's later dramatic fable,
The Dragon, whose hero, Lancelot—like Ferrero's Orlando—is an
idealistic knight-errant fighting for the freedom of docile slaves who do
not wish to be free. Over the years of accommodation to the Dragon's
totalitarian regime, the inhabitants of Shvarts's fairy-tale kingdom
have grown so accustomed to all forms of moral corruption that they
accept bribery, spying, informing, and even killing as normal, everyday occurrences. To these deformed human beings it seems only

Figure 3. Shvarts's *Naked King,* as portrayed by the Polish illustrator and stage designer Daniel Mróz, reveals the tyrant to be a senile deadweight patiently borne on the backs of his submissive subjects. From an edition of Shvarts's plays published by Wydawnictwo Literackie, Cracow, 1965.

natural that a young girl should be sacrificed yearly to the tyrant—much as Angelica is to be offered up to the Regent. After all, the towns-people reason, the Dragon is quite nice—a sentimental middle-aged gentleman, slightly deaf in one ear, who smiles frequently and "drops by like an old friend." And besides, he wards off all other dragons who might oppress them.

Evil in *The Dragon* is perfectly banal, existing solely because of the lethargy of those who endure it. When Lancelot challenges the passive citizens to resist and accuses them of collaboration—"But it turns out that you, my friends, are bandits too"—the populace turns against its savior as a troublemaker. A typical response is: "I was taught to be what I am."[26]

Debunking legends of dragons and heroes who are supernaturally powerful, Shvarts shows that tyranny persists even after the tyrant is killed, often in a more insidious form, because despotism lives in the hearts of the tyrannized. Once Lancelot has slain the dragon, the sick-ness of conformity turns out to be so deeply rooted that the system automatically continues; and the Mayor, who now becomes dictator, proves still more dangerous because he masquerades under slogans about democracy and freedom. Cowardice, a traditional comic vice, is given a new dimension: the collective guilt of complicity and the moral cowardice of capitulation are attributed to an entire people. Adapta-tion to the group, which in Bergson's theory is the proper corrective to folly, becomes under tyranny the mark of the greatest fools and scoun-drels. At the end of *The Dragon,* Lancelot concludes that it will be a long, hard struggle to bring freedom to such human beings: "The Drag-on has to be killed in each and every one of them"—a perception only slightly less melancholy than Orlando's dying recognition that the commedia masks do not wish to be saved from their own degeneracy.

Shvarts's third great parable, *The Shadow* (written when Stalin and Hitler were allies), presents a bleaker picture of a "mad, unhappy world" in which even the fairy-tale princess, like Angelica, is herself a corrupt betrayer of the naïve, honest hero. Those in power are preda-tory monsters and cannibals, afraid of everything and everyone, includ-ing themselves, and unwilling to forgive the scholar-hero for "being such a good man." In this universe of total distrust, false appearances are all that matters. "Smile, we're being watched" becomes the only expression of gaiety, and the executioner's block has been set up "in the pink drawing room, beside a statue of Cupid, and disguised with forget-me-nots."[27] The corruption lies so deep in human nature that the hero discovers that the tyrant is his very shadow and alter ego and that he must go to his death in order to live.

Melodrama—the alternate mode for the dramatization of tyranny—separates its characters into hateful villains and pitiable, innocent victims. Comedy, with its stress on mankind's universal participation in folly and vice, would appear to be the most suitable tool to kill the dragon in each and every one of us—or at least to expose the beast. It is for this reason that in the tyrant plays under consideration (written by firsthand witnesses of the European dictators), the element of pathos—an easy response to evoke when dealing with victims—is deliberately eliminated. In Chaplin's *The Great Dictator* (1941), on the other hand, despite the film's many brilliant moments, the comedy of the tyrant is severely flawed by the sentimental melodrama of the Jewish ghetto and the hero's optimistic belief in the goodness of the people and their ability to triumph. Chaplin's portrayal of dictatorship lacks any sense of terror, based, as it is, less on fundamental human flaws common to all than on the aberrations of a few lunatics. Brecht, who left the Jews out of *Arturo Ui* for good reasons, insists that "the comic element must not preclude horror."[28] In the comic depiction of tyranny, terror is an essential ingredient, but pathos sounds a false note.

A case in point is Shakespeare's prototypical tyrant play, *Richard III,* in which the comic scenes tracing Richard's rise to power through diabolical manipulation are founded upon the complicity of his victims. Crude comic justice emerges as Richard sends down the trapdoor all those who have abetted him in his many crimes and are thus equally guilty of murder and perjury. Even Anne, knowing the tyrant's crimes against her family, is culpable for accepting Richard against her better judgment; and, in fact, upon their meeting by the hearse of Henry VI, she curses herself if she should ever marry such a monster. Concentrating on the tyrant and his accomplices and not on his innocent victims, Shakespeare omits any presentation of the murder of the little princes (who are tainted only through the sins of their father), whereas the melodramatized stage and film versions by Colley Cibber and Laurence Olivier exploit the scene for its pathos.

The comic workings of higher arbitrariness in *Richard III* can be seen most fully in the scenes with Hastings, who first gloats over the unjust deaths of his enemies, Rivers, Grey, and Vaughan, and then smugly imagines that he stands high in the tyrant's favor. Asked by Richard what punishment those plotting against him deserve, the obsequious Hastings replies death, of course, thus dooming himself to be led off to instant execution. The tyrant's henchman gets his proper reward in a suitably ironic fashion.

The farce of Richard's rise to power is, to be sure, only a part of a much larger, serious drama of redemption for England. The comedy occurs primarily in Act III, where, in a series of mordantly funny episodes, Buckingham and Richard use every totalitarian trick to "persuade" the Mayor and Citizens of London to accept Richard as legitimate king. All the modern techniques of political violence, rabble-rousing, and propaganda are there: smears against rivals, trumped-up charges about dangerous associates, elimination of potential enemies, false promises and false laments for betrayed friends, accusations against the dead, predated death sentences, staged rallies (what Halévy calls "organized enthusiasm"),[29] provoked crises and fabricated states of alert (Gloucester and Buckingham appear "in rotten armor, marvelous ill-fitting" and pretend to drive off imaginary attackers), and feigned piety and reluctance to rule (Richard enters with "two right reverend Fathers," reading the Holy Book).[30] In all these stunts it is apparent that Richard can "counterfeit the deep tragedian" and is a master at manipulating reality and appearance through the equivocal and misleading use of language. To lull suspicion, the dictator knows how to feign geniality (as in Richard's good-humored inquiry about strawberries); to terrify, he can simulate a towering rage (as in his accusations against Hastings). All is fraudulent, for the tyrant is in essence an actor.

It is no wonder that Brecht sent his Arturo Ui to school to study with Shakespeare's Richard III, whose methods of eliminating opposition become a model for the Chicago gangster. "Doesn't he make you think of Richard the Third?" Brecht asks in the prologue;[31] and later, in order to play his role impressively, Ui takes lessons in speech and deportment with an old-fashioned Shakespearian actor. In actual fact, Hitler may have taken similar lessons, and the entire comparison between the Führer and Richard III is a natural one, as witness the following entry for 20 July 1935 from the diary of Harry Kessler, the "Red Count":

> Brückner [one of Hitler's adjutants] . . . said, "Man alive, have you still not noticed that the Führer is nuts?" Hitler always allows the murder of people with whom he is on friendly terms to be "wrested" from him. He tears his hair like a Wagnerian hero, makes a show of despair ("I really *cannot* permit that"), and finally "concedes" what he decided a week ago. "Richard III," I commented. "Much worse," replied Brüning, because the theatrical, sentimentally romantic, Wagnerian element enters into it.[32]

As the triad Hitler/Ui/Richard III reveals, the tyrant is a multiple sham, a parody of an authentic ruler (usurping his place) and a parody of an actor putting on a show (counterfeiting the tragedian). A comedian and clown by nature, the dictator must constantly perform before an audience. Put on the stage by a dramatist, such a ludicrous figure becomes theater-in-the-theater, a parody of parodies. And here is why the playwrights who portray tyrants find inspiration in commedia, Shakespeare, gangster films, fairy tales with ogres, and Punch-and-Judy shows.

TYRANNY AND THEATRICAL SPECTACLE

Tyranny is theater, and totalitarian regimes consist of ceremonies and rituals centering around the dictator and manipulated by him. In *The Arena of Ants,* a novel about German prisoners of war in America, James Schevill observes that "the Nazis were conquering Europe by theatrical spectacles, illusions, as much as the reality of industrial and military power. Masks are as necessary in politics as on the operatic stage."[33] Arturo Ui must learn to wear the mask of the tyrant; during the course of the play, particularly in the scene with the old Shakespearian actor, we see the man become the mask and watch Ui grow transfigured as he assumes what Hannah Arendt calls the dictator's "aura of impenetrable mystery."[34] Dr. Knock (especially as played by Louis Jouvet) wears an unfathomable mask of gravity from the start, never once letting on through the slightest gesture that the medical existence might be a common swindle and thereby convincing his patients that they are sick by the sheer force of his superb performance. In the film version of *Dr. Knock,* Jouvet transformed even the washing of his hands into an awesome and intimidating ritual, expressive of the doctor's absolute knowledge and power over others.

The tyrant's mastery of spectacle is a principal source of his power. "Do you know why people thought I was a great statesman?" Ferrero's Regent asks Orlando; "because I had cannons fired when I received the bankers who brought me money." Wahazar concocts special court rites that are a bizarre mixture of quack medicine, pseudoscience, modern technology and mystical belief. The dictator must offer his people a new religion of which he is the sole deity: a lonely, preposterous, terrifying, and sometimes pitiable ham actor. "I alone rule everything and I'm responsible for everything, and answer only to myself," his Onlyness screams. Megalomania and paranoia are the two poles between which the dictator oscillates.

THE RHETORIC OF TYRANNY

As an upstart, a nobody, arising out of nothing, with no warrant to rule, the modern tyrant must invent himself and his realm through his ability to devise names and symbols. Above all, the tyrant is the creation of his own perverted rhetoric. Diderot was the first to comment on the linguistic impact of totalitarianism: "Tyranny imprints a character of baseness on all kinds of productions; even language is not protected from its influence."[35] The tyrant's language is a grotesque debasement of normal speech, constantly approaching utter nonsense; for the playwright, this rodomontade becomes the key to the character's dramatic vitality. The dictator abuses words as he abuses his subjects; his repeated distortions have a hypnotic and almost magical power. The tyrant's torturing of language is his most extreme form of action, expressing his total personality. Ubu's invented insults and misshapen curses and profanity are the motive force behind his aggression and his ascent to power. In his first appearance as the dictator Hynkel haranguing the masses in absurd mock-German, Chaplin captures the essential linguistic madness of the tyrant. Gyubal Wahazar perpetually froths at the mouth and flies into hysterical rages that, like Hitler's, seem self-consciously staged performances. Witkiewicz's note, explaining how the frothing is to be done, furthers the impression that we are witnessing an act: "It's very easy to do by first stuffing one's mouth full of soda tablets or Piperazina flakes from Klawy's drugstore." Deliberately playing the buffoon, Richard III speaks a double-talk full of ironic wordplay and quibbles that say the opposite of what he intends. But as he begins to lose military and political control of the situation in Act IV, Richard no longer simply feigns anger— he actually flies into a screaming fit against the messenger who brings bad news as well as against his own subordinates.

The ancestor of all ranting dictators who froth at the mouth in frenzied rages is, of course, Herod the Great in the Christian mystery plays. Much as we enjoy seeing Chaplin as the Great Dictator raving insanely, so medieval audiences evidently delighted in the spectacle of Great Herod and other tyrant figures in the cycles (Pharaoh, Caesar, Augustus, and Pilate) blustering in comic fury. The medieval stage despot struts about the stage, swears, and speaks incomprehensible French;[36] he despises the multitude that he abuses, and his repeated calls for silence (addressed to the audience) suggest that he was hooted and jeered.[37] Much like his modern counterparts in drama, Herod accuses everyone of being a traitor and threatens to beat and break the bones of all his subjects, especially his own knights and retainers. There is every reason to believe that derisive laughter was the audience's response to such a base and clownish figure. In his essay on "The Comic in the Cycles," Arnold Williams points out that even the reactions of the brutish soldiers sent out by Herod to kill the Innocents were often comic: "In one cycle they enjoy the task, in another they feel it beneath them to kill babies and fight women. . . . It seems likely that the attack of the women was sometimes played for laughs."[38] In particular, the portrayal of Herod in the Wakefield cycle reveals all the possibilities for comedy inherent in the tyrant. Cruel and violent, stupid and cowardly, the Wakefield Master's Herod is a medieval Ubu who brags of his omnipotence over all creation, yet constantly gives way to impotent rage. This great dictator is an ignorant, mean, malicious monster who rages directly against the audience and menaces them with all the might of his great power.

For, despite his vain boasting, the medieval despot has, in fact, the full weight of authority, human and divine, to support his claims. The modern Herods, on the other hand, have no such sanctions and must fabricate the myth of their own omnipotence. The power of language to forge totalitarian myths and concepts is illustrated in Witkiewicz's *The Cuttlefish, or The Hyrcanian Worldview*.[39] A total fraud

Figure 4. Hyrcan IV, in the first postwar production of Witkiewicz at Cricot II in Cracow, 1956. Directed by the experimental artist, Tadeusz Kantor, *The Cuttlefish* was attack on the cult of personality and an important step in freeing Polish theater from tyrannical Stalinist controls. (Photo: K. Jarochowski)

in a world of total fraud, the tyrant-hero is a synthetic superman—"a very clever, but ordinary bandit" surrounded by a "depraved band of madmen and drunkards"—who proclaims himself ruler of the artificial kingdom of Hyrcania and calls himself Hyrcan IV (see Figure 4) Without a name or hereditary title of his own, the would-be dictator must first invent a country and then a world view to justify its existence. Wearing a helmet with a red plume and a purple robe that comes down to the floor, Hyrcan talks impressively and carries a huge sword; but beneath these trappings, he is an ordinary twentieth-century man in a dark business suit. The petty modern tyrant must impose himself on the world through theatrical illusion and gesture.

Improvising his realm and his values as he goes, Hrycan plans to rule over the inert masses—whom he despises as stupid cattle—by means of what he calls Hyrcanian desires. When challenged to explain the meaning of such a nonsensical phrase, the self-created despot reveals the true nature of totalitarian might: the power of the word to create the thing. "Once I give it definition, this empty sound will become a concept," the strong man declares. But Hyrcanian desires (daydreams of self-aggrandizement, as it turns out) cause Hyrcan to have a tantrum when he learns that his mother is a whore and that he may well be the illegitimate son of a Jewish banker. Deeply humiliated, the racist demagogue abruptly leaves the stage, muttering ominous threats; he is soon murdered by an anarchist artist who proclaims himself Hyrcan V and promises a government based on pure nonsense (see Figure 5). The same fabrication of myth plays a major role in the tyrant's rise in Toller's *Wotan Unbound.* The hero, an anti-Semitic barber named Wotan, is a compulsive reader of romantic literature who writes grandiose memoirs while in prison; at first a tool of financial and military interests, Wotan by the end of the play becomes transformed into a true dictator who screams maniacally that his book alone will save Europe.[40]

TYRANNY TODAY

With the deaths of Hitler, Mussolini, and Stalin (and their lesser confreres, such as Franco and Salazar), tyranny did not disappear from the earth, nor has the race of tyrants died out. After all, Idi Amin demonstrates better than any imaginable fictional character my central thesis that frightening despots are inherently preposterous. But in recent times tyranny has undergone a drastic demythification. For the most part, contemporary despotism is less colorful and spectacular than regularized and systematized. Tyranny has grown year by year more impersonal, more normal, and more efficient—and, therefore, even more dangerous.

Since the end of World War II and the vogue of the absurd, we have

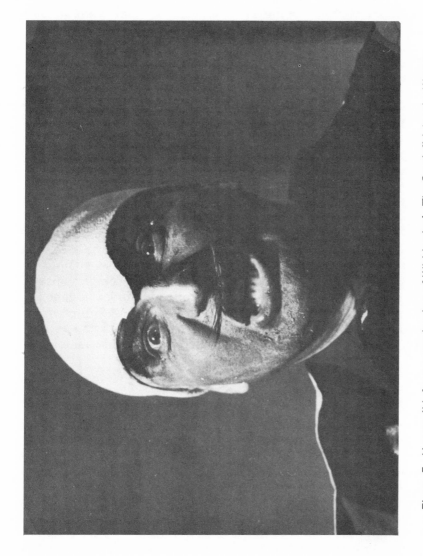

Figure 5. Hyrcan IV, from a production of Witkiewicz's *The Cuttlefish* by the Warsaw Student Theatre Sigma in 1966. "I'm creating supermen," Hyrcan screams. "Two, three—that's enough. The rest is a pulpy mass—cheese for worms."

had many comic parables and savage farces about totalitarian systems and the tyranny of the state. One thinks of Ionesco's *The Lesson* and *Rhinoceros* as well as Armand Gatti's *Le Crapaud-Buffle* and *The Tot Family* by the Hungarian István Örkény. Of contemporary playwrights, none has devoted more attention to the quiet, everyday workings of tyranny and its effects on the average tyrannized citizen than the Polish writer, Sławomir Mrożek (see Figure 6). Instead of flamboyant dictators, Mrożek presents the small victims of oppression who eagerly seek to justify their own submission to the power of power. In a whole series of parable plays—some short and some long—Mrożek lays bare the mechanism of tyranny as it operates in ideologies and institutions, in bureaucracies and social classes.

An early Mrożek one-act drama, *Striptease* (1961),[41] effectively illustrates the invisible tyranny that is the object of the playwright's ironic and detached scrutiny. Two official-looking gentlemen wearing dark suits and carrying briefcases unexpectedly find themselves trapped in an impersonal room into which a gigantic hand protrudes and forces them to remove their clothes (see Figure 7). One protests and argues eloquently; the other talks of inner freedom—but all to no avail. Regardless of their philosophical positions, both are compelled to submit to arbitrary power and strip off their own clothes and dignity before going to their destruction (see Figure 8). The tyrant is absent from *Striptease;* only a symbol is necessary to keep the system operating. In *Emigrés* (1975), in which the two characters are complementary figures in a theorem, AA observes: "Under a dictatorship, everyone is equal";[42] and Mrożek's parables are dedicated to demonstrating how tyranny strips supposedly civilized human beings of their pretenses and reduces them to a common denominator where certain universal laws hold sway.

In a recent trilogy of one-act plays, *Serenade—Philosopher Fox— Fox Hunt* (1977),[43] Mrożek makes his tyrants a rooster and a fox from an animal fable. The third section, *Fox Hunt,* is a richly allusive political parable about the shifting tides of power and the fate of those caught in the crosscurrents. In a new egalitarian regime, *all* the people—and not simply the king and nobles—have the right to hunt; in fact, everyone is required to go hunting, even Uncle, a sick old man in a wheel chair who does not know how to shoot and would prefer to stay home. The result of such "democratic" hunting on a mass scale is that there are no more wild animals left in the forest, except for one last fox desperately trying to save his hide. This fox—a clever farmyard bandit— has, therefore, brought with him into the woods a rooster—a petty hen-house tyrant—to serve as a decoy, hoping to convince the hunters that domestic animals would make good prey. The hunters are ready for the chase and urge the dogs on, the latter being bureaucrats with briefcases who keep careful count of the exact number of times they bark. Suddenly, in a surprising coup d'état denouement (already used to

Figure 6. An untitled drawing by Mrożek, who is a cartoonist as well as a playwright and story writer, shows the cooperative hierarchy by which the tyrant is raised aloft and the resulting precariousness of his position. From a book of Mrożek's cartoons, *Przez Okulary,* published by Iskry, Warsaw, 1965.

Figure 7. Mrożek's *Striptease,* in a production in Bialystok in 1962. The victims of tyranny follow instructions given by the anonymous powers represented by the giant hand. (Photo: J. W. Brzoza)

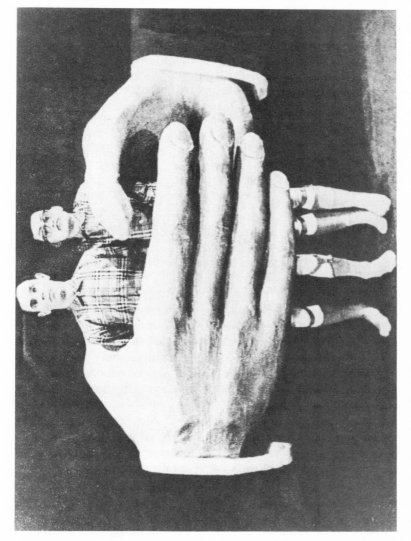

Figure 8. Another production of Mrożek's *Striptease*, at the Old Theatre in Cracow, 1962. Having capitulated to the inevitable, the two small officials find themselves caught in the grip of forces that will crush them. (Photo: W. Plewiński)

good effect in *Tango*), the terrifying howling of a pack of wolves can be heard offstage—evidently, not all wild animals are extinct. As the wolves draw closer and closer, the hunters rush for home in panic, and Uncle, abandoned by all, fires his shotgun twice wildly, accidentally killing both the fox and the rooster who had concealed themselves in a tree.

In the sharp twists of *Fox Hunt,* we see the comic laws of tyranny in operation. The higher power of arbitrariness blindly levels differences between greater and lesser figures in the hierarchy of oppression. Often cunning is helpless when confronted by brute force; wolves can replace hunters and even the feeblest are momentarily dangerous with gun in hand.

Comedy has no limits. The most monstrous tyranny of the twentieth century has been assimilated within its bounds. The Ubuesque follies and vices of dictatorship represent a subject of enormous importance for our age. Not only because tyranny has in the recent past been so widespread and wreaked such havoc on our fragile civilization. Not only as a warning of what may still come to pass if we are not vigilant. Not only as a picture of what prevails elsewhere, in other countries. But primarily because tyranny reflects in exaggerated form all that is wrong with the modern state. This view that despotism is the essence of all contemporary government finds eloquent expression in the words of Paul Valéry:

> Hence, the (political) mind, which under all circumstances is the opponent of man—contesting his liberty, his complexity, and his versatility—attains, in a dictatorial regime, to the fullness of its development. . . . Dictatorship merely completes the system of pressures and obligations of which modern man is the more or less conscious victim, even in the politically freest countries.[44]

The mirror and model of what already exists around us, tyranny, when viewed as a comic phenomenon, discloses follies and vices to which we are all subject; and the tyrant expresses our delusions, dreams, and fantasies of power. The little Jewish barber and Hynkel are identical twins in Chaplin's *Great Dictator*. The tyrant is *our* puppet, *our* inseparable shadow from whom we can never free ourselves entirely. Comedy offers no cure, but through laughter calls attention to the inescapable situation.

NOTES

1. In the discussion that follows, I am not concerned with the dramatic genre, comedy, but only with the comic treatment of tyrants wherever this occurs, even in plays that

as a whole would be classified as tragicomedy, history, or some form of serious drama. Likewise, I do not attempt to distinguish between farce and comedy or between satire and comedy. Because the subject of tyranny and comedy is a complex one, I have here attempted only to explore the basic relationships between the two.

2. Plato, *Philebus*, in *Theories of Comedy*, ed. Paul Lauter (New York: Doubleday Anchor, 1964), pp. 7–8.

3. W. H. Auden, "Notes on the Comic," in *Comedy: Meaning and Form*, ed. Robert W. Corrigan (San Francisco: Chandler, 1965), p. 62.

4. Elie Halévy, *The Era of Tyrannies*, trans. R. K. Webb (New York: New York Univ. Press, 1966), p. 266.

5. As might be expected, there is also a literature of comic dictators in Spanish that I have not been able to explore. For example, Ramón del Valle-Inclán, in both his plays and his novels, portrays hateful and ludicrous tyrants. Gabriel García Márquez's novel, *The Autumn of the Patriarch*, is a modern example of the genre.

6. Actually, the beginnings of the topic could be traced to the ancient world. Aristophanes, in *The Knights* and other comedies, ridicules the tyrannical demagogue Cleon, using many of the same techniques as the modern portrayers of dictators.

7. Quoted in Oscar Jászi and John D. Lewis, *Against the Tyrant* (Glencoe, Ill.: The Free Press, 1957), p. 44.

8. In Stanisław Ignacy Witkiewicz, *Tropical Madness: Four Plays*, trans. Daniel and Eleanor Gerould (New York: Winter House, 1972). Subsequent quotations come from this edition.

9. Wahazar dreams of the perfect totalitarian state, which, in Hannah Arendt's words, will come into being when "all men have become One Man." *The Origins of Totalitarianism* (New York: Harcourt, Brace & World, 1966), p. 477.

10. The chain reaction that Wahazar sets off in Albania bears out Paul Valéry's contention, made in 1934, that "dictatorship at present is contagious, just as, in the past, freedom was." *Collected Works*, X, trans. Denise Folliot and Jackson Matthews (New York: Pantheon, 1962), 245.

11. When Gyubal dies and is replaced by an inferior dictator, his victims lament that life has "lost its last remaining charm."

12. Northrop Frye, *Anatomy of Criticism* (Princeton: Princeton Univ. Press, 1957), p. 185.

13. Jules Romains, *Knock, ou le triomphe de la médecine* (Paris: Gallimard, 1947), p. 165. The ironic sense of this passage is lost in the English translations that I have seen.

14. Bertolt Brecht, *Collected Plays*, VI, trans. Ralph Manheim (New York: Vintage, 1976), 457.

15. Ibid.

16. Jacques Robichez, *Le Symbolisme au théâtre* (Paris: L'Arche, 1957), p. 360.

17. Leo Ferrero, *Angelica* (Paris: Editions Rieder, 1934). Both the play and the essay which accompanies it were originally written in French. Subsequent quotations are taken from this edition, and the translations are mine. Ferrero was killed in an automobile accident during a visit to the United States in 1933 when he was 30; *Angelica* was later staged by the Pitoëffs.

18. Quoted in Jászi, *Against the Tyrant*, p. 102.

19. Alfred Jarry, *Ubu Roi* (Paris: Fasquelle, n.d.), III, ii.

20. David Rousset, *The Other Kingdom*, trans. Ramon Guthrie (New York: Reynal and Hitchcock, 1947), p. 172

21. Nikolai Gogol, *Dead Souls*, trans. David Magarshack (Baltimore: Penguin, 1961), p. 206.

22. *The Trilogy of Alexander Sukhovo-Kobylin*, trans. Harold B. Segel (New York: Dutton, 1969), pp. 243, 260, 244, 243, 253.

23. Harold Segel gives valuable information about Sukhovo-Kobylin's use of French comic techniques in the introduction to his translation, op. cit., pp. xliii–xlv.

24. Ibid., p. 263.

25. In contrast, Brecht's *Arturo Ui* is so closely tied historically to the facts of Hitler's life that its resonance as a parable is limited. It applies to the Führer, but not to Stalin; it looks to the past, not to the present or future; and its approach to tyranny is retrospective rather than prophetic. For these reasons, it has been safely presented in the Soviet Union (in an outstanding production at the Leningrad Bolshoi Theatre) without encountering the many difficulties that Shvarts's plays have always experienced.

26. Yevgeny Schwartz, *The Dragon*, trans. Max Hayward and Harold Shukman, in *Three Soviet Plays*, ed. Michael Glenny (Baltimore: Penguin, 1966), pp. 151, 211, 215.

27. *The Shadow*, in *Twentieth-Century Russian Plays*, trans. F. D. Reeve (New York: Norton, 1963), pp. 434, 409, 444-445.

28. Brecht, *Collected Plays*, VI, 453.

29. Halęvy, *The Era of Tyrannies*, p. 266.

30. *Richard III*, III, v and vi.

31. Brecht, *Collected Plays*, VI, 198. Richard's courtship of Anne is overtly parodied in Ui's scene with Dullfeet's widow, but this is the least important analogue between Shakespeare's play and *Arturo Ui*.

32. Harry Kessler, *In the Twenties*, trans. Charles Kessler (New York: Holt, Rinehart and Winston, 1971), pp. 470–471.

33. James Schevill, *The Arena of Ants* (Providence: Copper Beech Press, 1977), p. 176.

34. Arendt, *The Origins of Totalitarianism*, p. 373.

35. Quoted in Jászi, *Against the Tyrant*, p. 105.

36. *The Wakefield Mystery Plays*, ed. Martial Rose (New York: Norton, 1961), p. 172.

37. A recent tyrant play that has enjoyed considerable success in New York, *Miss Margarida's Way* (1977) by the Brazilian playwright Roberto Athayde, attempts to provoke a similar kind of response. The play's only performer, a dictatorial and abusive schoolteacher, uses the audience as her class and the supposed object of her tyranny. Whereas Ubu Roi, based on a hated teacher from Jarry's childhood, becomes all tyrants, in *Miss Margarida's Way*, the concept of tyranny is reduced to a hated teacher. The idea is good, but the execution faulty. Miss Margarida has no mask or aura of mystery; her words inspire no fear and transform no one; her rhetoric degenerates quickly into commonplace obscenity, rather than becoming shaped into the imposing comic rant and invective necessary for the despot if he is to subdue others and convince them of his mission.

38. Arnold Williams, "The Comic in the Cycles," *Medieval Drama*, Stratford-Upon-Avon Studies 16 (London: Edward Arnold, 1973), p. 121.

39. *The Cuttlefish*, trans. Daniel and Eleanor Gerould, in *A Treasury of the Theatre*, II, 4th ed., ed. John Gassner and Bernard F. Dukore (New York: Holt, Rinehart and Winston, 1970).

40. For information about Toller's play as well as for other ideas on Hitler in film and drama, I am indebted to Alvin Goldfarb's unpublished essay, "Adolf Hitler as Portrayed in Theater and Film during his Lifetime."

41. Sławomir Mrożek, *Striptease, Dialog*, 6, 1961.

42. Sławomir Mrożek, *Utwory sceniczne nowe* (Cracow: Wydawnictwo Literackie, 1975).

43. Sławomir Mrożek, *Serenada, Dialog*, 2, 1977; *Lis Filozof, Dialog*, 3, 1977; *Polowanie na Lisa, Dialog,* 5, 1977.

44. Paul Valéry, *Collected Works*, X, 238, 244.

Black Humor:
To Weep with Laughing

MATHEW WINSTON

"Strange times, that weep with laughing, not with weeping." We might well appropriate this observation by Shakespeare's Timon of Athens exclusively to our time, did its context not remind us that Jacobean England and Periclean Athens were also strange in their own ways. But Timon's remark is an apt commentary on the literature of our day, when the forms that elicit tears and laughter—tragedy and melodrama, comedy and farce—have lost their distinctness and assurance. What has combined and replaced them is a strange but no longer peripheral variety of literature appropriately known as black humor.

"Black humor" was given its name by André Breton. When he used the phrase in his *Anthologie de l'humour noir* (1939), he did so almost superfluously, for he placed himself as squarely as his surrealist theories would allow in a European tradition that stressed the darkness of all comedy and especially of humor. The line can be followed in France from Charles Baudelaire's insistence in "De l'essence du rire" (1855) that "le comique est un des plus clairs signes sataniques de l'homme"[1] ("the comic is one of the clearest signs of the satanic in man") through

Jean-Paul Sartre's extended discussion of the sadomasochistic bases of comedy in his massive study of Flaubert, *L'Idiot de la famille* (1971). This notion of humor as dark, meditative, self-doubting, and full of the incongruities that are its special focus is alien to the English, who tend to equate humor with good humor; but it is at home on the European continent, as is witnessed by such works as Luigi Pirandello's *L'Umorismo* (1908, 1920) and by continued literary and critical emphasis in Germany on the humor of the grotesque and on *Galgenhumor* (gallows humor), which not coincidentally underlies Sigmund Freud's study of the comic. The continental attitude is perhaps best summed up by an old German saying: "Humor ist, wenn man trotzdem lacht" ("you have a sense of humor if you laugh anyway, despite the circumstances").

In the decades since Breton gathered miscellaneous writings under the vaguely defined heading of black humor, the concept has been applied to a steadily increasing number of works and media. French and German critics still tend to use *humour noir* and *schwarzer Humor* with specific reference to surrealism and to the authors Breton collected in his *Anthologie,* but more recent anthologies in these languages have included jokes, cartoons, and cabaret songs. The theater of the absurd has fit comfortably under the rubric of black humor, and its most important practitioner, Eugène Ionesco, has gone so far as to assert that "l'humour veritable est sinistre, mélancolique, macabre, c'est-à-dire: noir"[2] ("true humor is sinister, melancholy, macabre, that is to say: black").

The widest and also loosest extension of the phrase came when American critics picked it up, ignorant of its origins, and applied it to a seemingly new variety of American fiction of the late 1950s and early 1960s. A sampling of this fiction must begin with Vladimir Nabokov's *Lolita* and J. P. Donleavy's *The Ginger Man,* both of which were published in 1955 by the Olympia Press and took some time to make their reputation in America. James Purdy's *Malcolm,* William Burroughs's *Naked Lunch,* and Terry Southern's *The Magic Christian* were all published in 1959; John Barth's *The Sot-Weed Factor,* in 1960; Joseph Heller's *Catch-22* and John Hawkes's *The Lime Twig,* in 1961; Bruce Jay Friedman's *Stern* and Ken Kesey's *One Flew Over the Cuckoo's Nest,* in 1962; and Thomas Pynchon's *V.,* in 1963. These authors and this kind of writing have continued to shape American fiction to the present day.

As it has come down to us, then, the term *black humor* has been used in so many different ways and applied to such a diversity of works that it lacks any precision. The purpose of this essay is to define black humor and to show its utility in helping us to understand the body of experimental writing that has emerged since the Second World War: absurdist theater, postmodernist fiction, un-, anti-, and ir-realistic literature.

What is black humor? First and foremost, it is a tone in literature and related arts that combines horror and fun, the unsettling and the amusing, or, as Gerd Henniger has suggested, pleasure and guilt (*Lust und Schuld*).[3] The notion of tone in literature has met with critical objections in the past; yet they may be overcome by its usefulness in dealing with texts that are, for example, satiric or ironic without being satires or ironies and by the developing techniques of semiotics and of what the Germans call *Rezeptionsästhetik*, the study of how an author designs a work to obtain a desired response from his audience. A tone is the rhetorical effect of a work or a portion of a work on its reader or spectator. Tone is created through the handling of language and of visual and aural effects in art forms that are not restricted to the printed page, but it is also determined by the treatment of character, of plot, and of structure.[4]

We may illustrate black humor by way of several passages from earlier literature that prefigure that tone. I have not chosen these passages in order to legitimize the concept of black humor, as Martin Esslin did with a similar category in his *The Theatre of the Absurd* (1961), but rather to examine borderline cases that tell us a good deal about what black humor is and what it is not. The following selections depict death and mutilation in a macabrely funny way and so exemplify the disparity between content and form that is the hallmark of black humor. The contents provide the blackness, and the style mitigates that blackness with humor.

APPROACHES TOWARD BLACK HUMOR

In Sir Philip Sidney's *Arcadia* (1590) we are treated to the following description of a revolt by the peasantry against the nobility:

> Yet among the rebels there was a dapper fellowe, a tayler by occupation, who fetching his courage onelie from their going back, began to bow his knees, & very fencer-like to draw neere to *Zelmane.* But as he came within her distance, turning his swerd very nicely about his crown, *Basilius,* with a side blow, strake of his nose. He (being a suiter to a seimsters daughter, and therfore not a little grieved for such a disgrace) stouped downe, because he had hard, that if it were fresh put to, it would cleave on againe. But as his hand was on the grounde to bring his nose to his head, *Zelmane* with a blow, sent his head to his nose. . . . O (said a miller that was halfe dronke) see the lucke of a good fellow, and with that word, ran with a pitch-forke at *Dorus:* but the nimblenes of the wine caried his head so fast, that it made it over-runne his feet, so that he fell withall, just betwene the legs of *Dorus:* who setting his foote on his neck (though he offered two milche kine, and foure

fatte hogs for his life) thrust his sword quite through, from one eare to the other; which toke it very unkindlie, to feele such newes before they heard of them, in stead of hearing, to be put to such feeling.[5] (Bk. 2, Ch. 25)

Whatever horror of needless bloodshed and of civil war Sidney may convey elsewhere in the *Arcadia* and however callous his presentation may seem to us (and I have omitted his description of "a poore painter" who came to observe wounds and left with both his hands hewn off), it is clear that this scene is designed to make the reader laugh. It correctly assumes that the aristocratic audience for which it was written was not likely to sympathize with lower-class drunken bumpkins who ape their betters in the noble art of warfare, who initiate an attack, and who revolt against their proper masters. It also builds on the artistic context that has previously been established: the defenders are heroes whose story we have been following for hundreds of pages, whereas the rebels are stick figures whose existence is limited to a sentence apiece. Finally, it makes the rebels ridiculous: their inflated pretensions, the pratfall and the totally inadequate (and cowardly) offer of ransom are all the material of comedy, as is the caricatural attention to nose and ears. Sidney controls our perspective by these techniques and turns the killing of the rebels into a kind of Punch-and-Judy show or animated cartoon in which the shockingly violent contents are all but negated by the comic manner of their presentation.

This point of view is enlarged by Martin Decoud in Joseph Conrad's *Nostromo* (1904). Decoud's ironic detachment from the land of his birth reduces all its inhabitants to actors and their political struggles to a grotesque farce.

> Of his own country he used to say to his French associates: Imagine an atmosphere of *opéra bouffe* in which all the comic business of stage statesmen, brigands, etc., etc., all their farcical stealing, intriguing, and stabbing is done in dead earnest. It is screamingly funny, the blood flows all the time, and the actors believe themselves to be influencing the fate of the universe. . . . No man of ordinary intelligence can take part in the intrigues of *une farce macabre*.[6] (Pt. 2, Ch. 3)

He refers to a soldier-politician as *"un grotesque vaniteux et féroce"* (131) and says of the whole political situation, *"C'est funambulesque"* (131). He feels his attraction to a lady of that country is "like a ridiculous fatality" (133). But the perspective of black humor that Conrad describes here is shown to be a temporary aberration that depends on geographical and, above all, emotional distance. When Decoud travels to his native land and becomes involved with it, when he sees that the actors are people and the blood is real, his attitude has to change:

"Here on the spot it was not possible to dismiss their tragic comedy with the expression, *'Quelle farce!' "* (148).

The excerpts from the *Arcadia* and from *Nostromo* exemplify a limited kind of black humor—limited because one point of view completely dominates its latent alternative, because the perspective is momentary, and because the reader is ensconced in a network of normative values and assumptions that are reinforced by the rest of the work. We move a good deal closer to black humor when a scene maintains an equilibrium between two potential perspectives, as is both talked about and illustrated by Casimir Lypiatt, a character in Aldous Huxley's novel *Antic Hay* (1923):

> Yes, yes, I have come to admit everything. . . . That I was a ridiculous actor of heroic parts who deserved to be laughed at—and *was* laughed at. But then every man is ludicrous if you look at him from outside, without taking into account what's going on in his heart and mind. You could turn Hamlet into an epigrammatic farce with an inimitable scene when he takes his adored mother in adultery. You could make the wittiest Guy de Maupassant short story out of the life of Christ, by contrasting the mad rabbi's pretensions with his abject fate. It's a question of point of view. Every one's a walking farce and a walking tragedy at the same time. The man who slips on a banana-skin and fractures his skull describes against the sky, as he falls, the most richly comic arabesque. . . . But in this particular case, you must remember, I'm not a dispassionate observer. And if I am overcome now, it is not with laughter. It is with an indescribable unhappiness, with the bitterness of death itself.[7] (Ch. 19)

Lypiatt writes the above in a suicide note. Huxley takes a character he has shown us from the outside and encouraged us to laugh at and then switches perspectives on us so that we see his pain and something of his soul. Lypiatt's awareness does not lessen his misery. But the pain is mitigated for the reader; by this point in the novel we have seen enough of Lypiatt's bravura posturings to be relatively secure he will not kill himself, if only because suicide would wrench the tone of the novel too badly. He does not quite manage to become uncomic.

The passage from *Antic Hay* shows us that black humor need not involve the extremes of horror and farce or present a comical treatment of abhorrent material. Again, we are only moved in the direction of black humor because the reader can fairly well distinguish among the various perspectives and maintain his or her sense of norms. True black humor comes into its own when the normative point of view disappears, as in the following passage from John Hawkes's *The Cannibal* (1949), in which the demented neo-Nazi Zizendorf tells how he killed a potential betrayer of his cause, Stintz, by hitting the man with the nearest available object:

> I swung the tuba short. I should have preferred to have some distance and to be able to swing it like a golf club. But even as it was, Stintz fell, and half-sitting against the wall, he still moved for a moment.
>
> Two things were wrong: there was the lack of room and I had misjudged the instrument itself. Somehow thinking of the tuba as squat, fat, thinking of it as a mallet I had expected it to behave like a mallet; to strike thoroughly and dull, to hit hard and flat. Instead it was the rim of the bell that caught the back of Stintz's head, and the power in my arms was misdirected, peculiarly unspent. I struck again and the mouthpiece flew from the neck and sang across the room. I was unnerved only for a moment and when finally out in the hall, thought I would have preferred a stout club. Stintz no longer moved.[8]

Unlike the earlier passages, this one provides us with no guidelines. We must rely on the narrator, however much we may dislike and distrust him. The facts are appalling: a cold-blooded murder is committed by a mad individual for the sake of a despicable cause. On the other hand, the analytic detachment of the narrator, the curious instrument (in both senses of the word) selected for murder, the inadequate comparisons of the tuba to a golf club and a mallet, and the anatomical confusion of neck and mouthpiece, together with the silent and graceless fall of Stintz and the lack of blood and bone, all move us toward the comic.

The most extreme test of black humor is found later in the same novel when several pages are spent telling us in great detail how another of the characters cuts up the body of a young boy he has hunted throughout the book, has just killed, and intends to cook for dinner. Nothing could be more repugnant than this disgusting and macabre dissection of a helpless child. Yet when we look at it from a little distance, prepared by such scenes as the murder of Stintz, we may see that were anything else described or enacted in the same manner, it would be very funny. The ineptitude of the killer, who is disconcerted by his lack of light, instruction, and proper equipment, the way in which things drop out of his hands and fall on the ground would be appropriate to a farcical banquet served by the Marx brothers—if only it were a turkey dinner and not a child's corpse that was being prepared.

Many critics have insisted that the distinctive effect of black humor and of its related form, the grotesque, is that the reader must feel the humor and the horror simultaneously, but I find this formulation of our response inaccurate. It is indeed necessary that both potentials be present in the text and exert approximately equal claims, but it is unlikely that we respond to both at once. When we look at the various passages I have cited, we may react with amusement or with repulsion. Looking again, we may feel the opposite sensation; or our thoughts and emotions may shift as we move from sentence to sentence, from phrase to phrase, or even from word to word. The effect is similar to viewing an optical illusion in which one may see, for example, either a white table on a black background or two facing silhouettes separated by an intervening white space. You see the picture in one way, and then, by looking at it repeatedly or from a different angle, you become able to see the other image. Only after you have perceived both possibilities can you entertain the two potentials more or less simultaneously. In the case of the paragraphs I quoted from *The Cannibal,* the humorous is prime; in the scene I summarized, the blackness. But in neither instance may we correctly say, "This is intended *only* to be funny or *only* horrendous."

THE ROLE OF BLACK HUMOR

The comedy in black humor helps us overcome our fears. The examples cited support the validity of Freud's observation in "Der Humor" (1927), which Breton quotes approvingly in his *Anthologie:* "The grandeur in it [humor] clearly lies in the triumph of narcissism, the victorious assertion of the ego's invulnerability. The ego refuses to to distressed by the provocations of reality, to let itself be compelled to suffer. It insists that it cannot be affected by the traumas of the external world."[9] Freud was writing about the attitude of the humorous individual, the teller of a joke; and Breton, about the attitude of an author that is embodied in his text. When the work is successful, then the reader responds in kind.

If we may say that humor helps us cope with the "blackness" of the world, it is no less true that black humor also keeps us from the psychological safety and implicit superiority of a purely comic stance. It may bring us to what Samuel Beckett calls in *Watt* (1953) "the laugh of laughs, the *risus purus,* . . . the laugh that laughs . . . at that which is unhappy."[10] But this is by no means simple *Schadenfreude,* the pleasure one takes in another's misery, because it is a laugh that also laughs at one's own unhappiness, that of author, character, and reader. With its typical ambivalence, black humor reminds us of the pain and misery beneath what we are laughing at, which are not obviated by the laughter. To this extent it complicates our response to the literature we are reading and to the characters we are reading about. It is not a matter of *"ridi, Pagliaccio,"* of unveiling the true unhappiness beneath a jesting surface, but of showing that a person may both suffer and be ridiculous, depending on our perspective and on his own.

BLACK HUMOR IN CONTEMPORARY LITERATURE

The term *black humor* obviously serves a legitimate, if limited, function in describing this odd combination of conflicting responses. So far we have examined it only in borderline cases and in short excerpts. But when we look at contemporary literature, at what has often been called postmodernist literature, we find work after work dominated by black humor, by a polarity of conflicting responses that can alternate or coexist but that cannot be reconciled. And we find that the same treatment of the disparity between form and content that establishes the rhetorical mood is present throughout these books in a variety of ways and imposes analogous conflicts on the reader.

The literature of black humor frequently depicts horrible events, unhappy people, anarchy, and chaos. It uses language not merely to reproduce that disorder but also to play with it and thereby to structure it. Oskar Matzerath in Günter Grass's *Die Blechtrommel* (*The Tin Drum*, 1959) provides an excellent example of how language can move us in two opposing directions. He recalls the time in his childhood when he found the man who supplied him with toy drums murdered by Nazis and discovered that "der Weihnachtsmann war in Wirklichkeit der Gasmann" ("Santa Claus was in reality the gasman"). Recreating the memory of this violence, of his deprivation of the drums that were his means of expression, of the "braune Würste" ("brown sausages") left by the SA men who defecated in the toy shop, and intensely aware of the inadequacy of words to express all of this, Oskar writes:

> Ich weiss nicht, oh, weiss nicht, womit sie, zum Beispiel, die Därme füllen, . . . weiss nicht, aus welchen Wörterbüchern sie Namen für Füllungen klauben, weiss nicht, womit sie die Wörterbücher wie auch die Därme füllen, weiss nicht, wessen Fleisch, weiss nicht, wessen Sprache: Wörter bedeuten, Metzger verschweigen, ich schneide Scheiben ab, du schlägst die Bücher auf, ich lese, was mir schmeckt, du weisst nicht, was dir schmeckt: Wurstscheiben und Zitate aus Därmen und Büchern—und nie werden wir erfahren, wer still werden musste, verstummen musste, damit Därme gefüllt, Bücher laut werden konnten, gestopft, gedrängt, ganz dicht beschrieben, ich weiss nicht, ich ahne: Es sind dieselben Metzger, die Wörterbücher und Därme mit Sprache und Wurst füllen.[11]

> (I don't know, oh, don't know, with what, for example, they fill sausage casings, . . . don't know from what dictionaries they pick out the names for fillings, don't know with what they fill dictionaries as well as casings, don't know whose meat, don't know whose language: words signify, butchers

keep secret, I cut off slices, you open up books, I read what pleases my taste, you don't know what pleases your taste: slices of sausage and quotations out of sausage skins and books—and we will never learn who had to be stilled, had to become silent, so that sausage casings could be filled, books could become loud, stuffed, packed, quite densely filled with writing, I don't know, I suspect: it is the same butchers who fill dictionaries and casings with language and sausage.)

The *Därme* are not only sausage casings but also intestines, like those that produced the excretion of the SA men, and the "guts" from which a writer may create. The parallels in this passage make a connection that is frightening to think of, and the repetitions of "weiss nicht" and the run-on, broken syntax all reflect the angry confusion of Oskar. But at the same time the sentence makes us appreciate its mastery at using the devices of rhetoric: parallelism, antithesis, repetition, zeugma, chiasmus. An elaborate game is being played with and against the rules of language. Although there is little amusing about this passage, the reader can take pleasure in the exhibition of skill and in seeing how new verbal connections are made. In short, the prose is both a correlative to an anguished, violent world and a creative response to it that builds its own order, its own playground.

Verbal play—wit, puns, malapropisms—has always been one of the staples of comedy, and play with language is one of the elements that shows black humor's affinity with comedy. Although wordplay has seldom handled such deadly subjects before, it is the perfect means to convey disorder, for it breaks the accepted linguistic conventions of normal speech, and it is a means to play with the patterns and create a new form of its own. The variety in handling language is practically infinite, from the twisted clichés of Ionesco to the highly poetic prose of John Hawkes to the carefully asymmetrical and eccentric logic of Beckett, but it is the formal aspects of language and of linquistic structures that are made into a game the reader is invited to play. The message may be that there is nothing to say, that people are incapable of communicating with each other, that language fails miserably to correspond to the reality it tries to describe, but, paradoxically, it is only by mastering language that such doubt can assume artistic form, and it is only by a willingness to play with language and to risk the dangers of non-sense that the reader can appreciate and participate in these works.

Verbal play reminds us of the artifice of the work we are experiencing and, therefore, distances us from its mimetic referents. Although we may be moved by the characters and their predicaments, by the story told and the world depicted, we are repeatedly made aware that what we are dealing with is not reality but language. In many ways this reminder is frustrating. As William S. Gass expresses it in

"The Medium of Fiction": "That novels should be made of words, and merely words, is shocking, really. It's as though you had discovered that your wife were made of rubber: the bliss of all those years, the fears . . . from sponge."[12] Like the other arts, literature has increasingly turned to exploring its own medium as well as imitating the external world. Because literature's medium of language is intrinsically referential, it cannot escape reality; and black humor does not want to deny the horrors we face in our lives and in our nightmares. But language can be played with and verbal structures can be shaped, re-formed, in a way reality cannot. Language offers us that comfort or that compensation.

Like everything else in literature, characters are constructed of language. Those in black humor often acknowledge the fact, as does the narrator of Beckett's *L'Innommable* (1953)/*The Unnamable* (1958), who tells us he is "in words, made of words."[13] Their awareness that they are fictional or dramatic characters is one of the many devices used in this literature to distance us from them and thereby to help keep them comic, whatever they may suffer. In its presentation of character, black humor breaks away both from the realistic tradition, which situated character in its social setting, and from modernism, with its emphasis on probing the workings of the psyche. There is a tendency to flatten out character, perhaps most pronounced in the motiveless figures of the theater of the absurd and in the novels of recent American authors who have reacted against the Freudian assumptions of their predecessors. And a flat character is almost necessarily comic.

When the characters are more rounded, more fully developed, our perspective on them is continually changed, in the manner discussed in Lypiatt's suicide note, so that we do not know whether to take them seriously and extend our compassion to them or to maintain the distance that allows us to laugh at the silly clowns. Many of these characters are deformed. When the distortion is psychological, our distrust of their reliability modifies our sympathetic response to the tales they tell, especially in the case of an insane narrator whose reportage cannot be verified. When they are physically deformed, they confront us with the disparity between their own grotesque shapes and the individuals contained within those forms.

The characters in black humor may be aware of their dilemma, that on some level they are ridiculous, however anguished they may be and whatever terrible things may happen to them. Whether they are aware or ignorant, the simple humanity of a character in a book or the reality of an actor on stage always moves us toward sympathy, whereas the various techniques I have examined distance us and make the characters comic.

The plots of the fiction and drama of black humor walk the same tightrope. On the one hand, they correspond to the chaotic, disturbing, and often horrifying contents; on the other, they provide a framework that is reassuring, playful, and comic but that does not negate the contents. The simplest form is a plot that leads in a circle back to its beginning, so that although something seems to be happening along the way, when we get to the end, we discover that nothing has changed. In a work like Ionesco's *La Cantatrice chauve* (*The Bald Soprano*, 1950), virtually anything may happen without any logical or necessary connection with what has come before or with what follows, but this madness is contained by an extremely tight structure that offers an audience the safety and artistic pleasure of its boundary; unrestricted contents interplay with highly determined form.

The more complex kind of plot, which is also the other extreme (but equally atypical, abnormal), accepts the first part of a celebrated statement by Henry James and blissfully ignores or vehemently rejects the rest: "Really, universally, relations stop nowhere, and the exquisite problem of the artist is eternally but to draw, by a geometry of his own, the circle within which they shall happily *appear* to do so."[14] These plots refuse to fulfill our expectations that the intrigues of the story will be resolved, that a chronological sequence or series of cause and effect will emerge, and that the work will end at a resting point, most conventionally marriage or death. Thomas Pynchon's *V.* (1963) is a paradigm of this sort of plotting: it tells two loosely interrelated stories, one of which is presented achronologically and neither of which is brought to a conclusion. The broken sequences of a work like William Burroughs's *Naked Lunch* (1959) provide another variant.

In the past, modernist fictions have taken great liberties with plot sequence, but it has been possible for the reader to disentangle and rearrange them, if he were so inclined, and the breaks in narrative sequence were apt to represent the stream of thought of the narrative consciousness. In contemporary black humor, on the other hand, they are seemingly arbitrary, directed only by the whim of the author. That is to say, these works often do not present us with any kind of development, which is the *sine qua non* of what we usually call plot. The work does end, but it is unlikely to have a conclusion. Such a plot would indeed be chaotic were it not for the suggestions of patterns and motifs within these works, the possibility of interconnectedness that is always held out, though never in such a way as to let us establish a clear causal relationship or even to be sure a relationship does exist. In part, this situation reflects the disorder dealt with in the contents. But it is also potentially liberating; the reader is free to play with possibilities, to write his own conclusions, to rearrange the work as he sees fit. A genre that assumes there are no answers cannot provide us with solutions, but it can keep us from following in the rigidly preordained paths of most literary plot. It can invite us to participate in the satisfying game of creating forms at the same time as we recognize the completeness and arbitrariness of the shapes we forge. It can present us with a sky full of stars and let us have the fun of making constellations.

This aspect of play is also present in the literary forms used and created by works of black humor. Black humor, like all comedy, deals with disorder. The most traditional comedy, going back to the New Comedy of Menander, Plautus, and Terence, acknowledges and incorporates the mistakes, aberrations, and incongruities of life; but it contains them within a form where all mysteries and confusions—of class, gender, mistaken identity, and deliberate hypocrisy—are finally resolved. The authors of black humor have the problem of creating form while not trusting the stability of the "real" world and not being willing or able to ignore that instability. They start with the premise of Friedrich Dürrenmatt in his *Theaterprobleme* (1955) that "das Komische darin besteht, das Gestaltlose zu gestalten, das Chaotische zu formen"[15] ("comedy consists of shaping that which is without shape, of giving form to chaos"). Dürrenmatt's own works, which are at home in the realm of black humor, illustrate his contention. At its best, black humor fulfills Beckett's demand for a "new form . . . of such a type that it admits the chaos and does not try to say that the chaos is really something else."[16]

One approach black humor has taken toward such a form is to experiment with and parody the literary models of the past—the Western, the murder mystery, the historical chronicle, the epistolary novel, the philosophical and scientific inquiry, the scholarly edition, and science fiction. More radical experimentation involves playing with the formal possibilities of the stage and of the printed page—incorporating charts and prints, using different typefaces and alignments, introducing random factors, suggesting the reader choose in what order he reads the parts of a work, and so on. Such techniques elicit what we have seen are the typical dualistic responses of black humor: they distance us by calling attention to their own artifice, and they also make us into active participants in the work instead of passive spectators of it. They disorient us by their abuse of literary form, and they invite us to enjoy the joke. The same effect may be obtained by directly addressing the reader or spectator, even when he is insulted, as happens in John Barth's "Life-Story" (1968):

> The reader! You, dogged, uninsultable, print-oriented bas-
> tard, it's you I'm addressing, who else, from inside this
> monstrous fiction. You've read me this far, then? Even this
> far? For what discreditable motive? How is it you don't
> go to a movie, watch TV, stare at a wall, play tennis with
> a friend, make amorous advances to the person who comes
> to your mind when I speak of amorous advances? Can noth-
> ing surfeit, saturate you, turn you off? Where's your
> shame?[17]

In such a passage, any sense of suspense or illusion of verisimilitude is shattered, but the pleasures of mimesis are replaced by those of the game.

The techniques discussed here are not found only in works of black humor. Many of them are also used in postmodernist writings that are outside the scope of black humor because they do not possess its distinctive comic and playful effects, and there are many works that employ some of these devices and not others. The concept of black humor and the correspondences among language, character, plot, and form that I have delineated are functional insofar as they help us to focus on how these techniques come together in a work designed to create a mood of charged ambivalence in its reader or spectator. The test of my notion of black humor, as of any other literary concept, must be its applicability to individual novels and plays and its utility in enabling us to make significant connections and fine discriminations.

NOTES

1. *Oeuvres complètes*, ed. Marcel A. Ruff (Paris: Editions du Seuil, 1968), p. 372.
2. Cited in *Le Livre blanc de l'humour noir*, ed. Jean-Paul Lacroix and Michel Chrestien (Paris: Pensée Moderne, 1966), p. 13. See also Ionesco's "La Démystification par l'humour noir," *L'Avant-Scène*, No. 191 (Feb. 15, 1959), 5-6, which is reprinted in his *Notes et contre-notes*.
3. "Zur Genealogie des schwarzen Humors," *Neue deutsche Hefte*, 13 (1966), 18-34. See also the introduction to Henniger's *Brevier des schwarzen Humors* (München: Deutscher Taschenbuch Verlag, 1966).
4. This essay develops and complements ideas I have set forth in two previous pieces: "*Humour noir* and Black Humor," *Veins of Humor*, ed. Harry Levin, Harvard English Studies 3 (Cambridge, Mass.; Harvard Univ. Press, 1972), pp. 269-284; "The Ethics of Contemporary Black Humor," *The Colorado Quarterly*, 24 (1976), 275-288.
5. *The Countesse of Pembrokes Arcadia*, Vol. I of *The Prose Works of Sir Philip Sidney*, ed. Albert Feuillerat (Cambridge: Cambridge Univ. Press, 1963), pp. 312-313.
6. (New York: Signet, 1960), p. 130.
7. (New York: Harper & Row, 1965), pp. 238-239.
8. (New York: New Directions, 1962), pp. 173-174.
9. Trans. by James Strachey, *The Standard Edition of the Complete Psychological Works of Sigmund Freud*, Vol. 21 (London: Hogarth, 1961), p. 162.
10. (New York: Grove, 1959), p. 48.
11. (Neuwied: Luchterhand, 1974), pp. 165-166.
12. *Fiction and the Figures of Life* (New York: Vintage, 1972), p. 27.
13. In *Three Novels* (New York: Grove, 1965), p. 310.
14. "Preface" to the New York Edition of *Roderick Hudson* (New York: Scribner's, 1907), p. vii.
15. (Zürich: Die Arche, 1955), p. 46.
16. Tom F. Driver, "Beckett by the Madeleine," *Columbia University Forum*, 4 (Summer 1961), 23.
17. *Lost in the Funhouse* (New York: Bantam, 1969), p. 123.

From Pyrrhonic to Vomedic Irony

MORTON GUREWITCH

The title of this essay is both Greek and barbarous. I shall choose an Austrian to unlock the meaning of the Greek, and later I shall call upon an Englishman to clarify the significance of the barbarism. The Austrian is Arthur Schnitzler, who wove poignancy and wit, heartbreak and wryness into a number of interesting, unremarkable works but who managed once to create a masterpiece of ironic comedy: *Reigen* (1903), better known as *La Ronde*. This play, whose subject is the eternal, illicit vitality of sex, is often judged to be a sardonic depiction of human infirmity, a savagely satiric portrait of pitiable, cynical, mechanical hedonists making hay in a sick society. But that is nonsense. Schnitzler is not critically exposing and laughingly expunging (so to speak) a ludicrously unworthy aspect of human conduct. True, there are enough reformably ridiculous follies in Schnitzler's comedy to certify the presence of satire. But *La Ronde* is concerned not so much with the reformably ridiculous as with the irremediably absurd. (I cannot define the absurd with any novelty; it is the irrational, the disharmonious.) Schnitzler, that is to say, is not dedicating his laughter to the cause of human decency and progress. He is, instead, ironically tracing the potent wiles of inextinguishable, regressive impulse and extracting delight from the consequent wreckage of illusion.

The illusion *La Ronde* dispatches is romantic love and fidelity; the absurdity it underscores is lust's hegemony over man. The structure of the play, a ladder curving into a circle, ingeniously embodies Schnitzler's theme. The ladder reaches all the way from the proletarian crudities of the whore and the soldier to the aristocratic finesse of the actress and the count. At the same time, the comedy's circularity is achieved through interlocking erotic scenes that begin with the whore and the soldier and end with the count and the whore, who complete the roundelay. The irony of the circle is transparent: the bondage of sex equalizes all classes and careers; the same carnal compulsion drives everyone (or almost everyone—there are no ascetics in this play) to duplicitous rhetoric and bogus romance.

But that is not all. As the comedy's histrionic exhibitions of amorousness graduate from the soldier's crass, minimally disguised appetites to the actress's exquisitely dippy modulations on desire, the characters become more interestingly insincere. Indeed, competency in shamming becomes the most intriguing criterion of acceptable behavior in the play's erotic encounters. The romantic pretenses of the young gentleman and the young wife, for example, are funny primarily because these two lovers in the making fail to be more skillfully spurious; their rendezvous is soaked in the clichés of elective affinities, fated adultery, and so forth. It is true that they are also being satirized, rather gently, as hypocrites engaged in concocting theatrical feelings in order to justify a sexual liaison. But satire, which aims at the corrigible, is always secondary in ironic comedy, whose gaiety derives from the incorrigible.

La Ronde is an ironic comedy because it reveals the manner in which sexual desire forever forces us, despite differences in social background, profession, and sensibility, to camouflage naked instinct with the charlatanry of love. A further insight borne out by the play must not be neglected: the circle of the absurd may be broken by those capable of converting an animal craving into a species of charm, a quality of grace, a work of art. The one character in the comedy who is especially endowed with such transformational magic (though obviously she cannot match Schnitzler's own ironic feat) is the brainy, zany, irreverent actress, whose whimsical games of sex are marked not only by unpredictable fancies but by empathic expertise. Because the count, for example, is intermittently inclined to sadness (in the whore's bedroom he will ruminate, not too gloomily, on lost innocence), the actress becomes for the nonce a splendidly melancholy creature whose sexual appeal remains quite irresistible.

The actress's protean playfulness frees her not only from the blatancies of sex but from the illusions of love, which the comedy as a whole dissolves with an immense and yet subtle sense of fun. *La Ronde* does not communicate laughter pervaded by moral despair; it does not derisively mourn the failure of sincere, enduring love; it does not acidly satirize the dance of sex as a desecration of a spiritual goal. The romantic ideal, along with emotional profundity, is decisively undermined in Schnitzler's ironizing variations on sex, that unregenerate, irrational, indomitable—and highly comic—urge.

PYRRHONIC IRONY

The kind of ironic comeldy *La Ronde* exemplifies may be called Pyrrhonic, an epithet I borrow from Aldous Huxley's 1946 preface to *Brave New World* (1932). Huxley indicates in this preface that when he wrote his book, he was an "amused Pyrrhonic aesthete" who enjoyed the contrapuntal absurdities—pathological primitivism and pernicious utopianism—of two insane civilizations. As a Pyrrhonist, that is, a radical skeptic, Huxley highlighted the perversity of unstable individual aspiration and the madness of overstable societal organization. As an amused Pyrrhonist, he jested brilliantly with past, present, and future.

A Pyrrhonic ironist, whether short-term or long-term, may be described as a radical skeptic whose awareness of the absurd prompts him, under the aegis of comedy, to ruin reverence, desanctify values, and collapse ideals, all of which are, of course, rather wormy to begin with. As such, he is hardly the soul mate of the satirist, however intimate they may be. A traditional satirist (as against the contemporary nihilistic sort) is likely to treat irony as an instrument, not an attitude; a tool, not a temper. But even if he grasps irony as a vision, not merely a device, he usually subordinates his perception of ironic incongruity, as well as his flair for verbal irony, to his sense of the ridiculous and to a retaliatory, theoretically cleansing critique. (Dickens, for example, heaps up ironic incongruities and indulges in orgies of verbal irony whenever he satirically lacerates Pecksniff for his feints and hypocrisies in *Martin Chuzzlewit*.) The Pyrrhonic ironist, on the other hand, subordinates satiric motives for comedy to his sense of the absurd, which induces him to rate illusion, commitment, and historical change as inevitable, comedy-generating flops.

The Pyrrhonic ironist's credo, or rather anticredo—I disbelieve and am amused in my disbelief because it is absurd—alienates him not only from the religious existentialist (Kierkegaard treasures the right kind of irony as a constant challenge for the spirit, but he deprecates the unsalvational kind as an inability to distinguish between an agent of freedom and a force of destruction), but also from the nonreligious existentialist, whose relation with the absurd involves an anguish of self-metamorphosis the Pyrrhonic ironist knows nothing of. To illustrate the latter point: Sartre once placed a minor figure, the tutor of Orestes, in *The Flies* (1943) to show how a Pyrrhonic ironist's mind functions as an escape mechanism, grinding out divorces from reality. The tutor specializes in smiling skepticism and has, therefore, encouraged Orestes to disdain degrading exhibitions of unreason, especially the silly worship of gods. But it so happens that Jupiter's tyrannic presence in Argos, where Orestes now seeks his twisted and bloody roots, is nightmarishly pronounced. This fact transforms the tutor-ironist, who has managed to keep his cheeks rosy and his spirit snug while decimating the world's superstitions, into an ass. His skeptical bray is burlesquely impotent when he beholds the Furies threatening Orestes (what staggering evidence of the crude myths this ironist has customarily laughed away!) and can only regret that he isn't in Athens, for Attic reason is superb in explaining away culturally barbarous phenomena. In short, the tutor's irony approximates blinders; he has not the vision to cope with mystery, assimilate human pain, or understand the need for heroism.

Because Orestes is determined to liberate his tormented fellow citizens, he rejects his tutor's facile disengagement. Putting on the precious weight of commitment, he accomplishes his necessary murders and repudiates a reactionary Jupiter, thereby becoming (or so he is convinced) his people's savior. The play suggests that the ironist's untroubled self-extrication from the absurd is a form of inertia and irresponsibility and that only an existentialist grappling with the absurd can genuinely purge mankind of intimidating, deranged gods—that is, oppressive regimes and fearful mystifications. Pyrrhonic irony has rarely gotten worse marks. It is damned as an inauthentic, meaningless source of freedom, as a sheer cultivation of the void. In *Being and Nothingness* (1943), Sartre less caustically identifies the ironist, no longer asinine, as one who subtly establishes his personality as a "perpetual negation."

Yet the power of negation is a prime virtue for the gifted Pyrrhonic ironist (one not made of straw, like Orestes' tutor). Negation in his case is not sterile denial but a release from ideological victimization; not a mental miasma but an emancipation from misbegotten, obtuse, noxious affirmations; not a deadly sapping of vitality and devotion (which is what the revolutionary Sophia Antonovna maintains in Conrad's *Under Western Eyes*) but a detoxification of the absurd through comedies made from the flimsy stuff of illusion and certitude. This is precisely what Anatole France, the Ironic Frenchman, was once prototypically famous for. In subsequent generations of experiment and engagement, however, ironic mirth became the crime of insouciance, a retrograde detachment from human crisis, so that France's comic spirit was impugned for lacking grit and defeating promise.

Actually, a number of Anatole France's ironic gurus are neither chilly nor exceptionally passive. Nevertheless, a relatively cool Francean sage like Nicias, in *Thais* (1890), suggests that the Pyrrhonic ironist's heart, like that of Wilde's Lord Henry in *The Picture of Dorian Gray,* tends to be mostly brain, however genial his temperament. That is why Nicias would probably not subscribe to France's own dictum, expressed in *The Garden of Epicurus* (1894), to the effect that irony is the sweetener of life; pity, its consecrator. (This neat formula is shredded as humanistic folderol in Hemingway's *The Sun Also Rises.*)

For Nicias, irony is neither a cowardly apostasy nor a manly euphoria. It is, rather, a pleasurable and privileged atomization of reverence, governed by a blithe, lucid temper that immunizes one against the delusions of belief and the horrors of faith—the latter being incarnated in the sex-haunted holiness of the rabid monk Paphnutius. (*Thais* is the work that Rampion, the Laurentian character in Huxley's *Point Counter Point,* calls a boy's book, but one that is indispensable in getting at certain perverse bonds between piety and sensuality.) In short, Nicias typifies the Pyrrhonic ironist's distance of disinfection from an absurd world, although it should be added that he is not as aloof or as complicatedly disenchanted as, say, Axel Heyst's icily uninvolved father in Conrad's *Victory* (1915). Nicias, in fact, is a dilettante of tolerance. He is kind to all the truths he possesses, and he is convinced that he possesses them all, but he believes in none, for he regards them as toys of the mind that serve only to beguile men's eternal infancy.

All philosophic and religious systems, all sublunary bundles of truths are in the view of the Pyrrhonic ironist chiefly entertaining signatures of the absurd. The Pyrrhonic ironist, moreover, will at times apply his disintegrative skepticism to the very source of those signatures: the cosmos itself, the ultimate matrix of the absurd. One of the standard ways of engineering this sort of advanced demolition work is to invent demonic comedians to do the job. But ironic devils are scarcely all of a piece, if only because their infernal mordancy may be lamed by higher authority. Mephistopheles' sniping in *Faust,* for instance, is brilliant, but it is admittedly tethered to final good. In contrast, Ivan's devil in Dostoevsky's *The Brothers Karamazov* (1881) pokes truly subversive fun at an insanely Christianized universe. This devil, hallucinated by a feverish, self-tormenting Ivan, slyly and ingratiatingly presents himself as a cosmic underdog, frail, inadequate, abused. He claims that he became the devil only under duress, through some incomprehensible primordial decree; and he insists he is so baffled by the non-Euclidean fantasticality of the upper spheres that he is not at all certain there actually is a God—or even a devil. (Obviously, this devil does not mind spicing his revelations with the illogic by which he is so offended.)

What especially irks this untrustworthy devil is that he has been bamboozled into generating dissonance in human affairs. He was persuaded to do so after being informed that human history would come to a standstill if he did not stoke up enough irrationality and discord. This translates into a fiendishly ironic axiom: reason and harmony can only paralyze life on earth. Ivan's devil seems to be parodying God's gadfly doctrine in the heavenly prologue to *Faust,* which states that man needs the stimulus of error and obstacle to attain salvation. But the parody is nihilistic. Far from huzzahing God's shrewdness in arranging for an everlasting jangling of the human spirit on earth, Ivan's devil emphasizes the lunacy of a deity who could plot so shocking, so insulting, so reason-deprived and harmony-impoverished a course for mankind. The devil's message is the absurd's masterpiece: he himself is the suppressed savior of humanity (his role as villain of the universe is the cross he has to bear), whereas God (or, more accurately, unnamed supernal powers, with whom the devil may one day become reconciled if ever he is made privy to certain vital cosmic secrets) has inaugurated a wanton Christian theology of unreason and evil.

What juicier plums for Pyrrhonic irony than the incorrigible morals of the universe or the maniacal irrationalities of its makers? This metaphysical fruit lends its flavor to certain of Borges's fictions, in which teasing fantasies of the absurd echo, though with far greater intricacy, the suasions and gripes of Dostoevsky's great cosmic comedian. Yet such fantasies are apt to commingle with anguish, vertigo, or awe, so that an ironic purity of smiling denigration may be hard to pin down. However, in a fiction like "The Library of Babel," in the collection titled *The Garden of Forking Paths* (1941), absurdist lunacy can be richly mined, as when we learn of a Kafkaesque group of official inquisitors whose centuries-long search for a "clarification of humanity's basic mysteries" remains labyrinthine, profitless, dimly obscene, and perilously daffy. In this same epistle, the unwinking, faith-haunted narrator castigates the impious for believing that "nonsense is normal" in the Library (the universe) and that the constituents of this weirdly bookish place are very likely the product of a "delirious divinity." Unlike the narrator, the ironically attuned reader will welcome the impious as thoroughbred Pyrrhonists rather than desperate ignoramuses.

Those of Borges's bizarre, miniaturized comedies that imply irresolvable disgraces in the nature of infinity and eternity strikingly exemplify Pyrrhonic irony. Yet ironic comedy evokes a mad cosmos sparingly, simply because it cannot do very much with so unwieldy an object. It prefers the familiarity of terrestrial absurdities (sex, faith, truth, death, history, among others) whose longevity seems assured. Certainly, this is how ironic comedy operates in the world of the novel. The operation is not smooth, however, for as the absurd infiltrates the complexities of the novel, it becomes alloyed with noncomic materials, so that it acquires uncertain tonalities. We can see this happening in E. M. Forster's *A Passage to India* (1924), that remarkable work whose impurities of theme and attitude will probably never be rinsed out by criticism.

Insofar as comedy holds its own in Forster's novel, it is essentially satiric and ironic. Satiric because India is a repository of the ridiculous, overflowing with English colonial fatheads and volatile, fractious Indians—both sides, for the most part, being niggling, obscurantist, and rash. Ironic because India is rife with historical irrationalities, compounded by political, religious, psychological, and even physical anomalies that seem beyond resolving. (Compare *The Man Without Qualities,* the first volume of which was published in 1930. Like Forster's India, the Austro-Hungarian Empire in Musil's novel is an area of satire and a symbol of the absurd. The satire emerges from the bumbling busyness of the Collateral Campaign, a vast, factitious celebration of the empire; the irony emerges from the fact that the empire itself is a preposterous, collapsing monument to historical unreason.)

No wonder Forster dangles before us the twinship of mystery and muddle. What else can explain (of course, it is no explanation) the comic, but also noncomic, warping and blurring of convictions, feelings, happenings, impressions? If we inspect certain aspects of faith in this novel—the handling of faith is perhaps the surest litmus test for any ironist's sense of the absurd—shall we see mystery-muddle dissipate, or shall we see it thicken? And will a tone of lightness remain in force, or will it be ousted by gravity? Consider the quandary of Mr. Sorely, the younger and more enlightened of the novel's two marginal Christian missionaries. Mr. Sorely is willing to see monkeys and even jackals as recipients of God's infinite mercy; but he cringes at the idea of extending God's blessing to wasps, oranges, bacteria, and mud, which his theologically more generous Hindu friends are devoutly prepared to see God embrace. What are we to make of this? It would seem that both Christianity and Hinduism are being satirized for antithetical inadequacies: Christianity for being hedged round by insuperable country club discriminations; Hinduism for being intolerably messy in assigning redemptive capacities to, or guaranteeing God's concern for, fruit, filth, and wriggling microscopic entities. But beyond this thrust of satire one may perceive a delicate ironic erosion of the very ideal of religious charity and brotherhood.

Forster's reverential description of an elaborate Hindu ritual in the last section of *A Passage to India* is similarly ironized, for reverence is mixed with the kind of sovereign playfulness that sees men and mystics worshiping with disarming, loving gestures while remaining stranded in comic benightedness. It is all very tantalizing. Does the Hindu ceremony signify that God is really love, after all ("God si *[sic]* love" is perhaps more cockeyed than iffy), or does it suggest that God is an astonishingly littered void? Forster has it both ways: he is at once communicating the ineffable and the absurd. The result is that mystery-muddle is both dispelled and consolidated.

So much the better for Pyrrhonic irony (one might think), which thrives on indeterminacy and elusiveness. Yes, but the trouble is that Forster has already poisoned his final ambiguity by making the hideous echo in the Marabar Caves unforgettably reverberant. Moreover, the hundred Indias in the novel are not a colorful cultural hodgepodge; they concretize, if anything, a metaphysics of dissonance. Forster's comments on the cosmos's future cancellation of human divisiveness are intended to counterbalance such a metaphysics, but they are not very reassuring. For example, the image of the lowly punkah wallah, who is described as looking like a god though socially he is a scrap of refuse, prompts the narrator's reflection that divinity and garbage are from time to time bonded by nature to defy society's wicked class distinctions. Forster here recurs, with a slight change in terminology, to the cosmic impartiality that will finally do away with inequalities among men. But that power, ensconced somewhere in the illimitable, seems indecently divine in its neutrality. In any case, occasional hints that strife and alienation, so rampant in India, are not the key to ultimate reality do not jibe very well with reiterated ironic demonstrations that earthly uncertainties, disparities, and conflicts are virtually imperishable.

The Pyrrhonic comedy of incertitude, unreliability, and disharmony, which periodically blooms and is regularly suffocated in *A Passage to India,* is far more steadily and vigorously presented in Gide's *Lafcadio's Adventures* (1914), where ironic demoralizations become positively merry. Gide's aptitude for the absurd is more impish, if less profound, than Forster's, especially in his use of that slippery engine of irony: chameleonic truth. *Lafcadio's Adventures* is a novel dedicated to the ungraspable, to changing masks and shifting views and multiple fraud (fraud being, so to speak, uncertainty negatively consummated), particularly as it reveals the misguided efforts of the farcical savior Amédée Fleurissoire to rescue the supposedly kidnapped pope and expose his illegitimate substitute. What Amédée discovers is that truth and treachery are practically synonymous. Not surprisingly, the reader, swept along by an exhilarating insecurity that inside knowledge scarcely modifies, rides a crest of thematic fulfillment when Anthime Armand-Dubois, Amédée's scientific brother-in-law, ventures to suggest, in a fit of arthritic retributiveness, that a sham pope is perhaps only the prelude to a phony Almighty, who by implication must be lord of a swindling universe.

Instead of finding the pope, Amédée loses his virginity in a Roman brothel (nor is he unmarried to begin with). His missionary fiasco is completed when Lafcadio, impelled by a "gratuitous act," pushes the tortured ninny out of a moving train. Lafcadio himself is neither a buffoon nor an ironist. Yet he resembles Gide the ironist in the way he eschews sameness and stability. Several of Lafcadio's "uncles" have promoted his resilience by teaching him to despise utility and need (whimsy comes first) and to reject logic and consistency (unpredictability is preferable). Yet if Lafcadio's lightness of spirit is compatible with the ironic temper, his youthful love of novelty and risk is not.

Lafcadio has invented a philosophy of total possibility (which is strangely similar to the narrator's juggling with the infinite resources of truth-and-falsity). Its doctrine allows him, for example (in theory at any rate), either to kiss or to throttle an old Italian peasant woman. When his philosophic speculations are damaged by the unintendedly ugly killing of Amédée, Lafcadio is uncharacteristically immobilized by nightmare sensations. These are not likely to last, however, for at the end of the novel, in a typical erasure of omniscience (this deflation of authority, along with other roguish dismissals of narrative stereotypes, is one of Gide's major irony-engendering tactics), the narrator conjectures (but who knows?) that Lafcadio may well resume a life of curiosity and charming disrelationship. This is to say that Lafcadio's rejection of herdlike placidities may continue to parallel, in some extranovelistic realm, the ironic author's dismantling of absolutes and fixities.

Gide's ironic uncrowning of "truth" has been fraternally analyzed by Thomas Mann as a prankishly demonic relativism played out between the boundaries of anarchy and order. This analysis applies even better to the early Huxley, the Ironic Englishman who was to renounce the Pyrrhonic absurd (never quite successfully) in order to embrace the Perennial Philosophy. But it is Huxley's zestful desecrations of the ideal and his sardonic insinuations that life is a grotesque japery (these are more extreme ironic positions than Gide's) that give him a place in this essay, not his anthological recourse to an army of mystics.

Nevertheless, one early indication of Huxley's eventual journey from irony to faith ought not to be disregarded. In the final segment of *Antic Hay* (1923), Gumbril Jr., skeptical ex-pedagogue and some-time earwig ("below good and evil"), entertains the sirenic Myra Viveash with an encyclopedic patchwork of minutiae. After ranging disconnectedly from the mating rites of octopuses to family vaults in Italian cemeteries, he faintly qualifies his fragmentariness by implying that he may one day become a third-rate saint. This is a depressing glance at the future, for Gumbril is superlatively comic when he cannibalizes faith. Take, for instance, his early revelation in school chapel; here his inspiration springs not from a soul athirst (God, Gumbril concludes, is an unsatisfactory concept) but from uncomfortable buttocks. However, buttocks do get perversely connected to soul through the Greek *pneuma* (air, breath, spirit), for Gumbril has envisioned and intends to commercialize a sedentary man's paradisal pair of trousers, equipped with inflatable, pneumatic seats. Not a very noble vision, perhaps, but neither Gumbril nor his more cynical acquaintances can regard the kind of dream that is fueled by high-mindedness as other than pathetically, even stinkingly, obsolete in a disabused postwar world.

ROMANTIC IRONY

Of all the ideals that are comically eviscerated in *Antic Hay,* none is more hauntingly ironized than romantic love. Gumbril is aware that his love affair with Emily, who is possessed of a crystalline purity of spirit (and an odd history of virginity) offers a unique chance of redemption from his frivolous negativism and his quasi-Rabelaisian antics. But he is not really prepared to abandon irony or sensuality or mendacity for mystical quietude. Switching shabbily from Emily to the more provocative and coercive Myra, Gumbril works himself into a state of neurotic foolery that licenses him to blaspheme the great romantic lines by Arnold and Musset on the nexus between passion, pain, and beauty and to soil even further his experience of ecstasy by making a farcical joke out of Emily's preternatural sexual ignorance.

In this comic profanation of rapture, Huxley is exploiting the duality of romantic irony, which is a distinct variant of the ironic imagination. Romantic irony differs from Pyrrhonic irony in one all-important respect: Pyrrhonic irony is predicated on the failure of illusion in an absurd world; romantic irony, on the other hand, sustains the illusion it mockingly shatters. By pitting a comic, authentic antiromanticism against a genuine romanticism (or vice versa), romantic irony creates a union of mutually incompatible forces that allows dreams to survive their own destruction. Although in this connection we must pay homage to Friedrich von Schlegel, who calls, among other things, for a union of spontaneity and analysis, idealism and wit in romantic poetry, but whose invertebrate novel *Lucinde* (1799) fuses passion and play disappointingly, we must credit Byron with being the first great part-time comedian of romanticism. Byron's ambivalence, his romantic ardor and antiromantic cynicism, can scarcely be better illustrated than in the juxtaposition, in the first canto of *Don Juan* (1819), of two contrasting stanzas on the moon: the first makes the moon a peeping pander; the second, a sanctifying source of beauty and love.

In a similar vein, Heine merges two thoroughly discordant but equally compelling images in "The God Apollo," in the *Romanzero* (1851): one reveals a spellbinding, radiant, exiled god of harmony, surrounded by nine lovely muses (this image is a bit tarnished, however, by an Offenbachian element in the god's music); the other exhibits a shady, pork-eating ex-rabbi touring the country in the role of a Greek god, attended by squealing casino girls. The ideal is also wedded to its negation in Stendhal's romantic irony. In the introduction to *Love* (1822), Stendhal professes to be the first scientific, truly dispassionate analyst of this pathological condition; yet at the same time he celebrates the madness of love as the greatest of beatitudes. In his chapter "Werther and Don Juan," Stendhal assigns values and disvalues to Werther's romantic passion and Don Juan's antiromantic inconstancy, after which he gives the palm, with a nod to virtue rather than virtuosity, to Werther. He, nonetheless, leaves the impression that a Wertherian Don Juanism, which Julien Sorel will dramatize both gloriously and hilariously in *The Red and the Black* (1830), may combine the best of both amorous worlds. In the late, Baudelairean stage of romantic irony, queerer hybridizations occur. But by then romantic irony, often imaging life as a darkly comic curse, betrays a connoisseurship in voracious absurdity.

VOMEDIC IRONY

This brings us back to *Antic Hay* and to another variant of the ironic temper. (The early Huxley is clearly a complete ironist.) In the cabaret scene late in the novel, Gumbril and Myra find themselves beset by a sense of disconnection, hollowness, futility. It is at this point that Huxley introduces the novel's presiding deity (it presides over the closing chapters, at any rate): Nil, "world-soul, spiritual informer of all matter." Shortly afterwards, Gumbril and Myra witness a playlet of the absurd in which the utopian cravings of a monster are mortally scorned by a brutish world. This burlesque proof of the disfigurement and death of the ideal hardly arrests the dancing, epigrammatizing, and fornicating of two sophisticated escapees from Nothing. What they lack, however, is the exuberance of their friend Coleman, the diabolist who can depict London as an infernal city swarming with mephitic births, putrid copulations, and squalid deaths, but who can also vilify the human vomedy with near-apoplectic laughter. The human "vomedy," Huxley's felicitous typographical error for the human comedy (it occurs in one of his early essays), is a phrase that will serve to profile the most recent twist in the ironic temper.

Vomedic irony, as it may be called with pardonable ugliness, retains enough buoyancy to function as comedy. But its spirit of the absurd is so thoroughly amalgamated with bleakness, torment, and dread (Kafka's narratives of clownish-torturous bafflement come to mind) that it may seem to betoken the death of comedy. Yet Vomedic irony remains affiliated with certain ancient ironic insights that were intended to furnish a stimulus and a salve. Thus the point of Lucian's ironic wisdom in "Dialogues of the Dead"—life is a dream; life is a bubble; life hangs by a thread, erratically twitched by Chance and unpredictably slit by Death—is that one had better be candidly and cheerily resigned. In much the same way, the message of Montaigne's "Of Democritus and Heraclitus" rebukes defeatism. Exposed to the facts of disenchantment—nature is mutable; man, corruptible; the universe, chaotic—one had better learn to laugh; for in the face of unavoidable calamities, it is more enlightened to be flippant than furious, wiser to be mocking than miserable. In a word, disengagement and lightness provide a prophylactic against the absurd.

In the human vomedy, however, pessimism, nightmare, and nausea threaten to become overwhelming, so that the last-ditch verve, the uncannily resistant gaiety of Vomedic irony (which is often allied with farce) is, in effect, a prestidigitatory release from the shadows of destruction. In Beckett's *Molloy* (1951), the wit of entropy, the jokiness of decomposition, tenaciously and even miraculously alters or evicts what would otherwise be a purely morbid, if marvelously ingenious, depression. For Molloy, "it's misery to stay, misery to go"; yet traveling from one heap of muck to another gives him on occasion the sensation of being a gratefully ephemeral butterfly (whose energy is constrained by a crippled body and crumbling wings). In Céline's *Journey to the End of the Night* (1932), Bardamu is devirginized by the horror of war and immersed in the universal excrement of peace. Yet Bardamu's anxious, raffish, derisory survivalism and Céline's savage stylistic vivacity overcome the repulsiveness of reality.

In West's *Miss Lonelyhearts* (1933), the protagonist does not survive his own prolonged baptism of horror; yet the agonies Miss Lonelyhearts contends with in his column (witness the Gogolian case of teenage Desperate, born without a nose and hence unable to attract a boyfriend) are displayed with a grotesque funniness that de-emotionalizes the reader's sense of nausea. Moreover, Shrike, the contemptible newspaper editor whose vulgar, boisterous, corrosive cynicism makes Stavrogin's lethargically demonic irony in Dostoevsky's *The Possessed* (1871) seem almost Christlike in comparison, dissolves ideals with a cruel gusto that paradoxically helps the reader stave off tears, terror, and psychic vomiting.

Irony in its vomedic phase is a purgative for atrocities and humiliations, but Pyrrhonic irony is obviously closer to what one conventionally expects of comedy. Indeed Pyrrhonic irony least wrenches one away from such expectations when it abbreviates its distance of disinfection from an absurd world and becomes tolerant enough, even compassionate enough, to enter into a symbiotic, Chekhovian relation with humor's affection and affirmation. Pyrrhonic irony and humor are kissing kin in *The Magic Mountain* (1924), for example, where Mann, the Ironic German who preferred the title of humorist, deploys his extensive "equivocal" irony basically to reconcile the irreconcilable, to heal the absurd in the interests of harmony. Italo Svevo's ironic sportiveness in *The Confessions of Zeno* (1923) becomes a humorous indulgence of human foibles and foul-ups, many of which stem directly from Zeno himself, whose preoccupation with women, sickness, or last cigarettes reveals a mind cluttered with forgivable instabilities. *Ulysses* (1922) conjoins irony and humor rather more acrobatically. The novel is often manipulated by a devastating Pyrrhonic irony that makes a shambles of reality and reliability. Yet the central characterization of Bloom, appealingly miserable and kind, resiliently dignified, burlesquely aspiring, points to a humorous condonation and acceptance of man at the heart of Joyce's overcoordinated yet chaotic universe.

Still, ironic subversiveness and humorous yea-saying can hardly melt lexically into each other. It would be a mistake (however agreeable) to return, for example, to the language of Charles Lamb, who in "New Year's Eve" is troubled by reminders of unpalatable mortality and, therefore, ruminates on the precious things he wishes never to be weaned from: "Sun and sky, and breeze, and solitary walks, and summer holidays, and the greenness of fields, and the delicious juices of meats and fishes, and society, and the cheerful glass, and candlelight, and fireside conversations, and innocent vanities and jests, and *irony itself*—do these things go out with life?" It is Lamb who italicizes irony as a supreme delight. But, of course, he means by irony a playful obliquity of spirit, not a Pyrrhonic destruction of sweet security, just as he means, in speaking of absurdity in "All Fools' Day," not a cosmic violation of harmony and reason but a gentle, humorous aberration perpetrated by one or another innocent in a benign, if also shadowed, world. Devotees of "irony itself," like Lamb's "darlings of absurdity," are not yet wandering about among the world's lost tribes; but their comic zest, for good or ill, kicks up happy dust mainly in the realm of nostalgia.

4

Physical Deformity and Chivalric Laughter in Renaissance England

JOHN J. O'CONNOR

"We laugh at deformed creatures . . . ," says Sir Philip Sidney flatly in his *Defense of Poetry.* Modern readers who fancy they live in a more refined age are likely to be shocked, but Sidney is merely uttering a sixteenth-century cliché. He admits that such laughter is not delightful but rather a kind of "scornful tickling." The germ of much of what he says goes back at least to Aristotle, who in his sketchy comments on comedy in the *Poetics* defines laughter as a category of the ugly.[1] Aristotle's word is *aiskhrós,* which signifies the opposite of *kalós,* beautiful. In Greek the word can be applied to the spiritual as well as to the physical, as can Sidney's word *deformed.* Many humorous characters, like Jonson's Morose in *Epicoene,* may properly be called deformed. Nevertheless, that the Greek word is solidly anchored in the physical is clear from Homer's applying it to Thersites, the ugliest *(aískhistos)* man who came to Troy.[2] For Sidney and the Renaissance, the part of the *Iliad* where the crump-shouldered Thersites is soundly thrashed by Odysseus to the merriment of the Greek leaders was a comic touchstone.

Renaissance literature provides an abundance of instances where deformed creatures incite laughter. One need look no further than Shakespeare's Richard III, deformed, unfinished, sent, as he says, before his time into a world where dogs bark at him as he halts by. His crookback makes him literary brother to Thersites and, despite a world of differences between them, renders him almost inevitably comic. Although the stage provides many examples where some kind of physical ugliness or ungainliness is the root of comedy—Falstaff's belly, Bardolph's nose—for obvious reasons one does not expect to find extreme displays of physical deformity. Because it is often by looking at extremes that we learn where the limits of an idea are, the best place to look for deformed creatures is in chivalric romances, the most old-fashioned and convention-ridden literature of the Renaissance.

Chivalric romances often smacked of the Middle Ages, but perhaps for that reason they were very popular. Some now rank among the rarest books, for as they were often cheaply printed and held in low critical esteem, few readers treasured them up to a life beyond life. They were "popular" in a basic sense. Free of the physical limitations of the stage, they dealt with a world of the imagination. That world relied more on a sense of wonder than humor, but still there was a lot of humor in them. That it was often cruel may be the reason much of it has gone unnoticed or disdained. It is the kind of scornful tickling that depended heavily upon the ugly and misshapen and derived chiefly from two physical extremes, dwarfs and giants.

DWARFS IN CHIVALRIC ROMANCES

From ealiest times dwarfs were regarded with both ridicule and peculiar respect. They appear in accounts of the pharaohs and were sold in Roman times at prices far beyond those asked for slaves of normal size. Indeed, so desirable seemed the life of a dwarf that some parents attempted to stunt the growth of their children by enclosing them in little caskets (glossokoma).[3] During the Renaissance dwarfs were very fashionable at continental courts and were frequently intimates of royal and noble families. Perhaps they were regarded by aristocrats as an object lesson in humility, epitomes of the little state of man, living memento mori. Erika Tietze-Conrat's Dwarfs and Jesters in Art, a collection of paintings and sculptures of dwarfs and fools, is an intriguing record of the variety of ways in which dwarfs were seen.

In real life a certain amount of ridicule was inescapable. Italian dwarfs were often called Morgante or Morgantino, after the name of Pulci's giant, and dwarfs were sometimes used for purposes of grotesque spectacle. On one occasion, to amuse the ladies, Lucrezia Borgia had two dwarfs served up along with some fruit.[4] In Rome in 1566, Cardinal Vitelli gave a great banquet at which his guests were served by thirty-four dwarfs, almost all deformed.[5] In early seventeenth-century Paris, an outdoor performance at the Pont Neuf called *The Farce of the Hunchbacks* tickled onlookers. In it four hunchbacks, after being thrown into the river, emerged and engaged in a free-for-all.[6] When the Duke of Buckingham entertained Charles I and Henrietta Maria, a great pie was brought to the table, and at a propitious moment out popped a dwarf, to the particular admiration of the queen.[7]

Despite the Duke of Buckingham, England escaped most of this grotesquerie. Until the time of Henrietta Maria, dwarfs do not occupy a large part of the national consciousness. The few parts for dwarfs, as in Jonson's *Volpone* and Beaumont's *Knight of the Burning Pestle*, were played by boys. In 1636 dwarfs appeared in the mask *Richmond,* dressed as squires and bearing their masters' shields.[8] But nothing on the scale of the *Farce of the Four Hunchbacks* is to be found.

What Elizabethans knew about dwarfs doubtless came mostly by way of chivalric romances, so that literary tradition is a stronger force than historical fact. In these romances the dwarf always appears as grotesque, ugly, and, therefore, laughable. He is deformity in essence: infinite ugliness in a little room. When Birmartes first sees the dwarf Buzando, he bursts into laughter, for Buzando is "la plus layde & contrefaite personne, que Nature produit onques"[9] ("the ugliest and most deformed person Nature ever made"). Not only Birmartes but other characters who merely set eyes on dwarfs break into laughter. When the unusually tall Queen of Carmania ("shee did surmount all the knightes that were there foure fingers") enters a hall in formal array, leading a knight and followed by two dwarfs, one holding her train, the other carrying the knight's shield, which completely hides him, all those in the hall laugh.[10] In the infamous Canto 28 of *Orlando Furioso* a queen royally cuckolds her husband, one of the handsomest men in the world, by copulating with a dwarf, one of the ugliest. In Harington's English translation, the plate depicting the bizarre congress was notorious.

Though Sidney says deformity does not make for delightful laughter, writers of chivalric romances generally ignore delight and aesthetic subtlety. They portray dwarfs as almost always timorous or cowardly and, therefore, the more ridiculous. In *Palmendos* dwarfs are on one occasion sarcastically referred to as "these Myrmedons."[11] When Dardan the Dwarf leads Amadis to the castle of Arcalaus the Enchanter, he does so in fear and trembling. "Amadis tooke great pleasure to beholde his trembling, speaking thus merily to him. Feare not tall fellow, but let vs go down these staires" *(A de G,* I, 125). That Amadis, the epitome of knighthood, should resort to such unfeeling derision suggests that the line between cruelty and fun was not easy to discern.[12] Perhaps the demands of his allegory kept Spenser from making the Red Cross Knight's nameless dwarf-squire laughable, however timorous and cautious he may be.

Jibes at dwarfs are common in the romances, but so is cruelty. Dwarfs often find themselves batted around like tennis balls. Thus Troglador forces the dwarf Toydall to climb the topmast and tumble into the sea, where he nearly drowns.[13] Because he will not give up a letter that he is holding between his teeth, Buzando is whacked mercilessly by two churls at the command of a knight *(A de G,* VIII, Ch. 18). The dwarf Risdene is snatched off a ship by a huge bird and dropped on an island. Later he is suspended out a castle window, whence he falls onto the horns of a bull that gallops off with him.[14] Dardan is captured by Arcalaus and hung by one foot over a very smoky fire, an incident to which he often later refers and which never fails to draw laughter from Amadis and others *(A de G,* I, Ch. 19).

Dwarfs in this kind of fiction are supposed to be witty as well as laughable. On one occasion while the female warrior Alastraxerée is overthrowing several knights one after the other, a dwarf seated on an elephant makes pithy remarks that perhaps passed for wit in the sixteenth century, such as "Or deuinez si elle ne saulteroit pas bien mieux sur vn lict toute nuë" ("imagine whether she would not gambol even better naked on a bed") *(A de G,* IX, Ch. 28, fol.73ᵛ). When Amadis kills Dramis, the giant falls from his horse "as waightily, as if it had beene the fall of an Oxe. Get thee to all the Diuels, said Dardan the Dwarffe, my master is very well rid of thee . . ." *(A de G,* I, Ch. 43, p. 246). The dwarf Mardoquée, who on one occasion is made to engage in a wrestling match with the bumpkin Darinel for the delectation of his mistress and her friends, debates with him, too, about who is more handsome *(A de G,* IX, Chs. 34, 57). Mardoquée insists that beauty ought not be measured by the foot.

Although in medieval literature dwarfs sometimes possess strength, it has almost entirely disappeared by the sixteenth century. Nabot in *Gerileon of England* is a partial exception. He is described as "scarsely three Cubites in height," but he takes prisoner the King of Thrace. He keeps him in a miserable prison, gives him a little dirty water infrequently, and "when as hee purposeth to take his iourney anye where on Horsebacke, he causeth hym to bee brought foorth to crouche to the grounde, that he setting his foote vpon his backe, may make hym serue for a Stirrope to mounte on Horsebacke. . . ."[15] In thus anticipating a spectacular feat of Tamburlaine, little Nabot merely emphasizes his own absurdity. For a quality essential to the use of a human being as a horse block is gratuitousness. The tall, stalking Tamburlaine does not need a Bajazeth. Because Nabot does, he makes himself rather than the King of Thrace ludicrous. He is a dwarf acting like a giant.

GIANTS IN CHIVALRIC ROMANCES

For obvious reasons dwarfs in the romances are greatly outnumbered by giants. Dwarfs had limited uses. They might serve as messengers, rather unhelpful squires, or humorous hangers on, but few plots demand anything further from them. Many giants are not funny at all, but they make up in wickedness for what they lack in laughter. Moreover, some giants are not merely bestial, misshapen villains, but they become, like dwarfs, objects of ridicule and nasty chivalric humor.

Giants' names often suggest strangeness and disproportion and now and then a hint of a smile. *Nomen est omen,* it is said, and giant names are often gigantic. Some like Lurcon and Squamell suggest evil in a small bisyllabic way, but most giants have names of at least three syllables. Bustrafo, Mandroco, Franarco, Fulmineo, Candramarte, Barbario, Charonifer, Calfurnio, Briarostes, Brandimardo, and Monstruofuron represent some attempts to give a proper air of ferocity. Some writers apparently felt that even such names were not imposing enough, for many giants brandish two names. Grand Cardigan, Brandaman Campeon, Gedereon (or Geredeon) Brandembul, Furio Cornelio, Brontajar Danfania, Frandalon Cyclops, and Strangoulam-Boeuf presumably give the reader a mouth-filling sense of weightiness. A name like Alizar may seem at first tame by comparison, but it is usually followed by the awesome epithet *L'outrageux Roy.* Similarly, the giant Bergamo gains a degree of added ferocity from the addition "from the Taurus Mountains," and the formidable Famongomadan, as if that designation were not ample, is commonly referred to as the Giant of the Boiling Lake. Ardan Canileo also grows in readers' imaginations because *Canileo* means dog-lion, and he, like several ferocious giants in *Amadis de Gaule,* is a dog-faced denizen of the isle of Cynofale (a variant of Cyno-cephale, dog head). Inevitably in such Brobdingnagian names a touch of humor emerges, especially in such as Orbirrohell and Ortolomorgantell.

Giants are not always described. Perhaps the name alone is suggestive enough. Height is sometimes given precisely—as when we learn that Gedereon Brandembul is fifteen cubits tall—but then a second giant, we are told more vaguely, is so large that "he seemed to be a great tree" *(M of K,* V, fol. 221). When more detailed descriptions appear, they are often grotesque and ridiculous. For example, the giant Sallazart is thus introduced:

> For firste, he was so greate, that he by halfe exceeded the vulgare and common proportion of other menne: his hayres of his heade as blacke as a coale: neither was his Face any whitte fairer: wherein were twoo eyes that shinyng as well by night as by daie, would haue made the stoutest afraied: hauyng his browes a foote of good measure broade. The Nose a spanne long or more, the Mouthe stretchyng to his Eares, whiche with length laie on his Shoulders, like a Bloodhounde. And moreouer he had twoo long Tuskes or Teeth, sharpe as a Pike,

which raught fully halfe a Foote out of his Mouthe: his Chinne
was like the reste, whereon appeared no more haire then on
a Cow taile: for like a stinkyng Goate he had it hangyng to his
girdlestead. As for the reste, he was the finest Youth of the
worlde: but that he was great Bealied, and bigge Shouldred,
cariyng a Mountaine (as it were) vpon his backe *(G of E,* I,
fol. 87ᵛ).

As this description goes on, deformity grows more and more patently
ridiculous. As the reference to the cow's tail and the goat and the
sarcasm of "the finest Youth of the worlde" indicate, Sallazart is as
comic as he is fearful.

Moreover, giants carry on in a way that emphasizes the grotesque.
In battle they commonly roar like animals, and their rage is so extraordinary that they literally fume. The giant that Bellianis ultimately
kills blasphemes and, "foming like a Boare, and guided with a hellish
rage, most thicke smoke issued from the Vysor of his helme . . . ."[16]
One recalls how Orgoglio in the fight against Arthur "brayd with
beastly yelling sound" *(The Faerie Queene,* I, 8, 11). When the giant
Madaran is unhorsed, he begins "a letter vne fumée espesse de la
bouche & des nazeaux" ("to emit a thick smoke from his mouth and
nostrils") *(A de G,* XI, Ch. 13, fol. 25ᵛ). The great Corbalestre, apparently even more infuriated, ejects "la fumée par les yeux" ("the smoke
by his eyes"), and the prodigious Scaranfe emits "feu & fumée par le
nez, & par les oreilles" ("fire and smoke by his nose and his ears")
(A de G, XVII, Ch. 18, Fol. 97). As the fight goes against them, as it
almost always does in the end, giants rage against their gods, invariably pagan. The fire and smoke, the beastly roaring, and the blasphem-
ies frequently given in lurid detail provide a vision and cacophony the
reader could laugh at.

Because they are so animalistic and blaspheme so, they no doubt
deserve the cruelty—that apparently tickled readers—with which they
are killed. Heroes usually make giants suffer, and the suffering is
often attended by explicit laughter. Gerileon, for example, kills the
giant Ferclaste in typical fashion. When Ferclaste swings his mighty
club, Gerileon dodges so that "the Giaunte could not recouer again
his Club, beyng entred more then twoo foote into the ground." When
he tries to pull it out, Gerileon severs his right arm, then his left. Later
he cuts off one of the giant's legs "iuste in the gartering place: whereat
the Giaunte fell to the grounde" *(G of E,* I, fol. 55). The order in which
the giant's limbs are lopped off varies, but some form of cutting down
to size often happens, and it is commonly a laughing matter. When
Oceander cuts off both Grand Cardigan's arms, the narrator informs
us that the giant is left "in a pittifull pickle." In the same work, after
Ortolomorgantell overthrows Olbiocles and Phianora and lifts his club
to dispatch them both with one blow, Oceander steps in and cuts off

both the giant's arms. "Wherat *Olbiocles* . . . laughed a good," and
Ortolomorgantell is "quite dasht out of countenance" (*K of the Sea,*
pp. 124, 178). After Rosicleer lops off both Candramarte's arms at the
elbows, the giant swears revenge. He later sets on his sons to kill
Rosicleer. Infuriated by their lack of skill and courage, he reviles them:
"Thou vile and dastarde sheepe how lyke thou art to thy miserable
mother. . . ." *(M of K,* I, fol. 134).

Similarly, in other combats giants are treated ignominiously.
When Donzel del Febo knocks the great Herbyon off his horse, the fall
"made the Gyant weare his necke on the to side lyke a fidler" (*M of K,*
I, fol. 53ᵛ). When gigantic Bruno misses with his sword, Claridiano
retaliates by flooring him with his fist so that "his teeth fell out, leau-
ing his mouth all bloudie. . . ." Bruno has to return home "carrying all
his face wrapt and bound with bondes and rowles of linnen cloth, and
his mouth all to be plaistred" (*M of K,* V, fols. 172ᵛ-173). Attacked by
a giant after asking for food and lodging, Claridiano rises in the stir-
rups and beats in the giant's skull with his fists. Thereupon he laughs:
"Of truth I am a notable guest, for that before I doe enter into my
lodging, I doo paye the shot" (*M of K,* V, fol. 221ᵛ). When the monstrous Brandafuriel, "of a verie great stature and deformed," fights
Claverindo, his first blow with his "faulchin" misses and hits his own
horse on the head "yᵗ he cloue it in two peeces" (*M of K,* II, fol. 29).
The spectators all laugh because the stricken horse falls on the giant's
leg. Lurcon, run through the belly by Primaleon's lance, is dragged
dying around the lists by his horse (*Prim,* I, 130). When Amadis' lance
penetrates Famongomadan, "the tripes came out of his belly, and he
tumbled ouer and ouer" (*A de G,* II, Ch. 13, p. 87). The giant Madaran
in his fight with the Knight of the Phoenix is wounded so severely that
his entrails hang to the ground, and he has to try to avoid stepping on
them as he continues the fight (*A de G,* XI, Ch. 13, fol. 25).

A similar kind of black humor pervades episodes dealing with
giantesses, for deformity and its attendant laughter know no sexual
discrimination. The giantess Andandona is old, white-haired, and
deformed but very swift of foot. When she shoots darts at Amadis and
his men, they retaliate, and she runs off with arrows protruding from
her body, a sight at which they cannot help laughing (*A de G,* III, Ch. 2).
When the Knight of the Burning Sword comes face to face with the
one-eyed giantess, daughter of Frandalon Cyclops, she sneers at his
reputation. He answers by attacking her looks: "Par Dieu ma Dame, si
toutes les belles de ceste contree vous ressemblent, on ne iugera iamais
que ie soye venu par deça pour y faire l'amour, & moins encor'que
vous & moy soions enfans d'vn mesme pere" ("by God, my lady, if
all the beauties of this land look like you, one would never think that
I have come here to make love and still less that you and I are children
of a common Father") (*A de G,* VII, Ch. 19, p. 51). After the giantess
Malfadée is raped by Mascaron upon the dead bodies of her parents,

he dismisses her with a kick in the belly. Later, after Burning Sword severs Mascaron's head, she "la courut prendre, & à belles dents commença à la desrompre, ainsi que fait le Loup affamé l'Agneau qu'il a rauy du pasteur, dont le Roy Gradamarte se mist à rire . . ." ("ran to seize it and began to tear at it with her lovely teeth, just as the starving wolf the lamb that he has snatched from the shepherd, whereupon the king began to laugh") *(A de G,* VII, Ch. 37, p. 98). In view of Malfadée's sad history, Gradamarte's laughter may seem particularly callous, but the mere fact that she is a giantess puts her beyond the bounds of knightly sympathy. Like the daughter of Frandalon Cyclops, she does not look like one of the human race.

Some of the harsh treatment of giants of both sexes can be accounted for by the widespread assumption that they are allied to devils, and that may explain in part why they are so often laughed at. The devil on stage had long been a figure of fun as well as terror, and giants in chivalric romances became diabolic surrogates.[17] When the giant Darmaco impoverishes a lady and carries off her daughter, Palmerin is not at all surprised "in that Giants doe take a habit in treacherous dealings."[18] When such evildoers die, it is assumed they go straight to hell. Thus Alastraxerée, having killed the giant Brandinel, says: "va maintenant au lieu preparé de long temps pour toy & tes semblables" ("go now to the place long prepared for you and your kind") *(A de G,* IX, Ch. 8, fol. 21). Darmaco dies ignominiously as he is dragged and kicked by his horse and belabored also by Palmerin, who thus "sent his soule to the diuels, the patrons of his villainous life" *(Pal,* I, sig. G7). When Oceander kills Ortolomorgantell and his wife, he pierces them both "through the entrailes: wherewith falling on the floore, they impenitently yielded vp their sinne-bespotted soules into the blacke hands of *Belzebub,* their adopted Grandfather" *(K of the Sea,* p. 178).

The terrible monster called the Endriague is the offspring of an incestuous union between a giant and his daughter. At its birth "they swadled it vp in rich clothes, and gaue it to one of the Nurses to sucke: at whose brest it drew so strongly, and without any intermission, as, notwithstanding all her loud cryes, he sucked the very heart blood out of her body, so that shee fell downe dead on the floore. The like did the second, & the third, all of the Nurses instantly dying, not only by the poyson issuing from him, but also by the violence he did vnto them." Years later, when Amadis kills the monster, "the deuill came out of his body, causing such a clap of thunder, as the whole Island shooke with the sound thereof" *(A de G,* III, Ch. 10, pp. 99, 102). The entire episode is grotesque enough to be risible as well as fearful, and though for the seventeenth-century reader this may not have been delightful, it should have been at least nervous, laughter.

OTHER DEFORMITIES IN CHIVALRIC ROMANCES

Though giants and dwarfs make up the bulk of deformed beings who people chivalric romances, deformities of an intermediate range are also present. Primaleon of Greece meets and travels with a knight suggestively named Gibber, who is described simply as "hard-fauored and crump shouldred" (*Prim*, II, 9). One day while Flerida is at court, a strange misshapen knight appears in the company of a deformed lady. Because he speaks of the lady as though she is beautiful, all present laugh and jeer at him (*Prim*, II, 101 ff.). Old age may not be, properly speaking, a physical deformity, but it often appears so in these romances. On one occasion Esplandian and others see a hideous old hag, "vne femme tant vielle, caducque, & ridée, que ses deux tetasses luy deualoient iusques au dessouz du nombril" ("a woman so old, tottering, and wrinkled that her two dugs hung down below her navel"). Later Esplandian describes her in terms of mock admiration: "& toutefois elle a vn taint tant frais & delié, qu'a le bien contempler ie ne le vous pourrois mieux acomparer qu'a l'escorce de ces grands ormes qui seruent communément d'ombrages aux carrefours d'aucuns villages de la grand' Bretaigne" ("and yet she has a fresh and delicate complexion that upon close consideration I could not better compare for you than to the bark of those great elms that commonly serve as shade for the squares of some villages of Great Britain") (*A de G*, V, Ch. 37, p. 105; Ch. 39, p. 109). When the knight Ozalio without provocation kicks an old woman who is sitting before the palace, Palmendos breaks into laughter at the fun of it all.[19]

OTHER DEFORMITIES

There also occur various physical changes that might be classed as deformities. The knight Olbiocles is transmogrified into a boar; and the knights Maiortes and Trineus, into dogs. In some cases, knights and ladies are transformed like Fradubio (*Faerie Queene*, I, 2, 30-43) into trees. Sickness also works as a deforming agent. When the boy Frysol at age fourteen contracts a disease that makes him look like a leper, he is laughed at by his two jealous brothers (*Pal*, I, sig. O). Sometimes, even when no one laughs, a disease is so extravagant that it must have been intended as risible. One day while sniffing a flower, the daughter of the King of Malfada draws up into her nostrils a worm that causes putrefaction and a noisome odor. Thereafter she smells so bad that she is approachable only by the strong of will. The comic touch lies in her name: Zephira (*Pal*, II, sig. Q3). Her disease makes her resemble Alizar, l'outrageux Roy, whose breath is so vile that "qui ne le voyoit de pres, le pouuoit bien sentir de loing" ("whoever did not see him up close could smell him a mile away") (*A de G*, VIII,

Ch. 95, fol. 178). Zephira may also have reminded readers of the determined heroine Vienne in the romance *Paris and Vienne.* In an attempt to dissuade a too ardent suitor, she kept a small fowl in each armpit for days on end, long enough to accomplish her purpose.

Although in the sixteenth and seventeenth centuries skin color was not a major obsession, it occasionally surfaces in the romances. For example, Magadan, a Moorish king, is described as good and kind, "contre le commun naturel des noirs" ("against the common nature of blacks") (*A de G,* VII, Ch. 1, p. 1). The coupling of blackness with ugliness, and so with humor, occurs only once in the romances cited in this paper, in *Amadis de Gaule,* Book XII, Chapter 32. There a company of knights and ladies spend the night at a castle where a wedding is still being celebrated. The squire Sirind suggests to Gante, the attractive attendant to the newly wedded lady, that she come to his bed that night, and she pretends to agree. She then gets a black kitchen wench named Baruquelle to take her place by telling her that Sirind likes her. Baruquelle is described as "ayant les leures grosses, & reuirées, le nez tout aplaty, & les narines fort larges & ouuertes" ("having thick and protruding lips, a nose all flat, and her nostrils large and flaring"). In her whole person "n'auoit rien blanc que les dents" ("she had nothing white but her teeth"). Sirind has generously promised to share his luck with two fellow squires, and all night long the three take turns in the embraces of the woman they take to be Gante. At first light Sirind discovers that the one in his arms is ugly and black. Unable to keep from laughing, he tells his fellows that their Diana has been eclipsed and darkened by the light of day. Baruquelle runs off in vexation and shame, but the squires—and once the story comes out, the whole company of knights and ladies—laugh for days. As the point of the tale depends upon the comment about Diana (for Gante is supposed to be a virgin) being eclipsed, blackness is clearly an essential ingredient. Baruquelle's feelings are ignored because she is, like the daughter of Frandalon Cyclops, ugly and, therefore, beyond the pale. Though the Renaissance seems often to be color-blind, this tale indicates that that frame of mind was not absolute.

CRUEL HUMOR IN CHIVALRIC ROMANCES

The laughter directed at the ugly Baruquelle and at other "deformed" creatures, especially dwarfs and giants, underlines the black humor so common in the sixteenth and seventeenth centuries. Most of the instances cited above are obviously meant to be funny because the reader is told they are or because the characters laugh. Many similar instances exist where we may suppose that the reader knew enough to laugh without prompting. He enjoyed—if that is the right word—an area of laughter many modern readers would find alien or uncomfortable. Chivalric romances, which seem to many modern readers dull and tedious, had their moments of comedy—not very lighthearted perhaps, but in a dark world straws to be grasped at.

That a high proportion of the laughter in chivalric romances is malicious or sadistic should remind us of the ubiquity of such laughter on the stage and in other kinds of writing. Though the stage used almost no dwarfs and giants, their places in the ranks of deformity were taken by other types: the old, mad, diseased, betrayed, or ugly. A large number of old people in plays come off as comic because they are grotesque or misshapen. Old hags like Madge Mumblecrust (*Roister Doister*) and the loathly Dipsas (*Endymion*) and senior citizens like "old-huddle" Bilioso (*The Malcontent*) or Cleander (*Supposes*), who is reputedly "bursten in the cods," encourage the same kind of laughter as tormented dwarfs or half-disemboweled giants. Madmen or those pretending madness, like Hamlet, inhabit the strange gargoylesque world between laughter and pathos. Venereal disease is scarcely ever a serious problem but rather an excuse for scarred characters like Sir Pockhole in *Knight of the Burning Pestle* and for a deluge of puns on falling hair, French crowns, and decayed noses. The cuckold, that horned monster, the most feared of all deformities, seems to have been an unfailing inciter of guffaws. Finally, the stage had at hand all the tricks of makeup and dress that might suggest the alien, ugly, and hateful: the obvious butt of laughter. How many in the audience of *The Jew of Malta* must have roared with malicious glee when bottle-nosed Barabas tumbled into his own trap!

Other kinds of Renaissance literature share the habit of cruel humor, though often the victims may be not so much physically as ideologically repulsive. Renaissance readers must have laughed at the stripping of Duessa in the *Faerie Queene,* I, 8, 46–48. She is not only bestially hideous but, like Barabas, a political and religious alien. Her "neather parts," featuring a fox's tail "with dong all fowly dight," represent the gross Papist reality and in a religiously nervous age had to be funny. If there were malice in such laughter, it was taken to be righteous. Much the same frame of mind can be seen in Nashe's description in *The Unfortunate Traveler* of the slaughter of the Anabaptists. Though Jack Wilton is supposed to be the narrator, Nashe's voice comes through in all its sadistic glee, especially as he describes John Leyden and his ragtag followers praying before the battle. Nashe hated the Anabaptist innovation for its effrontery, its ignorance, and its divisiveness. It is a hideous deformity, and in the battle Nashe compares the Anabaptists to a bear torn to pieces by curs. He professes sorrow for the slaughter and wishes the bear "a suitable death to his ugly shape." Although in his description of the carnage Nashe tries to subdue his sense of humor, a certain ghoulish hilarity emerges in a rhetorical turn like this: "Their swords, their pikes, their bills, their bows, their calivers slew, empierced, knocked down, shot through, and overthrew as many men every minute of the battle as there falls ears of corn before the scythe at one blow."[20]

What Nashe felt about religious, Sidney apparently felt about political, innovation. In his *Arcadia,* Book II, Chapter 25, a mob of commoners rises up against Basilius, and Sidney describes the fight in a tone of amused contempt. As Zelmane and Dorus wreak havoc upon the ill-armed and inept rebels, their blows often have an ironic propriety. When a drunken miller attacks, Dorus cuts his throat and leaves him to "vomit his soul out in wine and bloud." Another rebel who has dreamed the night before that he "was growen a couple" is cut in half. A painter who wants to paint the battle between the Centaurs and the Lapithae and has come to this battle to gain fresh impressions has both hands cut off. In terms of chivalric romance, Sidney's sense of comedy is quite appropriate, for it is the many-headed mob, as blind and destructive as Polyphemus, that is the deformed monster of the episode. Thus the lopping off of the painter's hands, a treatment commonly reserved for giants, is right and proper.

Because they are so overt and unsentimental in their treatment of the deformed, chivalric romances illustrate with special clarity a habit of mind and a sense of humor common in the Renaissance. Ugliness or deformity habitually invited harsh and brutal treatment attended by laughter. Such black humor had deep and tenacious roots. Not only Homer but Aristophanes, Plautus, and numerous classical writers depended heavily upon comedy that sprang from the physically repulsive. In his *Philebus,* Plato implied that envy or malice is at the root of human laughter. During the Middle Ages occasions like the Feast of Fools ritualized grotesque fun. Even the assembled gods once laughed at misshapen Hephaestus. Surely a tradition so venerable must derive from a basic side of human nature. That modern society may no longer admit its propriety is less significant than that laughter of this kind has been a staple since time immemorial. As Horace remarks in one of his odes (IV, 9), "Vixere fortes ante Agamemmona/ multi" ("many brave men lived before Agamemmon"). It must be as true that many ugly men lived before Thersites. How ironic that chivalric romance, the least literary and most scorned of genres, should be so close to a classical view of human nature and so revealing of the beast within!

NOTES

1. *allà toû aiskhroû esti tò geloîon mórion* ("the laughable is but a part of the ugly"). S. H. Butcher, *Aristotle's Theory of Poetry and Fine Art* (New York: Dover Publications, 1951), pp. 20–21.

2. *aiskhistos dè anèr hupò Ílion êlthen* ("he was the ugliest man who came to Troy"). *Iliad,* II, 216.

3. Erika Tietze-Conrat, *Dwarfs and Jesters in Art,* trans. Elizabeth Osborn (New

York, 1957), p. 7.

4. Enid Welsford, *The Fool: His Social and Literary History* (Gloucester, Mass., 1966), p. 135.

5. Tietze-Conrat, p. 14.

6. W. L. Wiley, *The Early Public Theatre in France* (Cambridge, Mass., 1960), pp. 71-72.

7. The dwarf was Jeffrey Hudson, later Sir Jeffrey and a court favorite.

8. Allardyce Nicoll, *Stuart Masques and the Renaissance Stage* (New York, 1938), p. 205.

9. *Amadis de Gaule,* VIII (Paris, 1548), Ch. 18, fol. 31. Hereafter references to this romance will be abbreviated *A de G.* The editions used are as follows: Vols. I-IV (London, 1619); V (Antwerp, 1572); VII (Antwerp, 1573); IX (Paris, 1553); XI (Paris, 1559); XII (Paris, 1556); XVII (Lyon, 1578).

10. *The Mirror of Knighthood,* II (London, 1585), fol. 132. Hereafter references to this romance will be abbreviated *M of K.* The other editions cited are as follows: Vol. 1 (London, n.d.); V (London, 1583).

11. London, 1589, fol. 56.

12. In the Spanish edition Amadís de Gaula does not laugh at the dwarf. The English version as translated by Anthony Munday was entirely dependent on the French of Nicholas de Herberay, who made many additions and alterations in both language and spirit.

13. *The Knight of the Sea* (London, 1600), Ch. 2. Hereafter references to this romance will be abbreviated *K of the Sea.*

14. *Primaleon of Greece* (London, 1619), III, 130-145. Hereafter references to this romance will be abbreviated *Prim.* All volumes cited have the same place and date of printing.

15. *Gerileon of England* (London, 1583), I, fol. 5. Hereafter references will be abbreviated *G of E.*

16. *The Honor of Chivalry* (London, 1598), p. 74.

17. Alice B. Gomme, "The Character of Beelzebub in the Mummers' Play," *Folklore,* XL (1929), 292-293.

18. *Palmerin D'Oliva* (London, 1637), I, sig. G4ᵛ. Hereafter cited as *Pal.*

19. *Palmendos* (London, 1589), fol. 18.

20. Thomas Nashe, *The Unfortunate Traveler,* ed. Merritt Lawlis in *Elizabethan Prose Fiction* (New York, 1967), p. 473.

5

Jacobean Comedy and the Acquisitive Grasp

MALCOLM KINIRY

The broad economic and social changes that characterized England in the late sixteenth and early seventeenth centuries helped people its comedy. With the growing popularity of satire and of the comedies of London life, Jacobean dramatists drew increasingly on a fund of English stock characters who, though partly the products of ongoing theatrical traditions, also reflect real contemporary changes. Shylock, the Venetian moneylender, is replaced onstage by his English counterpart, the usurer who speculates in land. The profligate young gentleman who cannot hold on to his estate is recognized specifically as a victim of a nationwide pattern of enclosure (the take-over and fencing-in, strictly for private profit, of lands previously available to the general public). The Elizabethan figure of the frivolous knight, already rampant in a character like Sir Andrew Aguecheek of *Twelfth Night*, begins to appear in multiple variations soon after King James's wholesale creation of knighthoods in 1603. There is the sudden stage popularity of the wealthy widow who attracts a flock of upwardly motivated but precariously financed suitors. There is also the bourgeois wife who tries to use her husband's sudden wealth to vault into a social prominence far above his mercantile status. And there is the conniving, capitalist merchant—occasionally, as if to illustrate the thesis of R. H. Tawney's *Religion and the Rise of Capitalism* (1926), the merchant is explicitly a hypocritical Puritan.

According to a point of view with which I disagree, the close relation of these stock characters to contemporary life illustrates the conservative nature of Jacobean comedy, perhaps of all good comedy. Comic types such as the usurious landlord and the unscrupulous merchant, so the argument runs, express a widely felt moral aversion to the encroachments of capitalism upon a basically feudal system. Although such a view can help to explain the moral animus of many Jacobean comedies, it should not be used as a general framework or perspective for them all. I think that the arguments that equate comic values with social vision ultimately deprecate comedy—at least they cannot account for the most vital moments in many plays.

THE ANTIACQUISITIVE INTERPRETATION OF JACOBEAN COMEDY DISPUTED

Perhaps the most formidable (and certainly the most influential) view of Jacobean comedy remains L. C. Knights's *Drama and Society in the Age of Jonson* (1937). Knights describes a powerful moral tradition—inherited from the Middle Ages, kept strong in the citizen moralities of Dekker and Heywood, drawn upon in brilliant ways in the comedies of Jonson, and still alive in at least two of the comedies of Philip Massinger. Displaying "a sure grasp" of the actual conditions of the evolving English economy, the plays of that tradition are suspicious of the growth of capitalist enterprise and resentful of the alterations to an agrarian system. They unhesitantly endorse the customary hierarchies of social degree, and they use the new stock characters to express a deeply felt antiacquisitive spirit. The merchant's social-climbing wife and daughters in Massinger's *The City Madam* (1632), for example, illustrate the futile vanities of the *nouveaux riches*. Similarly, Giles Overreach, the usurer-villain of Massinger's *A New Way to Pay Old Debts* (1626), embodies the acquisitive enormities of a generation of newly landed capitalists.

The undoing of Overreach and the humbling of the city madam reaffirm the traditional antiacquisitive moral values of the community. "To write great comedy," says Knights, "one has to be serious about something."[1] Comedies like *A New Way to Pay Old Debts* and *The City Madam* are very good comedies, largely because they are clearly and seriously opposed to the changing shape of English society as it manifested itself in the early seventeenth century. Knights quotes as an example of Massinger's social and economic understanding this devious strategem by Overreach to divest Luke Frugal of his lands:

> . . . I'll make my men break ope his fences,
> Ride o'er his standing corn, and in the night
> Set fire on his barns, or break his cattle's legs:
> These trespasses draw on suits, and suits expenses,
> Which I can spare, but soon will beggar him.
> When I have harried him thus two or three year,
> Though he sue *in forma pauperis,* in spite
> Of all his thrift and care, he'll grow behind hand,
> . . . I will pretend some title: want will force him
> To put it to arbitrement; then, if he sell
> For half the value, he shall have ready money,
> And I possess his land. (2.1.37-44, 47-50)

Despite their melodramatic cast, these speeches draw special praise from Knights, for Massinger not only "observes the significant economic activities of the time" but he "sees their significance."[2]

One objection to the thesis of *Drama and Society* is that Knights's view of what is economically significant reveals an overreliance on Tawney, for whom the emergence of a class of irresponsible landlords was the central economic fact of the period. Actually, the dislocations of sixteenth- and seventeenth-century society are now attributed largely to demographic factors, whereas the new landlords—their greed notwithstanding—are seen as a neutral, perhaps even a stabilizing influence.[3] One of the dubious touchstones of Tawney's economic outlook (as taken up by Knights) is an abhorrence of social mobility within the class structure. One of Knights's frequent implications is that the entire fabric of society is threatened by such movement.

This is to underestimate both the durability and the flexibility of the English class system before and after the advent of capitalism. Lawrence Stone has compared the upper level of English society to a bus or hotel, which, though always full, is always full of different people; and he cautions against supposing that because "social mobility, upwards and downwards, was occurring at an unprecedented rate . . . the whole class structure was breaking down." On the contrary, the mobility of individuals is a permanent feature of the system:

> The apparent stability of class position is an illusion created
> by the slowness of change and the extraordinary stability of
> class character, resulting from the chameleon-like adaptabil-
> ity of new families. . . . The measure of the resilience of a class
> structure is its ability to absorb new families of different social
> origin and convert them to the values and ways of life of the
> social group into which they are projected.[4]

Chameleonlike adaptability is one of the resources of comedy. By emphasizing only those plays that treat mobility as a threat to social order, Knights ignores the resilience of society in absorbing its chameleons.

The most basic objection to Knights's thesis is that it rests upon an inadequate, though seductive, theory of comedy. That theory assumes that the movement of comedy is a return to social normality. The end of a well-written comedy restores a social equilibrium that has been temporarily upset by some disturbance or threat. An enticing biological analogy (if I may extrapolate freely) would equate the social world of a comedy with life as maintained by a healthy organism. Irritations are soothed; swellings subside; foreign particles are subjugated or expelled. By the play's end, for example, the straining social pretensions of the bourgeois wife in *The City Madam* have been deflated. Or the festering intrusions of Overreach in *A New Way to Pay Old Debts* have been counteracted. Such a theory supports the belief that comedy is a conservative ritual, a vehicle for managing the contradictions and misgivings of a community. In *A New Way to Pay Old Debts* the capitalist sins of the community are carried off on the crooked back of the usurious land-grabber, a scapegoat for the evils of a moneyed society.

As sufficient, indeed as appealing, as such a theory may be for the comedies of Massinger, the antiacquisitive tradition—if I may use this phrase to characterize Knights's view—provides far too narrow a base for evaluating other comedies, even some of those that share the same stock characters. Not all comedies insist on issues of social significance, nor do they all end with a return to normality. Some comedies do not fulfill a conservative communal function, and some very good Jacobean comedies are morally noncommital about the inroads of capitalism. In fact, in some plays the acquisitive impulse—the characteristically capitalist grab for money, land, or status—excites in its audience a participatory interest.

Against the citizen comedies of Massinger, Knights aggressively sets those of Middleton, so as to distinguish between those comedies firmly in the antiacquisitive tradition and those that merely reflect changes without any clear social perspective. Middleton, he says, "constantly gives us such glimpses of a society in the process of rapid reorganization," but he does so without moral direction.[5] Much to his credit, Knights is willing to quote one of Middleton's most energetic passages, the daydream of the woolendraper Quomodo in *Michaelmas Term* (1604–1606), which ends with the image of Quomodo and his family en route to his soon-to-be-acquired country estate:

> A fine journey in the Whitsun holidays, i'faith, to ride down with a number of citizens and their wives, some upon pillions, some upon side-saddles, I and little Thomasine i' th' middle, our son and heir, Sim Quomodo, in a peach-colour taffeta

jacket, some horse-length, or a long yard before us. There will be a fine show on's, I can tell you. (3.4)

Of this and other such passages of luxuriating citizen aspirations, Knights observes that such ambition "is not set in the light of a positive ideal of citizen conduct" and that "its implications are not grasped and presented."[6] But here comedy's reach exceeds its social grasp. Or, to redirect Knights's favorite critical metaphor even more perversely, Quomodo's vitality as a comic character derives from his enthusiasm for a much more literal form of grasping.

Some of the shortcomings of the antiacquisitive tradition can be illustrated by its marginal relevance to other socially resonant comic situations. Consider, for example, the lively confrontation between a usurer and a widow in Beaumont and Fletcher's *The Scornful Lady* (1610-1616), a comedy written for the children of the Queen's Revels. Here Morecraft, a forerunner of Giles Overreach, is trying to woo a merchant's widow by denigrating her dead husband, a rich importer:

> Sweet widow leave your frumps, and bee edified: you know
> my state, I sell no Perspectives, Scarfes, Gloves, nor Hangers,
> nor put my trust in Shoo-ties: and where your husband in an
> age was rising by burnt figs, dreg'd with meale and powdered
> sugar, saunders and graines, wormseed and rotten reasons
> [=raisins], and such vile tobacco, that made the foot-men mangie;
> I in a yeere have put up hundreds; inclos'd my widdow, those
> pleasant meadowes, by a forfeit morgage: for which the poore
> Knight takes a lone chamber, owes for his Ale, and dare not
> beat his Hostesse: nay more—[7]

Morecraft is a stock usurer. The self-praise of his talents for enclosure and for mortgage making, those two most notorious disrupters of people from land, places him firmly as a villain. Still he is not quite from the same moustache-twirling mold as Overreach. Beaumont and Fletcher are not much interested in singling him out as the embodiment of destructive capitalist ambitions. For one thing, the picture of the society he is disrupting does not lend itself to secure moral feelings. The image of "the poore Knight"—hardly the Luke Frugal whom Giles Overreach victimizes—does not evoke much sympathy for the victims of Morecraft's acquisitiveness. If money were not so tight, the dispossessed knight still would be slugging ale—only he would feel more free to beat his hostess.

The main joke, of course, is that the usurer can belittle the enterprises of another committed capitalist, the merchant. In the recognition that the importer and the usurer are only degrees apart, we can, if we like, credit Beaumont and Fletcher with a grasp of economic reality. But an appreciation of Morecraft's hypocrisy is only one dimension of the comedy. There is also a perverse and pleasing logic to Morecraft's condescension toward the retailer. Morecraft's own achievement is a triumph of scale and of style, reminiscent of the boast of Volpone that he has gained his wealth "no common way" ("I use no trade, no venture. . . . I blow no subtle glass, expose no ships/ To thret'nings of the furrow-faced sea"[8]). Even though Morecraft's list of miscellaneous "Shoo-ties" has the exhilarating extra effect of characterizing the merchant as a figure of formidable energy, his disdain for soiled hands and mere petty corruptions is persuasively grand. Part of Beaumont and Fletcher's comic accomplishment is that Morecraft can successfully appropriate the manner of an established aristocrat while belittling a capitalistically kindred spirit.

There is rich comedy, too, in the widow's reply. Amusingly, she makes no effort to dispute Morecraft's disparagements of her late husband. Indeed in those, at least, Morecraft has struck a responsive chord:

> My husband was a fellow lov'd to toyle, fede ill, made gain his exercise, and so grew costive, which for I was his wife, I gave way to, and spun mine owne smocks course, and sir, so little— but let that passe. Time, that weares all things out, wore out my husband, who in penitence of such fruitless five yeares marriage, left me great with his wealth, which if you'le bee a worthy gossip to, be knighted Sir. (2.3.29–35)

The comic effect depends upon the widow's marvelously colloquial evocation of life—including economic life—and it really makes no moral judgments at all on capitalist enterprise. It is not her husband's acquisitiveness that comes under the widow's disapproval, but rather his devotion to the work ethic for its own sake and at the expense of all pleasure. In her pregnancy metaphor ("great with his wealth") she sees her own widowhood as a form of capitalism, an opportunity for fruitful investment. Even her interruption is eloquent—in "but let that passe" she turns away from her vengeful satisfaction with her old sexual infidelities; yet the sour memory of her marriage fuels her determination to profit as well as she can from it. This is unlike the social ambitiousness of the merchant's wife and daughters in *The City Madam,* whose ambitions are presented only as garish vanity, a longing after coaches and gowns. There is cunning but no vanity in the widow's own acquisitiveness, especially as it is set against the sober acknowledgement of "time, that weares all things out."[9]

It is her cunning and sobriety, as well as her wealth, that make the widow attractive to Morecraft. In his eyes her one flaw is her determination to marry a knight, a flaw only because her ambition seems misplaced. It is almost as easy to purchase a knighthood as it is to impoverish a knight, but it is seldom worth the expense. After the widow has left the stage, Morecraft considers, for a moment, the possibility of buying a title:

> Shee's rich and sober, if this itch were from her: And say I bee at charge to pay the Footmen, and the Trumpets, I and the Horsmen too, and be a Knight, and she refuse me then; then am I hoyst into the Subsidy, and so by consequence should prove a Coxcombe: Ile have a care of that. (2.3. 145–150)

Once entered in the king's subsidy book, he would be liable to any number of royal levies. Morecraft looks at the trumperies of title and the lure of social advancement with the eye of a preacher looking at worldly vanities, though his spur is not righteous indignation. To purchase a knighthood is to take a step toward economic impotency. His is an incisive but decidedly amoral recognition that a social rise is not a universal good.

I am not suggesting that Morecraft attracts our sympathy. He never loses the villainous aura that attends a stage usurer, but the very conventionality of that role leaves us free to observe other solid qualities. Both Morecraft and the widow begin to come alive as full-bodied characters as we learn how well-met are their intelligences. We lose sight of their larger but more elusive significance as embodiments of capitalist changes. I can imagine an argument that, anxious to praise this scene but deferential to the moral terms of Knights, contends that Morecraft and the widow are vehicles of satire, that they are satirically placed in a world of cutthroat capitalist ambitions. It is the sort of argument that can be made more plausibly with some of the comedies of Middleton, but that there, too, soon wears thin. Whatever its satirical overtones, a scene like this one from *The Scornful Lady* is fascinating primarily because we find ourselves caught up in the complications of getting and spending; we are not inclined, nor at leisure, to make general moral observations about the debilitating powers of money.

The exchange between Morecraft and the widow suggests two further objections to Knight's morality-bound evaluation of Jacobean comedy. First, stock characters often serve contradictory comic functions. On the one hand, they produce a reflex sort of comic reaction. By conforming to type, such characters allow the playgoer indulgent laughter—the reaction of a superior being toward one who cannot choose but behave with laughable predictability. On the other hand, however, stock characters also provide the innovative dramatist with an opportunity for ingenuity, for putting new flesh on familiar bones. Through nuance and invention such a dramatist is able to thwart and alter our ceremonialized expectations. We are delighted by the vitality of the unforeseen. The surprisingly supple-minded qualities of both Morecraft and the widow frustrate the tendency to see them as representative or ritualized figures.

The second objection is that the antiacquisitive tradition over-stresses the idea of a comic pattern, particularly the importance of a play's ending. Many comedies owe their energy not so much to the unity or outcome of their actions as to the verve of their individual vignettes. In the routine of a stand-up comedian, the overall impression may depend partly on his ability to establish a rhythm for the whole performance, but the best jokes often succeed independently of their context. So in some comedies the most vital comic moments often tend to float free of their encompassing action. The confrontation between Morecraft and the widow is a good example of such a moment, for Morecraft's first brash appearance has little in common with his feeble and unengaging presence later in the play.[10]

Despite this last objection that the antiacquisitive tradition under-values the comic vignette, I would not want to forsake comic movement as a criterion. The best comedies integrate their vital moments with some unified movement of plot. Still, a further objection to the antiacquisitive tradition is that it favors only one sort of plot movement—the return to social normality. But the equilibrium achieved by the comic ending need not entail a return, after some challenge, to the *status quo*. To revert to the biological analogy of society as organism, there is also the equilibrium that attends fusion, growth, or readjustment. It is even possible to assert, with Northrop Frye, that "the movement of comedy is usually a movement from one kind of society to another" and to point specifically to the type of plot resolution that "causes a new society to crystallize around the hero."[11] Certainly, one of the patterns in which a comedy can move is in an ascending line, according to an additive principle that allows the comedy to end when it has reached some climactic plateau. The play-ending marriage is one example of a convention that can accommodate this rising pattern as easily as that of a challenge and return. For though marriage usually represents the reassertion of the traditional social order, it can also signal—as it does for Petruchio in *The Taming of the Shrew*—a coup, a solid acquisition, an accomplishment to which the rest of society will have to adjust.

JACOBEAN COMEDIES OF INTRIGUE
AND THE ACQUISITIVE IMPULSE

Oddly, some of the best vehicles for the frankly acquisitive impulse and for a less moralized treatment of capitalist changes are intrigue comedies, plays that often hinge on the efforts of disreputable characters to bilk their social betters. I say, "Oddly" because some of the best intrigue comedies seem to conform to Knights's conservative view of comedy as community safeguard. A figure like Mosca in Jonson's *Volpone* advances by exploiting the corruptions and vanities of others and then finally falls victim to his own acquisitive impulses. In the end, social pretensions have been leveled, the threat to order vanquished, and society purged, presumably, of its unhealthy excess. Alexander Leggatt, however, has argued convincingly against this point of view by contending that intrigue comedies, regardless of their outcomes, exert an amoral, possibly even a subversive, appeal. We follow the schemings of the comic intriguer with a straightforward delight in the trickery, both for its own sake and because it flouts conventional morality.[12]

To illustrate how detailed but morally detached a social view is possible within the intrigue framework, I would like to look at *The Puritan* (1606), a comedy performed by the children of Paul's.[13] Once attributed to Shakespeare but now exiled to anonymity,[14] it serves as an especially good example of a popular sort of Jacobean comedy that, unencumbered either by literary aspirations or by moral commentary, excites a direct fascination for various forms of acquisitiveness. *The Puritan* is usually dismissed offhandedly as a crude satire against Puritans, but I think that its satire has been overstressed and its tone miscalculated, whereas the range, quality, and distance of the play's social observation seldom have been noticed. I will consider the play at some length, partly because it is so little known, but mostly because its vitality springs from such an illustrative array of social detail.

The intriguer of *The Puritan* is George Pyeboard. Loosely based on the jestbook characterization of George Peele, Pyeboard (a "peele" is literally a pie-board, a wooden shovel for taking pies from the oven) is an indigent ex-scholar who has come to London to live by his wits. Overhearing the lamentations of a Puritan widow and her daughter, he devises an elaborate plan to trick the women into marrying one of his unemployed soldier-friends and himself. The two pose as a seer and a conjurer and are eventually so successful in their performances that they win the women. Before they can be married, however, they are betrayed by one of their friends, a soldier who is bitter that he has received no reward for helping them in their deception.

Although such a plot summary is certainly enough to show, as Baldwin Maxwell once tersely observed, that the play is not Shakespeare's,[15] it does little to illustrate its comic strengths. I would like to single out four features in particular that help to distinguish *The Puritan* as a vital but morally detached comedy, one that dispassionately displays several varieties of the acquisitive grasp. The first feature is the muted and qualified nature of its Puritan satire. When Pyeboard first overhears the widow, she is in the midst of a lamentation:

> O, out of a million millions, I should ne'er find such a husband;
> no he was unmatchable, unmatchable. Nothing was too hot,
> nor too dear for me. I could not speak of that one thing that I

had not. Beside, I had keys of all, kept all, receiv'd all, had money in my purse, spent what I would, went abroad when I would, came home when I would, and did all what I would. O, my sweet husband! I shall never have the like. (1.1, p. 232)[16]

The satirical pitch of such a passage is clear enough. The widow mourns the diminution of her financial, possibly even her sexual, indulgences. Yet she stirs little indignation. She is a stock character, but she is also an inventive variation on the widow figure—neither the blatant hypocrite like the title character of Chapman's *The Widow's Tears* (1605-1606), nor the shrewdly assured realist of *The Scornful Lady.* Her sorrow is not the less sincere for its financial underpinnings.

As for the dead capitalist himself, he becomes, in his wife's evocative reminiscences at least, a figure of formidable energy. He, too, is presented as a kind of stock character, but at an odd and amusing distance. Pyeboard himself, in his guise as seer, takes the opportunity to compose the Puritan's image out of the satirist's clichés. Your husband is now in purgatory, he assures the widow:

> 'Tis but mere folly now to gild him o'er
> That has but past for copper. Praises here
> Can not unbind him there. Confess but truth;
> I know he got his wealth with a hard gripe:
> O, hardly, hardly . . .
> He would eat fools and ignorant heirs clean up;
> And had his drink from many a poor man's brow,
> Even as their labour brew it. He would scrape
> Riches to him most unjustly: the very dirt
> Between his nails was ill got, and not his own.
> O, I groan to speak on't; the though makes me
> Shudder, shudder! (2.1, p. 240)

Part of what makes this speech such fun is that the satire is deflected aimlessly away. The richest comic qualities in such a passage come from the inapplicability of the sentiments to the speaker. Pyeboard's mock-indignation is a cloak for his grudging admiration of the Puritan's hard, hard grip. His wife pays the departed perhaps the ultimate compliment when she reacts excitedly to the revelations at the end of the play, "O wonderful! Indeed I wonder'd that my husband with all his craft, could not keep himself out of purgatory." Puritan acquisitiveness is hardly the object of hot-blooded, or even cold-eyed satire here.

A second sort of acquisitiveness can be glimpsed in a brilliant scene that the dramatist embroidered from his jestbook source. At one point Pyeboard is seized by a trio of constables, who detain him for the rent he owes his most recent landlady. At first he tries to put them off by pretending to be a gentleman, but, failing that, he persuades his captors to accompany him to the home of a real gentleman, who, he extemporizes, has promised to pay him for composing a masque. Pyeboard chooses a gentleman's house at random, knocks, enters, and in a hasty aside takes the gentleman into his confidence. He pretends to show him his idea for the masque, the gentleman signifies his approval, and the two of them leave the room, ostensibly to fetch the money, but actually to let Pyeboard escape out the back door. Puttock, Ravenshaw, and Dogson, the three constables, are left to contemplate the gentleman's hangings and the maps on his wall:

> Sirrah serjeant, these maps are pretty painted things, but I could never fancy them yet; methinks they're too busy, and full of circles and conjurations. They say all the world's in one of them: but I could ne'er find the Counter in the Poultry [i.e., the jail, called the Counter, near the poultry market in Cheapside].

The scene is a marvelous bid of social comedy. Puttock and the other officers embody, with their limited grasp, the parochial mentality. Crafty in their petty corruptions, they are nevertheless wholly in awe of the gentleman and wholly in ignorance of the mercantile ways of the world.

The gentleman himself is evidently one of the chameleon-gentlemen who have effectivey disguised their sudden rise in status. The city home suggests a business career, as do the maps on the wall. He is addressed as "your worship," a title that at least vaguely suggests a political appointment, the most common vehicle for a marked social advancement. His servant even answers the door complaining of the need for a porter, a sign perhaps of a still evolving household. I bring up these points about the likelihood of the gentleman's being newly arrived only to emphasize how slight an importance his longevity as a gentleman could have for others. What effectively marks him as a gentleman is not his claim to lineage but his aristocratic manner and, more importantly, his substantial house. He is a gentleman simply by virtue of his acquisition. "We will attend his worship," says Pyeboard in the hallway, before confiding to the audience:

> Worship, I think; for so much the posts at his door should signify, and the fair coming-in, and the wicket; else I never knew him nor his worship. (3.5, p. 245)

A third and equally tough-minded version of acquisitive grasping in *The Puritan* is Pyeboard's own futile attempt to climb the social ladder. Nothing can come of nothing, and Pyeboard's sheer wit, though it is enough to keep him a step or two out of debtor's prison, is

not enough finally to raise him. Leggatt, whose judgments about citizen comedies are elsewhere so persuasive, dismisses *The Puritan* in a
succinct footnote because its comedy, he feels, is flawed by the way
the action turns so sharply against its intriguer. Throughout the play
we have been encouraged to hope for Pyeboard's success, and when he
fails, we are merely disappointed.[17] But I think that the comedown of
Pyeboard is an aspect of the play's sober view of social change. His
precarious height is simply too difficult to maintain—he falls more out
of physical necessity than for the sake of a moralistic conclusion. And
like the fall of anyone who lands on his feet (Pyeboard is not imprisoned at the end of the play), his is comically apt.

Finally, against Pyeboard's fall is set the unspectacular rise of
three knights, who in the end win the widow and her daughters. Their
marriages represent no large social leap; in fact, they only help to
strengthen the status the knights had already nominally attained. They
indicate the gradualness of most social mobility, the small acquisitive
victories achieved by marriage. In rewarding the knights at the end of
the play, the dramatist once again demonstrates his flare for comic
innovation. Despite his name, one knight, Sr. Oliver Muckhill, is a
clear departure from his foppish stereotype. He is a dignified figure,
calm when at first rebuffed and gracious when finally accepted. It is
he who deftly manages the play's conclusion by converting the soldier's
betrayal of Pyeboard to his own direct benefit. His strategy is another
of the comic dramatist's subtle social touches. Rather than reveal the
fraud to the widow himself, he prevails upon a nobleman whom he has
managed to keep slightly in his debt. The noble, with one magisterial
sweep, reveals Pyeboard's deception and urges the women to marry the
knights. They are "men of estimation," he gently quips, men, he goes
on to say, "who have long wooed you, and both with their hearts and
wealth sincerely love you" (5.5, p. 257).

That it is possible to love "with" one's wealth is a sentiment well
outside the antiacquisitive tradition but well within the grasp of comedy. It is one of a complex of keen but only mildly satirical social observations in *The Puritan*. The supple financial tentacle by which
Muckhill is able to retain the services of the nobleman illustrates a
delicate shift in social power. The old hierarchies prevail, even as they
are being gradually infiltrated by new individuals. Muckhill's gentle
grip is a version of the Puritan's more tenacious one and of the other
anonymous gentleman's secure possession of his household. By contrast, Pyeboard, who is socially more agile than mobile, realizes that
he cannot hold on to very much, partly because "the multiplicity of
scholars, hatch'd and nourished in the idle calms of peace, makes
them, like fishes, one devour another" (1.1). Even this grim and familiar economic explanation is cheerfully subordinated to a broader
comic outlook.

In arguing against the antiacquisitive tradition as a perspective for evaluating Jacobean comedies, I have also questioned the more general idea that comedy is inherently conservative. Any comic movement—to reinvoke a proposition of Northrop Frye that I quoted earlier —brings with it a new society. Even the social world at the end of *A New Way to Pay Old Debts,* though the movement of that play is essentially restorative, is not the same world as before Overreach's intrusion. To say this is not necessarily to accept Frye's other proposition that at the end of a comedy a new society crystallizes around the comic hero. *The Puritan* is one example of a comedy in which a new society crystallizes to the exclusion of the hero. But whoever are the recipients of the changes, comedy presents a world of shifting relationships, a society that is always becoming a somewhat different society.

There is, nevertheless, a sense in which all comedy is conservative. For though the social world of a comedy is subject to continual change, the change proceeds in familiar patterns. The shifting and readjustment of individuals goes on, but the hierarchies of social relationships remain similar. In this sense, I think, the views of Knights are not conservative enough. For by seeing capitalism as a threat capable of transforming society in a fundamental way, Knights underestimates the elasticity of both society and comedy. Capitalism brings to Jacobean comedy a spurt of energy. It suggests a new set of stock characters and provides new opportunities for vigorous confrontations, and it accelerates the vital social changes that are always the concern of comedy.

NOTES

1. *Drama and Society in the Age of Jonson* (1937; rptd. London: Chatto and Windus, 1951), p. 296.
2. Ibid., p. 277.
3. See the introduction by Lawrence Stone to R. H. Tawney's *The Agrarian Problem in the Sixteenth Century* (1912; rptd. New York: Harper & Row, 1967), pp. xi-xii.
4. Lawrence Stone, *The Crisis of the Aristocracy, 1558-1641* (Oxford: Clarendon Press, 1965), pp. 38-39. Stone has borrowed the hotel and bus comparisons from Joseph A. Schumpeter, *Imperialism and Social Classes,* trans. Heinz Norden (New York: Augustus M. Kelley, 1951), p. 165.
5. *Drama and Society,* p. 267.
6. Ibid, p. 266.
7. *The Dramatic Works in the Beaumont and Fletcher Canon,* gen ed., Fredson Bowers, *The Scornful Lady,* ed. Cyrus Hoy (Cambridge: Cambridge Univ. Press, 1970), II, 488-489. Subsequent references are included in the text. "Saunders" are a parsley-like vegetable, and "Perspectives" are optical glasses that produce trick effects.
8. *Ben Jonson,* ed. C. H. Herford and Percy Simpson (Oxford: Clarendon Press, 1937), V, 25-26. But Beaumont and Fletcher's speech is not meant to carry Jonson's moral reverberations. Unlike Volpone, Morecraft makes no paradoxically exalted claim of purity by disavowing capitalist methods altogether. Volpone goes on to say, for instance, that "I turn no moneys in the public bank/ Nor usure private," a boast to which Morecraft does not aspire.
9. Clifford Leech in "Three Times Ho and a Brace of Widows," in *The Elizabethan Theatre,* III, ed. David Galloway (Hamden: Archon Books, 1973), p. 32, speaks of the conventional "comic vulnerability" of widows and cites the Dutchess of Malfi as one who overrides the stereotype. The widow in *The Scornful Lady* is another.

10. One of Knights's objections to Middleton is that his best comic scenes seem detachable from their dramatic contexts (see *Drama and Society,* p. 266). I do not think such detachability is necessarily a fault in comedy.

11. *The Anatomy of Criticism* (Princeton: Princeton Univ. Press, 1973), p. 150.

12. *Citizen Comedy in the Age of Shakespeare* (Toronto: Toronto Univ. Press, 1973), p. 150.

13. That each of my major examples is a comedy written for a private theater raises an issue too complicated to discuss here. Generally speaking, however, the antiacquisitive tradition is most characteristic of the public theater comedies, the "Theatre of a Nation," which Alfred Harbage in *Shakespeare and the Rival Traditions* (New York: Macmillan, 1952) contrasted with the less public-spirited children's plays, the "Theatre of a Coterie." Lately, Harbage's dichotomies between public and private theaters have been criticized as far too severe; see, for example, Michael Shapiro, *Children of the Revels* (New York: Columbia Univ. Press, 1977). I am not suggesting that less moralistic attitudes toward acquisitiveness surfaced solely in the private theaters.

14. D. J. Lake, *The Canon of Thomas Middleton's Plays* (Cambridge: Cambridge Univ. Press, 1975), pp. 109–135, argues for Middleton as the author of *The Puritan.*

15. "The Puritan, or the Widow of Watling Street," in *Studies in the Shakespeare Apocrypha* (New York: King's Crown Press, 1956), p. 113.

16. All quotations from *The Puritan* are from *The Disputed Plays of William Shakespeare,* ed. William Kozlenko (New York: Hawthorn Books, 1974). Kozlenko's text is a photographic reprint of *The Doubtful Plays of Shakespeare,* ed. Henry Tyrrell.

17. *Citizen Comedy in the Age of Shakespeare,* p. 74, n. 12.

PART 2

COMIC THEORY:
HEGEL,
THE PSYCHODYNAMICS
OF LAUGHTER,
AND
COMIC DEVALUATION

Hegel's Theory of Comedy

ANNE PAOLUCCI

The comic, it has been said, is the ultimate refinement of art, the "purest" of the purely aesthetic artistic experiences, beyond which art has nowhere to go without ceasing to be art. Like religion and philosophy, art may indeed begin—as Aristotle alleged—with wonder; but its end comes with the excitement of self-confident or self-assuring laughter. The end comes with the representation of persons, happenings, and/or things that are comical in themselves, that make us smile or laugh sympathetically, recognizing that they were intended to make us do so. We do not find such comic awareness where there has not been a self-conscious effort to make us experience it—and that is so because the genuinely comic has not, like the tragic, a nonintentional counterpart in the nonartistic sphere.

Of course, the great difficulty—one might even venture to say, the traditional difficulty—in generalizing about comedy and the comic lies in the fact that we do not have, in this sphere, an Aristotelian legacy to defend or attack, supplement or amend. Of Aristotle's fragmentary *Poetics,* it has been aptly said that it contains "a greater number of pregnant ideas on art than any other book."[1] On comedy and the comic, however, it is virtually silent, offering only the barest promise of a theory: not remotely enough to serve as a guide or challenge to subsequent criticism. Some modern critics rejoice in the fact that, with respect to comedy, there are "no authorities to get in the way; none of the age-old assumptions to overcome; few widely held prejudices to discard; and no attractive, but false, critical positions to mislead us." Yet there are also a variety of pitfalls yawning in the way of intelligent criticism here, not the least of which is the danger of entering upon a treadmill—the perspective from which always seems so various, so beautiful, so new, until its repetition becomes obvious. And the worst danger is, as Robert W. Corrigan observes in his excellent anthology *Comedy: Meaning and Form,* that, precisely for want of the kind of guidance that Aristotle provided with respect to tragedy, the modern unencumbered venturers in the sphere of comic theory too often run the "risk of missing the subject altogether."[2]

Had Aristotle left us a theory of comedy, we might at this point have presumed to introduce our subject with the directness of A. C. Bradley's lecture on "Hegel's Theory of Tragedy," which begins:

> Since Aristotle dealt with tragedy, and, as usual, drew the main features of his subject with those sure and simple strokes which no later hand has rivalled, the only philosopher who has treated it in a manner both original and searching is Hegel.[3]

Bradley held the Chair of Poetry at Oxford and was in the midst of delivering the lectures on Shakespearean tragedy that raised him to eminence as one of the greatest interpreters of Shakespeare when he sought to define his own theory of tragedy by comparing and contrasting it with Hegel's—"to the main ideas" of which, as he explained, "I owe so much that I am more inclined to dwell on their truth than to criticize what seem to be defects."[4] But with the true disciple's absolute preference for truth, Bradley gave himself fully, in that lecture on Hegel, to the task of criticism, seeking first to supplement and then to amend the Hegelian theory. At the close of the lecture, he said with candor:

> I leave it to students of Hegel to ask whether he would have accepted the criticisms and modifications I have suggested. Naturally I think he would, as I believe they rest on truth, and I am sure he had a habit of arriving at truth. But in any case their importance is trifling, compared with that of the theory which they attempt to strengthen and to which they owe their existence.[5]

Bradley, it has been noted, refrained altogether from theorizing about comedy.[6] Yet it is generally acknowledged that his "Rejection of Falstaff" in the *Oxford Lectures on Poetry* contains one of the profoundest treatments of humor in all literature and also that, as Professor E. F. Carritt has demonstrated at some length in his *Theory of Beauty*, the profoundest insights of that "inimitable essay" owe their being to Hegel's direct influence.[7]

Bradley knew how to read and use Hegel. In his lecture on Hegel's theory of tragedy, he warns his audience repeatedly that the theory is part of an organic, philosophical whole, saying at one point: "I cannot possibly do justice in a sketch to a theory which fills many pages of the *Aesthetik;* which I must tear from its connections with the author's general view of poetry and with the rest of his philosophy," and at another point: "His theory of tragedy is connected with his view of the function of negation in the universe. No statement therefore that ignores his metaphysics and his philosophy of religion can be more than a fragmentary account of that theory."[8] Bradley's words apply with equal rigor to Hegel's theory of comedy, which, as we here propose to show, is also part of Hegel's view of the function of negation in the universe.

THE PLACE OF COMEDY IN THE HEGELIAN SYSTEM

An initial difficulty in studying Hegel's view on comedy lies in the fact that he traces, defines, and circles back to his subject in many different passages of many works. His main contribution to the development of a philosophic theory of comedy is, of course, to be sought in several hundred pages of his voluminous lectures on *Aesthetics*. But there are also briefer discussions in almost all his other works, ranging from the early *Phenomenology of Mind* through the *Encyclopedia* to the posthumously published lectures on the *Philosophy of History,* the *Philosophy of Religion,* and the *History of Philosophy*. Even in his treatise on *Natural Law,* which is otherwise highly technical in its exposition, Hegel manages to climax his discussion of the moral imperative of practical reason with several pages on the nature of the comic spirit that serve, incidentally, to justify Dante's characterization of his great poem as a *commedia*.[9]

The point here is that to appreciate fully and correctly Hegel's view on any given subject, including comedy, one should have, ideally, a grasp of the large philosophical canvas. Short of such a grasp, the discussions on comedy, scattered as they are in so many different places, may seem fragmentary and abortive. Still, even a novice learns to appreciate individual insights quickly enough; and where the subject matter is familiar to him, he soon recognizes the validity of the Hegelian analysis and lingers over it with profit. For some, unfortunately, the experience of reading Hegel is nothing more than a series of such insights, a kaleidoscopic fragmentation that is never properly redeemed by the effort needed to understand the full implications of Hegel's intellectual world. Thus abstracted from their implied base, many of Hegel's observations often are interpreted as the very opposite of his intended meaning.

We cannot enter here on a discussion of the phenomenological base of the Hegelian theory of knowledge and how it is shaped critically in Hegel's discussion of aesthetics. For our present purpose, it will suffice to point out that the Hegelian discussion of comedy contains the two characteristics of the Hegelian method generally: (1) firm adherence to the notion of an organic logical necessity that directs the evolution of the Idea in all its manifestations and (2) conviction that the historical process in which the Idea unfolds and reveals itself is a dialectic of extremes, spiraling into and out of inherent contradictions. The foci of *universal* and *particular* are linked under tension, as opposites, in the *individual,* the unity of which is thus what might be characterized as an essentially *elliptical* unity; and the oscillations that result—the orbiting toward meaning through seemingly contradictory tendencies, swinging from peaks into valleys (*apogees* and *perigees*), from dark ages into enlightenments (*aphelions* and *perihelions*)—preclude the common view of a "progressive" linear thrust forward and upward toward "perfection." And individual human experience here parallels the course of historical cultural development. In each of us the Idea works itself into light through a process of self-shattering inner rejection, which makes possible a spiritual fusion of the many self-contradictory masks of willfulness each of us wears and sheds at any one moment. In these terms, the Hegelian dialectic, with its seeming paradoxes, is the very heartbeat of thought.

One need not revert to the clichés of the Hegelian manuals to grasp the importance of the sort of triads to which we have alluded. From both a phenomenological and an historical perspective, each is a complete moment of awareness and becomes, almost by necessary reaction, the first term of a new triad, and so on. For instance, in the sphere of drama, both tragedy and comedy are represented to us as a dialectical tension of opposites, with comedy triumphing in the life of thought only when the tension of tragedy has become too much to bear and the unity of the tragic personality is shattered so profoundly that art can no longer piece it together. But more important than the method of the dialectic as such is Hegel's application of it, in which he brings to bear an incredible knowledge of specific facts and thorough acquaintance with the individual works of particular authors.

For Hegel, comedy takes on crucial meaning and plays a vital role as the "universal dissolvent" that clears the stage of history of all the accumulated debris of anciens régimes or outworn conventions and standards. Its specific dramatic expression may be as varied as the number of comic poets; farce, sarcasm, ridicule, irony, all kinds of laughter and *humor* in the restricted modern sense, surface in comedy with the necessity to clear away the one-sided insistence on prejudices of all kinds, formal beliefs, and misdirected actions. Hegel notes parallels between comedy and tragedy here. In both, a crucial opposition is set up between absolute and one-sided claims; but whereas in tragedy that one-sided insistence inspires awe because of the substantive and truly ethical content that is threatened (for example, *Antigone, Richard II*), in comedy such insistence is merely laughable and absurd because it is not the *substantive* content of true values that is at stake, but only the *excesses* and *contradictions* that have rendered the ethical content inoperative (for example, *The Clouds, Henry IV, Parts I and II*).

Comedy, in other words, is the other side of the coin: the absolute standards of tragedy are undermined as society loosens up, comes to recognize and tolerate its idiosyncracies, turns back upon itself, and reverses its former rigorous position—as indeed the Athenians did with respect to Socrates, after his death finally acknowledging their own fatal excesses with and through comedy. The rigorous confrontations of the tragedies of Aeschylus and Sophocles give way to the more immediate sensibilities of Euripides and finally to the laughter of Aristophanes. Comedy is the exhaustion of an age and clears the way for what follows; it is historically a *negative* force, the final statement of a given equation. In its individual dramatic expression, however, it appears as a *positive* force, an art form in its own right, beyond history, in which the comic poet traces the refracted, multifaceted reflections of his age, drawing upon his own personal and immediate experience, as well as the myriad situations and characterizations of his time, in order to expose sham and restore through ridicule and laughter a proper balance.

Through his genial description of human follies and hypocrisy, the comic writer is thus able to create an entire world, richer in its particulars than the world of tragedy, a world at once recognizable and renewed through a comic catharsis not altogether different from that of tragedy. What in tragedy produces catharsis through the immediacy of *fear* (identification with the notion of suffering and of man's vulnerability) and the distance of *pity* (recognition of special circumstances not applicable to all) surfaces in comedy as *laughter* (or, more precisely, the immediate response to the folly of excesses through which the audience expresses, often only visibly with a smile, its acceptance of the truth of the exaggerations depicted) and *ridicule* (the distance between the "knowing" spectator and the "foolish" protagonist). Comic catharsis, it may, therefore, be said, prepares our own hearts, as well as the stage of history, for the restoration of essential values in a new social structure.

Precisely because it exaggerates the oscillation between extremes that characterizes the Hegelian approach generally, the concept of comedy provides an excellent introduction to the Hegelian world. In this respect, the discussions of comic subject matter in the chapters of Hegel's *Aesthetics* that focus on the symbolic, classical, and romantic (modern) forms of art, together with the treatment of comedy as a sub-genre of the third or dramatic voice of poetry, are of central importance. Yet wherever the idea of the comic surfaces in his treatment of other subjects—phenomenology, psychology, economics, law, religion, politics, history—we get illuminating observations that bring the force of those other subjects to bear on comedy at the same time that they give us a broadened sense of the entire Hegelian canvas of thought through a mosaic of penetrating cumulative insights.

Briefly, therefore, but always with a masterful command of the large idea and particular details, Hegel explores for us, in a variety of contexts, the distinction between irony and the genuinely comic spirit; the determinant importance of content rather than form in distinguishing the varieties of comedy (and of the comic generally) in both its ancient and modern development; the nature of comic characterization, diction, thought, and feeling; the part that audiences are made to play in recognizing and responding to, and thereby completing, the different possible comic effects; and the ultimate moral and political as well as artistic function of comedy as it relates to tragedy, enriching his argument throughout with references and examples from Molière, Aristophanes, Plautus and Terence, ancient satyric drama, Spanish comedy, and Shakespeare—who is here exalted to the same position of absolute superiority that Hegel accords him with respect to tragedy. It is Shakespeare who emerges as the unassailable "master" of modern comedy, the dramatic poet who "outshines all others" in this field. Hegel's procedure in all of this is altogether empirical and inductive. He moves only very gradually from *particular* instances of works of art directly appreciated to the definition of *universal* principles, which then serve him as the basis for classification, analysis, and critical or reconsidered appreciation of *individual* works of art in their social and historical contexts, apart from which they lack genuine individuality in Hegel's sense of the term.

But before taking up the constituent themes of the Hegelian approach to comedy, we need to make a final introductory comment about comedy and tragedy and the function of negation in the Hegelian universe. The opposition in human relations that triggers comedy certainly bears a close resemblance to the conflict of substantive values found in tragedy; yet the comic resolution is both artistically and morally more demanding. Comic action is full of contingencies and accidents, conflicting motives, projects, ambitions, intrigues. Instead of the cataclysmic upheavals of necessity that bring the tragic opposition to resolution, comedy gives full rein to individual idiosyncrasies, particularized intentions, and quirks and habits and mannerisms in rich profusion. Yet it remains true at the same time to an unwavering serious purpose: its spiritually liberating task of exposing the world's follies through that proprium of man—which is his capacity (unknown to beasts below him and to angels above him) to laugh. In comedy, as in tragedy, we are offered assurance of the ultimate indestructibility of substantive values; but to give us that assurance, the characters of comedy do not have to suffer the kind of internal erosion that is exhibited in the protagonists of tragedy. The comic heroes, says Hegel, are free and invulnerable in themselves and can, therefore, focus on whatever stirs their fancy and pass judgment on all things without losing their equanimity.

AESTHETIC IRONY AND THE COMICAL

It deserves to be stressed, I think, that when Hegel first speaks of the comical in his lectures on aesthetics, it is to distinguish it sharply from aesthetic irony, with which it was then, as now, often confounded. Having traced the development of the modern concept of art through Kant, Schiller, Winckelmann, Schelling, etc., Hegel quite early in his lectures takes up the widely current notion of the artist's life as a life of ironic detachment, of self-conscious retreat from the present state of mind or heart into the depths of the infinite ego. It is that willful retreat, Friedrich von Schlegel held (following Fichte's lead), that makes possible the romantically modern "artist's life"—for which there is no ancient and certainly no medieval or even Renaissance precedent. "With respect to beauty and art," writes Hegel, Schlegel's idea "receives the meaning of living as an artist and forming one's life *artistically*. But according to the principle before us, I live as an artist essentially only when everything I do or say, with respect to any content whatever, remains for me a mere 'put-on' or show, assuming a shape which is wholly within my power." Others, looking on, may take that show seriously. But that means simply that those "others" are not yet free artists in their own right; that they are not yet able to "see in all that usually has value, dignity, and sanctity for mankind, simply a product of one's own power of caprice"—the power whereby a genuinely free artist "is able to set his seal on the value of such things and determine for himself whether or not they shall be of importance in his life" (B/124–125).[10]
The viewpoint of the man or woman skilled in living the ironical artist's life (Hegel observes, not without a touch of the same sort of irony) is, of course, the viewpoint of *Godlike geniality* or, more precisely, that of the divinely *creative* genius who, having liberated himself from art's ancient bondage of *mimesis,* or mere imitation, knows himself to be wholly free with respect to every possible content of his life and art. Confronted by any merely objective thing, he has an absolute confidence that he "can annihilate as well as create it" with

equal ease. The one who has attained the standpoint of such Godlike geniality, writes Hegel,

> looks down in superiority on all other mortals, for they are pronounced *borné* and dull, inasmuch as law, morality, and so forth retain for them their fixed, obligatory, and essential validity. The individual who thus lives his artist's life does not, of course, on that account deny himself relations with others. Quite the contrary, he insists on having friends, mistresses, etc., but as genius he simply cannot permit any such relations to have a determinate bearing on the reality of his life and actions, or to retain any significance of universal value in their own right; his attitude toward all such relations is, in sum, ironical. (B/126)

Hegel observes that this irony was an "invention" of Friedrich von Schlegel, though he was by no means alone in its celebration. So long as the ego clings to such a standpoint, "everything appears to it as without worth and futile, excepting its own subjectivity" (B/127), which values itself most, of course, precisely when it has willfully emptied itself of all positive content and is thus, in its ironically hollow utterances, most like sounding brass or tinkling cymbal.

If, however, the ego is in time no longer able to *enjoy* simply its own emptiness in prolonged intimacy, a disquiet comes over it, and it becomes what Hegel calls the "*morbidly* beautiful soul" that yearns to fill its "abstract inwardness" with solid, substantial, essential interests, yet dares not act to satisfy that longing, dares not "do or touch anything for fear of surrendering what it has so long prized as its inner harmony." A *truly* beautiful soul, says Hegel, *acts* and is actual. The *morbidly* beautiful soul, on the other hand, lacks the strength to fill its dissatisfaction and empty longing with a content of substance. Taken abstractly, this sort of irony

> borders closely on the principle of comedy; yet, granting a measure of affinity, the comic must be essentially distinguished from the ironical. For the comic must be limited to showing that what is brought to nothing is something inherently null, a false and self-contradictory phenomenon; for instance, a whim, a perversity, or particular caprice, set over against a mighty passion; or even a *supposedly* reliable principle or rigid maxim may be shown to be null. But it is quite another thing when what is to be shown as null is *in reality* substantive, moral, and true. . . . Therefore, in this distinction between the ironical and the comic, what is essentially at issue is the content of what is to be brought to nothing. (B/128–129)

By way of illustrating his meaning, Hegel observes that there is nothing truly comic in attempts to show the nullity of, say, a Cato, who "can live only as a Roman and republican." Cato is not null in himself; and where art insists on the contrary, it makes itself essentially null. Irony, in other words, tries to show that worth itself (not merely pretended worth) is worthless and, as a corollary, that the worthy are truly worthy—ironically—only when, from their lofty station of ironic creative genius, they reveal how profoundly aware they are of the worthlessness of true worth. That is what makes them, in their own eyes, the "best and the brightest"—the *schöne Seele* of the morbid variety, in Hegel's sense. The treatment of fallen "heroes" of recent political history comes to mind in this connection, but perhaps the most vivid example of the ironic creative genius who indulges what is "best and brightest" in himself to the point of self-destruction is Shakespeare's Hamlet. Hegel's discussion here, together with his scattered references to that enigmatic and elusive masterpiece of dramatic characterization—ironically tragic, not comic—deserves close and serious scrutiny.[11]

THE PERSONAE OF ANCIENT AND MODERN COMEDY

In his long discussion of the "independence of character" of figures drawn from heroic ages, Hegel notes that only princes can be represented as essentially tragic characters. With respect to tragic willfulness—ancient, medieval, or modern—the mass of common people can only be spectators, a chorus of onlookers responding with conventional judgment. When epic or tragic poetry reaches into that mass for its heroes and heroines, the result—and it is usually fully intended—is invariable mock epic and mock tragedy. The genres that can appropriately draw upon the lower classes of civil society for their characters, writes Hegel, are those of comedy and the comical in general. In comedy, he says, "individuals have the right to 'spread' themselves however they wish and can." In their willing, if not in their acting, "they can claim for themselves an independence" that is manifestly contradicted by their actual social condition and that is "immediately annihilated by themselves" in action. (K/192)

Comedy thus finds its proper subject matter in all that is petty, perverse, exaggerated, inflated, vain, ridiculous, foolish, and hypocritical, skirting around the positive core of substantive values but never probing it. Hegel stresses that these negative moments are found in both comedy and tragedy, but he notes also that what is negated in both is never anything substantively positive *as a whole*. In tragedy, the protagonist is always pressing a one-sided claim that cannot validate itself so long as it remains one-sided. In comedy, what is negated is always a vain and empty claim. The result, in one case no less than in the other, is thus the negation of a negation—a catharsis, in other words, that prepares the human heart, if not the times, for a positive reaffirmation of moral and cultural values. And that is quite the contrary of the ironic effect, where the intent is to triumph over "everything that is excellent and substantive." What distinguishes the comic from the tragic approach to this catharsis of negation is made most obvious, according to Hegel, in the treatment of the leading personages of the best ancient comedies—which are, of course, the plays of Aristophanes.

Introducing his most pointed discussion of the comic genius of Aristophanes, Hegel says: "What is comical is a personality or subject who makes his own actions contradictory and so brings them to nothing, while remaining tranquil and self-assured in the process." This is followed immediately by an extended observation to the effect that comedy, in fact, "has for its basis and starting point what tragedy may end with, namely an absolutely reconciled and cheerful heart." The possessor of that heart may repeatedly frustrate his own purposes by the means he uses to attain them; yet he does not on that account lose his "peace of mind." On the other hand, this is only possible if we are made to see that, for him, as well as for us, those purposes really have no substantive value. Then comes this classic Hegelian observation, which is supported, philosophically, by the full force of his view of the function of negation in the universe:

> In this matter we must be careful to distinguish whether the dramatis personae are comical in themselves or only in the eyes of the audience. The former case alone can be counted as really comical, and here Aristophanes was a master. On these lines, an individual is portrayed as comical in the strict sense only when it is obvious that he is not serious at all about the seriousness of his aim and will, so that this seriousness always carries with it, in the eyes of the individual himself, its own destruction. . . . The comical therefore plays its part more often in people with lower aims, who are what they are, and have not the least doubt about what they are and what they are doing. But at the same time they reveal themselves as having something higher in them because they are not seriously tied to the finite world with which they are engaged but are raised above it and remain firm in themselves and secure in face of failure and loss. It is to this absolute freedom of spirit which is utterly consoled in advance in every human undertaking, to this world of private serenity, that Aristophanes conducts us. If you have not read him, you can scarcely realize how men can take things so easily. (K/1220-1221)

Hegel then proceeds to explain that, whereas true comedy draws the interests that it exhibits in this way from the spheres of genuine morality, religion, and even art—that certainly was the practice in the old Greek comedy—it is never by virtue of acting seriously that truly comic characters fail to realize such interests. It is always by "subjective caprice, vulgar folly, and absurdity" that the protagonists of comedy "bring to nought actions which had a higher aim." (K/1221)

And here, especially, Hegel reminds us that "Aristophanes had available to him rich and happy material partly in the Greek gods and partly in the Athenians." The "humanized" Olympians contain in their very concept a contrast between the divine and the human that is essentially comical, particularly when they are represented as acting on motives of manifestly human pride while insisting on their "divine significance." But it is especially the follies of the Athenian masses and their demogogic spokesmen, the absurdities of the war against Sparta, the new morality of the Sophists, and especially the new direction given to tragedy by Euripides that Aristophanes likes to dissect. In all his best comic portrayals—Socrates teaching Strepsiades and his son in *The Clouds;* Dionysius descending to Hades to fetch up a tragedian in *The Frogs;* the heroes and heroines of *The Knights, Ecclesiazusae,* and *Peace*—the keynote that resounds is the

> self-confidence of all these figures; and it is all the more imperturbable, the more incapable they obviously are of accomplishing their undertaking. The fools are such naive fools, and even the more sensible of them also have such an air of contradiction with what they are devoted to, that they never lose this naive personal self-assurance, no matter how things go. It is the smiling blessedness of the Olympian gods, their unimpaired equanimity which comes home in men and can put up with anything. In all this Aristophanes is obviously not a cold or malignant scoffer. He is a man of most gifted mind, the best of citizens to whom the welfare of Athens was always a serious matter. (K/1222)

Aristophanes does not, in fact,

> turn into ridicule what is truly of ethical significance in the social life of Athens, namely genuine philosophy, true religious faith, but rather the spurious growth of the democracy, in which the ancient faith and the former morality have disappeared; what he exhibits, in other words, is sophistry, the whining and querulousness of tragedy, the inconstant gossip, the love of litigation, and so forth, and these are placed before us, as opposed to true political life, religion, and art, in their suicidal folly. (O/iv, 304)

The all-pervasive corruption in institutions and individuals is contrasted, by Aristophanes, with the true values to which lip service is given, so that what we have in that lip service finally "is a mask concealing the fact that real truth and substance are no longer there, but have been handed over to subjective caprice."

Aristophanes himself, however, belongs to the same movement of spirit that he criticizes, Hegel observes. And with that, we are brought face to face with the ultimate negative significance of all genuine comedy. In unmasking the "subjective caprice" of the new philosophers, tragedians, rhetoricians, etc., Aristophanes is actually bringing to completion the very triumph of what he unmasks. For all the profundity of its insights, there is implicit in the Aristophanic comic sense "one of the greatest symptoms of Greek corruption, and thus these pictures of a wholly unperturbed sense of 'everything coming out right in the end' are really the last great harvest of this gifted, civilized, and ingenious Greek people." In this respect, the comic treatment of Socrates— or what we might venture to call the Aristophanic "rejection of Socrates"—is particularly significant, says Hegel. And in his lectures on the *History of Philosophy,* as well as in those on the *Philosophy of History,* Hegel dwells on that "rejection" to trace in it the signs of inherently inevitable decay confronting the Greek world of beauty, truth, and freedom. With Socrates, tragedy indeed walks off the stage into the actuality of history; but the Greek spirit can find in that moment a good-natured, good-humored, purposeful redemption of its contradictions by portraying Socrates himself as comically self-conscious in a Falstaffian sense of the self-destructive side of his own philosophical method.[12]

But comedy in which the characters appear comical to themselves as well as to others is not the only kind of comedy. Hegel notes that a second type eventually arose among the Greeks, in which characters are dramatically betrayed by their authors, with the result that they appear comical only to others. Aristophanes, the "comic author par excellence," adhered strictly, in all his plays, to his original principle. "But in the new comedy of Greece," writes Hegel, "and later in Plautus and Terence the opposite tendency was developed, and this has acquired such universal prominence in modern comedy that a multitude of our comic productions verges more or less on what is laughable in a purely prosaic sense and even on what is bitter and repugnant." Hegel is thinking of Molière here and, therefore, hastens to explain that when he uses the term *prosaic* comedy, he does not mean to suggest that such comedy is necessarily an inferior form of the genre. Writing particularly of Molière's best comedies, which are by no means "to be taken as farces," Hegel explains:

> There is a reason for prose here, namely that the characters are deadly serious in their aims. They pursue them therefore

with all the fervor of this seriousness and when at the end they
are deceived or have their aim frustrated by themselves, they
cannot join in the laughter freely and with satisfaction but,
duped, are the butt of the laughter of others, often mixed with
malice. So, for example, Molière's Tartuffe, *le faux devot,* is
unmasked as a downright villain, and this is not funny at all
but a very serious matter; and the duping of the deceived Org-
on leads to such painful misfortune that it can be assuaged
only by a *deus ex machina.* . . . There is nothing really comical either about the odious *idée fixe* of such rigid characters
as Molière's miser whose absolutely serious involvement in his
narrow passion inhibits any liberation of his mind from this
restriction. (K/1233-1234)

Molière's departure from the Aristophanic model is intentional.
But from the time of the New Comedy of Greece and its Roman imita-
tors there has been another tendency of an inferior sort that has by no
means always been pursued intentionally; and that is the tendency that
results in the comedy of intrigue, for which Plautus and Terence provided what have remained the principal models. Hegel's discussion of
the varieties of comic intrigues might easily have been illustrated out of
Shakespeare, for here, too, Shakespeare is a master; but, no doubt, because he treats it as an inferior genre, he prefers to cite examples of
what he calls the Spanish "mastery" of intrigue. Where the hand is not
sure in fashioning comic characters—and that is rarely the case in
Shakespeare—one turns for a substitute to ancient and fashionable
models or works out ideas of one's own for "carrying out a well-con-
structed intrigue." Generalizing, Hegel observes that intrigue of a
comic variety usually arises "from the fact that an individual tries to
achieve his aims by deceiving other people." One variety of intrigue
shows us the deceiver pretending to share the interests of other characters in the play and to be laboring to further them; but this "false fur-
therance" usually backfires, so that the deciever finds himself caught
in a trap that he has himself set. Another variety shows us the deceiver
putting a "false face on himself in order to put others in a similar per-
plexity." But the variations on this sort of coming and going, in and out
of deceptions, are virtually limitless.

Citing Spanish examples, which have much in them that is "attractive and excellent," Hegel is concerned however to stress that "intrigues and their complications" are not to be regarded as inherently
comical, any more than the interests of love, honor, loyalty, etc.,
on which they are usually built are inherently comical. Tragedy makes
use of the same interests and complications. But whereas in tragedy
such interests are plainly substantive and "lead to the most profound
collisions," in comedy, writes Hegel, they are, as motives, "clearly
without substance from the start—as for example a prideful unwilling-

ness to confess a long-felt love which at last finds itself just for that reason betrayed—and can therefore most appropriately be annulled in a comic fashion."

What makes the genuine comedy of intrigue comical is not plot as such, therefore, but the nature of the interests and values at stake and the characters of the chief personages involved. In modern comedy, the characters who "contrive and conduct intrigues are usually—like the slaves in Roman comedy—servants or chambermaids who have no respect for the aims of their masters, but further them or frustrate them as their own advantage dictates and only give us the laughable spectacle of masters being really the servants, or the servants masters." In most intrigues of this sort, "we ourselves, as spectators, are in on the secret; and because we are not in the least threatened by the deceits and betrayals, often pursued against the most estimable fathers, uncles, etc., we can readily laugh over every contradiction implicit or obvious in such treacheries." (K/1234-1235)

Hegel notes that this sort of modern comedy, for the most part, lacks anything even remotely resembling the "frank joviality that pervades the comedies of Aristophanes." What that frank joviality provides in the old Greek comedy is the possibility of a genuinely cathartic effect upon the observer. In modern comedies, the effect of intrigue is often altogether repulsive, particularly where the "cunning of servants, the deceitfulness of sons and wards, gains the victory over honest masters, fathers, and trustees who have not been actuated by prejudices and eccentricities." But just as we are being tempted to conclude that Hegel altogether prefers ancient Aristophanic comedy to anything the modern world has produced in the genre, we get this important reservation:

> Nevertheless, in contrast to this essentially prosaic way of treating comedy, the modern world has in fact developed a type of comedy which is truly comical and truly poetic. Here once again the keynote is good humor, assured and careless unconcerned gaiety despite all failure and misfortune; and with this, the exuberance and dash of what is at bottom pure tomfoolery and, in a word, fully-exploited self-assurance. As a result we have again here (but on a profounder level, in a more intimate depth of humor, the sweeping compass of which includes a much broader sector of human society as well as subject-matter) what Aristophanes achieved to perfection in his field in Greece. As a brilliant example of this sort of thing I will, though without going into detail, once again emphasize the name of Shakespeare. (K/1235-1236; O/iv, 348)

I have already suggested, with a reference to the Aristophanic "rejection of Socrates" in *The Clouds,* that the great parallel between

Aristophanic comedy and modern comedy is to be sought in Shakespeare's comic treatment of Falstaff; and I have in mind particularly what A. C. Bradley has called, in his thoroughly Hegelian Oxford lecture on the subject, "The Rejection of Falstaff." When he says that the "bliss of freedom gained in humor is the essence of Falstaff" and that the main source of "our sympathetic delight" in the "immortal Falstaff" is his "humorous superiority to everything serious and the freedom of soul enjoyed in it,"[13] Bradley is echoing what Hegel says specifically about the heroes of Aristophanic comedy. But if we trouble ourselves to gather together all that Hegel says incidentally about Shakespeare's comic heroes, we get an even clearer impression of how much Bradley has gained from Hegel as an interpreter of Shakespearean comedy.

It is, for instance, in his general discussion of Shakespeare's capacity to represent his tragic heroes as poets in their own right—with a "free imaginative power" by means of which they are "enhanced above themselves"—that Hegel interrupts himself to make a similar observation about "Shakespeare's vulgar characters, Stephano, Trinculo, Pistol, and the absolute hero of them all, Falstaff," who, although they "remain sunk in their vulgarity, are at the same time shown to be men of intelligence with a genius fit for anything, enabling them to have an entirely free existence and to be, in short, what great men are." (K/585-586) Hegel uses almost the very same terms to characterize the comic treatment of Cervantes's Don Quixote and the entire world of Ariosto's *Orlando furioso*. In Hegel's assessment, Cervantes and Ariosto rank beside, and just below, the creator of Falstaff as the greatest comic geniuses of the modern world—in whose work we can trace a romantic equivalent of the dissolution of Greek society that made possible the plays of Aristophanes. (K/590-592)

TRAGEDY, COMEDY, AND THE "END" OF ART

Though the principles of comic dissolution remain the same, there is a world of difference between the values at stake in Aristophanes' *The Knights, Peace, The Clouds, The Frogs, The Birds, Ecclesiazusae,* etc., and those at stake in the comic masterworks of Ariosto, Cervantes, and Shakespeare. Comic dissolution follows tragedy's last effort to save the substantive values of an age. As Hegel repeatedly expresses it, tragedy destroys the individual in order to reconcile the substantive values that his one-sided willfulness has brought into conflict. Comedy, on the other hand, spares personality in the last resort, when its sacrifice can no longer suffice to reconcile and thus save the once substantive values that society as a whole no longer has the will to sustain. These two fundamental features of action—which are tragic when personality sacrifices itself for serious things and comic when it triumphs over the ruin of serious things that are beyond salvation—provide, according to Hegel, the one truly consistent basis for distinguishing the two major dramatic genres. The characters in comedy also dissolve finally, but "it is in their own laughter that they dissolve" and then only "after their laughter has dissolved everything else." (K/1199) Triumphing in its own dissolution, subjective personality challenges art itself to dare to represent that dissolution as defeat, without sacrificing itself as art.

A. C. Bradley makes this very point in the concluding paragraphs of his lecture on Falstaff, and he does so in words that clearly anticipate what T. S. Eliot will later venture to say about *Hamlet,* namely, that here we must simply admit that "Shakespeare tackled a problem which proved too much for him."[14] With his Mona-Lisa remark about the Mona-Lisa character of Hamlet, Eliot may have meant to suggest that Shakespeare there pressed the capacities of tragic art to their absolute limits and perhaps a little beyond. But we don't have to surmise Bradley's meaning where he says of Shakespeare that "in the creation of Falstaff he overreached himself" and that "he was caught up on the wind of his own genius, and carried so far that he could not descend to earth at the selected spot." That is a thoroughly Hegelian judgment, the rationality of which is supported by the entire *Aesthetics.* For Bradley, as for Hegel, Shakespeare's drive to overreach his own artistic genius, in Falstaff as well as in Hamlet, is by no means an artistic defect. Shakespeare, says Bradley, could easily have brought his high-flying Falstaff down to the ground at any selected spot; but, had he chosen to do so, we could hardly have regarded it an "achievement beyond the power of lesser men." Shakespeare's achievement, says Bradley, "was Falstaff himself, and the conception of that freedom of soul, a freedom illusory only in part, and attainable only by a mind which had received from Shakespeare's own the inexplicable touch of infinity which he bestowed on Hamlet and Macbeth and Cleopatra, but denied to Henry the Fifth."[15]

Hegel is Bradley's source for that insight and judgment, except that Hegel presses the argument at least one step further to conclude that we must look not to tragedy, even on the heights of *Hamlet,* but rather to comedy—comedy of the order of Shakespeare's Falstaff—for the ultimate aesthetic catharsis, beyond which art is powerless to move us. Just after he has concluded his treatment of modern comedy, with the final tribute to Shakespeare that has already been cited ("Als glänzendes Beispiel dieser Sphäre will Ich zum Schluss auch hier noch einmal Shakespeare mehr nur nennen als näher charakterisieren"), Hegel brings the entire course of his lectures on aesthetics to a close in two brief paragraphs that sum up its argument and clearly define the place of comedy in the whole. "Now, with this development of the kinds of comedy," he writes, we have reached the real end of our inquiry. We began with symbolic art where personality struggles to find itself as form and content and to become objective to itself. We proceeded to the plastic art of Greece where the Divine, now conscious of itself, is presented to us in living individuals. We end with the romantic art of emotion and feeling where absolute subjective personality moves free in itself and in the spiritual world. Satisfied in itself, it no longer unites itself with anything objective and particularized and it brings the negative side of this dissolution into consciousness in the humor of comedy. Yet on this peak comedy leads at the same time to the dissolution of art altogether. (K/1236)

One need not labor either the originality or the impressive consistency of that statement. No one reading Hegel's pages and coming to this final conclusion can doubt even for a moment what he considered to be the most profound (though possibly not the most aesthetically perfect) expression of art. It is that of romantic art, of art on the verge, and even beyond the verge, of transcending itself as art. To suggest that Hegel depreciates art in rising to this conclusion is to have misunderstood all that he has said about architecture, sculpture, painting, music, and epic and lyric poetry, as well as tragedy and comedy. What he means, of course, very simply, is that when artistic power has stormed the highest heights, when it has aimed to do and has done much more than reason can ask of it or allow it to do, it must say, finally, with Shakespeare's Prospero—

> This rough magic
> I here abjure. . . . I'll break my staff,
> Bury it certain fathoms in the earth,
> And deeper than did ever plummet sound,
> I'll drown my book. (*The Tempest,* 5.1. 50-57)

CONCLUSION

The foregoing pages have attempted to place the Hegelian theory of comedy in its proper perspective by identifying its characteristic property (in the peculiarly human capacity to smile and laugh), by distinguishing it from irony, by comparing its ancient and modern forms, and, in a more general way, by contrasting it with tragedy and relating it, in some measure, to the large Hegelian system. The subject, needless to say, deserves a great deal of expansion, far beyond what we have attempted here. An anthology of Hegel's writings on the subject, doing full justice to the wealth of illustrations he introduces, would closely match in size a volume like *Hegel on Tragedy,* which runs to 400 pages.

The intention here, of course, has been to focus upon the underlying or, rather, organizing theory. Hegel's method (as we noted at the outset) is, however, essentially empirical and inductive, so that it would have done violence to his aesthetic attitude had we started out with a summation of principles taken out of context, abstracted from what is, in effect, a very large body of sensitively critical literary analysis and comparison, focused constantly on the content and forms of the individual works of art themselves. Still, by way of summary, I should like to set down what amounts to an outline of points essential to the Hegelian theory, some of which have had to be glossed over, if not altogether neglected, in the main discussion.

The comic attitude, it must be said, is an essentially artistic attitude that has no merely natural, nonartistic counterpart. As the inner force that enables us to smile, it works as a dissolvent with respect to everything in life that tends to keep us from smiling. The comic is not to be confounded, however, with the ironic. The difference consists in the fact that the truly comic attitude restricts itself to showing that what dissolves beneath its gaze is something inherently null, a false and contradictory thing, idea, situation, or character that has already spent its substance.

In comic art (as in symbolic, classical, and romantic art generally), therefore, it is the content, not the form, that is the determinant thing. The form of the individual work of art must not be something added to the content, externally, but precisely that form that the already artistically determined content requires for its full expression. This is, of course, contrary to the "new criticism" or Crocian view, according to which art is form and nothing but form. In the case of comedy, says Hegel, the determinant content is the triumph of subjective personality in situations of conflicting interests and values that lead, in the case of tragedy, to the destruction of personality.

From what has just been said, it follows that comedy can indulge itself best with characters that do not have the responsibilities of princes or statesmen. A prince who ought never to have been a prince can be comical, but it is better for comic effect to bring lower-class characters into play—characters who can "put on airs," spread themselves transparently. When they negate themselves, together with their apparent interests and values, such characters reveal the requisite negation of a negation, which is the essence of comedy. Hegel finds this kind of comic effect in Dutch and Flemish painting, too.

But the comic attitude is not a merely rational attitude; it is an overriding emotion, or *pathos* in the Greek sense. Pathos—overriding feeling—is the true domain of art, says Hegel. Comic as well as tragic characters succeed in drama only when they possess, or rather are possessed by, true pathos.

Genuine comedy first appeared, according to Hegel, when the Greeks, for whom beauty was truth and truth beauty, ceased to be satisfied emotionally with that ideal identity. The beauty of classical art lost its reason for being when the Greek spirit, within itself, came to experience an overwhelming disquiet and dissatisfaction. That was the mood—the critical, sophistic, Socratic mood—of the times that gave rise to Aristophanic comedy. Although he was himself full of the critical spirit of Socrates, as also of Euripides, the great Greek comic playwright carried the dissatisfaction of his age beyond itself in the same direction. Aristophanic comedy can, therefore, be characterized as the expression of dissatisfaction with dissatisfaction; with its "rejection" of Socrates and Euripides, and so on, it negates the negation, triumphing over it serenely in the process. But here Hegel is at pains to distinguish the genuinely comical from the satiric, which is bitter and critical without reconciliation, without redemption, and without poetry.

The world of true comedy is a world where subjective personality makes itself absolute master of all. It raises poetry to a peak of subjective self-confidence without objective support. It is art's last bloom. It smiles a self-assured smile, and then there is a fall into prose. Art loosens its hold on all that it has theretofore taken seriously, so that its *aesthesis* is then able to transform itself into religious *ecstasis* and, sometimes preferably, into scientific *sophia*.

Aristophanes gives us characters who are comic in and for themselves as well as for us. Later Greek comedy and the Roman masters of the genre—Terence and Plautus—departed from his example. They could not rise to the poetry of true comedy and so contented themselves with characters that are laughable only for others, not themselves. They gave us slaves who trip up their masters, sons and daughters who deceive their fathers, humorously. But because the characters deceived are not essentially null, the laughter has to be pursued either in slapstick fashion or through the ins and outs of elaborate intrigues, more often than not contrived by deceived deceivers.

Although most of the modern world's comedy has been of this kind, it has, nevertheless, managed not merely to match, but even to surpass, the poetic mastery of Aristophanes in Shakespeare. The comic world of Shakespeare is more intense than that of Aristophanes because the truth of romantic art, to which it is prepared to sacrifice ideal artistic beauty, is higher than the truth of classical art. Shakespeare is the culmination of romantic art. In his *Hamlet,* he pushed the poetry of tragedy so far that those who apply ideals of classical beauty to its interpretation are tempted to judge it a failure; and in his comic characterization of Falstaff, he does the same—and more. In his high comedy, Shakespeare indeed validates Hegel's assertion that art's ultimate triumph consists in its own romantic effort to transcend itself as art.

NOTES

1. W. D. Ross, *Aristotle* (London, 1930), p. 290.
2. Robert W. Corrigan, ed., *Comedy: Meaning and Form* (San Francisco, 1965), p. 2.
3. A. C. Bradley, "Hegel's Theory of Tragedy," *Oxford Lectures on Poetry* (Bloomington, Indiana, 1961), p. 69.
4. Ibid., p. 81.
5. Ibid., p. 92.
6. E. F. Carritt, *Theory of Beauty* (London, 1923), p. 312. Carritt says: "To the barrenness of most accounts of humour I have found three grateful exceptions; ... Mr. A. C. Bradley's 'Rejection of Falstaff' ... is a perfect illustration, by a concrete instance, of the truth; but he refrains from theorizing. The two theories are those of Hegel and Bergson."
7. Ibid., p. 316.
8. Bradley, p. 69.
9. G. W. F. Hegel, *Natural Law,* trans. T. M. Knox, introduction by H. B. Acton (Philadelphia, 1975), pp. 104–108.
10. G. W. F. Hegel, *Aesthetics: Lectures on Fine Art,* trans. T. M. Knox, 2 vols. (Oxford, 1975); *The Philosophy of Fine Art,* trans. F. B. B. Osmaston, 4 vols. (London, 1920); *The Introduction to Hegel's Philosophy of Fine Art,* trans. Bernard Bosanquet (London, 1886). Quotations have been slightly adapted by the author in most cases, in accordance with the text of the German: *Asthetik,* ed. H. G. Hotho, 1842, and reedited by F. Bassenge, 2 vols. (Berlin, 1966). The references in the text are to the translation used as a "base" (*K, O,* or *B*), followed by page(s); for this initial reference (B/124–125), read, "Bosanquet translation, pp. 124–125."
11. Most of Hegel's comments on *Hamlet,* scattered throughout his works, are collected in *Hegel on Tragedy,* ed. (with an introduction) Anne and Henry Paolucci (New York: Anchor Books 1962; reissued New York: Harper Torchbook; reissued New York: Greenwood Press, 1978, hardcover). See Index under "Hamlet."
12. *Hegel on Tragedy,* "Socrates" in Index.
13. Bradley, "The Rejection of Falstaff," *Oxford Lectures on Poetry,* pp. 262 and 269.
14. T. S. Eliot, *Selected Essays* (London, 1932), p. 146.
15. Bradley, p. 273.

Smiles and Laughter: Some Neurologic, Developmental, and Psychodynamic Considerations

HERBERT J. LEVOWITZ

Man alone suffers so excruciatingly
in the world that he was compelled
to invent laughter.
   Nietzsche, The Will to Power

Quite accidently, my focus was engaged by a television news report of a man and wife returning to their community after having won the million-dollar lottery. She was greeted with shrill shrieks and tearful embraces from other women, whereas the man's good fortune evoked deep guffaws and hearty slaps on the back from his male counterparts. The scarcely concealed aggression, enveloped in laughter, fostered the speculations for this paper: What is the neurobiologic mechanism of laughter, and how vulnerable is it to interruption? What are the developmental factors that modify and contribute to the multipurpose functions of this mechanism? What are the psychodynamic functions of laughter for adults?

 The extensive scientific literature on laughter is complicated by contradictions and endless, dissenting opinions. What follows will fit comfortably into the weave of that fabric, but we still hope to avoid B. Stolberg's view of the expert as "a person who avoids the small errors as he sweeps on to the grand fallacy."

It is our view that laughter is an exclusive possession of Homo sapiens and that the neurologic integration requisite for laughter is diffusely represented in cortical and subcortical areas of the brain. Although this formulation is similar to the view of the essential neurologic substratum for language offered by Noam Chomsky,[1] laughter would appear to have a more extensive and more primitive neurologic organization than language. As with animals, the somatic and autonomic expressions of emotions, both pleasant and unpleasant, are integrated in subcortical areas of the brain. The participation of a cortical linkage in man uniquely allows our species to use cognition and higher mental functions in the coproduction of laughter and the comic.

Those cerebrovascular accidents (strokes) that result in extensive aphasias most often spare the ability to laugh. In fact, extensive neurologic damage extending all the way from crippling mental retardation through cerebral palsy does not manage to obliterate the mechanism of laughter. Excessive and often uncontrollable laughter is seen in organic brain disease. However, diseases affecting subcortical nuclei (Parkinsonism) are known to mask out the facial expressions of emotion.

As a psychiatrist treating mostly children and adolescents, I have seen laughter obliterated by altered states of consciousness (stupor, coma) and those early profound depressions of infants subsequent to nutritive and affective deprivations. The marasmus and "laser-beam" staring of the anaclitic depression of infancy reveals the absence of smiling and laughter despite neurologic intactness. Severe vegetative depressions and catatonic states share this picture of absence of smiles and laughter without neuroanatomical disruptions (but with altered neurobiochemistry). An area for investigation would be our speculative formulation that the autonomic and somatic (motoric) components of laughter are integrated in the subcortical areas deep in the brain, and diseases of these structures will efface the expression of comic affect. The emotional and cognitive, and indeed conscious, components of laughter are widely elaborated in the cerebral cortex and are eliminated by intense psychological states. It is the competent coordination of these two neural structures that gives exclusively to man a sense of humor and the ability to laugh.

SMILES AND LAUGHTER IN INFANCY

Born the most immature of all animals, human beings have the greatest potentiality for development. In fact, nature appears to delay the structuring of the human brain in order to increase outside influences (parental culture, customs, and values). The neurological and psychological are interwoven as personality is molded in a stimulating environment, and experience and upbringing are imprinted structurally in the brain. Thus, the prolonged period of growth and development helps to program inputs and alterations in the person's ultimate personality and psychic functions—and laughter obeys this same pattern. The earliest smiles from the newborn are often related to satiation and relaxation of oral muscles after sucking. Later when this same facial expression is seen on the mother's face, the child associates and interprets it as a pleasurable state. Mother and child communicate as the parent is alerted to the well-being of the offspring, and the baby can projectively identify the happy state he or she sees in the mother. Throughout life, smiling and laughter still retain some of this expressive, communicative quality, informing others of our own species about our feelings of pleasure and euphoria.

The newborn's postprandial smile rapidly becomes an emotional indication of expected need fulfillment and tension abatement. With time, those external stimuli that are associated with inner tension releases will be heralded by the baby's smiling. René Spitz has described the "smile response" as a "sign of recognition of a complex of stimuli, without recognition of the face as a person, and the initial instrument of exchange or contagion between the infant and its human partner,"[2] the source of its gratification. Smiling becomes the earliest scaffolding of pleasurable reciprocal exchange.

In the absence of language and cognitive capacities, all of the baby's infantile cravings must achieve gratification through the motoric system. Activity broadcasts the baby's needs, and through motor activity (ingestion, grasping) they are gratified. The resultant intense inner gratification may elicit smiling. Blatz and his colleagues have demonstrated that smiling—and to an even greater extent laughter—occurs in babies as a general reaction to intense gratification of any kind and becomes rapidly linked to motoric activities.[3] Edith Jacobson speaks of "smiling, the mild twin of laughter . . .[and laughter] as a much stronger reaction becomes more specifically tied up to experiences in the realm of the motor system itself."[4] The child when observing fast movements participates in the experience, not actually but emotionally, and finds release instead in laughter.

Laughter is elicited in children after the second month of life by short and especially rhythmical exteroceptive stimuli, known as tickling. The child views the tickler as a playful attacker and the tickle partly as a threat and partly as sexual excitement. The tickler reassures the child of no harm intended by grinning and laughing—it's all in fun. As Edmund Bergler notes, "tickling . . . is one of the few ways in which masochistic feelings of being overwhelmed can be enjoyed by the child without guilt. But we say ironically, 'I'm tickled to death,' intuitively sensing the masochistic danger which lurks beneath the playful surface."[5]

SMILES AND LAUGHTER IN CHILDHOOD

Motor stimulation as such does not produce laughter unless the suddeness of the stimuli and speed of the movements can engender "a thrill . . . of anxious tension mixed with quickly increasing pleasure which dissolve the fears"[6] of possible hurt. A typical game that elicits laughter from the less-than-one-year-old is to move one's hand up his or her supine body with increasing speed, at first accompanying the movement with slightly threatening sounds and facial expressions and terminating in tickling and laughing at the baby's neck. After a stage of frightened thrill, the child bursts into laughter. (This is analogous to the amusement park roller-coaster ride; the speeding downside thrill alternates with shrill laughter when slowed at the heights or valleys.) As Blatz noted, "Laughter and smiling may be considered as socially acceptable tics . . . accompanying the resolution of conflicts that have for a shorter or longer period kept the individual on the horns of a dilemma"[7] (will I be hurt or gratified?). The anticipation of pleasure will play a role in comic phenomena so that the expectation of a joke, a funny picture, a happy ending contributes to the "anticipation of amusement" that counteracts our fear of disappointment. More recent neurophysiologic exploration[8] has strongly supported the notion that feedback from the facial musculature helps to tell the brain that it is having a good time, and the simple act of smiling may help induce a happy state of mind.

As the developing crawler and toddler masters his or her body apparatus, overcomes gravity, and learns about the environment, each new epistemological triumph may be accompanied by a burst of toothless grinning and laughter. Jean Piaget has alerted us to the spontaneous laughter that accompanies this "data input process" (assimilation) and formulated a pleasure-in-mastery hypothesis that can best be observed during the sensorimotor period of development of the first two years of life.[9] Immense pleasure seems to be derived from the child's initial understanding of some previously confusing events, or accomplishment of some previously unmastered physical task, or from the "assimilation" of some novel object or event into the child's sensorimotor schemata. As noted by Jerome Kagan, "the smile signifies a cognitive success following some doubt over that success . . . a feeling of uncertainty followed by resolution."[10]

The cognitive triumph of the baby in pulling a box open with its finger or catching a rolling ball or retrieving an object that was momentarily out of sight forms an embryonic part of the laughter that will later accompany the cognitive aspect of "getting the joke" or solving puzzles and brain twisters. Our ability to conceptualize the two meanings of double entendres and comprehend incongruities and unusual verbal representations forms a bridge to childhood life—the intrinsic pleasure involved in cognitive "assimilative" acquisitions of the child is the same as the pleasure involved in the cognitive activity in understanding humor.

Early childhood affords the developing person respite from the realistic cares and problems of reality. The young child's play consists largely of motor behavior and is often accompanied by laughter. The sheer joy of bodily movement and mastery of motor skills through play utilizes developmental factors mentioned above. Martha Wolfenstein has emphasized that as the child progresses from one cognitive or developmental level to the next, what is humorous and laughter-producing also manifests a meaningful progression.[11] A basic motive in humor initiated by children is the overcoming of distress and momentary release of frustration. With the increasing awareness of restrictions in the expression of hostile and early sexual impulses (oral voracity, anal preoccupations), the child learns to use the joke as a modified expression of these impulses. The use of a joke facade allows the vicariously enjoyed "forbidden" to get past the inner and outer censors. Children, after the time of the difficult education to cleanliness, laugh at the production of "dirty noises," especially as the production of such onomatopoetic skills is learned to be forbidden. Glee over the expression of the naughty and relief that retaliation commensurate with the guilt is not forthcoming both find an energic overflow into laughter.

Children will laugh upon observing quick and staccato movements and at the observation of movement errors, such as falling or stumbling by others. A silly motion is funny to a child when it has achieved competency in movement repertoires. The role of mastery in young children's humor was noted by Ernst Kris, because, in order to experience the comic, "a preliminary condition is complete control over the function in question. An absurd movement on the part of another person will seem funny to the child only when it has itself mastered the movement."[12] As Edith Jacobson noted, "having established his feeling of superiority, he may now relax and permit himself to participate in the experience again through a similarly uncontrolled but socially accepted and harmless motor release, the outburst of laughter, which represents both, pleasure and narcissistic triumph, and in addition is an outlet for aggressive impulses."[13] At later stages of development, youngsters will laugh not only at movement errors, but also at errors of thinking, as their own powers of thought are firmly established. Adults will add laughter at moral mistakes and enjoy the same inner superiority and mildly aggressive denigration of misdoers.

Around the time of entering school, youngsters become increasingly capable of verbal humor emancipated from motor ability. Children five or under, when asked to tell something funny, might jump up and down or begin to topple over or roll around while saying something funny; saying "a funny" and acting funny are intertwined. But with the outset of the sixth year, children acquire a repertoire of verbal jokes, related with a minimum of motoric activity. Fantasy and nonsense allow a gleeful flight from the demands of reality. Anxiety over the expression of the forbidden and frustration with the restraints of society will be momentarily undone through the medium of humor. The frightening is rendered manageable by joking and through counterphobic derision. Telling a humorous story repeatedly allows the child gratification through a reenactment of the mastery over anxiety. Sometimes, as a substitute for tears, laughter will replace crying. It is possible to defend against the anxiety attendant on painful feelings through a joke with its camouflaged reassuring meanings—"you are not dangerous; I am powerful and triumphant."

With the achievement of higher levels of mastery and understanding of one's world and with the acquisition of new challenges, worries, and hurts, the capacity to comprehend and produce verbal jokes will progress through various stages, taking on more complex psychic functions. Normally inhibited erotic and hostile ideas will find temporary release through the joke, and the pent-up instinctual energy will burst through in the form of laughter. As Sigmund Freud commented, "humor is not resigned; it is rebellious. It signifies the triumph not only of the ego, but also of the pleasure principle."[14]

SMILES AND LAUGHTER IN ADULTHOOD

At this point, preparing to comment on the function of laughter for adults, I had in mind to say, as they do in "Monty Python's Flying Circus," "and now, for something completely different . . ." It can't be said, because laughter for adults is not completely different from what it is for the growing human organism, but an outgrowth of the earlier developmental pathways. "The child within the adult" still needs that mechanism that will supply moment-to-moment relief from the tasks of apperception of reality, restraining hostile urges towards our fellow creatures and retaining pristine cleanliness from erotic drives. Some mechanism that affords us "little murders," small narcissistic triumphs, and momentary moral superiority will not be left to the province of childhood.

Verbal jokes are extraordinary complex products of man's mind. Even though it has been described as the least known of Freud's works by his biographer Ernest Jones, *Jokes and Their Relation to the Unconscious* (1905) remains the most telling exploration in the psychoanalytic literature of man's sense and use of humor. Freud theorized that the source of laughter at a joke is the release of energy otherwise bound up in ongoing psychic work. The psychic work needed to retain "the burden of intellectual upbringing" and not abandon it in a return to childlike thought requires energy; psychic energy is also expended in maintaining repression of primitive urges and bizarre, animalistic thoughts (primary process); the repressive lid is also mounted over unacceptable sexual and aggressive impulses by psychic-work energy (cathexis). Through the joke, verbal expression is given to the forbidden and made conscious in a disguised form, and primitive unrealistic gratifications are allowed. The sudden release of energy (countercathexis) otherwise bound in psychic work spills over in the motoric and respiratory components of laughter with its accompanying pleasurable sensation. Thus, according to Freud, the joke, the comic formulation, and the witticism foster laughter, because "the conditions are present under which a sum of psychical energy which has hitherto been used for cathexis is allowed free discharge."[15]

Adults need to avoid the guilt and shame that would come about by too nakedly expressing their sexual and aggressive urges and too openly protesting their own superiority. Humor, wit, and irony provide a pathway. The pseudoaggression inherent in a joke slides past the conscience (superego), and the energy freed as we abandon our usual repression of our base urges is delivered up in laughter. Even watching a comic film, according to Edith Jacobson, "permits the onlooker, after a tentative identification, to quickly detach himself from the suffering hero, and by unloading on him all the inferiority he dreads having in himself, the sins and weakness of the past which he has long since mastered . . . he discharges his affects and his own mobilized infantile impulses in laughter and pleasure in the hero's being hurt."[16] Laughter provides intermittent victories for the ego and enables the individual to avoid the pain of continued psychic work without relief. As Martin Grotjahn has noted, laughter and a sense of humor develop in stages and gradually throughout our lives. Every step is connected with mastery of some new challenge and anxiety; each conflict mastered at a developmental stage is marked by a growth of the sense of humor. "So people are proud of it . . . it's the mark of distinction of having achieved strength and maturity."[17] In a less benign note, Freud has interpreted humor as a spiteful triumph of narcissism and the pleasure principle over the miseries of life.

SUMMARY

At the outset of life, smiles and laughter provide testimony to our states of pleasure: the pleasure of affective and nutritive gratification, the pleasure of the mastery of our body apparatus, and the pleasure of acquisition of a sense of reality. During the course of life, smiles and laughter accompany those triumphs whereby we avoid suffering narcissistic injuries and suffering the continued expenditure of energy to maintain an adult facade free of infantile and instinctual imperfections.

The earlier role of laughter is fused to the latter through the sense of pleasure that is achieved. The avoidance of suffering, even for intermittent moments, is so important to our species that its mechanism is neurologically spread out in the brain, insuring its survival through most neurological catastrophes.

NOTES

1. Noam Chomsky postulates that experience elicits, but does not form, the innate structures of language. A neurological substratum universally present in all intact children accounts for our capacity to create language. See Noam Chomsky, *Aspects of the Theory of Syntax* (Cambridge, Mass.: M.I.T. Press, 1965).

2. René Spitz and William Cobliner, *The First Year of Life* (New York: International Universities Press, 1966).

3. W. E. Blatz, K. Allin, and D. Millichamp, "A Study of Laughter in the Nursery School Child," *University of Toronto Studies: Child Development Series*, VII (1936), 31.

4. Edith Jacobson, "The Child's Laughter," *Psychoanalytic Study of the Child*, II (1946), 39-60.

5. Edmund Bergler, *Laughter and the Sense of Humor* (New York: Intercontinental Medical Book, 1956), p. 181.

6. Edith Jacobson, p. 43.

7. Blatz, Allin, and Millichamp, p. 31.

8. G. Schwartz, R. Davidson, and F. Maer, "Right Hemisphere Lateralization for Emotion in the Human Being," *Science*, CXC (1975), 286-288.

9. Jean Piaget, *Play, Dreams and Imitation in Childhood* (New York: The Norton Library, 1962), and Jean Piaget and Barbara Inhelder, *The Psychology of the Child* (New York: Basic Books, 1969).

10. Jerome Kagan, *Change and Continuity in Infancy* (New York: Wiley, 1971), p. 157.

11. Martha Wolfenstein, "A Phase in the Development of Children's Sense of Humor," *Psychoanalytic Study of the Child*, VI (1951), 336-350, and "Children's Understanding of Jokes," *Psychoanalytic Study of the Child*, VIII (1953), 162-173.

12. Ernst Kris, "Ego Development and the Comic," *International Journal of Psychoanalysis*, XIX (1938), 77-90.

13. Edith Jacobson, p. 47.

14. Sigmund Freud, "Humor," trans. James Strachey, *Collected Papers* (New York: Basic Books, 1959), Vol. V, 215-221.

15. Sigmund Freud, *Jokes and Their Relation to the Unconscious*, Standard Edition, ed. James Strachey, VIII (London: Hogarth Press, 1960), p. 148.

16. Edith Jacobson, p. 59.

17. Martin Grotjahn, *Beyond Laughter* (New York: McGraw-Hill, 1957), p. 258.

Humor's Devaluations in a Modern Idiom: The Don Juan Plays of Shaw, Frisch, and Montherlant

MARGARET GANZ

> *DON JUAN. How is that very flattering statue, by the way?*
> *Does it still come to supper with naughty people and cast*
> *them into this bottomless pit?*
> *ANA. It has been a great expense to me. The boys in the mon-*
> *astery school would not let it alone: the mischievous ones*
> *broke it; and the studious ones wrote their names on it.*
> *Three new noses in two years, and fingers without end. I had*
> *to leave it to its fate at last; and now I fear it is shockingly*
> *mutilated. My poor father!*[1]

No one would confuse the tone of the speakers in the above quotation with that of characters in an earlier Don Juan play. Twentieth-century whimsy and deprecation are here exercising themselves on ultimate matters, though not without forebears, as witness Nikolaus Lenau in his 1841 dramatic poem chiding the Statue for managing "Die Nase in die Nachwelt frech zu strecken" ("impudently to poke a nose into posterity").[2] Here in Shaw's *Man and Superman* (1903) the use of "flattering" could suggest traditional satire, but the devaluation involved in "Does it still come to supper with naughty people" sounds the characteristic note of *humor,* toying in this instance with the question of the legend's power. Not only have the dimensions of that legend been playfully reduced to those of a tale fit only for scaring children, but with Ana's reply the infirmity of such a purpose is revealed. Shaw, even bolder than the wittily disabused Rostand will be in *La Dernière nuit de Don Juan,* 1921 ("The Last Night of Don Juan"), tosses off (among other prophetic matters in his dream sequence—will Freud himself be more eloquent on man's destructive instincts?) a just anticipation of the Commander of Calatrava's fate in the modern world. Indeed, the most devoted daughter of the twentieth century would be hard put to subsidize anatomical repairs and the expunging of graffiti for a monument to spiritual assumptions so vandalized by modern truancies.

It is the techniques of humor proper—involving as they do a subtle devaluative process—that underlie the modern handling of the Don Juan material in three significant instances. Indeed one should not assume that the comic impulse in dealing with this material is only to laugh away the skeletons of the spiritual past with burlesque and satiric thrusts, throwing in as fit subject for jests, along with the traditional cowardliness and expediency on matters spiritual of the servant figure (already the sport of Tirso, Molière, and Mozart), the hypocrisy (Shaw), sexual timidity (Max Frisch), or hunger for renown (Montherlant) of the paternal authority figure. To ignore the stance of humor is vastly to underestimate the richness and ambiguity comedy can attain when its manifestations are provoked by the destiny of absolutes.

The modern metamorphosis of the defiance and retribution motif in the Don Juan material (the invitation to supper of the murdered Commander's stone Statue and its arrival to drag Don Juan to hell after a lethal handshake) illumines then not only the dubious fate of absolutes but the kind of comic strategy to encompass that fate that the specific mode of humor allows. The other, more familiar aspect of the material—the hero's fleshly conquests, with their suggestions of adolescent gratification in Tirso, of libertinism in Molière, of romantic idealization in Gautier and Lenau among many—of course also receives the attention of modern comedy, which could hardly work changes on the Avenger without also exercising itself on the figure of the Seducer. In so doing, comedy often adapts earlier works (sometimes even earlier words, as for example, those of Molière's Pauvre) to its own whimsical purposes as much to challenge erotic as metaphysical assumptions. It is quite prepared, in fact, to turn matters upside down and confront us with a Don Juan who "is the quarry instead of the huntsman" (Shaw's terms [497] *before* he has abandoned his victims). But its elusive ways are best traced in its manipulation of the supernatural elements, deeply rooted in folklore and in considerable part responsible for the popularity of the Don Juan legend and drama.

Largely antedating the birth of the Don Juan matter, these elements, in which rebellious challenge and drastic punishment figure significantly, are most vulnerable to the modern impatience with superstition and consequent impulse to deride. Yet they also inspire a very different comic emotion, for they reflect such ageless psychological conflicts, terrors, and threats involving authority, transgression, and condemnation as humor especially has long tilted with. In its excursions, this particular comic mode has sought to achieve that mastery of "distressing affects" whose complexity and "grandeur" Freud stressed, even as he termed humor "the highest of . . . defensive processes."[3] By the intuitive acceptance of imaginative vagaries that satire and farce often withold, humor has also effected that whimsical tolerance and sustained that precarious balance between tears and laughter long noted by critics of English and German comic writing. The contemporary Swiss playwright Max Frisch is more humorist than satirist in *Don Juan oder die Liebe zur Geometrie,* 1962 ("Don Juan or the Love of Geometry") as he acknowledges fantasy's claim to greater solidity than fact for a popular imagination. His disabused Don Juan, busy concocting his legend, reassures the Bishop that success must attend a fabrication so firmly grounded on folkloric precedent:

> . . . seien Sie getrost: die Geschichte ist glaubwürdig, keineswegs originell, ein alter Sagestoff, eine Statue erschlägt den Mörder, das kommt schon in der Antike vor, und die Verspottung eines Totenschädels, der dann den Spötter in Jenseits holt, denken Sie an die bretonischen Balladen, die unsre Soldaten singen; wir arbeiten mit Uberlieferung—[4]

> (. . . rest assured: the story is believable, in no way original, an old Saga matter, a Statue strikes down the murderer, it already appears in classical antiquity, also the mocking of a death's head, which then fetches the mocker into the other world, think of the Breton ballads our soldiers sing; we are working with tradition—)

Playful reworkings of the Don Juan material like those that Frisch, and Shaw before him, have given us maintain the connection between its two main elements: what Otto Rank in *Die Don-Juan Gestalt,* 1924 ("The Don Juan Legend") termed the popular fantasy aspect (the seducer's enviable triumphs) and the tragic reality (the sinner's guilt and punishment). But the qualitative difference in the comic approach is very significant. It no longer merely relieves the terror of impending catastrophe, the annihilation of the sinner by divine judgment, as it formerly did through the coarse, naïve jests of Tirso's Catalinon or the ridiculous terrors and greed of Molière's Sganarelle. Humor now exercises its techniques on the fate of catastrophe itself in the modern world. It is its doom that humor now playfully proclaims and offsets, yet with an achieved mastery of loss that involves, like other humorous exercises in conquering despair, "a great expenditure of psychical work."[5]

Such a particular comic approach upholds Rank's diagnosis of "a progressive *devaluation of the material*" in the later Don Juan works. Whether such devaluation "corresponds to the conquering of the guilt feelings" for the "Oedipal orientation" of "one who has foundered on the mother complex"[6] (an opinion Rank himself would revise later) is far more problematic. That in Shaw—and Montherlant—the once fierce, ultimately deadly interaction of Don Juan and Commander has become nothing more, or less, than amiable is probably in part a comic protective device against Oedipal guilt or against Oedipal disillusionment.[7] But the ramifications of this altered relationship are much wider. Given a modern recognition that drastic options and resolutions (last judgments and salvations not only in spiritual but psychological terms) are ever harder to procure, the rapprochement of Seducer and Avenger in these twentieth-century plays functions as a humorous strategy to renounce absolutes and, in so doing, defuse the threat of despair.

Humor has, of course, long charted possible responses to the at once disquieting and ludicrous fate imposed by diminished alternatives. Dickens's Dick Swiveller of *The Old Curiosity Shop* is a prince of humorists, gently mocking his state as he contemplates how a pair of gloves—to be bought on credit like his dinner and boots—effectively shuts off his last access to the streets of London. In the archetypal gallows-humor joke (so suggestively rehearsed by Freud), the condemned man, noting of his imminent Monday execution that the week was indeed beginning well, gamely jostled reality in the face of a demise imposed by the external world. The modern convict, in the larger sense of all Denmark as prison that that "developed Don Juan" (493), as Shaw calls Hamlet, understood so well, similarly chooses a jesting denial as alternative to a demise imposed by his inner despairing world. The widest meaning of condemnation suggests that both modes of forging a comic reassurance out of distress are the province of the humorist.

Twentieth-century options being what they are, humor's defensive playfulness has indeed come into its own. Regarding his Don Juan, Frisch notes, "Als Parasit in der Schöpfung . . . bleibt ihm früher oder später keine andere Wahl: Tod oder Kapitulation, Tragödie oder Komödie" (97). ("As a parasite in creation . . . early or late no other option remains to him but death or capitulation, tragedy or comedy.") Yet the play itself shows us these ultimate choices no longer clearly demarcated in our later time of disabused expectation. Marriage, the particular comic trap and final judgment of the Don Juan of Shaw and Frisch, marks not only the traditional worldly compromise and reconciliation of comedy, but an abdication of alternatives hardly less epochal than a descent to hell. "What we have both done this afternoon," the affianced John Tanner proclaims (really speaking for himself) "is to renounce happiness, renounce freedom, renounce tranquility, above all, renounce the romantic possibilities of an unknown future . . ." (686). Only in the death that his wish-fulfilling dream vouchsafes him can he as Don Juan ascend to heaven[8]—the absolute of contemplation—from a sensuous hell that with some exceptions curiously looks like life. As for Frisch's Don Juan, he finds that conjugal existence has a rattling way of undermining one's pursuit of the fourth dimension and that a wife coming to dine can in her own attractive way be almost as daunting, if not as drastic, as a Commander. The divestiture of tragic dimension endured by these heroes as they descend into the matrimonial abyss is, of course, in tune with the modern experience of denudation and loss. Don Juan's twentieth-century options are then not to marry or to burn (in the cataclysmic sense!) in order to resolve the dilemma of the seducer's life—but of course to capitulate *and* die in a different sense, in that tragicomic state of matrimonial entanglement and metaphysical bereavement to which one might (freely) apply Auden's whimsical emendation of a line from "September 1, 1939": "We must love one another or die" to "We must love one another and die."

For an important realization about that ultimate executioner—the marmoreal Commander—has played havoc with traditional alternatives. The possibility of his *not coming* to supper in a Don Juan drama (here again Lenau anticipates some twentieth-century versions) has rightly been judged from one vantage point to be as devastating as his relentless avenging tread formerly was. Yet in another sense that failure obligingly to descend from the pedestal-machine, arousing, in Camus's felicitous phrase about Don Juan's realization of the Commander's absence, "la terrible amertume de ceux qui ont eu raison"[9] ("the terrible bitterness of those who have been right"), is a complex comic paradox, as the very overtones of this ironic statement suggest. Shaw, Frisch, and Montherlant in *La Mort qui fait le trottoir* [*Don Juan*], 1958 ("Death the Streetwalker") have, each in his own way, conveyed the comic reverberations of this failure to "show" (in twentieth-century parlance). But beneath the contrasting approaches to this theme lies the central psychological experience of *desertion* to which the strategies of humor have to a certain extent always been directed.

Freud, discussing Heine's alleged deathbed statement to a priest regarding the possibility of divine forgiveness: "Bien sûr qu'il me pardonnera: c'est son métier" ("Surely he will forgive me: it is his occupation"), goes beyond noting the comic disparagement in the use of *métier* to a fine intuition of the joke's "purpose," which, even if Freud does not say so, is quintessentially humorous:

> . . . in the dying man, *as he lay there powerless*, a consciousness

stirred that he had created God and equipped him with power so as to make use of him when the occasion arose. What was supposed to be the created being *revealed itself just before its annihilation as the creator* [my italics][10]

So terrible a realization—of ultimate abandonment to one's own resources—has liberated the comic spirit. Yet only the sublimity of humor, rising superior to that metaphysical gallows, will suffice. Freud's own whimsical reaction to the discovery that the date he had (on no other than neurotic supposition) assumed would be that of his death had come and gone—"That shows just what little trust one can place in the supernatural"[11]—is, like Heine's comment, subtler than it seems. It encompasses a paradoxical mixture of relief and rue at desertion by more than human certainties. Here, too, there is self-conscious amusement at one's own expense that external forces have not obligingly buttressed one's assumptions of a regulated cosmos, assumptions one was arrogantly testing even with the stake of life itself, hoping to win— and lose.

How to come to terms with the recognition that man, having wrought an ultimate executioner and deliverer in his own image, has now to rise to the task of himself exercising the prerogatives of office is one of the great comic quests of twentieth-century literature (psychoanalysis, musing long on superego, has been struggling in its own mode to resolve the challenge). One need only think of the gyrations of Beckett's Estragon and Vladimir, thrown back on their ingenuity in the face of the intuition that "nothing happens, nobody comes, nobody goes . . ." to conceive of the humorous victory in admitting that cosmic retribution might indeed be something, a token that sense rather than subjectivity prevails in the movements of life. Through the ironic exasperation of his Don Juan, Frisch toys with the basic absurdity of such disappointed expectations:

> Jetzt sind es zwölf Jahre schon, Eminenz, seit dieses Denkmal steht mit den peinlichen Spruch: DER HIMMEL ZERSCHMET- TERE DEN FREVLER, und ich, Don Juan Tenorio, spaz- iere dran vorbei, sooft ich in Sevilla bin, unzerschmettert wie iregendeiner in Sevilla. Wie lang, Eminenz, wie lang denn soll ich es noch treiben? Verführen, erstechen, lachen, weiter- gehen. . . . Es muss etwas geschehen . . . es muss etwas gesche- hen! (67)

> (For twelve years now, your Eminence, this monument stands with its painful saying: MAY HEAVEN CRUSH THE TRANS- GRESSOR, and I, Don Juan Tenorio, promenade past, as often as I am in Seville, as uncrushed at any in Seville. How long, Your Eminence, how long then shall I carry on thus? Seduce,

stab, laugh, walk on. . . . Something has to happen . . . something has to happen!)

"An expectation that has turned to nothing," the principle that Kant, Freud reminds us, uses to define the comic, is, of course, just as applicable to the tragic experience. But humor transcends the anticlimatic manifestations of comedy and tragedy to encompass both modes. Invested with what Pirandello in *L'umorismo* ("On Humor") has termed the *"sentimento del contrario"* (*"feeling of the opposite"*),[12] the humorist divines that an expectation that has turned to something, as Mendoza in Shaw's play suggests to Tanner, may be as unfortunate as an expectation that has turned to nothing. Adapting Wilde's witticism from *Lady Windermere's Fan,* Shaw has Mendoza say, thinking of his own failure to win Louisa Straker: "Sir, there are two tragedies in life. One is to lose your heart's desire. The other is to gain it. Mine and yours, Sir" (685). Both "tragedies" are integral to Tanner's experience, however, much as he denies having any "heart's desires," for he has—another case of coalescing alternatives—two desires of the heart: to flee Ann and to be trapped by her. The intertwining of two such potentially tragic options—to win and to lose—can, under the aspect of forfeited eternity, become the central preoccupation of humor. Incongruous conjunctions are grist to its mill, as are incongruous yearnings, defeats, and victories, a truth glimpsed by Montherlant in his own handling of a Don Juan who is "ensemble fidèle et infidèle" ("simultaneously faithful and unfaithful") and "ne renonce à rien" ("renounces nothing").[13]

In the treatment by Shaw and Frisch of the characteristic Don Juan theme—the rush to and from erotic desire—the rush to and from the alternative desire, contemplation, with its narcissistic reverberations, is an integral humorous element.[14] As for the rush to and from judgment, the compromise capitulation of marriage has become central to it. Yet earlier artists working on the Don Juan matter had also, whether consciously or not, shadowed forth the impulse to incite and flee judgment, reflected in the taunting invitation to supper, as under the domination of desire. We may not be prepared to claim with Otto Rank that "in the figure of the Stone Guest" (earlier presented by him as an embodiment of the ego ideal) "appears the mother herself, coming to fetch the son,"[15] but the psychological ambiguities in a drama of retribution in which Eros and Death are such central protagonists cannot be denied. (If nothing else, the perceived connections between the Commander and the Elder Hamlet, between the minister of revenge seeking a victim and the victim seeking an avenger, should suggest complexities.[16])

DON JUAN AND THE COMMANDER

Some psychological answers to the elusive Don Juan-Commander relationship, both in its traditionally awesome and more recent comic manifestations, may lie in the richly ambiguous traffic, with its erotic overtones, of ego and superego. That this traffic, in Freud's view may, under special circumstances, be *central to humor,* sheds light on the modern entente between Don Juan and his former judge. But the subtle connections Freud has generally established for that traffic (for example, with the threat and lure of annihilation in *The Ego and the Id* and with the transfer to metaphysical authority of parental power and love in "The Economic Problem of Masochism")[17] illumines the equivocal nature of Don Juan's provocation of his destiny in the much earlier versions. In Tirso, Don Juan's confusion between the death age will bring him ("tan largo me lo fiáis" ["you are giving me such a wide berth"] he arrogantly retorts to threats of death as punishment) and that which moral justice will swiftly deal out with its stony handshake suggests a psychic denial of retributive fears whose reverse element may be a rush toward their fulfillment not devoid of erotic implications. Don Juan's shaking hands with Death, as, deviously in Tirso and passionately in Mozart, he has asked to grasp hands with Love, may thus go beyond a dramatically ironic descent from gratification to punishment.

When we consider our comically recast relationship of Don Juan (destroyer-victim) and Commander (victim-avenger), Freud's brilliant supposition that in humor the superego may exercise a benign function, addressing "kindly words of comfort to the intimidated ego," is suggestive. That the superego may here encourage the ego *by allowing its own otherwise severe demands to be mocked by it*—in the sense of playfully dismissed—would be in line with Freud's hypothesis of the superego's reduction of the threatening world to a child's play in comforting the ego.[18] In keeping with such a hypothesis, the traditionally mingled effect of humor—sad and amusing at once—may well in modern times derive additional impact from the ever more pronounced and more equivocal experience of metaphysical loss (awe of ideals and absolutes) and realistic gain (reassurance regarding ultimate judgments) that underlies its manifestations in an absurd world. He would be the most gifted modern humorist who could best transfigure the "terrible amertume" lurking in the realization of one's worst suspicions about abandonment—the loss of protection, salvation, *and* punishment as indications of love—into gain by managing to convert an ambiguous, mingled emotion into a narcissistic pleasure. That "triumph of narcissism" Freud speaks of, that "victorious assertion of the ego's invulnerability" that accounts for the "grandeur" of humor has probably always had as its underlying tone a nostalgic affirmation of the safety of lonely self-reliance and defeated aspirations. In such versions of Don Juan as Shaw, Frisch, and Montherlant have given us, the triumphs of playfulness, whimsy, and clowning rest more than ever on the defeats of disillusion, loss, and abdication.

DON JUAN AND MARRIAGE

For Shaw and Frisch the grand, if fleeting, victory over essential griefs takes a very similar comic form. It is in keeping with Nietzsche's assignment of a true place in comedy, as Denis de Rougemont reminds us,[19] to the philosopher *married,* with Socrates' marriage a conscious ironic demonstration of that verity. Shaw's Don Juan, philosopher and revolutionist, not only amiably avers that he became famous for running away from sexual engagments, but contends that he was forced to do so because "the lady's impulse" had been "solely to throw down my fortifications and gain my citadel" (629). The reversal of sexual assumptions by this witty accusation is as evident as the laugh it wins is easy. The comic dimensions change, however, when we realize that the move is from the physical to the mental and spiritual. It is not the sexual citadel that is threatened but the seat of that "moral passion" whose rise in Tanner has all the marks of a superego's birth. This altered state that Tanner in Act I despairs of defining for the divertingly conventional, amoral, and tough-minded Ann Whitefield will still be vainly defended by him at the conclusion of the last act as Ann sweeps him off his feet (though the actual swooning is hers). Even here, however, the humorous effect depends on Tanner's perception of the absurdity not just of his dilemma of desire, but of the figure he cuts in this different drama of star-crossed lovers: the uneasy narcissist at bay with only rousing rhetoric to delay the inevitable:

> But why me? me of all men! Marriage is to me apostasy, profanation of the sanctuary of my soul, violation of my manhood, sale of my birthright, shameful surrender, ignominious capitulation, acceptance of defeat. I shall decay like a thing that has served its purpose and is done with; I shall change from a man with a future to a man with a past; I shall see in the greasy eyes of all the other husbands their relief at the arrival of a new prisoner to share their ignominy. (680)

That the juxtaposition of two alternatives represented by the terms *philosopher* and *married* could only yield a comic experience is a central assumption in Frisch's Don Juan play. Even more impish than Shaw (and prepared to explore the reverberations of the experience a significant step further), Frisch shows us a philosopher who, more desirous of journeying into "Hölle" ("Hell") than "Ehe" ("wedlock") has descended to the conjugal state in spite and because of self. He has thereby secured, in luxurious country seclusion—à deux, hélas—the right to exercise his "moral passion" for the contemplative purities of geometry, safely hidden away from the long despised conventional world and a new generation that is inexorably and with impunity trivializing Don Juanism. His going John Tanner one better (and worse) by at the last producing an heir only enriches the humor of unlikely conjunctions and baffled transcendence.

The traditional contradictions of dramatic irony play no small part in the capitulation of Frisch's Don Juan, which is enriched with baroque contingencies. Absurdity pursues him, from the initial Hamletlike rebellion against an official wedding with Donna Anna (he can hardly swear eternal love after just failing to recognize his intended in their passionate encounter in the park) through the later wearisome vicissitudes of a Don Juan's occupation. Like Tanner, he has been driven to a matrimonial fate he flees, but, even more than his predecessor, he is ridden by contraries on his circuitous way. By the significant age of thirty-three, this seducer longs for that monastic cell despised by Lenau's hero but so clearly envisaged by Camus for his. Yet the faithful whore Miranda, who had singled him out at the brothel because he preferred to play chess and loved geometry, will snare him, her power over the man of her choice arising partly from her discovery that, like Eliza Doolittle, she can do without him.

In this contrarious adventure of existence, as Frisch suggests, seduction itself has been the idealist's only alternative. By successfully impersonating Anna (not without some masterful sewing adjustments she owes to the madam, Celestina), Miranda has in the early part of the play sent her Ferdinand off on a seducer's career. This Don Juan has erroneously assumed through the years that a heart thoroughly broken by the second demonstration of the at once embittering and consoling unreliability of love's knowledge might well be delivered from conventional obligations. After all, a well-advertised seducer's career has been the safer option for a tormented idealist and putative philosopher who, in hewing to principle earlier (he could not count on love and wanted no love to count on him), had driven his best friend and his beloved Anna Ophelialike to suicide. Ultimately, however, the tragic prerogatives of the young must be abandoned; only the comic alternative of settling down (being kept by the titled and enriched widow of a grateful brothel client juggles the paradoxes further) is left to the mature Don Juan.

That settling down, that descent of sorts, spells new knowledge: that the paradoxical punishment of the married philosopher entails not only that he be bedded down here in his "Gefängnis" ("prison"), yet "mit vierundvierzig Zimmern" ("with forty-four rooms") the Bishop hastens to remind him, and ample room to roam and study; not only that he desire "der Mensch allein" ("Man alone") to be "das Ganze" ("all in all") (88) and yet be troubled by and lonesome for women, but more important still, that he must forgo a grander resonance of retribution. In a world where no paternal ghost threatens descent into the fiery abyss, the only appearance one can count on, and exasperatingly late, is that of a wife. Well might Frisch's Don Juan mutter under his breath his Shavian forebear's Marlovian-Miltonic jest: "wherever ladies are is hell" (604).

In Frisch's play it is the hero's earlier management of the final judgment scene in the traditional Don Juan drama (devising a theatrical spectacle of his edifying demise for presentation to a doltish audience is procuring a convenient alibi to escape the boredom of a seducer's life and fame) that is the most telling element in the humorous reworking of the material. Having Don Juan commission the part of the Commander to be enacted by Miranda's former employer, the *madam à tout faire,* Celestina, is not just satirical iconoclasm on Frisch's part. For the disabused humaneness of this descendant of Shaw's Mrs. Warren and the absurdity of her experience recall to us the central dilemma of belief and doubt humor is here addressing. She, so proudly committed to the sanity of her business and her cunning common sense, ultimately finds she has overestimated her clients' desire to recuperate from "falschen Gefühlen" (22) ("false emotions"). She can convince no citizen of what Shaw would call "the Philistine world," not even the now materialized Leporello, of the falseness of a catastrophe to whose artifice she has so magisterially contributed. Because Leporello, only a realist of the cowardly variety, can easily slough off intimations of spiritual desertion, Celestina warns him of the heady effect of the nearby convent she is visiting: "Ich kenne dich: ein bisschen Klostergarten, ein bisschen Vesperglöcklein, und schon wirst du weich. Demnächst glaubst du noch selbst daran, dass er in der Hölle sei." (81) ("I know you: a bit of cloister garden, a bit of Vesper bell, and you will soon weaken. Next even you yourself will believe it, that he is in Hell.") In humorous exasperation with people whose belief, she says, is merely their refusal to know (the now pious Elvira, for instance), Celestina announces to Leporello what the next conjugal act will in one sense prove true, that Don Juan is in hell. As Frisch concludes this act by feeding his Leporello the exact words of his Molièrean counterpart ("Voilà par sa mort un chacun satisfait . . ." and so on.) ("Now is each one satisfied by his death . . ." and so on), modern self-consciousness takes its leap into the comic abyss to portray Don Juan in the toils of "le plus épouvantable châtiment du monde!" (83) ("the most dreadful punishment in the world!").

DON JUAN AND FINAL JUDGMENT

Like Shaw, Frisch has glimpsed in the Don Juan material the humorous possibilities, so essentially connected with the theme of marriage, of what we have called the rush to and from judgment (with annihilation as punishment).[20] Behind the high jinks in the faked melodrama of the Commander's arrival at the banquet and Don Juan's descent into the abyss to the tune of *"das bestellte Halleluja"* (*"the ordered Halleluja"*) lurks a reality at once ironic and humorous: not only is the moral catastrophe "Nichts als Theater" (79–80) ("nothing but theater"), but the chief *sufferer* has become the *impresario*. Telescoping the centuries, Frisch playfully suggests that the origin of the Don Juan legend is, of course, an inspired hoax: in the last act the drama of Don Juan's journey to hell by Father Tellez-Tirso has just come off the press and is both perused and impatiently tossed into a corner by its protagonist-architect while waiting, as we know, for his wife to come.

This humorous havoc playing with the traditional Don Juan material is in line with other modern iconoclasms on this very subject. To hear Shaw's Statue praising wine and women (his countertenor blending in Mozart's toast with the Devil's operatic baritone); Rostand's Don Juan, sentenced to the hell of enacting his destiny in a puppet show, intoning: "C'est moi le fameux Burl .... Le fameux Burlador! ... Burlador ..." ("It is I the famous Burl .... The famous Burlador! ... Burlador ..."); and Anouilh's Ornifle trying to improve on Molière with "Je crois que deux et deux ne font pas quatre. ..." ("I believe that two and two do not add up to four. ...") is to experience not only the sound but the texture and taste of twentieth-century disillusion and—what Otto Rank so brilliantly sensed and traced in the latter part of his psychoanalytic study of Don Juan—its particular kind of *literary self-consciousness* (Rank himself would be impaled in Montherlant's play for certain ideas on Don Juan!)

To be conscious of the self in the twentieth century is to be thrown back upon the self—and what better metaphor for that state than the phenomenon of a Don Juan no longer like Tirso's hero "a devout believer in an ultimate hell," as Shaw puts it (489), but forced instead himself to stage apocalyptic matters in the absence of an appropriate metaphysical establishment. That such a fate approximates the situation of the modern artist-philosopher, left as it were the task of fabricating hoaxes, his territory of expression hemmed in by time, is in line with earlier romantic identifications of the Don Juan figure and the artist. But "artist" must be understood in its widest sense. He who has trafficked between the sensual world and mental activity (between what Shaw terms "Romance and Ascetism, Amorism and Puritanism" [499]) and been left cheated of the immortality not only a more impressive audience but a more grandiose theater might allow must find conjugality—the embrace by and of institutional sanctities, procreative injunctions, and what the modern psychologist gracelessly calls "object relations"—at best settling for less in the absence of more.

Not Don Juan alone but his initial adversary, the Commander, guardian of parental ideals and matrimonial demands, is now enlisted to convey that dismaying truth under the aspect of comedy in the modern Don Juan play. Montherlant, often more sardonic than humorous, allows his coarse and naïve Commander to prattle of conjugal ideals with the Philistine cynicism of a very married man: "La vérité est dans un seul être dont on tire par l'affection, la pratique, le temps, des accords de plus en plus profonds. Du moins j'ai lu cela dans les livres. Rien ne ressemble davantage à une peau qu'une autre peau" (1044). ("Truth resides in one being from whom one draws forth, through affection, practice, and time, ever deeper harmonies. At least I have read that in books. Nothing resembles one skin more than another skin.") Yet he has been anticipated by Shaw's humorous vision of his Commander, the Statue—bad father (like Shotover in *Heartbreak House,* he cannot recall his own daughter)—and indifferent husband, who knows he has enthusiastically peddled his conjugal balderdash on the effect at eighty of the "one white hair of the woman I loved" (640) to countless amorous prospects with hardly less brio than an accomplished Don Juan. Moreover both Commanders, the one fatuously and the other wryly, proclaim their moral occupation as messengers of divine retribution gone. The vainglorious satisfaction of Montherlant's Commander in his projected tomb rests, after all, on its very inscription: "martiale, virile, enfin digne de moi: *'J'y suis. J'y reste.'* " (1034) ("martial, virile, in short worthy of me: 'Here I am. Here I remain.' ") Beyond jests about hellfire making him sneeze and impish self-praise regarding his handsomeness as an art work, Shaw's Statue has challenged the sturdiness of absolutes in his announcement that the frontier between hell and heaven "is only the difference between two ways of looking at things" (647).

Humor lurks at the threshold of wearied, despairing self-consciousness, befriending the relativity of absolutes, the twilight of alternatives. Though Shaw often jostles his characters into proclaiming reassuring ambiguities and releases skyrockets about progress through the life-force and the philosopher's goal as "Nature's pilot" (646), a fundamental skepticism underlies even as it provokes his comic strategies. Comedy is his inevitable medium because he is a skeptic about that other absolute, the tragic experience—did he not maintain that people like Hedda Gabler do not, in fact, kill themselves but live on to plague others? Here in the dream sequence he is not wholly unprepared to endorse the Statue's relativism; to accept Don Juan's reduction of Nature, Time, and Death to the merely human dimensions of "pandar," "wrecker," and "murderer" (639); or to allow the Devil (ironically quoting Tennyson's *In Memoriam* as Scripture) his full due as he suggests just how metaphoric and relative heaven and hell have become for the modern consciousness:

> . . . men get tired of everything, of heaven no less than of hell . . . when you have a thousand times wearied of heaven, like myself and the Commander, and a thousand times wearied of hell, as you are wearied now, you will not longer imagine that every swing from heaven to hell is an emancipation, every swing from hell to heaven an evolution. Where you now see reform, progress, fulfillment of upward tendency, continual

*ascent by Man on the stepping stones of his dead selves to
higher things,* you will see nothing but an infinite comedy of
illusion. (644–645: italics mine)

In Frisch and Montherlant, we have seen the Statue's inscription
used for comic purposes that tell much about altered values and modes.
Shaw anticipates such later devaluations as he toys with the words of
Mozart's Commendatore: "Di rider finirai pria dell' aurora" ("You will
finish laughing before dawn") and "Ribaldo audace!" ("Audacious
ribald!"). Ennui rather than heavenly castigation now threatens the
unrepentant sinner, but his identity seems to have become quite flex-
ible. When the Statue impugns Don Juan's fencing talents, claiming
he would have won had his foot not slipped, we are in the realm of
farce; but when Don Juan impishly retorts: "Audacious ribald: your
laughter will finish in hideous boredom before morning" (618), the comic effect is complex and elusive. It is Don Juan's turn to issue a warning—to the new arrival who has chosen the hell of beauty and pleasure
uninterrupted by human frustration. Yet the Statue might well retort
in kind to the heaven-bound Juan. Humor, using the language of past
beliefs, reworks it to plumb the depths of its losses. Defying heaven
(the original Burlador), rejecting it (Shaw's Statue), yearning for it
(Shaw's Don Juan) may actually invoke the very same punishment—
abandonment by meaning to the reality of what Shaw, anticipating Pirandello, has his Devil call "an infinite comedy of illusion."

How to transmute the "hideous boredom," Adam's curse in an absurd world, into laughter is the complicated charge of humor, as it
formerly had the task of countering the hideous apprehension evoked
by an apparently meaningful world. If Don Juan's growing older (not
invariably, yet frequently) in the successive stages of the legend indeed
approximates the preoccupations of an aging world, then jesting in the
face of a steadily deepening disfunction in man and universe is the ultimate alternative, as Frisch suggests in his comment on the drastic
fate of Don Juan only forestalled by the comic vision:

> Hinter jedem Don Juan steht . . . die Langeweile eines Geistes,
> der nach dem Unbedingten dürstet und glaubt erfahren zu
> haben, dass er es nie zu finden vermag; kurzum, die grosse
> Langeweile des Schwermut, die Not eines Herzens, dem die
> Wünsche ersterben so das ihm bloss noch der Witz ubrigbleibt;
> ein Don Juan, der keinen Witz hat, würde sich erhängen. (100)

> (Behind every Don Juan stands . . . the boredom of a spirit
> which thirsts after the absolute and thinks it has come to know
> that it can never find it; in short, the great boredom of melan-
> choly, the need of a heart, whose wishes perish, so that only wit

remains for him; a Don Juan without wit would hang himself.)

That the comic view is perhaps the only remaining option might appear to be challenged by Montherlant, as one of the epigraphs to his Don Juan play proclaims life "une comédie qu'il faut bien prendre au tragique" ("a comedy one is bound to take in tragic terms"). Yet humor's capacity to encompass contrary states and to dwell near tragic territory makes it still a viable mode in this treatment of the Don Juan material. Montherlant does not so much vindicate his assertion as suggest the interchangeability of comic and tragic as attributes of life and modes of dealing with it. When Don Juan's illegitimate son Alcacer thinks with self-satisfied indignation of other comedies in which sons scheme to do their fathers out of money, Don Juan's reminder that the two of them are, of course, in a tragedy is the very way to raise doubts about the appropriateness of such distinctions.

To reflect what Montherlant terms "un *ondoiement* perpétuel, moral et physique" (1080) ("a perpetual *undulation,* moral and physical") is tantamount to granting that life is a tragedy that one must come to terms with comically. One of the carnival workers in the play, overhearing Don Juan's meditation on his sensual decay, his failure to remember the past, and his apprehension of the future, greets it with giggles, "Parce que c'est triste" (1047) ("Because it is sad"). It is he and his friends who will provide the play with its Statue, a mere "carton pâte" ("pasteboard") monster fabricated to scare Don Juan from his house for purposes of petty thievery (by his absence the real Commander does justice to the motto of his monument). At the end of the play, however, the arch Commander comes or, rather, surfaces, as the black mask Don Juan has used to hide his wrinkles becomes incorporated with his face, shadowing forth a skull. Yet here, too, the response of Don Juan cuts against the tragic grain with "A la bonne heure!" ("All right!") and a rush to the pavements of Seville in pursuit of an ultimate erotic transaction.

"Quelqu'un me dit 'C'est une farce.' Quelqu'un: 'C'est une pièce âpre.' C'est une pièce âpre et une farce" (1081) ("Someone says, 'It is a farce,' another, 'It is a harsh play.' It is a harsh play and a farce") noted Montherlant, going on to defend in his Don Juan play the alternation of "la gravité, voire le pathétique, et la bouffonnerie, le seriéux et la boutade" ("gravity, indeed pathos, and buffoonery, the serious mode and the quip"), suggesting the difficulties of playing for and pleasing the French public "ancré dans le dogme des 'genres tranchés' " ("anchored in the dogma of 'sharply delineated genres' "). Despite the referenses to the ancestry of Don Juan from Mephistopheles through Punch to Faust, the invoking of Shakespeare, and of Charlie Chaplin's power to amuse and move at the same time, Montherlant's own comments remain unhelpful, for he merely contends for the alternations of tragicomedy or the more conventionally mixed effects of comedy itself. That his work really suggests a mutual infiltration of the modes, corresponding to a larger dissociation of metaphysical assumptions, could well have made a general audience uneasy. Not unused to coarse physical or sexual comedy, such an audience might have accepted that this Don Juan has chamber pots emptied on him while waiting for an assignation or his backside pricked with a pin by the Commander's wife during the duel, that his invitation to supper is really a gracious offer to provide the Commander with an assignation. But a vaudevillian routine about closing one's eyes so that the policeman will not see one that veers into a jest about wearing a mask so that death will not see one disquietingly alters the moral temperature and comic pace. Such is also the effect of parodies more impishly nostalgic than blasphemous: Don Juan greeting the failure of a girl to arrive with "le pavé me l'a donnée, le pavé me l'a reprise, que la volonté de Dieu soit faite" (1037) ("The pavement giveth, the pavement taketh away, may God's will be done").

In Shaw and Frisch, external catastrophe has become internal capitulation, a descent from ideal striving to human bonds, from sensual pursuit to conjugal discipline. The punishment is giving up narcissistic gratification, whether fed by "moral passion" or hurt at love's blindness. Don Juan must abnegate the private self to live more maturely in a public world, which comprises not only betrothal (the conclusion of *Man and Superman*) but procreation (the conclusion of Frisch's *Don Juan*). But for Montherlant's hero it is no longer a question of growing up but of growing old—he is sixty-six—no longer a question of dying to the self but of dying in the most literal of terms, and not because of transgression but because time has almost worked its indifferent will. What of Eros when the light sinks and the sky will not release comets much as one stares at it? That is the question for this Don Juan. Worse for him than for Shaw and Frisch's protagonists, who are relatively freer of theological haunting, religion, which once caused him indignation, has become "quelque chose de comique" (1030) ("something comical"). "Dieu ce n'est pas sérieux" (1028) ("God is not a serious matter") he notes at another moment, like his Molièrean predecessor unable to give in the name of divine love, a possible indication that he has not finished smarting at the intimations of desertion. The Don Juan who here answers the Commander's accusation in the duel scene that he has merely lived in the world of appearances by nearly echoing the temptation to despair extended by Shaw's Devil ("Il y a le monde des apparences. Ensuite il n'y a rien" [1048] ["There is the world of appearances. And then there is nothing"]) will later comment in similar terms on the arrival of the pasteboard Commander: "Je savais bien qu'il n'y a pas de spectres. Il n'y a pas de fantastique: c'est la réalité qui est le fantastique" (1077) ("I knew there were no spectres. The fantastic does not exist: reality is the fantastic").

This Don Juan is then a different protagonist—a bitter clown, whose changeableness (only a Commander naïvely committed to moral absolutes risks calling him insincere) is as fundamental as the sparseness and finality of his conflict between desire and despair. In the familiar rhythms suited to questioning flowers about one's erotic destiny, Don Juan musingly intones at a point of danger: "Une pensée pour l'amour . . . Une pensée pour la mort . . .—" and so on (1054–1055) ("One thought to love . . . One thought to death . . .—"). More even than John Tanner, hardly unmindful of the self-absorption that pulls the rug from under him at some of his most triumphant moments, or Frisch's Don Juan, who knows that his paradisiacal prison has been wrought by the inescapable needs of his ego, Montherlant's hero acknowledges his narcissistic absorption. "Allons! tout le monde vieillit" (1047) ("Come on! Everybody ages") the good-natured, conventional Commander burbles. "Non, moi seul" ("No, only I do") Don Juan counters with a comic self-deprecation Tanner might envy.

That humor can grow in the crannied wall of Montherlant's brooding is a great tribute to its powers. It comes more glancingly but always presupposes that whimsical self-consciousness that is Shaw's high virtue. Here an adolescent bravura—shades of Tirso—with its appropriate expletive "Flûte" ("Nuts!") gamely mocks the spectacle of the aged seducer Don Juan knows himself to be, at once acknowledging and transfiguring the ignominies of decay into near-Falstaffian impudence and jests. Waiting for an assignation with an adolescent girl, Don Juan notes: "Elle ne viendra pas: je desserre mon ceinturon" (1019) ("She won't come: I loosen my belt"); being told another prospect has a broken tooth, he exults, "Mais une! c'est tout juste ce qu'il faut" (1022) ("Just one! Precisely what is needed"). The very password for his meeting with the Commander, whom he is to instruct in the art of seduction—"Mort aux jeunes!"—is not as happy an invention as Falstaff's ironic battle cry on Gadshill, ". . . down with them! cut the villains' throats! . . . they hate us youth!" but it is, like that of the aging knight, a jest at his own expense, in the face of his own decline. More largely even, such comic assertions playfully undercut, instead of savaging as Montherlant sometimes does by sarcasm, assumptions about love, fidelity, selflessness, and generosity—the standard accumulations of the youthful idealist that time has a way of absurdly sifting. Montherlant is here true to Camus's statement: "Dans l'univers que Don Juan entrevoit, le ridicule *aussi* est compris" ("The universe as perceived by Don Juan *also* comprises the ridiculous").

Humor's twentieth-century subject and the circumscribed nature of its triumphs in bracing to wisdom an all too vulnerable and nostalgic world were prophesied by Pirandello, projecting as the humorist's appropriate subject a Prometheus aware that his antagonist Jupiter "is no more than a vain phantasm . . . the shadow of his own body projecting itself as a giant in the sky, precisely because of the lighted torch he holds in his hand," and yet unable and unwilling to extinguish torch and shadow, which remains "terrifying and tyrannical, for all men who fail to realize the fateful deception." Despite the brevity of its affirmation, however, humor remains the grandest strategy to offset dismay. Pirandello notwithstanding, Prometheus, depicted by a humorist, would go beyond "pondering sadly his lit torch" to tangling playfully with "the fateful cause of his infinite torment."[21] Don Juan, whom Shaw through Hamlet (493) indirectly associates with Prometheus,[22] has in his modern persona undertaken a different defiance and bearded a different antagonist from those in former times even if, like the traditional Don Juan, he still chafes at the restriction of emotional freedom and the tedium of conventional concerns.

Camus, claiming that Don Juan can hardly be sad, not only speaks of his laughter as "l'insolence victorieuse," but observes that whereas the sad are justified either by ignorance or hope, "Don Juan sait et n'espère pas. . . . Il fut triste dans le temps ou il espéra" ("Don Juan knows and does not hope. . . . He was sad at the time when he still hoped"). It is the impressive achievement of humor that its particular "insolence victorieuse" is an ambiguous phenomenon, rooted in continuing intimations of humility and defeat. That comic mode has long been attuned to offsetting disappointment, rejection, and loss through the victory of the imagination and the celebration of incongruity. In the modern world humor has confronted the ultimate of judgments—absence of meaning—and exercised its techniques to counter this special betrayal.

That the apocalyptic aspects of the Don Juan matter would bear the main weight of humorous transformation was inevitable. A Commander shorn of inexorable virtue and ghostly prerogatives, a Don Juan in flight from sensual desire and tempted by conjugality, and, not least, a relationship between the two that substitutes mutual affection or amused tolerance for deadly enmity—such are the humorous devaluations that in Shaw and Frisch, and partly in Montherlant, allow a certain mastery over the erosion of meaning. More safety would be less: an ambivalent reassurance that forgoes wholly denying or repressing loss is the guarantee of humor's sublimity. Montherlant, less to the humorous manner born than the other two playwrights, deals more traditionally with his hero's seductive ubiquity (neither Shaw's nor Frisch's hero would subscribe to the dictum "C'est par ses passions qu'on est sauvé" [1033] ["It is through one's passions that one is saved"] without vast mental reservations regarding the meaning of "passions"). At moments, however, Montherlant also shows that characteristic humorous flair for snatching jests out of despair. All three works suggest to us that, in view of its formidable modern task, humor more than ever deserves Freud's praise as "one of the highest psychical achievements."[23]

NOTES

1. Bernard Shaw, *Man and Superman,* in *Complete Plays with Prefaces* (New York: Dodd, Mead, 1962), III, 608. References in this essay will also be made to the Prefatory Letter ("To Arthur Bingham Walkley"). For an anticipation of Shaw's approach to the Statue see his short story "Don Giovanni Explains" in *Short Stories, Scraps & Shavings, The Collected Works of Bernard Shaw* (New York: Wm. H. Wise, 1932), especially pp. 104-105, 110-113.

2. Nikolaus Lenau, *Don Juan,* in *Lenaus Werke* (Berlin: Deutsches Verlagshaus, Bong & Co., n.d.), II, 338. All translations in this essay are mine.

3. *Jokes and Their Relation to the Unconscious* in *The Complete Psychological Works of Sigmund Freud,* trans. James Strachey (London: The Hogarth Press and the Institute of Psycho-Analysis, 1971), VII (1905), pp. 228, 229, 233. The material dealt with here is from this elaborate work's last section, which Freud devotes to humor proper rather than to jokes and to the comic.

4. Max Frisch, *Don Juan oder die Liebe zur Geometrie* (Frankfurt am Main: Suhrkamp, 1962), p. 72. This edition is of a 1961 revision of a 1952 work and includes Frisch's "Nachträgliches" (supplementary notes), to which references are also made in this essay. For another, brief exploration of the Don Juan theme, see Frisch's *Die Chinesische Mauer* ("The Chinese Wall") (Frankfurt am Main: Suhrkamp, 1972; earlier eds. 1947, 1955), pp. 21-23, 55-56, 91. On the nature and significance of such folkloric elements as Frisch alludes to in both plays and their role in the fashioning of the Don Juan material, see Georges Gendarme de Bévotte, *La Légende de Don Juan* (Paris: Hachette, 1906), pp. 37-49, and the detailed study of this subject, Dorothy Epplen Mackay's *The Double Invitation in the Legend of Don Juan* (Stanford: Stanford Univ. Press, 1943).

5. *Jokes and Their Relation to the Unconscious,* p. 230.

6. Otto Rank, *The Don Juan Legend,* trans. and ed. David G. Winter (Princeton, N.J.: Princeton Univ. Press, 1975), pp. 106, 96.

7. For the possible connection between the "disappointment of Oedipal wishes" and the development of humor, see Lucile Dooley, "The Relation of Humor to Masochism," *Psychoanalytic Review,* 28 (1941), 41-45.

8. The pervasiveness of this particular mode of transcendence in Shaw's work has been dealt with by Arthur Ganz in "The Ascent to Heaven: A Shavian Pattern," *Modern Drama,* XIV (December 1971), 253-263.

9. "Le Don Juanisme" in *Le Mythe de Sisyphe* (Paris: Gallimard, 1972), p. 104.

10. *Jokes and Their Relation to the Unconscious,* pp. 114-115.

11. This comment to Ferenczi is cited by Ernest Jones in *The Life and Work of Sigmund Freud* (New York: Basic Books, 1957), III, 390.

12. "Every feeling," Pirandello notes, "every thought, or every impulse that arises in the humorist immediately splits into its contrary: every affirmative into a negative, which finally ends up assuming the same value as the affirmative." *On Humor,* trans. and ed. Antonio Illiano and Daniel P. Testa (Chapel Hill, N.C.: Univ. of North Carolina Press, 1974), p. 125. See also pp. 5, 12, 109.

13. "Notes" to *La Mort qui fait le trottoir (Don Juan)* in Montherlant, *Théâtre* (Paris: Gallimard, 1972), p. 1081.

14. That humor and contemplation are subtly related is indicated in Alfred Winterstein's comment that in humor "the destructive instinct seems to be sublimated . . . as intellect, and assumes specifically the form of *contemplation;* in playful superiority it depreciates not only reality and its dangers but, in addition, those individuals for whom these things are significant." "Contributions to the Problem of Humor," *Psychoanalytic Quarterly,* 3 (1934), 305.

15. Rank, p. 96.

16. In this regard Rank's references to the motifs of the stone sarcophagus (with "ponderous and marble jaws") and the unearthing of the skull (ibid., pp. 74, 76) are especially illuminating, as is his discussion of *Hamlet* in *Psychology of the Soul,* trans. William D. Turner (New York: Barnes, 1950), pp. 61-70.

17. The unusual relationship between ego and superego in humor is a hypothesis central to Freud's essay "Humour," a 1928 reworking of ideas from the last section of *Jokes* which deals specifically with humor (see note 3). For this very significant essay, see *The Future of an Illusion, Civilization and its Discontents, and Other Works,* XIX (1927-

1931), 160–166. See pp. 54–59 of "The Ego and the Id," and pp. 167–170 of "The Economic Problem of Masochism" in *The Ego and the Id and Other Works*, XIX (1923–1925).

18. In line with our suggestion, see Dooley, p. 45. Rather unconvincing is Edmund Bergler's revisionist argument that in humor the ego, despairing of kind treatment by the superego, fights back against its betrayer and torturer by a satisfying, if fleeting, narcissistic retreat from reality. See "A Clinical Contribution to the Psychogenesis of Humor," *Psychoanalytic Review*, XXIV (1937), [34]–53 and *Laughter and the Sense of Humor* (New York: Intercontinental Medical Book Corporation, 1956), pp. x, 165–166, 201. The pertinence of the superego's tolerance is enhanced by Ernst Kris's suggestion that the comic "can scarcely make the eternally forbidden its object (if it does, it is wont to produce a painful effect) but that this must be found in something which is even now held in esteem, *is even now represented in the superego.*" "The Psychology of Caricature" in *Psychoanalytic Explorations in Art* (New York: International Universities Press, 1952), p. 186. For Kris's comments on humor proper, see a significant footnote on p. 187 and in "Ego Development and the Comic," pp. 204, 205, and particularly pp. 212–213.

19. *Comme toi-même: essais sur les mythes de l'amour* ["As Yourself: Essays on the Myths of Love"] (Paris: Albin Michel, 1961), p. 129. See pp. [102]–159 for provocative discussions on the relation of Don Juanism to the thought of Kierkegaard and Nietzsche.

20. The fascinating subject of the connection between procreation and the fear of personal annihilation in the loss of the soul (familiar to some readers from Freud's essay "The Taboo of Virginity") is explored in connection with Don Juan's role as a diabolical bearer of fecundity in Rank's drastic revision of his study of Don Juan: *Don Juan: Une Etude sur le Double* (Paris: Denoël & Steele, 1932). That in some of the folkloric tales the encounter with a ghost is experienced by someone about to get married suggests the pervasiveness of the connection.

21. *On Humor*, p. 141.

22. For a brief but interesting discussion of Don Juan as "un Prométhée chrétien, temporel et moral" ("a Christian Prometheus, temporal and moral"), see Micheline Sauvage, *Le Cas Don Juan* ["The Don Juan Phenomenon"] (Paris: Editions du Seuil, 1953), pp. 156–157. The larger question of temporality and its relation to Don Juanism is explored with admirable thoughtfulness in the whole of this study.

23. *Jokes and Their Relation to the Unconscious*, p. 228.

 **PART 3**

SHAKESPEAREAN
COMEDY:
TWELFTH NIGHT
AND
AS YOU LIKE IT

The Season of *Twelfth Night*

RALPH BERRY

Twelfth Night is the statutory comedy, as often as not, in a summer festival season. Any moderately dedicated playgoer must have seen it several times and passed up many more chances. Like *Hamlet,* it tends to be absorbed into the general textures of the current theater, and it is not usually associated with revolutionary productions. Moreover, it is not the focus of any great academic or theatrical debate. Its meaning is not in doubt: *Twelfth Night* is widely accepted as a supreme harmonizing of the romantic and comic, sweet and astringent. The admirable production, then, is held to be one that holds these elements in balance. It is in the inflection that a production gives to *Twelfth Night* that the special interests lies, and this inflection has undoubtedly modulated in recent years. Broadly and crudely, *Twelfth Night* used to be funny and is now much less so. What has happened?

I want to describe two models of *Twelfth Night* productions, old and new. The seamless fabric of theater history does not often lend itself to radical departures; yet I think I can point to a date for the founding of the New Model *Twelfth Night:* 1969. For the old, I shall turn to the late nineteenth century and synthesize a few productions. This is less for their antiquarian interest that for their continuing influence. The nineteenth century reveals in caricatured form contours of a *Twelfth Night* that were recognizable until quite recently and are still visible in the outer provinces of theater.

THE OLD MODEL

The essence of the old model was its direct appeal to laughter and romance. Of Augustin Daly's production in New York, 1894, Odell tells us : "Moonlight was brought into play as never before in this comedy; Viola dreamed on a bench as Orsino's minstrels warbled Shubert's 'Who is Olivia (Sylvia)?'"[1] The *New York Herald Tribune* has this:

> The scene is Olivia's garden. The time is evening. Viola, disguised as the minstrel Cesario, having received an intimation that perhaps her brother, Sebastian, has not drowned, has spoken her joyous soliloquy upon that auspicious thought, and has sunk into a seat, in meditation. The moon is rising over the distant sea, and in the fancied freshness of the balmy rising breeze you can almost hear the ripple of the leaves. The lovelorn Orsino enters, with many musicians, and they sing a serenade, beneath the windows of Olivia's palace. The proud beauty comes forth upon her balcony, and parting her veil, looks down upon Viola . . . Not a word is spoken and not a word is needed. The garden is all in moonlight; the delicious music flows on; and . . . the curtain slowly falls. It was a perfect triumph of art, in the highest and best vein.[2]

It is, however, through the appeal to laughter that this piece must be gauged. The old promptbooks give us a fair idea of the mechanisms of production.

Take the great drinking scene (2.3). The main thrust of production was to play up the drinking, singing, and general merriment. The standard stage direction was

> *Table and 3 chairs discovered. Tankards and long clay pipes on tables.*[3]

Feste, incredibly, might be the life and soul of the party. *"Clown jumps over table, and all three dance in circle."*[4] Some interpolated songs were usual. Sir Andrew sang

> Christmas comes but once a year
> And therefore we'll be merry[5]

after the catch, which has the double effect of defining the title more closely and allying it with the spirit of simple revelry. This spirit dominated the scene's end. A hallowed interpolation (after "Come, knight") was

| SIR ANDREW. | Sunday, Monday, Tuesday, Which is the properest day to drink? |

SIR ANDREW.)
SIR TOBY.   } This is the properest day to drink!
CLOWN.   )

Note the upbeat ending, after Shakespeare has written in a downbeat cadence (matching the opening). Henry Jewett's production (Boston, 1915) went further, with much business of people sliding around in the dark, falling candles, and the ominous direction *MUSIC PIANO JOVIAL*.[6] The general commitment to revelry was unquestioned.

This comes out, naturally, in the garden scene (2.5). This scene has to be played quite straightforwardly for laughter: as one prompt has it, *"Bns of Bobbing from behind Trees all thro' this."* [7] But the ruthless insistence of the Neilson prompt on the laugh quota is interesting. After Malvolio's exit from the garden the play-text reads

OMNES. Ha! ha! ha! [Shades of Greyfriars]

And following Maria's entrance and Sir Toby's "Wilt thou set thy foot o'my neck?" *"all laugh and keep it up as long as possible."* There is a similar instruction to Fabian after Malvolio's cross-gartered scene. It is really an anticipation of canned laughter. Fabian is the audience's stalking-horse, and he dramatizes the risibility of the play.

There is, I think, a hint of realization by the producers that the laughter-elements need to be "protected," or played up.. There is no real need for cuts aimed at shortening the piece—*Twelfth Night* is not long—so all cuts tend to reveal a shaping impulse. Sir Toby's "I would we were well rid of this knavery. If he may be conveniently delivered, I would he were, for I am now so far in offence with my niece that I cannot pursue with any safety this sport to the upshot" (4.2.72-76) disappears from Irving's prompt.[8] Thus a singularly unpleasant passage, which markedly qualifies our view of Sir Toby as a jolly dog, yields in the interests of a rounded stereotype.

Malvolio presents a central challenge to Sir Toby's view of the action, and solutions vary. Irving played his virtually uncut, taking his chances for pathos for all they were worth. (He notes *"crying"* in his prompt for "Ay, good fool" in the prison scene.) Daly cut Malvolio totally from the fifth act; the prison scene was his last. But cuts in Malvolio's final appearance were common. Neilson cut his "And tell me, in the modesty of honour" to "That e'er invention played on?

Tell me why!" Olivia's "Alas, poor fool, how have they baffled thee" goes, together with Feste's bitter "whirligig of time" speech: thus some painful elements are expunged. Malvolio's "I'll be revenged on the whole pack of you" is in response to Fabian's "on both sides passed." This shows an awareness of the problem. Feste is to be "protected" against his own words, and Malvolio is less pathetic—the fewer words he has, the less poignant his plight is.

As so often in the nineteenth century, Feste's "whirligig of time" speech seems to have been felt rather strong, even though elsewhere a coarse communal sensibility is evident. Neilson, as we have seen, cut it. Jewett left it in, but followed Feste's "revenges" with *Laugh. Bns. Mal. down C. and turn up tear off chains. Mal. music for exit."* "Malvolio music . . . " Still the direction identifies the problem.

The conclusion formalizes the old view of *Twelfth Night*. It was customary to interpolate these lines for the Duke (after Malvolio's exit):

> And now after twelve nights of tastes and pleasures,
> Let me commend you to your dancing measures.

A dance followed. Thus an invocation to revelry, and *not* Feste's down-beat "When that I was, and a little tiny boy," ended the play. In short, the old model took every opportunity to play up the farcical and comic elements; it softened the asperities of Malvolio's humiliation; it projected, finally, an apotheosis of romance, good humor, and social accord. But it strained somewhat at the text to achieve these effects. One senses a directional awareness that the play is not so easy or so reassuring as all that.

THE NEW MODEL

The new model, to my observation, starts edging into view in the 1950s. Historically, I am content to relate it to the profound shift in sensibility that occurred in the English theater around 1956. That was the *annus mirabilis* of Suez and of Osborne's *Look Back In Anger*: theater historians, however much they fret at the cliché, agree that "*Look Back In Anger* came to symbolize the urgent need for change."[9] Of course, one can find earlier evidence of productions with modernist elements, of a performance (say) that restored Sir Toby to the knighthood.[10] But I prefer to limit my case here to a couple of critical reactions. So intelligent a critic as Laurence Kitchin writes (in 1960), "*Twelfth Night*, even in the drinking scene, is not farce."[11] He would not have needed to say that a few years later. One locates social time through the *démodé,* and Muriel St. Clare Byrne is especially dismissive of an Old Vic production that got it wrong. "Farcical" is the word that recurs in her long review.[12] Malvolios who cross-garter *both* legs together will no longer do.

That was in 1958. In the same year, Peter Hall, as we should expect, got it right. His Stratford production was costumed in a Cavalier style that suggested, a shade ominously, Van Dyck. Robert Speaight took the point: "Mr. Hall had conceived his Illyria in some English autumn not too long before the outbreak of the Civil War."[13] *Autumn* is, conceptually, the key word: it comprehends the gold and russet brown of Lila de Nobili's set and the subliminal notion of nostalgia for the golden age, the pastoral antebellum world. 'What luckless apple did we taste,/To make us mortal, and thee waste?" Years after, Hall's successor at the Royal Shakespeare Company, Trevor Nunn, had no doubt that this *Twelfth Night* was "definitively right. He had touched a Chekhov-like centre in the play; it was unarguable."[14] Yet at the time, critics felt that Hall's casting took certain liberties. The focus of displeasure was Geraldine McEwan's Olivia. This actress has since become best known as a comedy of manners specialist—she has played very successfully in Congreve, Lonsdale, Maugham, for instance—and her poseuse Olivia, complete with giggles and squeaks, centrally undercut the romantic tradition.[15] Olivias used to be played in the county matron manner. For the rest, Sir Toby (Patrick Wymark) was a gentleman. (To take Sir Toby seriously is a sign of a modern production.) Malvolio (Eric Porter) was a recognizable human being. Above all, Max Adrian's intelligent and melancholy Feste dominated the play in the 1960 revival. His final envoi was "a distant and elegant pavane."[16]

The casting of *Twelfth Night* is open to a wide variety of options; the text is extraordinarily elastic.[17] I don't want to discuss these options in detail, but I stress the dualism of the matter: *Belch* (with its Humours, stereotypic suggestion) or *Sir Toby*. (We could remember Elgar's epigraph for his *Falstaff,* "a knight, a gentleman, and a soldier.") Olivia plays well as a *grande dame* or as an aristocratic ingénue. More than that, some parts seem designed as functional variables, as spaces left open for the director to fill. Fabian is the leading instance. Neutral and unaligned, he can be played old or young, plain or tuppence colored, English or Welsh ("I would exult, *mun*"). Maria, as we shall see, turns out to be another variable. But any discussion of individual parts is apt to incur the danger of missing the point. The point lies in the constellation of relationships, in the overall system of checks and balances. If you want a melancholy Feste, someone has to cheer us up; if you plan a bleak *Twelfth Night,* you need a Feste with a certain charm.

That leads us to the initial production of the contemporary era, John Barton's Royal Shakespeare Company of 1969 (revived in 1971). Much admired and much contested, this is a directorial statement that rests solidly on the title: *Twelfth Night*. It is curious that this has been so widely interpreted as an unequivocal call to revelry. In fact, most people understand perfectly well that the *last* day of the Christmas festivities finds one sated. One more party, and then thank God for work. The mood is caught beautifully in 2.3, when Sir Toby wants the party to go on when everyone else wants to go to bed. So the title states a central dualism: a feast, an end to feasting. The play, as a set of casting options, seems sited over this dualism. And, astonishingly, Barton demonstrates this point through Maria.

Who is Maria? There'a a question about her social position that is functionally puzzling. She is some kind of companion: a younger daughter of local gentry? Is she in Olivia's household to get married or because she has failed to get married? Does she rank with the servants or the great family? Evidently, she's on the blurred edge of the class lines, above and below Malvolio. When Viola/Cesario puts the boot in ("No, good *swabber*, I am to hull here a little longer"), Maria has no answer to the social insult. She is usually cast as a soubrette, pert and bouncy. Barton made her an elderly spinster. (First Brenda Bruce, then Elizabeth Spriggs.) This Maria "is ageing, left on the shelf; she waits desperately for the word from him, and what she often gets is a dusty answer. The words 'Tis too late to go to bed, now' are spoken to her."[18] Sir Toby, a well-born failure, is intelligent enough to be aware of his own parasitism. But he is Maria's last chance. So there's an elegiac quality at the heart of even the comic action.

The act of presentation of this *Twelfth Night* was genuinely original. The 1971 revival had it perfectly gauged; the audience takes its seats to find Richard Pasco's Orsino listening to his musicians. Presently an aural disturbance comes upon the music. It grows louder and is identified as the sound of the sea crashing upon the shore. This sea is the background to the action; it enters into the imagery of Orsino's opening speech ("Receiveth as the sea") and intermittently returns to the audience's consciousness. The sea implies a sense of the canon's unity. It intimates that *Twelfth Night* is the beginning of the long swell that culminates, beyond the breakers of the tragedies, in the final romances. This *Twelfth Night* understands, and is conscious of, *The Tempest*. For Richard David, "the sound of the sea reverberating through key-moments in the play" served "to remind us of that sense of the changes and chances of life that is surely intrinsic in the mood of the play as in its basic situations."[19] Robert Speaight had experienced a sharper sense of "the howling of the gale outside the gilded cage of Orsino's palace; reality at odds with romanticism . . ."[20] It is a metamorphosis of that calm, untroubled seascape that Daly provided for the New Yorkers of 1894.

John Barton's *Twelfth Night* is the classic of recent times; and its statement, though modulated in later productions, has not I think been seriously challenged since. Basically, he takes the play seriously.

From that perspective, endless variations remain possible. Take the relationship between Sir Toby and Sir Andrew. It is, on Sir Toby's part, contemptuous, exploitative, and sadistic. And it ends in the unequivocal "Will *you* help? an ass-head and a coxcomb and a knave, a thin-faced knave, a gull?" Now how far is the director prepared to go in acknowledging the truth of this latter transaction? In the old days, no problem: Sir Andrew simply looked shocked at Sir Toby saying such *terrible* things. In the Regent's Park production of 1972, Sir Andrew stood stock-still for a long second, head bowed, as of one pondering an irrevocable decision. He than marched off like an automaton stage *left,* casting no glance at Sir Toby. Sir Toby limped off stage *right.* The audience could have no doubt that the friendship was permanently shattered.

Illusion, clearly, is what the director now perceives in this network of relationships. The concept became an emblem in Peter Gill's Royal Shakespeare Company production of 1974, which I take to be the latest important version of the modern statement. The figure of a golden Narcissus hangs over the stage, the only pictorial element in a bleak box. The program cites, of all people, R. D. Laing:

Narcissus fell in love with his image, taking it to be another. . . .

> Jill is a distorting mirror to herself.
> Jill has to distort herself to appear undistorted to herself.
> To undistort herself, she finds Jack to distort her distorted image in his distorting mirror.
> She hopes that his distortion of her distortion may undistort her image without her having to distort herself.

The atmosphere is vibrant with erotic undertones: Orsino's bisexuality is marked, and at least one critic had no doubt that Orsino was ready to grope the nearest, anytime.[21] A boyish Viola (Jane Lapotaire) contributes to the general sexual confusion. Maria's maturity has now become an RSC orthodoxy; Sir Toby is a gentleman and intelligent, a decision that invariably imparts a stereoscopic depth to his scenes. David Waller has since explained, in interview, that his reading of the part is based on "I hate a drunken rogue." "And it seems quite clear to me that he's referring quite consciously to himself."[22]

The bleaker elements were intensified in this *Twelfth Night.* Barton had allowed himself a Feste with a certain Celtic charm (Emrys James); but Gill's Feste, Ron Pember, "hinted always at a radical's social distaste for the antics of privilege . . . He was discomforting, an outsider, almost malevolently saturnine, defying the sentimental response to Malvolio's plight by pressing home his final accusations with heartless accuracy in Act V . . . Pember sang his songs with the gritty voice of the modern unaccompanied folk-singer."[23] There's more than a hint of Brecht in this. But there could in any case be no question of minimizing the effect of the final scene, given the major casting decision of this production: Nicol Williamson's Malvolio.

Nicol Williamson's salient characteristic is his capacity to portray pain. It is of a voltage that sets him apart from any other actor on the English stage. Not that his Malvolio was unfunny. His accent—which critics varied in finding Welsh, Scots, and veering from one to the other—placed him in the Baptist/Presbyterian tradition of the intolerant Nonconformist preacher on the make. More subtly, it placed him as an outsider (Illyria is set in the effete south of England). This Malvolio took his chances suberbly in the garden scene, but his final humiliation was shattering. Michael Billington's verdict is precise: "But what Williamson does so brilliantly is to blend high comedy and deep emotional pain . . . he tears Maria's epistle into miniscule fragments before departing to his own permanent, private hell, all dignity destroyed."[24] Williamson seems to have experimented with his final line during the production. When I saw it, the line was inaudible, spoken through the hands covering his face. Robert Speaight writes of a "fourfold repetition."[25] The wound is open, and Orsino cannot heal it. The shock waves travel through the entire action.

Narcissism, eroticism and alienation, illusion ending in anguish: is this the last word of the current era on *Twelfth Night?* I don't think so; it appears to me rather as an overcompensation, an emphatic rejection of a stage cliché that had hardened into a lie. The modern statement on *Twelfth Night* has its textual justification: one has to ignore a great deal to build a production around the celebration of cakes and ale, and the play has to respond to certain tendencies of our era. To cite a few, a taste for dark comedy has long been prevalent. The most influential (upon the stage) of recent Shakespearean writers, Jan Kott, treated *Twelfth Night* in a chapter entitled "Shakespeare's Bitter Arcadia."[26] Moreover, the "problem plays" have, so to speak, territorially expanded. *Measure for Measure* and *Troilus and Cressida* are played far more often than ever before, and they now look like mainstream Shakespeare, not aberrations.[27] Then again, we ought not to ignore the oblique impact of Chekhov.

I earlier cited Trevor Nunn's identification of the "Chekhov-like centre" of the play, and the point is worth pursuing. One often uses the word *Chekhovian* fairly loosely to indicate an autumnal atmosphere of agreeable but rather futile people discussing, in an aimless way, what to do next. The word tends to move away from its moorings. *Chekhovian* means "like Chekhov," and his importance on today's stage goes beyond his actual productions. Quite often one sees a *Twelfth Night* with 2.3 played as a homage to Chekhov: the sense of lateness and futility, the pauses, the alternation of manic gaiety and brooding, the inconsequentiality and missed connections:

SIR TOBY. Does not our life consist of the four elements?

SIR ANDREW. Faith, so they say; but I think it rather consists of eating and drinking.

SIR TOBY. Th'art a scholar; let us therefore eat and drink.

The scene—it occurs in Olivia's household but comes over as a tavern scene—reminds us of the tavern scene in *2 Henry IV*, as the old Falstaff fondles Doll Tearsheet, "do not bid me remember mine end," and recalls the RSC's Chekhov-oriented production of the mid-sixties. (I think it true that contemporary taste prefers the second part of *Henry IV* to the first, and this used not to be so.) It is not in question that Chekhov is the father of Beckett and Pinter; he is important today in a way that Ibsen is not. Not everyone will go all the way with Christopher Booker's judgment: "It is for our recognition of this melancholy, arid picture that I believe we have quietly elevated Chekhov into the supreme 'serious' playwright of our age."[28] We have, nonetheless, to acknowledge him as an unseen presence in the world of comedy. Through him, one catches at the implications of "autumnal." The subtext of autumn is winter: and one wonders, with Nunn, if winter is not after all the right season for a setting of *Twelfth Night*.

Chekhov, if you like, is a surface presence. But there is an underground subsidence that affects even more our view of *Twelfth Night*. The practical joke has vanished. I don't mean that it has ceased to exist, but its sanctions have. Our ancestors, as the memoirs testify, took a robust pleasure in the playing of practical jokes. The fondness for them persisted through the nineteenth century. In the last generation or so, the relish for them has ebbed away. As I take it, we know too much about the sadistic undercurrent of much practical joking to be at ease with it. It is one of the social changes of our lifetime that the historian should learn to document. Its passing means that the entire network of assumptions sustaining the old *Twelfth Night* has collapsed. And that raises the whole question of what is called, for want of a better word, comedy. The theory of comedy is the search for a better word. Perhaps all theoreticians of comedy should take their lead from Aristotle, who passed up the opportunity of making up his lecture notes into a book, opting for the easier field of tragedy. His reviews have probably gained from that heroic evasion. A modern production of *Twelfth Night* is obliged to redefine *comedy*, knowing always that its ultimate event is the destruction of a notably charmless bureaucrat. There it is, and it happens. Do we laugh at it?

Twelfth Night, which appears as a machine for inducing laughter, discloses itself in the end as a machine for suppressing it. One is always aware of mixed responses in the theater, of laughter in the wrong places. It's a general hazard of playgoing, and one accepts it without comment. But once, at a repertory production under a man who knew his business, I understood it as the dramatist's design: what had seemed an imperfection of theater experience became the truth of the play. Malvolio's entrance in Act V created a storm of laughter. The interventions of Fabian and Feste and the dawning awareness of Olivia became the implacable advance of a reality that stifled laughter. The laughter of others, but not oneself, became the experience of the drama. One by one, the laughs ceased, like lights going out in the house, as the edge of the great play, dark as logic, moved over the consciousness of the audience. It received in total silence the destruction of Malvolio, and the strained half moment that followed "I'll be revenged on the whole pack of you" bore the meaning of the play. That silence, that end of laughter, is today's *Twelfth Night*.

NOTES

1. George C. D. Odell, *Shakespeare From Betterton To Irving,* 2 vols. (1920; rptd. New York: Dover, 1966), II, p. 442.
2. November 28, 1894. Cited in John Russell Brown, *Shakespeare's Plays in Performance* (Harmondsworth: Penguin, 1969), p. 244.
3. Augustin Daly, New York, 1869. The promptbook for this production is now lodged at the Folger Shakespeare Library, Washington, D.C. In this and the next five notes I give the Folger call mark for the promptbook: TN, 9.
4. Adelaide Neilson, London, 1878. Folger: TN, 18.
5. Ibid.
6. Folger: TN, 30.
7. Neilson, loc. cit.
8. Henry Irving, London, 1884. Folger: TN, 13.
9. John Elsom, *Post-War British Theatre* (London: Routledge & Kegan Paul, 1976), p. 75.
10. The phrase is Kenneth Tynan's. I take it from his review of a 1948 production, reprinted in his *A View of the English Stage* (Frogmore, St. Albans: Paladin, 1976), p. 70.
11. Laurence Kitchin, *Mid-Century Drama* (London: Faber, 1960), p. 45.
12. *Shakespeare Quarterly,* 9 (1958), pp. 523–524.
13. *Shakespeare Quarterly,* 12 (1961), p. 427. This relates to the 1960 revival.
14. See Ralph Berry, *On Directing Shakespeare: Interviews with Contemporary Directors* (London and New York: Croom Helm and Barnes & Noble, 1977), p. 60.
15. "Some gaiety is lost," felt Rosemary Anne Sissons in the *Stratford-upon-Avon Herald,* April 25, 1958.
16. Robert Speaight, "The 1960 Season at Stratford-upon-Avon", *Shakespeare Quarterly,* 11 (1960), p. 450.
17. For two admirable discussions of the casting options, see Brown, op. cit., pp. 222-228, and Arthur Colby Sprague and J. C. Trewin, *Shakespeare's Plays Today: Some Customs and Conventions of the Stage* (Columbia, South Carolina: University of South Carolina Press, 1970), pp. 92–97.
18. Gareth Lloyd Evans, "Interpretation or Experience? Shakespeare at Stratford," *Shakespeare Survey,* 23 (1970), p. 135.
19. Richard David, "Of an Age and for All Time: Shakespeare at Stratford," *Shakespeare Survey,* 25 (1972), p. 167.
20. Robert Speaight, "Shakespeare in Britain," *Shakespeare Quarterly,* 20 (1969), p. 439.
21. B. A. Young, *The Financial Times,* August 23, 1974.
22. Quoted by Peter Thomson, in "The Smallest Season: The Royal Shakespeare Company at Stratford in 1974," *Shakespeare Survey,* 28 (1975), p. 145.
23. Ibid., pp. 145-146.
24. *The Guardian,* August 23, 1974.

25. Robert Speaight, "Shakespeare in Britain, 1974," *Shakespeare Quarterly,* 25 (1974), p. 392.

26. Jan Kott, *Shakespeare Our Contemporary,* 2d ed. (New York: Doubleday, 1967).

27. A discussion of the "problem" play category ought, in my view, to begin with *The Merchant of Venice* before continuing with *Twelfth Night.*

28. Christopher Booker, "Mirror of our Melancholy", *The Daily Telegraph,* February 26, 1977.

Comic Premises of *Twelfth Night*

MAURICE CHARNEY

The title of this play, *Twelfth Night, or What You Will,* gives critics a special latitude of interpretation. It is *What You Will,* or whatever you wish it to be. I recognize the presumption, then, of my title, which claims to disclose the comic premises of the play. If the play means "what you will," then the critic's will is determined by his own value system. Perhaps this is just a generous way of explaining how the critic's wish fulfillments are acted out in literature. In a splendidly malicious essay, Sylvan Barnet demonstrates that Charles Lamb's view of the play is much influenced by the fact that his own father was a household servant something like Malvolio.[1] Lamb's essay "On Some of the Old Actors," first published in 1822, laid the groundwork for a tragic—or at least tragicomic—view of Malvolio and of the play. The theatrical tradition has followed Lamb in regarding *Twelfth Night* as a dark comedy, an "autumnal" play (in Ralph Berry's phrase).

Lamb writes specifically about the Malvolio of Robert Bensley, who acted the part at the turn of the century. This discussion comes just after the description of Mrs. Powel as Olivia, whose "fine spacious person filled the scene"[2]—we are emphatically in a different era of personal beauty. To Lamb,

> Malvolio is not essentially ludicrous. He becomes comic but by accident. He is cold, austere, repelling; but dignified, consistent, and, for what appears, rather of an over-stretched morality. . . . But his morality and his manners are misplaced in Illyria. He is opposed to the proper *levities* of the piece, and falls in the unequal contest. Still his pride, or his gravity, (call it which you will) is inherent, and native to the man, not mock or affected, which latter only are the fit objects to excite laughter. His quality is at the best unlovely, but neither buffoon nor contemptible. His bearing is lofty, a little above his station, but probably not much above his deserts. We see no reason why he should not have been brave, honourable, accomplished. (p. 134)

This reads like an idealized portrait, which Robert Bensley beautifully realizes: "Bensley, accordingly, threw over the part an air of Spanish loftiness. He looked, spake, and moved like an old Castilian. He was starch, spruce, opinionated, but his superstructure of pride seemed bottomed upon a sense of worth" (p. 135). Lamb's conclusion, therefore, is inevitable: "I confess that I never saw the catastrophe of this character, while Bensley played it, without a kind of tragic interest" (p. 136).

I have been quoting Lamb in such loving detail only in order to confute him. I am genuinely disturbed by the feeling abroad that comedy is not enough, that it is, in Richard Levin's satirical phrase, "no laughing matter."[3] We have been thoroughly indoctrinated in the belief, first formulated in Aristotle's *Poetics,* that tragedy is "more serious" than other genres and, therefore, more significant, more profound, more meaningful as an imitation (or "mimesis") of human experience. In Shakespeare studies there is a whole subindustry of criticism devoted to discovering dark implications, tragic overtones, ironic undercutting in otherwise lighthearted romantic comedies. Somehow in *Twelfth Night* the wind and the rain—"For the rain it raineth every day"—of the Clown Feste's final song have given a final warrant for a tragic perspective on this play, and the fact that this song appears again in *King Lear* seems to clinch its darker significance. But the wind and the rain and the vagaries of daily life and the ages of man are all traditional topics of comedy.

With due apologies, therefore, to a pluralistic "what you will," I offer my own comic premises of *Twelfth Night*—in other words, a set of assumptions about comedy that underlie the play and shape its comic perspective. Most obvious of all is the title, *Twelfth Night,* which marks the festive occasion. Twelfth Night, or January 6, climaxes the twelve days of feasting, revelry, and celebration that begin with Christmas. Twelfth Night is the feast of the Epiphany, when the Magi, guided by a star, do homage to the Christ-child in His manger in Bethlehem. It is a joyous occasion. Unfortunately, none of this has any literal relation to Shakespeare's play, although various claims have been made for the fact that the play was acted on Twelfth Night as part of the general festivities.[4] Shakespeare's title has strong comic associations and falls in the same general category as *Much Ado About Nothing, All's Well That Ends Well,* and *As You Like It.* The subtitle, *What You Will,* has more than a little resemblance to *As You Like It:* both are a general invitation to license, indulgence, and unrestricted revelry.

TWELFTH NIGHT AND COMIC FESTIVITY

Even though we cannot allegorize *Twelfth Night* as a play of the Epiphany, we can still understand its title as a commitment to festivity and the values of carnival. Robert Herrick's poem *"Twelfe night, or King and Queene"* (from *Hesperides,* 1648) offers a pleasant and homely commentary on Shakespeare's Twelfth Night play, as the occasion would have been understood in the early seventeenth century. The poem turns on the folk custom of choosing a king and queen of the Twelfth Night festivities. Whoever finds the bean in his portion of the Twelfth Night cake becomes the king, whereas the finder of the pea becomes the queen:

> Now, now the mirth comes
> With the cake full of plums,
> Where Beane's the *King* of the sport here;
> Beside we must know,
> The Pea also
> Must revel, as *Queene,* in the Court here.
>
> Begin then to chuse,
> (This night as ye use)
> Who shall for the present delight here,
> Be a *King* by the lot,
> And who shall not
> Be a Twelfe-day *Queene* for the night here.
>
> Which known, let us make
> Joy-sops with the cake
>   [i.e., cake dunked in wine];
> And let not a man then be seen here,
> Who unurg'd will not drinke

To the base from the brink
A health to the King and the Queene here.

Next crowne the bowle full
With gentle lambs-wooll
  [a drink made with hot ale and the pulp
  of roasted apples, sugared and spiced];
Adde sugar, nutmeg and ginger,
  With store of ale too;
  And thus ye must doe
To make the wassaile a swinger
    [i.e., something forcible or effective,
      especially something very big—a "whopper"].

Give them to the King
And Queene wassailing;
And though with ale ye be whet here;
  Yet part ye from hence,
  As free from offence,
As when ye innocent met here.[5]

Typical of Herrick's love of paradox is the desire for the Twelfth Night feast to be both "innocent" and a "swinger" at the same time. His lilting insistence on "here" is matched by a detailed emphasis on preparing the "lambs-wooll" punch that will be the demurely inebriating basis of the festivities. The catechistic dialogue between Toby and Andrew in Shakespeare's play is entirely in the spirit of Herrick's poem:

TOBY. Does not our lives consist of the four elements?
ANDREW. Faith, so they say; but I think it rather
    consists of eating and drinking.
TOBY. Th' art a scholar! Let us therefore eat and
    drink. Marian I say, a stoup of wine! (2.3.9-14)[6]

Toby's final imperative makes it clear that eating is subordinated to drinking.

In the same festive spirit is Toby's much-quoted reply to Malvolio: "Dost thou think, because thou art virtuous, there shall be no more cakes and ale?" (2.3.114-115). In its immediate context (and not as a famous quotation), Toby's question shows that he is genuinely worried that the sober and censorious Malvolio will bring the party to a sudden end. The Clown, too, insists on one of the ingredients of Herrick's "lambs-wooll": "Yes, by Saint Anne, and ginger shall be hot i' th' mouth too" (2.3.116-117). In the context of festive revelry, the Twelfth Night participants are not mere drunkards—God forbid such an offense to the spirit of folklore and cultural anthropology—but ritual celebrants;

and the wassail bowl filled with its elaborately concocted "lambs-wooll" punch provides a suitable conclusion to the twelve strenuous days of Christmas festivity.

TWELFTH NIGHT AND ITS ASSOCIATION WITH HOLIDAY

Twelfth Night announces a festive occasion. My second premise comes from the subtitle: "What You Will." This heralds the comic values of license, self-indulgence, and wish fulfillment associated with holiday and special occasions. Holiday is not everyday, and there is a mood of extended possibility, even hyperbolism and excess that would not be tolerated in ordinary experience. Wonder is an important effect of comedy, an emotion that matches the pity and fear associated with tragedy. Strange, splendid things happen to you in comedy if only you are sufficiently open and receptive—"loose," as we might say.

Thus Sebastian, the twin brother of Viola, is suddenly wooed—in error, of course—by the lovelorn Olivia. His reaction is entirely typical of festive comedy, where the irritating question of identity does not dare to raise its ugly head:

> What relish is in this? How runs the stream?
> Or I am mad, or else this is a dream.
> Let fancy still my sense in Lethe steep;
> If it be thus to dream, still let me sleep! (4.1.60–63)

Without a moment's hesitation, the intensely practical Sebastian fully commits himself to the world of "fancy" (or imagination) and dreams, his former self steeped in Lethe, the river of forgetfulness in classical Hades. His final exclamation declares his allegiance to dreams and the delightful rewards they bring rather than to the more parsimonious world of a shipwrecked orphan in Illyria.

Sebastian's enlightenment is very much in the spirit of Antipholus of Syracuse in *The Comedy of Errors,* who, although a stranger in Ephesus, suddenly finds all the good things in life thrust forcibly upon him, including the lovely Adriana, who insists that he is her husband. Like Sebastian, Antipholus of Syracuse reacts with characteristic generosity:

> To me she speaks, she moves me for her theme;
> What, was I married to her in my dream?
> Or sleep I now, and think I hear all this?
> What error drives our eyes and ears amiss?
> Until I know this sure uncertainty,
> I'll entertain the offered fallacy. (2.2.182–187)

Antipholus does not raise intrusive and disturbing—and irrelevant—questions about his own identity. He makes the only possible choice available to the comic hero: he will "entertain the offered fallacy." Even though he knows it to be a delusion, he accepts it because it is offered; to refuse the good things that are freely given is to violate the comic spirit.

We know, therefore, that Sebastian cannot and should not and will not rebuff Olivia's erotic advances, even though Olivia is taking the initiative with her bemused and wondering partner:

> OLIVIA. Nay, come, I prithee. [A slight hesitation on
>   Sebastian's part is only good manners.] Would thou'dst
>   be ruled by me!
> SEBASTIAN. Madam, I will. [Sebastian is not in a position
>   to make either objections or specific stipulations.]
> OLIVIA.   O, say so, and so be. (4.1.64–65)

Olivia's final alliterative line represents an emotional high point for her, who had previously so many doubts and hesitations about falling in love with Viola. The six strong monosyllables—"O, say so, and so be"—make an ecstatic, scene-ending couplet.

TWELFTH NIGHT AND THE POSITIVE VALUE OF LOVE

A third premise arises directly from comic festivity: that love is a positive value, that lovers are archetypal comic characters, and that the purpose of comedy is not only to incite and nurture love—especially young love—but to bring lovers through the maze of comic intrigue to the marriages that typically end comedies, with their joyous feasting, dancing, revelry, and the promise of offspring. Complications are introduced, as in the mix-up of the twins in *Twelfth Night,* for the sole purpose of a gratifying resolution at the end. As Lysander announces in *A Midsummer Night's Dream,*

> For aught that I could ever read,
> Could ever hear by tale or history,
> The course of true love never did run smooth. . . . (1.1.132–134)

But the obstacles are necessary for the fulfillment, according to Prospero's pedagogic plan for Ferdinand and Miranda:

> They are both in either's pow'rs. But this swift business
> I must uneasy make, lest too light winning
> Make the prize light. (*Tempest* 1.2.451–453)

Love must not be a "swift business"—Prospero means specifically that the lovers must not consummate their passion before marriage—because being in love is an emotional entanglement and commitment delicious in itself. Once the lovers are no longer innocently rapt and the "prize" they seek is won, they enter an entirely different stage in their relationship. In Northrop Frye's terms, at the end of comedy the lovers by marriage enter a new society in which they will be the parents against whose authority they had earlier rebelled.[7]

We are so distracted by Malvolio in *Twelfth Night* and by the undue importance conferred upon him by the critical and theatrical tradition that we tend to forget that the play is about falling in love. Orsino is hopelessly in love with Olivia; Viola (disguised as Cesario) is desperately in love with Orsino; Sir Andrew Aguecheek is foolishly in love with Olivia; Maria is shrewdly in love with Toby (and manages to win him by the success of her practical joke); and, most importantly, Olivia falls in love with Viola-Cesario, the boy-girl emissary of Orsino, who is entirely interchangeable with her twin brother, Sebastian, whom Olivia, with her own priest at hand, manages to snare in marriage. The play begins with Olivia earnestly mourning her dead brother—surely a grief that is, in the words of Claudius, an "obstinate condolement" *(Hamlet* 1.2.94), especially because we have just heard Viola's optimistic hopes for her "dead" brother. The frozen and formal Olivia is thawed by love, and we are permitted to follow the steps of her erotic entanglement with charmed interest. All thoughts of her dead brother disappear as the androgynous Viola-Cesario woos not for Orsino but for himself/herself.

The love-at-first-sight convention simplifies the erotic psychology, but is no less convincing than any other convention. Olivia is smitten despite—perhaps because of—her own elaborate defenses. She understands the messenger's prepared role, his "line." "Are you a comedian?" (1.5.180), she asks guardedly, intending the word in its older, general sense of "actor," as in modern French, but with some inescapable connotations of someone not in earnest—Cesario is speaking for Orsino. The love orator protests too much, but the damage has already been done, so that it hardly matters what Cesario says. Once Olivia is in love, she is securely and unwaveringly in love. That is the special attraction of the comic convention. In characteristic fashion, Olivia is more concerned with herself than with the love object. She probes this new perturbation of spirit that she feels with delighted preoccupation:

> Not too fast; soft, soft,
> Unless the master were the man. [There is some
>   confusion in her mind between master and servant,
>   although "man" is supremely ambiguous. She has
>   taken Orsino's "man" for her "master."]

How now?
Even so quickly may one catch the plague? [Love
   at first sight is like the sudden onset of a
   communicable and fatal infection.]
Methinks I feel this youth's perfections
With an invisible and subtle stealth
To creep in at mine eyes. (1.5.294-299)
   [Here, as always in Shakespeare, love is a
   physical attraction. The physical beauty of the
   love object enters at the eye and ensnares the
   soul. This is standard erotic psychology conveniently modeled on Plato.]

Olivia's conclusion indicates her acceptance of her fate: "Well,
let it be" (1.5.299), which is analogous to Hamlet's newfound stoic
fortitude: "The readiness is all. Since no man of aught he leaves
knows, what is't to leave betimes? Let be" (5.2.223-225). The blind
Cupid with his arrows is a minion of Fortune, so that the lover must
yield to irresistible pressures. In her final soliloquy in the scene, Olivia
finds that being in love raises all kinds of uncertain dualisms between
"eye" and "mind," physical attraction and spiritual worth:

I do I know not what, and fear to find
Mine eye too great a flatterer for my mind.
Fate, show thy force; ourselves we do not owe.
What is decreed must be—and be this so! (1.5.309-312)

No matter how passive Olivia feels in the hands of some larger force,
she now actively pursues the fate that has been thrust upon her. The
optimistic cast of "be this so!" is entirely different from the earlier
"Let it be." Olivia has definitely cast her lot as a comic heroine, who
will vigorously seek the consummation of a fortuitous love.

TWELFTH NIGHT **AND THE NEGATIVE VALUE OF SELF-LOVE**

If love is a positive value in comedy, then self-love is a negative
value. Our fourth premise is that comedy seeks to confute self-love
in all its forms. The action of *Twelfth Night* involves the transformation
of self-love into love of another, especially for Orsino and Olivia.
Malvolio, of course, is never touched by these mollifying influences,
and he is rigorously excluded from the harmonious ending of the play.
His final threat, "I'll be revenged on the whole pack of you!" (5.1.380),
is a mark of his outcast status in the new society of the happy ending.
There is no place for Malvolio in the feasting and marriages with which

the play ends, just as there is no place for Shylock in *The Merchant of Venice* or Jaques in *As You Like It*—there have to be some meaningful limits to the inclusiveness of comic reconciliation. Malvolio, Shylock, and Jaques have learned nothing from their discomfiture—they have emphatically not been put out of their humors—and the new society is better off without them. They can not be facilely converted to the values of comedy, and it is to Shakespeare's credit that he doesn't try.

Malvolio is not so isolated at the beginning of *Twelfth Night* as he is at the end. He is, after all, Olivia's steward. When he comes to put down the spirit of cakes and ale in Act II, Scene 3, he speaks in his mistress's name and with all of her authority: "My lady bade me tell you that, though she harbors you as her kinsman, she's nothing allied to your disorders" (2.3.95-98). Presumably he is speaking on instruction when he goes so far as to invite Toby to decamp: "If you can separate yourself and your misdemeanors, you are welcome to the house. If not, and it would please you to take leave of her, she is very willing to bid you farewell" (2.3.98-101). This kind of talk does not make it seem so preposterous that Malvolio might believe in Maria's plot: that his mistress is in love with him. "There is example for't. The Lady of the Strachy married the yeoman of the wardrobe" (2.5.39-40)—whoever the mysterious Lady of the Strachy (or is it starchery?) might be.

But Olivia is quickly transformed by love, as is Orsino, too, under Viola's subtle influence. Orsino cannot possibly remain the ridiculous, mooning figure of his opening aria, chewing on "music, moody food/ Of us that trade in love" (*Antony and Cleopatra* 2.5.1-2), as Cleopatra phrases the malady. Malvolio, however, never changes at all, and he is just as presumptuously incapable of love at the end of the play as he was at the beginning. Olivia understands his problem almost as soon as he appears in the play: "O, you are sick of self-love, Malvolio, and taste with a distempered appetite. To be generous, guiltless, and of free disposition, is to take those things for birdbolts [blunt arrows used to shoot birds] that you deem cannon bullets" (1.5.90-93). Malvolio is an agelast, a man incapable of laughter; he is also terribly literal-minded and totally lacking in imagination. He can neither laugh nor love—the two seem to go together—in fact, he cannot understand anything outside his own self-serving and self-aggrandizing perspective. Maria's ingenious plot against Malvolio plays on his inordinate vanity and social climbing.

He is enamored of the idea of being married to Olivia, but he does not pant after her body as a good comic hero should. The life-force does not flow in Malvolio, whose blood, like Angelo's in *Measure for Measure*, "Is very snow-broth; one who never feels/ The wanton stings and motions of the sense" (1.4.58-59). Malvolio's sexlessness is a mark of his exclusion from the world of comedy. He muffs his one direct invitation from Olivia, or at least that's the way he understands the double entendre. Convinced that her steward is mad, Olivia asks comfortingly: "Wilt thou go to bed, Malvolio?" The steward is obviously flattered by his lady's solicitude, but he doesn't seize the occasion to gather rosebuds while he may: "To bed? Ay, sweetheart, and I'll come to thee" (3.4.30–32). An awfully tepid answer for someone who purports to be an ardent lover, cross-gartered, smiling, in yellow stockings—the full carnival regalia.

Instead of feeling Olivia's "perfections/ With an invisible and subtle stealth/ To creep in at mine eyes" (1.5.297–299), as Olivia says of Cesario, Malvolio in love has no perturbation at all, but grows more complacent and more self-satisfied. As Fabian puts it, "Contemplation makes a rare turkey cock of him. How he jets under his advanced plumes!" (2.5.30–32). In other words, the strutting rooster haughtily surveying his imagined domestic kingdom. That is why Lamb's sympathies for the noble and ill-used Malvolio are so misplaced and so hostile to the spirit of comedy. Malvolio is indeed "an overweening rogue" (2.5.29) as he imagines himself already three months married to Olivia, lording it over the household in his "branched velvet gown" (2.5.48). His moralistic dialogue with his kinsman Toby is insufferably insolent and humble at the same time, in the true Dickensian mode: "'Cousin Toby, my fortunes having cast me on your niece, give me this prerogative of speech'" (2.5.70–72). His officious, circumlocutious speech is hostile to the free-flowing energy of comedy. Although we may admit, with Toby, that the joke has gone too far and is beginning to backfire, I think we cannot feel for Malvolio the kind of tragic compassion we feel for Othello. Like Rosencrantz and Guildenstern, Malvolio should not come near our conscience; his defeat, like theirs, "Does by [his] own insinuation grow" (*Hamlet* 5.2.59). In terms of the dynamics of comedy, Malvolio and his negative values need to be confuted and driven out in order that the new society at the end of the play may come into existence. Malvolio troubles the comic kingdom of Illyria.

TWELFTH NIGHT AND THE LANGUAGE OF COMEDY

All of our premises are not merely theoretical formulations, but are acted out and embodied in the play. From this dramatic representation emerges a final proposition: that the language of comedy is an autonomous and self-contained system, that words are often used for an expressive and celebratory purpose. The Clown is Olivia's "corrupter of words" (3.1.37), and the fact that he exercises an official function in the play indicates how significantly *Twelfth Night* is a play of words. Feste threads his way through the play and does a good deal to set the tone and establish comic values. Viola, in fact, delivers a curious soliloquy justifying the Clown's role:

> This fellow is wise enough to play the fool,
> And to do that well craves a kind of wit.
> He must observe their mood on whom he jests,
> The quality of persons, and the time;
> And, like the haggard [a wild, untrained hawk],
>   check at [be distracted by and hunt] every feather
> That comes before his eye. This is a practice
> As full of labor as a wise man's art.... (3.1.61–67)

Viola deploys all the commonplaces of the "wise fool" tradition to explicate Feste's very self-conscious art. The clown, like the wild hawk, pursues every opportunity for jest that presents itself and not just the one grand proper occasion. The clown, like the hawk, is a professional hunter.

Much of Feste's part is marked by an adroit use of words and styles to impress his auditors. In speaking to Viola, the Clown disdains words of ordinary discourse: "Who you are and what you would are out of my welkin; I might say 'element,' but the word is overworn" (3.1.58–60). And the Clown makes merciless fun of Sebastian's fancy word *vent*: "Vent my folly? He has heard that word of some great man, and now applies it to a fool. Vent my folly! ... I prithee now, ungird thy strangeness, and tell me what I shall vent to my lady. Shall I vent to her that thou art coming?" (4.1.12–17). By displacement, the discourse turns on Sebastian's word rather than on his message.

Sir Andrew is especially amenable to the power of words, which is one of the most charming indications of his childlike natural folly. Viola-Cesario's parodic wooing of Olivia in the high style seems awfully grand to Sir Andrew:

> VIOLA. Most excellent accomplished lady, the heavens rain
>   odors on you.
> ANDREW. That youth's a rare courtier. "Rain odors"—well!
>   (3.1.86–89)

The next exchange is even more impressive to the simple knight:

> VIOLA. My matter hath no voice, lady, but to your own most
>   pregnant and vouchsafed ear.
> ANDREW. "Odors," "pregnant," and "vouchsafed"—I'll
>   get 'em all three all ready.   (3.1.90–93)

Vouchsafe is one of Osric's words in *Hamlet* (5.2.170), and even if Sir Andrew is squandering his money on wooing Olivia, he is at least learning the discourse of an elegant courtier. We can imagine that he will return to his native place with these high-flown words, like a bag of gold coins, to be used only on suitably distinguished occasions.

Sir Andrew is a lovable comic reflector. His nostalgic declaration "I was adored once too" (2.3.181), as Toby is now by Maria, his true-bred "beagle" (179), arouses not pathos but comic indulgence, because Andrew is an adorable gull. It is in the spirit of the abbreviated and besotted autobiography of Silence in *Henry IV, Part 2:* "Who, I? I have been merry twice and once ere now" (5.3.40–41).

Language as a comic premise in *Twelfth Night* affirms how often the words assert comic values as well as execute the business of the play. I won't advance any portentous claims about metalanguage as the standard-bearer of metadrama, for the play so obviously acknowledges its own fictive assumptions. As Fabian puts it, with excessive explicitness: "If this were played upon a stage now, I could condemn it as an improbable fiction" (3.4.133–134). What he means literally is that the plot against Malvolio succeeds so admirably well that one might be inclined to confuse the mirthful reality with an "improbable fiction." Fabian is self-consciously putting us on our guard against the enticing illusions of stage plays. Thus there is an inner drama of the comic language in *Twelfth Night,* an intricate matrix of puns, double entendres, festive abuse, and very exuberant nonsense. The play both demonstrates and celebrates the powers of language to capture a shifting and elusive reality.

One important and obvious point is that the play is oral. Its words are spoken rather than read (although, *faute de mieux,* we do read them), so that the language has a phonetic immediacy not associated with print. This would account for much more extensive wordplay than is available to the eye alone. Far be it from me to press puns on unwilling recipients, but the only practical rule to follow is that if it sounds like a pun to you, then it is a pun even if others don't get the point. Consider how often the Clown addresses Olivia as "madonna" in Act I, Scene 5 of *Twelfth Night.* The word occurs nine times in this scene (and once in 5.1.299), but never again in Shakespeare. It is clearly an unusual word that calls attention to itself in Act I, Scene 5. It threads its way very self-consciously through Feste's discourse, but the punning undertone on *mad* does not become explicit until the ninth example in the scene, where Feste speaks of Toby: "He is but mad yet, madonna, and the fool shall look to the madman" (1.5.136–137). Those three *mads* are capped by a fourth as Malvolio enters and begins unwittingly: "Madam" (138). If *mad, madonna, madman,* and *Madam* do not constitute wordplay, then the spoken word has lost its vitality.

One of the most vigorous affirmations of oral discourse in *Twelfth Night* is Toby's put-down of Malvolio: "Sneck up" (2.3.94). This is the only example of the expression in Shakespeare, and it seems especially appropriate for one who, by his own admission, is a "notorious geck and gull" (5.1.345). The *Oxford English Dictionary* lists *sneck* as chiefly Scottish and Northern dialect. Because a *sneck* is the latch of a door or gate, *sneck up* probably means something like "Shut up." The unusual word defines the urgency of the situation. For those not skilled in Scottish and Northern dialects, the sound of "Sneck up" is enough to indicate its abusive appropriateness in context: "Bug off."

Feste is a specialist in double-talk and comic nonsense, for which he has no more appreciative audience than Sir Andrew, who makes an effort to remember everything he has ever heard in this wonderful world of Illyria: "In sooth, thou [i.e., Feste] wast in very gracious fooling last night, when thou spok'st of Pigrogromitus, of the Vapians passing the equinoctial of Queubus" (2.3.22-24). Despite the vast commentary collected in the Variorum *Twelfth Night,* these words can mean whatever we choose to associate with them. For me the Vapians are the vapid people, of whom Supervacuo in *The Revenger's Tragedy* must be the unacknowledged leader. The Clown is an expert in Rabelaisian mock-learning on the authority of his mythical sage Quinapalus, who observes with sly wit: " 'Better a witty fool than a foolish wit' " (1.5.35). The "old hermit of Prague, that never saw pen and ink" (4.2. 13-14) is another of the Clown's authorities. He is obviously a guru firmly established in the oral tradition, whose vatic pronouncements have been taken down by his disciples. The Clown quotes what the old hermit of Prague "very wittily said to a niece of King Gorboduc, 'That that is is'; so, I, being Master Parson, am Master Parson; for what is 'that' but that, and 'is' but is?" (4.2.14-17). This is the true mystical doctrine of identities, as in Antony's description of the crocodile for the drunken Lepidus: "It is shaped, sir, like itself, and it is as broad as it hath breadth; it is just so high as it is, and moves with it own organs. It lives by that which nourisheth it, and the elements once out of it, it transmigrates" (*Antony and Cleopatra* 2.7.43-47).

After Feste's warm-up as the old hermit of Prague, he is ready to take on the mad Malvolio in the guise of Sir Topas, the Parson. Their first wit combat turns on the Pythagorean doctrine of the transmigration of souls: "What is the opinion of Pythagoras concerning wild fowl?" (4.2.51-52) asks the mock-solemn Sir Topas to test the reasoning powers of his subject. Malvolio must play straightman to the Clown's Mr. Interlocutor, so that whatever he says is wrong. The Clown-Parson concludes with some relish: "fear to kill a woodcock, lest thou dispossess the soul of thy grandam" (4.2.60-61). Because a woodcock was a traditionally simple and foolish bird, like our snipe, Malvolio's Pythagorean lineage is not so subtly insulted.

As Fabian, in a reconciling spirit, expresses it at the end of the play, this is only "sportful malice" (5.1.367) to repay Malvolio for "some stubborn and uncourteous parts/ We had conceived against him (363-364). But the comic conclusion is the Clown's: "And thus the whirligig of time brings in his revenges" (5.1.378-379). The whirligig image, as a type of comic fortune, leads directly to the wind and the rain of the Clown's concluding song. This is not a tragic statement, as some have misunderstood it, but only an account of the ups and downs of "man's estate." Again we have the comic equivalences announced by the "old hermit of Prague": "A foolish thing was but a toy" (5.1.393), or trifle, and "Tosspots," or drunkards, "still had drunken heads" (405). All's one, nothing can be done, "A great while ago the world begun" (407), but the final line is the actor's flattering epilogue to his audience: "And we'll strive to please you every day" (410).

CONCLUSION

So much remains to be said about this splendid play that I feel I may have worked myself into a tight corner by attempting so strenuously to demonstrate that it is a comedy. Who ever doubted it? My five premises, however, assert that *Twelfth Night* is not only a comedy, but also a festive comedy, which follows the holiday, carnival spirit set out so vigorously in Mikhail Bakhtin's book on Rabelais, *Rabelais and His World,* and C. L. Barber's book on Shakespeare, *Shakespeare's Festive Comedy: A Study of Dramatic Form and Its Relation to Social Custom.*[8] To recapitulate my argument, *Twelfth Night* lends itself naturally to festive comedy because its title asserts a festive occasion: the twelfth day of the Christmas festivities, associated particularly with the feast of the Epiphany. The subtitle of the play, *What You Will,* establishes the values of holiday over everyday and comic license over decent propriety and order. Only on Twelfth Night or some other festive occasion are the rules of ordinary life suspended and the wish fulfillment of "what you will" can take over. This is, of course, best expressed in the primacy of love as a comic subject. The festive occasion is extraordinarily favorable to lovers, just as it is equally dangerous to narcissists and self-lovers like Malvolio. The force of love confutes sexless agelasts. Finally, the play floats freely in a lively comic idiom, cultivated especially by the professional jester, Feste, and applauded by the wonderfully natural Sir Andrew Aguecheek, a foolish innocent.

If I count correctly, there are five unnumbered comic premises in this conclusion. Five is an arbitrary number, and I could wish to cite fifty to prove the comic vigor of *Twelfth Night.* If the play has tragic overtones—and I think it detracts from the scope of comedy to need to make such an assertion—it is only tragedy in its restricted sense of the rough and tumble of fortune, the wind and the rain, and the vicissitudes of daily existence. Thus, when Maria threatens that the Clown "will be hanged for being so long absent" (1.5.16-17), the Clown accepts his fate with proverbial good will: "Many a good hanging prevents a bad marriage" (19). This cheerful agreement to take things as they come—a cheerful irony, really—is the essence of the comic spirit of *Twelfth Night.*

NOTES

1. Sylvan Barnet, "Charles Lamb and the Tragic Malvolio," *Philological Quarterly,* XXXIII (1954), 178-188. Barnet notes that Lamb's contemporaries saw Bensley's Malvolio as comic—grotesque, perhaps, but definitely not tragic.

2. *The Works of Charles & Mary Lamb,* ed. E. V. Lucas (London: Methuen, 1903), II, 133. All quotations are from this edition.

3. Richard Levin, "'No Laughing Matter': Some New Readings of *The Alchemist,*" *Studies in the Literary Imagination,* VI (1973), 85-99.

4. See Leslie Hotson, *The First Night of "Twelfth Night"* (London: Rupert Hart-Davis, 1954). Although one may disagree with Hotson's specific conclusions, his reading in contemporary documents offers a lively background to the occasion of the play.

5. *The Poetical Works of Robert Herrick,* ed. L. C. Martin (Oxford: Clarendon Press, 1956), p. 317.

6. *Twelfth Night* is quoted from the Signet Classic Shakespeare edition, ed. Herschel Baker (New York: New American Library, 1965). Other plays of Shakespeare are quoted from the paperback Signet editions, general editor Sylvan Barnet.

7. See Northrop Frye, "The Argument of Comedy," *English Institute Essays 1948* (New York: Columbia Univ. Press, 1949), which is expanded in the *Anatomy of Criticism* (Princeton: Princeton Univ. Press, 1957, pp. 163-186).

8. Mikhail Bakhtin, *Rabelais and His World,* trans. Helene Iswolsky (Cambridge, Mass.: M.I.T. Press, 1968). This translation is so poor as to be almost unreadable. C. L. Barber's *Shakespeare's Festive Comedy* was published by the Princeton University Press in 1959 and was reprinted in a paperback edition in the Meridian series by World Publishing Company, Cleveland, Ohio, in 1963.

The Sweetest Rose: *As You Like It* as Comedy of Reconciliation

CHARLES FREY

Laughter has no content. Or, rather, a sense of humor that leads to laughter is its own content. Theories of humor and its mode of expression in comedy tend, therefore, as they attempt comprehensiveness, to become theories of pure form, issuing, most often, in grand generalizations concerning golden means, avoidance of absurdity or of mechanical action, and rules of right proportions; that is, we all know, in one sense, what comedy is about; its content is always the same—love, sex, death, money, class, generational conflict—just as its result is always to expose those who would alter relations that must obtain to foster the huge ongoingness of life. Yet we need comic theory, as well as endless debate about it, because although we know that a sense of humor is somehow a sense of proportion and propitiation celebrating the ongoingness, still we do not know precisely what leads to or underlies it. While some laugh, others stay aloof.

Shakespeare's comedies, however—at least such romantic ones as *Much Ado About Nothing* and *As You Like It*—are supreme among their genre in that they evoke nearly universal laughter. Audiences bring to such comedies varying tastes in humor; yet few individuals remain aloof. Why? What accounts for Shakespeare's power to take us all in? I believe that *As You Like It* delights us partly because it addresses itself so successfully to the very question of individuated versus universal tastes. The play makes us laugh sympathetically at our differences while reconciling them toward common ends such as fellowship and marriage. End and source become one, moreover, in a vision of love as both a mean and means of reconciliation as well as a generative principle of differentiation. In what follows I explore only a few of the varied ways in which Shakespeare makes the substance of his comedy out of reconciling individual and universal tastes.

I

If the play's title is meant to suggest only an inconsequential relativism of tastes, an analogue to *Much Ado About Nothing* or to *What You Will* or to Lodge's remark in his preface to *Rosalynde,* "If you like it, so," then the play means to disarm interpretation in advance. But the title may do more than bow to quirks of individual preference. It may say not merely, "Take it as you like," but also, "This is what you, the collective audience, like." The title may thus hint that the play embraces not only relativism but reconciliation. This sort of ambivalence between or paradoxical union of *like* as differentiated taste and *like* as comparable taste appears in the Epilogue, where Rosalind charges the women in her audience to "like as much of this play as please you" but then charges that *between* the men and women "the play may please." Even if we allow for the pun on *play,* the point is made that there should be room for both individuation and sharing of the pleasure.

I dwell, perhaps too solemnly, upon this point because it hints at the distinctive metabolism of this astonishingly complex drama and its equally complex effect. *As You Like It* affirms the humor of finding that one's likes, though unique to oneself, are nonetheless shared with and thus *like* the likes of others. So trembling and difficult is the balance maintained in this play between individuation and harmonization, between the concrete and the universal, that solemn interpretation can hardly hope to remain as gracefully poised. One is defeated before one starts. One can, however, begin by disengaging from the sorts of approaches to *As You Like It* that stress its discontinuities, its relativity of likings, at the expense of its wholeness; for this is the most persistent mistake made with the play: to find a critic-analytic play that suits, perhaps, a critic-analytic mind.

Some kinds of solemn analysis we cannot take seriously. Consider the British headmaster who published, in 1818, a volume entitled *The Progress of Human Life,* analyzing and praising Jaques's speech upon the seven ages of man as if it were the final summation of human wisdom, noting, for example, how the adjectives applied to the babe "mewling and puking in the nurse's arms" so perfectly describe what the headmaster called the "imbecility" of infancy.[1] This educationist never noted the dramatic context of the speech, the "melancholy" nature of the speaker, or the satiric nature of the seven depictions; yet he felt entitled, delightfully enough, to "correct" the baseless fabric of Shakespeare's theatrical vision by imagining Shakespeare, at the last, pointing raptly to Bible pages promising a new heaven and new earth.

Others would moralize the spectacle of *As You Like It* into quaintly secular terms. Writing on the "descent to sexual realities" in Shakespeare's romantic comedy, a recent critic seeks to praise Rosalind in these terms:

> Emotionally committed to femininity yet sexually experienced in both male and female attitudes, she remains witty and skeptical enough never to be trapped in an inexpedient role. She thus deserves our closest attention as the most successful model for women in Shakespeare.

And the whole play is seen as

> a complex investigation of the interaction of the conscious mind with its emotional drives and the physiological equipment with which it finds itself arbitrarily endowed.[2]

Again, the play is translated out of the theater and converted into a didactic tract. Both the schoolmaster and psychological critic seem objectionably serious about *As You Like It* because they appear, almost, not to "get" the joke or, if they do, to focus upon the tensions of wit and miss the resolutions of humor. They remain too intent upon divisions and dissociations of the play, its analytic processes that, in the full drama, open up a space for connective metaphor and synthesis, providing the initial shock of wit amazed at life's incongruities only to move beyond into the afterglow of humor, the process of accepting and making things even.

A special mode of excessively relativistic analysis threatens the would-be director of *As You Like It*. When "love," so-called, is divided among eight individualized lovers, what hope can there be for unity of focus or judgment? Was not Shakespeare working a piece of dramatic whimsy or at least purposeful ambiguity out of his source novel, such whimsy as digesting the name Saladyne and coming up with the equally oily Oliver, such ambiguity as he made inhere in most of the main characters? Is Duke Senior silly? Or wise? Is Adam comic? Or dignified? Is Touchstone truly central? Is Jaques really melancholy? Is Celia bland? Or vivacious? Is she a vital character in her own right? Or, because present but silent, like Touchstone, much of the time, more of a sardonic chorus, disengaged from the action and helping to distance it for us? Is Orlando a straight man? Or a wit in his own right? Is Rosalind gracious, a gentlelady, not particularly comic, in the style of Helena Faucit? Or maddeningly coy, in the style of Elisabeth Bergner? Or winningly insecure in the style of Vanessa Redgrave? And how is she to divide herself into Rosalind and Ganymede? How much of each role is present in her exchanges with Orlando?[3] However one resolves these questions—and in the theater they must be resolved—one must seek fidelity to the overall progress of the action. The play, after all, does move in a direction. The first scenes are scenes of emptying the stage, and the last are scenes of filling it up. What becomes scattered gathers together again. The relativism is not final.

II

Let us take a closer look. *As You Like It* opens with Orlando's complaints of stifling confinement. Orlando is growing physically, and the spirit of his father, as he says, "grows strong" within him; yet Oliver "stays" him at home and "bars" him the place of a brother, so that he begins to "mutiny against this servitude." To the warring verbal images of growth versus confinement, the play adds the visual images of Orlando physically grappling first with Oliver and then with Charles the Wrestler. One senses that the court is a place of opposed energies grinding against each other until that which is good can gasp free. The second scene parallels the first. Rosalind, in the position of Orlando, enters as he did on the theme of a lost (in her case, banished) father. Celia, in the position of Oliver, establishes by contrast a loving sisterly relation with Rosalind—"I could have taught my love to take thy father for mine." Celia becomes inversely analogous to Oliver when she offers all of her inheritance to Rosalind. The girls then proceed to a friendly grappling of wits as they "devise sports," and the parallel between the two scenes is continued when Celia inquires of the entering LeBeau, "What's the news?", much as Oliver had inquired of the entering Charles, "What's the new news?" As protagonists of the two scenes begin to merge, so do themes. It is facetiously suggested that LeBeau thought wrestling a sport for Rosalind and Celia to engage in, and, after Orlando overthrows Charles, Rosalind and Orlando become mutual champions in the "wrestling" of their affections. The competitive closeness of the court is held before us as Duke Frederick, toward the end of the act, declares his mistrust of Rosalind and argues to Celia:

> Thou art a fool; she robs thee of thy name,
> And thou wilt show more bright and seem more virtuous
> When she is gone. (1.1.76–78)

Shakespeare's dramas, like the bulk of the world's stories, tend to originate in family quarrels, and an almost incestuous overcloseness or excessive interdependence within families is often the motivating force of his comedies and tragedies alike. Says LeBeau, "There comes an old man, and his three sons—"; Celia responds, "I could match this beginning with an old tale."[4] The play itself began by referring to Sir Rowland and his three sons. *King Lear* begins, in the fashion of LeBeau's tale, with an old man and his three daughters. Sibling rivalry, in short, is a prime cause of such drama: a brother or sister (one of which most of us are) seeks not just a superior claim to parental affection but also *differentiation* from siblings, an independent identity and life. We remember the recurrence of Biblical narratives based upon brother rivalries as between Cain and Abel or Jacob and Esau or Joseph and his brothers. *As You Like It* opens with the words, "As I remember, Adam," and the play goes on to suggest an atmosphere from Genesis with its Cainlike rivalry in Adam's garden and with Orlando, who speaks of his father's "blessing" on his brother and then imitates Jacob in leaving his father's house and journeying to a land of shepherds, where he wins his bride as Jacob won Rachel. We find, in addition, overt reference to the Prodigal Son, who was also afflicted with a jealous elder brother; that is, the genial biblicality of the play's opening suggests, without any allegorical strain, a kind of primitive, mythic entanglement of siblings who first wrestle in rivalry until one or more disengages to seek a fortune and, indeed, a separate self out in the "world." In *As You Like It*, initial entanglements provide the urge for the divisions that later dominate.

The chief spectacle of the first portion, the wrestling match, presents an emblem of affairs at the "envious court." A grappling of overclose relations, in which vertical alignment, fall, or overthrow is the issue, suits the themes of brothers' displacements and of falling in love. The court is a little world of fallings and failings presided over by Fortune's wheel, a world in which men like Orlando are not being made but rather marred and men like Charles, the Duke, and Touchstone's knight swear by their nonexistent honor, a world of the "broken music" of rib breaking, in which amity cannot yet replace enmity, in which even Rosalind is counseled to wrestle with her own affections lest she fall for Orlando.

After the wrestling match, we see the central characters uncoiling, as it were, from the envious court out into a wider "world" of Arden forest, the ways of which are to be continually anatomized. In the post-Edenic Arden, explosive energies of the court context are received, absorbed, and filtered through a variety of prisms, so that a wide spectrum of human appetites and conduct is spread forth for general survey. In his speech that opens the second act, Duke Senior sets the style of Arden. His praise of life amid nature's adversities in preference to the "painted pomp" of court is done in the Arden style of confrontation and comparison. The Duke compares and converts the icy fang of biting winter's wind into tongues of talking trees. Nature, which had seemed an all-consuming swallower, turns out to be a redemptive force issuing from sermonic mouths of brooks and trees and stones. Arden encompasses both negative and positive extremes, plus the range between, and it has a habit of converting negative extremes to positive or of suggesting that the negative is but a version of the positive waiting for metamorphosis. Travelers who arrive famished convert their impressive hunger to expressive poetry and song. Even Celia, Touchstone, and Oliver find that what seems at first a bleak desert place changes its character as they revive and change theirs—to lovers. Orlando first feels in Arden the fang of hunger, the "thorny point /Of bare distress" (2.7.95-96), but soon puts poetic tongues on trees or, as Rosalind describes it, "odes upon hawthorns and elegies on brambles" (3.2.352-353). Shakespeare rather harps upon the idea of Touchstone's couplet—"He that sweetest rose will find /Must find love's prick, and Rosalind" (3.2.109-110). The "prick" of love must have its innings *and* its outings.

III

Arden's wit seems at first only explosive, relativizing, analytic, marking out distances between extremes. It is a bit absurd for the Duke to speak of smiling while shrinking with cold, just as it is more than a little absurd for Jaques to moralize the herd of deer into a thousand similes of human ill-fashion. It is the habit in Arden to anatomize the body of the world and, in an excess of emotion, to overdissect and overcompare people, ideas, lives. One thinks of Jaques's seven ages of man, his seven kinds of melancholy, and Touchstone's seven types of lies. But Orlando, too, has the analytic itch, as he devises a "Rosalind of many parts" (compare Phebe marking Ganymede in "parcels"), and Rosalind herself gets constantly at apparent divisions and relativities in life:

> Time travels in divers paces with divers persons. I'll tell you who Time ambles withal, who Time trots withal, who Time gallops withal, and who he stands still withal. (3.2.302-305)

> No, no, Orlando, men are April when they woo, December when they wed. Maids are May when they are maids, but the sky changes when they are wives. (4.1.138-141)

A giddy excess of long pent-up energy seems to engender on every side lists, anatomies, and hyperbolic pilings on. Silvius tells Corin:

> If thou remember'st not the slightest folly
> That ever love did make thee run into,

Thou hast not lov'd.
Or if thou hast not sat as I do now,
Wearying thy hearer in thy mistress' praise,
Thou hast not lov'd.
Or if thou hast not broke from company
Abruptly as my passion now makes me,
Thou hast not lov'd.
O Phebe, Phebe, Phebe!   (2.4.31–40)

Touchstone gives three answering "I remember's," implying an equivalence between the naïve and affected sentimentalism of Silvius and Touchstone's own bawdy cynicism. This sense of equivalence in opposites is caught nicely by Touchstone's later summary:

And so from hour to hour, we ripe, and ripe,
And then from hour to hour, we rot, and rot,
And thereby hangs a tale.   (2.7.26–28)

The distinctive metabolism of the play inheres in its special attitude toward its own constant anatomizing. The style of division, opposition, and confrontation implies, on the one hand, a witty recognition of life's incongruities. But the diversity and relativity continually dredged up are expressed, paradoxically, through unifying devices of repeated phrases, balanced structures, echoing sounds. Making things even far outweighs, in the end, an apparent relativity of preferences. This is a meaning of that wonderful exchange in which Touchstone's relativities of court and country values encounter Corin's stolid unity of view:

COR. And how like you this shepherd's life, Master Touchstone?
TOUCH. Truly shepherd, in respect of itself, it is a good life;
    but in respect that it is a shepherd's life, it is naught. In
    respect that it is solitary, I like it very well; but in respect
    that it is private, it is a very vile life. . . . Hast any philosophy
    in thee, shepherd?
COR. No more but that I know the more one sickens the worse
    at ease he is; and that he that wants money, means, and content
    is without three good friends; that the property of rain is to
    wet and fire to burn; that good pasture makes fat sheep; and
    that a great cause of the night is lack of the sun. . . . (3.2.11–28)

Tautologies of nature render ridiculous man's subjective quibbling over whether the glass is half full or half empty. The four pairs of lovers, in similar fashion, reveal highly diversified styles of love, but all are in love. Shakespeare's comedy builds on the fact that it makes all the difference in the world to the individual lover exactly whom he or she is getting, but it makes very little difference to society. So long as weddings and babies result, society cares almost nothing for the varieties and mix-ups of particular loves. And so the play celebrates, beyond the diversity of those who gather in Arden, the general dance of their gathering.

IV

It is true that *As You Like It,* like all drama, is founded upon conflict, and in clashing attitudes toward court and country and in clashing romantic and unromantic attitudes to love lies much of the wit of the play. But critics, more adept at discussing tensions of wit than syntheses of humor, tend to overstate the final place of conflicts in *As You Like It.* One critic would make of Arden a "bitter Arcadia" in which men and women long to escape burdens of sex roles for return to a mysterious fount of androgynous godhead. Another critic would have us see Rosalind as motivated by a "will to dominate." The play, we are told, "focuses on the mating dance of a masterful female round her captive male," and "virtually all the relationships manifest a sense of unease, of latent or open hostility."[5]

To pretend, however, that the play leaves us with satiric wit debate is as perverse as to find that its great achievement is in depicting seven ages of man. No more can the relationships and debates be fixed in static opposition than can life be fixed in seven stages. Though, as Celia says, "it is as easy to count atomies as to resolve the propositions of a lover," this is a play, finally, not about the incorrigible divergence and shifting of likings, but about the possibility of harmonizing them. As a central image of the play's opening portion is the circle of partisan spectators around the locked wrestlers, so the recurring visual image of the central portion is the circle of foresters enjoying song. All of the songs are dialectical in that, on the one hand, against leisure and love they admit rough weather and faithlessness, but, on the other hand, they are all occasions for merriment. That Jaques can find melancholy in the merry notes of the first song only authorizes us to find merriment in his parody that calls "fools into a circle." Despite winter, feigning friendships, and foolish loves, the songs insist, "this life is most jolly."[6] Even the song of the deer-hunters (4.2), which suggests that all men must fear the horns of cuckoldry, is a song of celebration; the burden of love's metamorphoses can be borne without laughing the life force to scorn. The only real enemy recognized in the play is divisive time, which measures the lateness of lovers for their meetings and renders life "but a flower." Still, our counsel is to "take the present time" and its gifts of renewal. Lovers can still love the spring.

When Orlando throws down Charles, Duke Frederick shouts, "No more, no more." But the awareness of more, of all the possibilities of repetition and flowering increase, dominates the play. The characters display engaging appetites for excess. All Arden is ardent, greedy for an unending more. Thus Jaques approves the song of Amiens:

> More, more, I prithee more.
> AMI. It will make you melancholy, Monsieur Jaques.
> JAQUES. I thank it. More, I prithee more. I can suck melancholy out of a song, as a weasel sucks eggs. More, I prithee more. (2.5.9-13)

The word *more* is used more often in *As You Like It* than in any other Shakespearean comedy.[7] It is as if the characters, emerging from cramped quarters of court or winter, would find, in terms of Duke Senior, "more pageants than the scene wherein they play in." Says Rosalind-Ganymede to Orlando:

> I will be more jealous of thee than a Barbary cock-pigeon over his hen, more clamorous than a parrot against rain, more new-fangled than an ape, more giddy in my desires than a monkey.
> (4.1.141-145)

The play seems in its overall tone to be serenely delighted with every excess. Celia, the laughing victim of Rosalind's "petitionary vehemence" to know if it's Orlando she has seen, responds:

> O wonderful, wonderful! And most wonderful wonderful!
> And yet again wonderful! And after that out of all whooping.
> (3.2.188-190)

But the play never is out of whooping.

In *As You Like It,* rhetorical figures of repetition and structural elaborations of set themes are so pervasive as to constitute a distinctive and indelible style. Rosalind, of course, loves to say the same thing in varied ways: "Is his head worth a hat? Or his chin worth a beard?" (3.2.201-202), or: "What said he? How looked he? Wherein went he?" (3.2.216-217). In order to answer Rosalind "in one word" as demanded, Celia asks for "Gargantua's mouth." In truth, it is Rosalind who has, in the play, the mouth of Gargantua. No one can or would want to still her fondness for euphuistic elaboration. When Orlando politely inquires, "Who ambles Time withal?", Rosalind answers:

> With a priest that lacks Latin, and a rich man that hath not the gout, for the one sleeps easily because he cannot study, and the other lives merrily because he feels no pain; the one lacking the burden of lean and wasteful learning; the other knowing no burden of heavy tedious penury. (3.2.313-318)

The special music of *As You Like It* is this habit of mildly or wildly varying a single theme: "sleeps easily"—"lives merrily," "because he cannot
study"—"because he feels no pain," "lacking the burden"—"knowing
no burden," and so on. Editors are uncertain whether to set many of the
speeches as prose or verse. This is a play wherein they are variations of
a single impulse, a play filled with refrains and burdens. Orlando asks
Rosalind for the marks of a lover, and she replies:

> A lean cheek, which you have not; a blue eye and sunken, which
> you have not; an unquestionable spirit, which you have not;
> a beard neglected, which you have not. . . . (3.2.363–366)

Rosalind tells Phebe to take Silvius:

> Cry the man mercy, love him, take his offer;
> Foul is most foul, being foul to be a scoffer. (3.5.61–62)

The refrains and burdens have a way of drawing attention to the common
theme within, a way of suggesting that a tautology lurks at the base of
relativity. All eight lovers, no matter how apparently diverse their natures
and attitudes, are in love. A rose is a rose is a rose is a rose.

But we do not want simply to behold the unity of human desires.
As You Like It continues to mean, "Take it as you like it, according to
your individual preferences," as well as, "This is as everyone likes it;
this is the common denominator that pleases all tastes." Touchstone
may even mock the play's propensity to say in many ways only one thing.
As he takes Audrey away, he tells William:

> To have is to have: for it is a figure in rhetoric that drink,
> being poured out of a cup into a glass, by filling the one doth
> empty the other. For all your writers do consent that *ipse* is
> he. Now you are not *ipse*, for I am he.
> WIL. Which he sir?
> TOUCH. He sir that must marry this woman. Therefore you
> clown, abandon—which is in the vulgar leave—the society—
> which in the boorish is company—of this female—which in the
> common is woman. . . . I will bandy with thee in faction; I
> will o'er-run thee with policy; I will kill thee a hundred and
> fifty ways. (5.1.39–56)

Elegant, empty variation may bespeak a monochromatic mind. Again
we have Touchstone closing the scene with a stutter: "Trip Audrey,
trip Audrey. I attend, I attend)) (5.1.62).

Even Rosalind's love of elaboration flows from her singleness of
purpose. Cupid, she says, was "begot of thought, conceived of spleen
and born of madness." Her force of elaborative imagination stems from

fecund love and is a way of defining such love. She opens up a space for desires to play in, a space in which to metamorphose the close wrestling into broad measure of the dance. Her expansive energies lift the mind of the play from obsessive focus upon a single envious space to the variety and spaciousness, yet also the connectedness, of diverse lives. As she says of her own intellect:

> The wiser, the waywarder. Make the doors upon a woman's wit, and it will out at the casement; shut that, and 'twill out at the keyhole; stop that, 'twill fly with the smoke out at the chimney.
> (4.1.152-156)

No wonder that Rosalind is Shakespeare's most talkative woman. Beatrice, in comparison, speaks some 2,400 words, a mere 11 percent of her play; and Viola is in much the same position. Helena and Portia rise to the totals of 3,600 and 4,600 words, respectively. Even Cleopatra in her infinite variety only speaks 4,700 words, less than 20 percent of her play's total. But Rosalind speaks some 5,700 words, almost 27 percent of all those in the play. (She speaks, moreover, in excess of 1,300 different words. It is not surprising that Orlando seems a trifle bland in comparison with his relatively restricted stock of 700.[8]) Rosalind needs to speak enough and waywardly enough to turn the polarities of the play in a circle. As Ganymede she tells Orlando:

> I will weep for nothing, like Diana in the fountain, and I will do that when you are disposed to be merry. I will laugh like a hyen, and that when thou art inclined to sleep. (4.1.145-148)

Rosalind teaches Orlando to see that what seems arbitrary in love may betoken the constant pressure of love's impulse and its desire to respond to the kaleidescopic amplitude of life.

Once the relativity of liking and the liking of relativity are well established in the play, then the underlying unity of human nature is adduced:

> PHEBE. Good shepherd, tell this youth what 'tis to love.
> SIL. It is to be all made of sighs and tears,
>   And so am I for Phebe.
> PHEBE. And I for Ganymede.
> ORL. And I for Rosalind.
> ROS. And I for no woman. (5.2.82-86)

Diverse lovers chant a single verse. Shakespeare hints at this natural perspective in his overlapping use of names in the play: two Fredericks, two Olivers, two Jaques. All are convertible—psychically, religiously. One's analogues abound. A clown, Touchstone, meets a clown, Corin, and another clown, William. An apparently hypothetical "old religious uncle" materializes as an "old religious man" in Arden forest. Those critics who take too seriously the wit of the play, its patterns of opposition, confrontation, and relativity, are like those who might throw up their hands in surprise upon meeting their double, but never extend their arms for a humorous embrace. Difference remains more real, more precious than sameness; the shocks of wit overpower the sympathies of humor.

The final pleasure of *As You Like It* does not reside simply in the space opened up for metaphors and behaviors of incongruity, but rather in a harmonization of disparate impulses, in strangers' meetings becoming lovers' matings. As our perspectives open out, we become aware of hidden sympathies and correspondences. "Then," said Aristotle, describing one source of comedic pleasure:

> since that which is according to nature is pleasant, and kindred things are natural to each other, all things akin to one and like one are pleasant to one, as a rule—as man to man, horse to horse, youth to youth; whence the proverbs: "Mate delights mate"; "Like to like"; . . . and so forth.[9]

This is the view that makes earthly things even and gathers them together in order and delight. In *As You Like It*, the vertically aligned wheel of Fortune, alluded to in the first act, yields to the horizontal circle of the final dance, where likes join likes in Arden's own sanctifying circle.

V

If some critics, then, speak too solemnly of *As You Like It*, it is because they choose to remain in realms of incongruous wit, because they find more to say about satire, ridicule, and the unromantic than they have to say about humor, sympathy, and romance. The wheel of fortune and the odds for high and low provide ready material for the discursive intellect, but what's to say about a dance? This is not to deny that, in a variety of ways, other interpreters have recognized the basic health of the play, the way it reconciles opposing positions, assimilates disparate and relativistic views into a commonalty. We have been shown how classical and Christian perspectives are combined, how reassurance underlies the perturbation, how a comprehensive philosophy emerges from the cross-qualifyings, and how the play gives to raw energy and even outrage a transforming elegance and beauty.[10] But rarely, if ever, is enough stress given to the diachronic drive of the play as opposed to its supposedly synchronic structure of ideas.

Nor will it do to say that Shakespeare gives us humor, as opposed, say, to Jonsonian satire.[11] Shakespeare moves us by moving *from* satire *to* humor. There is plenty of satire in *As You Like It.* We have to accept the presence of the unromantic sniping at the romantic, of the thorn as well as the rose. Shakespeare added to Lodge's story the complex invectives and abrasions of Jaques and Touchstone for a reason. We need to look for the drama of the play, its going from the seemingly incommensurate and relative to the all-likes and from like as quirky preference to like as shared pleasure. The process, the dramatic process and progress of finding sympathetic common denominators within apparently hopeless diversity, of finding human connection among wholly individual preferences—this is the gist of it. And it is why this mild, often bland, serene, supremely gentle play finally calls forth such stunning claims from some interpreters. It works, they say, a conversion of the will; it alters perspectives; it truly changes us.[12] Does not the play indeed hint at a largeness of effect, a kind of conversion? The charmed circle of the forest offers escape *and* salvation. Its denizens, we recall, "have with holy bell been knoll'd to church." Its "heavenly Rosalind" was devised by "heavenly synod." She claims a religious uncle and proves she can conjure even as the god Hymen can. The forest's powers to convert an Oliver and offer a "monastic" nook to such as Duke Frederick and Jaques are not the greatest of its wonders, for Orlando becomes as much the new Adam (bearing the old) in Arden as he was Hercules at court. When he sheds his falsely romantic self-concern, when he tames the "green and gilded snake" and finds "kindness, nobler ever than revenge," then Rosalind can cease to counterfeit. After melding their Petrarchan, pastoral, fleshly, and prideful loves into versions of marriageable love, the couples to be wed are like enough, as Jaques says, to be couples "coming to the ark." Though all have chewed the "food of sweet and bitter fancy," all commit themselves to wed and thus to find a single "blessed bond." By the end of *As You Like It,* a society has matured and not only matured but become, perhaps like the society of the audience before it, much more likable.

VI

Shakespeare's way with *As You Like It* depends for its success upon our regaining a measure of confidence in life's beneficent wholeness. We enter the theater immersed in local strivings, our heads buzzing with sociopolitical trivia of who's in and who's out. Shakespeare seems willingly to begin his play in the same environment of Fortune's City. But he drives us away from fortune into nature, from relativities of rank and luck toward happy glimpses of teleological harmonies. Busy plotting and intellectual machinations aimed at atomistic gains give way to quieter resolutions of fellowship and song. Thus it is not surprising that the same critic who notes a "curious stillness at the heart of the play" also notes a "subordination of plot in the traditional sense to an intricate structure of meetings between characters, a concentration upon attitudes rather than action."[13] Characters, moreover, who are realistically English in type and manner, who are often victims of Fortune and butts of wit, seem at first unsuited to the nearly idyllic natural settings to which they come, but Shakespeare "softens" the humor, shades the bright light of wit, favoring gentler emotions of contentment rather than the "ebullition of outward merriment."[14] In *As You Like It,* despite the range of characters, action, and language, we achieve a serene vision of continuing blessings; we reach a source and end, a reason for going on. There is in Arden "a timeless world beset by time" where "voices of maturity" counsel just perspectives on human folly and promote a willingness to proceed with the major businesses of life.[15]

It has been suggested that, though "Shakespeare had no comic theory," a kind of teaching, a comic morality, is to be found embedded "in the whole substance of his comedies."[16] A combined questioning and acceptance throughout Shakespeare of overarching purposes in life accords well with the ethos of his comedy. In his Preface of 1765, Samuel Johnson defends Shakespeare's powers of "exhibiting the real state of sublunary nature" in which "many mischiefs and many benefits are done and hindered *without design.*" A few lines later, however, Johnson refers to "the successive evolutions *of the design.*"[17] Therein lies, surely, one key to the secret of Shakespeare's comedy. He makes us muse: How can the seemingly undesigned fit a design? How can mistake and folly seem so embraceably happy? How can chance be so choice? And how is it that we may achieve "a point of view in which love is known for its absurdity, and yet retained with laughing certainty at the centre of human experience . . ."?[18]

Because, lastly, love and its discontents are at the center of Shakespearean and probably most other comedy, comic theory involves, inevitably, social theory. The question is often: Who deserves to propagate and thrive? And in what style? It has been argued that English Renaissance theorists applied a class concept of decorum in assigning comedy to the common errors of the meaner sorts of men.[19] Such comedy, one might conclude, will celebrate, even as it attempts to purify, the great coming on of the middle class. In part, it does. But Shakespeare, in *As You Like It* and elsewhere, elevates his comedy, dramatizing romance and the fortunes of its nobility. He favors, in his late comedies particularly, plots in which generational succession is threatened: a Prince or Duke appears unlikely or disinclined to marry (*Twelfth Night, All's Well, Measure for Measure*), or the King or Duke has or appears to have only female issue (*As You Like It, Pericles, Cymbeline, Winter's Tale, Tempest*), so that special, nearly symbolic, prominence is accorded marriage as guarantor of societal continuity. The central marriage, moreover, often requires nobility to marry beneath itself or at least to entertain the offered fallacy that it is so doing. Each "crisis of degree" is solved in its own way, but always the result is to remind audiences that, in and through marriage, the varied powers of class and sex may be made more even and, in the phrase of Hymen in *As You Like It,* may "atone together."[20] Through such means as these, Shakespeare makes his comedy of reconciliation remarkably complete.

NOTES

1. John Evans, *The Progress of Human Life: Shakespeare's Seven Ages of Man: Illustrated by a Series of Extracts in Prose and Poetry. For the Use of Schools and Families: With a View to the Improvement of the Rising Generation.* (Chiswick: Charles Whittingham, 1818), p. 43. *As You Like It* is quoted from the new Arden edn. of Agnes Latham(London: Methuen, 1975).

2. Hugh M. Richmond, *Shakespeare's Sexual Comedy: A Mirror for Lovers* (Indianapolis: Bobbs-Merrill, 1971), pp. 138, 145.

3. Some of these problems are usefully discussed by, among others, Agnes Latham, Intro. to Arden *AYL,* pp. lxix-lxxxii, and John Russell Brown, *Shakespeare's Dramatic Style* (New York: Barnes & Noble, 1971), pp. 82-94. On Helena Faucit's Rosalind, compare Helena Faucit Martin, *On Rosalind* (Edinburgh: Wm. Blackwood, 1884), and Charles H. Shattuck, *Mr. Macready Produces As You Like It; A Prompt-Book Study* (Urbana, Ill.: Beta Phi Mu Chapbook 56, 1968), pp. 55-57. Elisabeth Bergner's performance may be seen in the 1936 film produced by Paul Czinner. Vanessa Redgrave's Rosalind may be heard on the recording by the Royal Shakespeare Company (Caedmon 210).

4. An old tale such as the fourteenth-century romance of *Gamelyn,* which contributed to Lodge's source story as well as to legends of Robin Hood.

5. For the notions of "bitter Arcadia" and desires for androgyny, see Jan Kott, *Shakespeare Our Contemporary,* trans. Boleslaw Taborski, rev. ed. (London: Methuen, 1972), pp. 217-236. The unromantic Arden of hostile competitiveness is that of Ralph Berry, *Shakespeare's Comedies: Explorations in Form* (Princeton: Princeton Univ. Press, 1972), pp. 175-195. See also James Smith, *Shakespearian and Other Essays* (Cambridge: Cambridge Univ. Press, 1974), pp. 1-23.

6. "In the songs of Shakespearean comedy, the grimmest facts of human experience are transmuted by the lyric art, relegated to their proper place in the natural scheme of things, and thereupon dismissed, their sting having been drawn." Cyrus Hoy, *The Hyacinth Room: An Investigation into the Nature of Comedy, Tragedy, & Tragicomedy* (New York: Knopf, 1964), p. 37.

7. I exclude romances, such as *Cymbeline* and *The Two Noble Kinsmen.* See Marvin Spevack, *The Harvard Concordance to Shakespeare* (Cambridge, Mass.: Belknap Press, 1973).

8. See Marvin Spevack, *A Complete Concordance to the Works of Shakespeare* (Hildesheim: Georg Olms, 1968), Vol. 1.

9. Lane Cooper, *An Aristotelian Theory of Comedy* (New York: Harcourt, Brace, 1922), p. 137.

10. On classical and Christian perspectives in the play, see Richard Knowles, "Myth and Type in *As You Like It,*" ELH, 33 (1966), 1-22, and René E. Fortin, " 'Tongues in Trees': Symbolic Patterns in *As You Like It,*" *Texas Studies in Literature and Language,* 14 (1973), 569-582. Reassurance amid perturbation is Alfred Harbage's general concept of As They Like It. See *Shakespeare and the Rival Traditions* (1952, rptd. Bloomington: Indiana Univ. Press, 1970), p. xiii. Harold Jenkins, "As You Like It," *Shakespeare Survey,* 8 (1955), 45, and Latham, op. cit., p. lxxxv, *inter alia,* get at larger views engendered of contradictions. See also David Young, *The Heart's Forest: A Study of Shakespeare's Pastoral Plays* (New Haven: Yale Univ. Press, 1972), esp. pp. 71-72. On elegant outrage, see E. M. W. Tillyard, *The Nature of Comedy and Shakespeare,* The English Asso. Presidential Address, 1958 (London: Oxford Univ. Press, 1958), pp. 14-15. To critics impressed with the play's religious dimension must be opposed one who sees "nothing in it of our relation to powers supra-human—nothing of astral determinism, nothing of

any divinity. . . ." Warren Staebler, "Shakespeare's Play of Atonement," *Shakespeare Association Bulletin,* 24 (1949), 103. David Young, *Heart's Forest,* p. 71, says: "*As You Like It* is, in fact, almost all style"; Warren Staebler, 105, says there is "little playing with words and no playing with words solely for the play as in other comedies." Yet a recent critic insists with regard to *As You Like It:* "Readers may differ among themselves as to the exact tone of the play, but the areas for interpretive disagreement are small." Michael Jamieson, *Shakespeare: As You Like It* (London: Edward Arnold, 1965), p. 68.

11. The opposition of Jonsonian satire and Shakespearean humor is a commonplace. See Helen Gardner, "As You Like It," orig. in *More Talking of Shakespeare,* ed. John Garrett (London: Longmans, Green, 1959), rptd. in *Twentieth Century Interpretations of As You Like It,* ed. Jay L. Halio (Englewood Cliffs, N.J.: Prentice-Hall, 1968), p. 58, referring to Nevill Coghill's well-known essay "The Basis of Shakespearian Comedy" in *Essays and Studies* 3 (1950). 1–28. Compare Willard Smith, *The Nature of Comedy* (Boston: Gorham Press, 1930), pp. 146–167, and esp. p. 166. Dover Wilson, *Shakespeare's Happy Comedies* (London: Faber & Faber, 1962), pp. 21–23, says that Shakespearean comedy lacks social criticism. Allan Rodway, *English Comedy* (London: Chatto & Windus, 1975), p. 98: "Generally speaking, Shakespeare seems to promote integration with nature, Jonson with society. In the one a *sharing* is offered, in the other a *warning.* Shakespeare relies not on one comic view, but on a comic sense of relativity. Consequently he creates characters whom one may laugh *with,* who are funny in themselves. . . ." See also Elder Olson, *The Theory of Comedy* (Bloomington: Univ. of Indiana Press, 1968), p. 89.

12. Tillyard, *The Nature of Comedy and Shakespeare,* p. 15: "For all its apparent ease no play of Shakespeare includes more or masters its content more magnificently." To Albert Cirillo, "*As You Like It:* Pastoralism Gone Awry," *ELH,* 38 (1971), 39, *As You Like It* suggests an ideal that "can only exist in the impetus for a conversion of the will that lets us see things, not necessarily as we like them, but as they should be, and as they are." For David Young, *Heart's Forest,* pp. 71–72, the play offers its audiences a "remarkable widening of judgment, a new tolerance," something close to an "Olympian amusement and understanding." Notice that none of these testimonials suggests much of a call to action. Sixteenth-century theory of comedy was, to be sure, didactic, but it was not really incitory. Thomas Lodge saw the intent of comedy to be praise of God as well as the "'imitation of life, the mirror of custom, the image of truth.'" (From Lodge's *Defence of Poetry* (1579) as quoted in Marvin Herrick, *Comic Theory in the Sixteenth Century* (Urbana: Univ. of Illinois Press, 1950), p. 223.) Yet it has been well argued that comedy, concerned as it is with formal limits, tends to be more revolutionary than tragedy. See James Feibleman, *In Praise of Comedy: A Study in Its Theory and Practice* (London: George Allen and Unwin, 1939), p. 200.

13. Anne Barton, " 'As You Like It' and 'Twelfth Night': Shakespeare's Sense of an Ending," in *Shakespearian Comedy,* Stratford-upon-Avon Studies 14, ed. Malcolm Bradbury and David Palmer (London: Edward Arnold, 1972), p. 162.

14. In this sentence, I am following Allardyce Nicoll, *An Introduction to Dramatic Theory* (New York, Brentano's, 1923), pp. 178–179.

15. For the idea of "voices of maturity" in *As You Like It,* see R. A. Foakes, 'The Owl and the Cuckoo: Voices of Maturity in Shakespeare's Comedies," in *Shakespearian Comedy,* p. 124.

16. Kenneth Muir, "Didacticism in Shakespearean Comedy: Renaissance Theory and Practice," in *Review of National Literatures,* 3 (1972), 52.

17. *Samuel Johnson on Shakespeare,* ed. W.-K. Wimsatt, Jr. (New York: Hill and Wang, 1960), p. 29 (emphasis supplied).

18. G. K. Hunter, *Shakespeare: The Later Comedies* (London: Longmans, Green, 1962), p. 32, referring to *As You Like It.* M. A. Shaaber, "The Comic View of Life in Shakespeare's Comedies," in *The Drama of the Renaissance: Essays for Leicester Bradner* (Providence: Brown Univ. Press, 1970), pp. 176–177: "Shakespeare's comic view of love is based on the acceptance of it—on the acceptance of all of it, its component of folly as well as its component of glory." As William Empson puts it, speaking of love's truth and feigning in *As You Like It,* in *Some Versions of Pastoral* (1935, rptd. New York: New Directions, 1968), p. 139: "Two ideas are united which in normal use are contradictory, and our machinery of interpretation so acts that we feel there is a series of senses in which they could be more and more truly combined."

19. Vernon Hall, Jr., *Renaissance Literary Criticism: A Study of Its Social Content* (New York: Columbia Univ. Press, 1945), pp. 180–185.

20. On the "crisis of degree" in Shakespeare, see René Girard, "Levi-Strauss, Frye, Derrida, and Shakespearean Criticism," *Diacritics,* 3 (1973), 34–38. In Shakespeare's pastoral romance, particularly, we find the move from Fortune's City to nature an escape in part from a patriarchally dominated world to one in which women such as Rosalind, Marina, Imogen, Perdita, and Miranda are enabled to gain a more independent footing and to assert upon other court expatriates an influence that redeems nature and restores civility. Shakespeare's later comedy thus shares with much of his tragedy (*Lear, Othello, Macbeth, Antony and Cleopatra*) the theme of lusty proud, martial male ego confusing and humbling itself through woman's love, but at the same time rising to a higher nature and civility.

PART 4

CONTEMPORARY
COMEDY:
STOPPARD-WILDE,
BEHRMAN,
AND
CANDY

12

Travesties and the Importance of Being Stoppard

COPPÉLIA KAHN

In an interview given shortly before the premiere of *Travesties* (1975), Tom Stoppard said he was trying to contrive "the perfect marriage between the play of ideas and farce or perhaps even high comedy" and compared *Travesties* to his previous play *Jumpers* (1972) as "a serious play dealt with in . . . farcical terms."[1] It is this paradoxical mixture of the serious and the comic that also distinguishes *The Importance of Being Earnest* (1895). Oscar Wilde enters *Travesties* not merely through the historical curiosity of Joyce's involvement in a production of his finest play in Zurich during World War I. Rather, in style and substance— and for both Wilde and Stoppard, style is substance—*Travesties* is closely allied to Wilde's aesthetic and to *The Importance of Being Earnest* in particular. By interweaving his play with Wilde's, Stoppard gains more than jokes, travesties, shifts of perspective, and a rudimentary plot. Through the constant evocation of Wilde's drawing-room world of high wit, Stoppard mirrors his own conception of art as play. To see what he is saying about art in *Travesties,* we need to turn back for a moment to *The Importance of Being Earnest* and to notice its subtitle: "A Trivial

Comedy for Serious People."

The play has often been understood and applauded as a satire of Victorian solemnity and earnestness. Eric Bentley points to "the contrast between the elegance and savoir-faire of the actors and the absurdity of what they do," calling it "a fact of sociology and history."[2] Undoubtedly, the play can be read as social satire consistently and with pleasure. Algernon's seriousness about meals and the calmness with which muffins should be eaten; Lady Bracknell's preference for ignorance, that delicate exotic fruit whose bloom must not be touched, over education; Gwendolen's insistence that Algernon follow convention and propose to her on his knees even though she has already confessed that she loves him passionately—throughout the play Wilde seems to depict a society that confuses tenacious adherence to ritual and tradition with real feeling, knowledge, and belief. Victorian social life, he seems to be saying, is the opposite of what it pretends to be; it is mere posturing with nothing really earnest behind it.

But a reading of *The Importance of Being Earnest* mainly as satire that sets out to criticize social reality for being based on pretense and artifice seems at odds with Wilde's avowed beliefs. As is well known, his critical writings preach the idea that art not only has no direct connection with nature or social reality but is by definition superior to it. "Art never expresses anything but itself," he says, meaning that it doesn't hold the mirror up to nature or chronicle the age, and "the only beautiful things, as someone once said, are the things that do not concern us," that have no practical use and no social import.[3] His longest, most ambitious essay, "The Critic as Artist: With Some Remarks upon the Importance of Doing Nothing" (1890), puts forth in logical argument the same views of art that *Earnest* presents indirectly in the form of high comedy. Cast as a dialogue between two immensely overeducated young men, Gilbert and Ernest, and set in "the library of a house in Piccadilly, overlooking the Green Park," at many points it echoes the witty paradoxes of Jack and Algernon (particularly when Gilbert, Wilde's mouthpiece, declares, ". . . we are born in an age when only the dull are treated seriously, and I live in terror of not being misunderstood").

Seriously enough, in this essay Wilde argues at some length that because Life, "being terribly deficient in form," is a failure from the artistic point of view, "it is through Art, and through Art only, that we can realize our perfection." It is not the artist alone, but also and equally the critic, who realizes this perfection, through his contemplation of art. From the viewpoint of "that practical organization of life that we call society," the critic does nothing but cultivate himself as an exquisite sounding board of impressions gleaned from art.

> For emotion for the sake of emotion is the aim of art, and emotion for the sake of action is the aim of life. . . . Society, which is the beginning and basis of morals, exists simply for the concen-

tration of human energy, and in order to ensure its own con-
tinuance and health stability it demands of each of its citizens
that he should contribute some form of productive labour to the
common weal, and toil and travail that the day's work be done . . .
while, in the opinion of society, Contemplation is the gravest
sin of which any citizen can be guilty, in the opinion of the highest culture it is the proper occupation of man.[4]

Algernon and Jack are the comic versions of Gilbert and Ernest, the
critics who exist to do nothing at all, which Wilde calls "the most difficult thing in the world." As Algernon says, "It is awfully hard work
doing nothing. However, I don't mind hard work when there is no definite
object of any kind." Instead of contemplating Aristotle's *Poetics,* Turner's paintings, or Ruskin's prose as Gilbert and Ernest do, they contemplate Gwendolen and Cecily or cucumber sandwiches and Belgrave
Square, and they do so in the serious spirit of pure play that is the social
equivalent of the critic's sublimely disinterested cultivation of art. As
Johan Huizinga points out in his brilliant study of the idea of play, *Homo
Ludens,* the readily posited opposition between the playful and the serious is, in fact, neither conclusive nor fixed. Though playing is specifically separate from real or serious life, though it is "pretending" and
"just for fun," within its own sphere play itself proceeds seriously,
according to rules, spatial and temporal limits, conventions: "play demands order, absolute and supreme." Play is superfluous; it has no
biological or material purpose, though it may take on cultural functions
in rite or ceremony. But though it is fundamentally opposite to all that
is rational, purposeful, and socially functional, therein lies its peculiar
value and meaning; it is useful in its uselessness, an activity desired
only for itself, like Wilde's art for art's sake.[5]

Wilde conceived his comedy as a demonstration of paradoxes that
define life as play:

> It is exquisitely trivial, a delicate bubble of fancy, and it has
> its philosophy. . . . That we should treat all the trivial things of
> life seriously, and all the serious things of life with a sincere
> and studied triviality.[6]

Algernon's declaration, "Well, one must be serious about something, if
one wants to have any amusement in life," is indeed serious, for to separate the serious from the trivial in Wilde's play is to violate its nature.
He means the sincere and studied triviality with which his characters
approach marriage and muffins, handbags (with or without handles)
and parentage to be no less trivial for being studied and no less serious
for being trivial. Life for Gwendolen or for Jack is an elaborate series of
profoundly deliberate and artificial poses demanded by well-established
conventions and rituals. As such, it is analogous to play, and, as play,

it is like art itself as Wilde conceived it. In his view, it is not important to be earnest—to tell the truth about life or oneself—but to be Ernest; to create, if necessary by lying, an artificial identity, attitude, or style that serves no rational end but only expresses some personal vision (such as a preference for the name Ernest) and thus improves upon reality.

One of Wilde's major essays, "The Decay of Lying" (1889), boldly sets forth the idea that "lying, the telling of beautiful untrue things, is the proper aim of Art." Wilde's liar is like his artist, in that he imagines and creates for the sheer pleasure of it, without regard to self-interest, truth, or social utility. Style, the essence of art, is the artist's lie about nature, his distortion, exaggeration, or misrepresentation of it; and the liar is the social equivalent of the artist and "the very basis of civilized society" who knows that "truth is entirely and absolutely a matter of style."[7] Style in dress, manners, and conversation is that art that any man or woman may practice—a disinterested, useless, purposeless but supremely well-ordered sort of play, seriously trivial.

STOPPARD AND THE MODE OF TRAVESTY

For Stoppard, the literary mode of the travesty is a similarly serious— and funny—sort of play, with styles, with the visions they express, with ideas of art and its relation to society. The word *travesty* comes from *trans-vestire,* "to change clothes"; in sixteenth-century French and Italian usage, it meant disguise, the staple comic device, that may involve the audience as well as the characters in a game of guessing who is who. In the literary sense, *travesty* means to clothe a character or situation from a known literary work in the "dress" or style that specifically makes it ridiculous or grotesque, that debases it. The gamelike or play element is retained, for the reader or audience must guess what author, style, or genre is being travestied in order to get the comic point.[8]

It is a travesty to place Wilde's decorous, perfectly upper-class and artificial drawing-room comedy characters amidst the actual revolutionary ferment of Zurich in 1917, eccentric and foreign as it is, and equally a travesty of the real historic importance of Lenin, Joyce, and Tzara to mix them up in the farcical confusions of Wilde's courtship plot. (The real Tzara, of course, set out to travesty Western culture in its totality; so he cannot be said to be travestied in the same sense as the others.) Of the characters in Stoppard's play, only Lenin and Nadya are allowed to retain their identities and points of view consistently; the others shift into various verbal costumes, changing their identities by changing their speech.

One form of verbal identity not only contradicts but also mocks another in successive travesties. For example, after Carr's opening monologue as his elderly self, he turns into his Wildean younger self, civilly conversing with his butler, as does Algernon with his in the opening scene of *Earnest,* and echoing Algernon's witty aphorisms. Tzara then makes his entrance, announced as "Mr. Tzara" and speaking the lines Wilde wrote for Jack but in a Rumanian accent approximating the real Tzara's, thus travestying Wilde's exquisite English speech. After opening pleasantries modeled on Wilde's, Carr and Tzara fall into a discussion of art in which Carr represents the Wildean viewpoint ("It is the duty of the artist to beautify existence") and Tzara, the dadaist ("It is the duty of the artist to jeer and howl and belch . . ."), but, like Carr's memory in his monologues, the train of conversation jumps the rails frequently, running out of Wilde's drawing room into rough terrain. Tzara abandons logical discourse to chant "articulately" "Dada dada dada . . ." and Carr abandons polite speech for gutter invective: "My God, you little Rumanian wog—you bloody dago—you jumped-up phrase-making smart-alecy-arty-intellectual Balkan turd!!!"[9]

Stoppard's travesties of style are, of course, inseparable from his travesties of ideas in the erratic and explosive debate on art running through the play. In general, conversations about art in Act I question its validity or seriousness in the context of World War I, whereas those in Act II question it similarly in relation to another cataclysm, the Russian Revolution. Both these political events, costing countless lives and shattering the pieties on which European culture had been based, serve to put the question to art in the bluntest possible form: what right has it to exist when men are dying by the millions and whole societies are turning upside down?

In the first discussion between Carr and Tzara (from which I have just quoted), Tzara leads off in typical dadaist fasion by claiming that the war has destroyed all belief in the traditional values on which rational arguments for civilization have been based. Dada exists partly to make this plain by travestying all forms of rational or artistic expression in this now specious and debased civilization. As antiart, it is thus the only true art. Carr counters with a breathtaking claim, "Wars are fought to make the world safe for artists"; art is the capstone of "civilized ideals" and the cause for which the war is being fought. Tzara replies with a travesty of historical causality, purporting to show that the war began because the heir to the throne of Austria-Hungary attempted to circumvent a ridiculous bit of royal protocol by riding through Sarajevo side by side with his wife. Suddenly, the whole debate collapses as Carr slips into the traditional soldiers' lyric, "We're here because we're here because we're here," voicing the utter futility of justifying the war in a mindless, gaily helpless acceptance of it, while simultaneously Tzara chants "dada," the credo of his position. The two sides of the argument have joined and become indistinguishable.

In their next conversation, Carr utterly reverses himself and lashes out against "the idea of the artist as a special kind of human being," whereas Tzara disarmingly defends the artist as "the priest-guardian of the magic that conjured the intelligence out of the appetites." But then he turns this argument on its head, too, for art has now been corrupted by paymasters and patrons, and the artist paints only to eat—and shit. Thus: "Without art man was a coffee-mill, but *with* art, man—is a coffee-mill! That is the message of Dada—dada, dada dada..." It is now impossible to tell whether dada stands for the supremacy of art or the negation of art or, paradoxically, for both.

Round three begins with a set-to between Tzara and Joyce in the most obstreperous statement so far of the clash between dada and an orthodox conception of art as the Holy Grail of civilization. Tzara smashes crockery to symbolize the destruction of the temple of art, moving Joyce to a paean that tersely evokes the power of art to transform and eternalize the ephemera of life. Not surprisingly, he chooses the same example as Wilde uses to illustrate a similar point in his essay "The Critic as Artist," the Homeric epic. "What now of the Trojan War if it had been passed over by the artist's touch? Dust," says Joyce, and Wilde offers a prose poem recreating the whole Homeric world, concluding

> Phantoms, are they? Heroes of mist and mountain? Shadows in a song? No: they are real. Action! What is action? It dies at the moment of its energy. It is a base concession to fact. The world is made by the singer for the dreamer.[10]

Joyce rests his case on a typically boastful claim for his own version of the *Odyssey,* which he states with a crucial distinction: "Yes, by God *there's* a corpse that will dance for some time yet and *leave the world precisely as it finds it.*"

Like Wilde, Stoppard implies here that any comparison between action that effects a change in the real world and art that creates an imaginary world is inappropriate. It is perfectly true that art makes no difference, and that is the only argument for its continued existence. Though Joyce is made to exit from this encounter drawing a rabbit from his hat, in a parody of his own statement "An artist is the magician put among men to gratify—capriciously—their urge for immortality," when Stoppard brings the first act curtain down, he vindicates Joyce's boast. Carr evokes the last moments of his fantasied legal victory over the Irish nuisance:

> I dreamed about him, dreamed I had him in the witness box, a masterly cross-examination, case practically won, admitted it all, the whole thing, the trousers, everything, and I *flung* at him— "and what did you do in the Great War?" "I wrote *Ulysses,*" he said. "What did you do?"
> Bloody nerve.

Carr's conviction that he did something better by fighting is, of course, a comic irony. Joyce's art lives on, whereas Carr, the consular nonentity, survives only through the grace of Stoppard. The first two stages of the debate involved playful reversals and inconclusiveness. In this finale, affirming the sublime indifference of the artist to social action, Stoppard abandons his neutrality for the moment and stands by an art that flouts social imperatives and exists only for itself "to leave the world precisely as it finds it."

The debates of Act I are intensely agonistic. Though they begin as debates, observing the rules of logic and polite social intercourse, they soon turn into flytings—exchanges of personal abuse between two poets attacking each other, scurrilous and vulgar. As agons, however, they are inherently playful, that is, devoid of purpose save for the purpose of argument itself. The spokesmen exchange positions capriciously, or their opposing viewpoints collapse in identical nonsense. No points are firmly won; no questions, resolved. Stoppard simply maintains the pleasurable uncertainty and tension of the contest, without allowing it to become so serious that we want it to be settled, until the Act I curtain, when he comes temporarily to a *point d'appui.* The play actually concludes with Carr suggesting a perpetual agon continuing the debate:

> I learned three things in Zurich during the war. I wrote them down. Firstly, you're either a revolutionary or not, and if you're not you might as well be an artist as anything else. Secondly, if you can't be an artist, you might as well be a revolutionary ...
> I forget the third thing.
> *(Blackout.)*

As Huizinga demonstrates through a wide range of examples, primitive social life "normally rests on the antagonistic and antithetical structure of the community itself," revealed in summer-winter combats; heroic contests of strength, skill, and bravery; or contests of words—bragging and scoffing matches. Such agonistic games are at once a basic structure of social life and a typical form of play.[11] Thus, in form as well as content, Stoppard's play mirrors play itself.

In Act II, Stoppard adopts an altogether different strategy from that in Act I. In the driest historical prose, all connectives in strict logical order and no puns, Cecily lectures on the inception of the Russian revolutionary movement. This solemnity is shortly travestied by the resumption of the plot of *The Importance of Being Earnest,* but it reenters the play in Nadya's account of Lenin's flight from Switzerland and his responses to art as man and as revolutionary. Stoppard's treatment of Lenin is consistently respectful of historical fact; in the published text of *Travesties,* he states, "Nearly everything spoken by Lenin and Nadezhda Krupskaya herein comes from his Collected Writings and from her *Memories of Lenin.*" He is also quite explicit in the stage directions for the scene in which Lenin outlines the role of literature in revolutionary society, describing the "much reproduced photograph" of Lenin addressing a crowd in a public square in May 1920 and specifying that his Lenin on-stage should resemble it as much as possible. The question arises of why Stoppard should depict Lenin with such conspicuous seriousness and fidelity to history when no other character escapes incessant comic metamorphosis and mockery. (For a brief moment, it might seem that the actual Lenin provides his own travesty, when Nadya quotes his letter instructing a comrade to find two Swedish deaf-mutes resembling him and Zinoviev to lend them their passports for the proposed trip to Russia.) Broadly, Stoppard wants to give reality, society, historical fact, social action, and earnestness, as opposed to Wildean "Ernest-ness," their full measure here, in order to strengthen by stark contrast his own romp-ing and irreverent revision of cultural history. He underlines this dis-tinction between the two realms, which he has mingled freely before, in the staging:

> (The corner of the Stage now occupied by Tzara and Carr is independent of the Lenins. It can no longer be said that the scene is taking place "in the Library." Carr and Tzara might be in a café; or anywhere.)

Thus, Lenin's most important moments in the second act, his speech about literature and his confession of music's power over him, are frozen in historical truth; and the remaining brief exchanges between Carr and Tzara float free even from the putatively real setting of Zurich.

More specifically, the actual Lenin embodies that conflict between artistic freedom and social necessity that Stoppard sees as essential to art, a conflict expressed in the great disparity between Lenin's hectoring, predictably ideological speech, and his candid, heartfelt confession Staged as an enactment of the "justly famed image" of Lenin addressing a crowd, the speech is written in an Orwellian doublespeak of isms, in which freedom for literature means party control of it:

> We want to establish and we shall establish a free press, free not simply from the police, but also from capital, from careerism, and what is more, free from *bourgeois anarchist individualism!* These last words may seem paradoxical or an affront to my audience. Calm yourselves, ladies and gentlemen! Everyone is free to write and say whatever he likes without any restrictions. *But* every voluntary association, including the party, is also free to expel members who use the name of the party to advocate anti-party views.

On the other hand, when Lenin describes his response to music and his ambivalence about that response, he uses simple, passionate language:

> I don't know of anything greater than the Appassionata.

Amazing, superhuman music. It always makes me feel, perhaps naively, it makes me proud of the miracles that human beings can perform. But I can't listen to music often. It affects my nerves, makes me want to say nice stupid things and pat the heads of those people who while living in this vile hell can create such beauty. Nowadays we can't pat heads or we'll get our heads bitten off. We've got to hit heads, hit them without mercy, though ideally we're against doing violence to people . . . Hm, one's duty is infernally hard.

Although Lenin excludes art in the traditional or bourgeois sense from the revolution, he himself is moved by it. He prefers Pushkin to Mayakovsky, respects Tolstoy's "traditional values as an artist" while criticizing his political views, and is moved to tears by *La Dame aux camélias* and Beethoven. His poignant renunciation of the pleasure art gives restates Stoppard's main point: if art's nature and purpose can be defined at all, they exist wholly apart from social utility, of which they are usually subversive. A highly theatrical, sentimental moment, with Beethoven's sonata played in the background, Lenin's speech makes us aware of art's social costs, of how, from the revolutionary point of view, it co-opts and forestalls social justice.

In Act I, Tzara the Rebel and Carr and Joyce the Traditionalist opposed each other; in Act II, a more ironic confrontation takes place between the two rebels, Tzara and Lenin or, more precisely, Cecily as Lenin's convert and Carr as an intelligent commentator on his ideas. Cecily's simple and unequivocal quotations of socialist doctrine, "The sole duty and justification for art is social criticism. . . . Art is a critique of society or it is nothing!" seem to make a place for dada in the revolution, dada with its determination to smash the bourgeois rationalism and elitism supporting art at all levels. Tzara touchingly assumes that "artists and intellectuals will be the conscience of the revolution," believing that even though Lenin "is a reactionary in art . . . he is moved by a vision of a society of free and equal men." The dadaist imagines a society in which artists will be free to pursue the same kind of irrational, antisocial, anarchic play that he is devoted to. Interestingly enough, at this point the consciously barbarous dadaist becomes allied with the Wildean aesthete, for both demand total freedom for the artist to pursue his own ends and assume tacitly that society owes him a living, though at the same time they conceive that his aims subvert social purpose and organization. Even Carr knows better than that and repeats a point he made in Act I: Tzara as an artist is "an amiable bourgeois," member of a privileged class whose "work" produces no material benefits for society; whose work, in materialist terms, is play. Lenin in his own voice dashes Tzara's hopes at the same time as he touches on the common ground shared by dada and the revolution:

> We must say to you bourgeois individualists that your talk about absolute freedom is sheer hypocrisy. . . . The freedom of the bourgeois writer, artist or actor is simply disguised dependence on the money-bag, on corruption, on prostitution.

The revolutionary and the dadaist both oppose bourgeois privilege, but the revolutionary insists that art become "a cog in the Social Democratic mechanism," whereas the very soul of dadaism is its rejection of socially defined meaning or purpose for art, its insistence on total freedom not to define itself at all.

Stoppard's view of art as civilized play, the necessary counterweight to what is real or serious in a social sense, lies somewhere between these two. In *Travesties,* he argues that art must always be at counterpurposes with society or it is not art. Consequently, any one conception of its status in society can never be endorsed because it will then become co-opted for some social purpose and cease to be art. When Carr tells Tzara, "I don't think there'll be a place for Dada in a Communist society," Tzara replies, "That's what we have against this one. There's a place for us in it." Thus though Stoppard insistently poses the question of the social role of art, he refuses to answer it. He mocks Joyce's Homeric high priest of art and Tzara's barbaric yawper and Lenin's "cog in the Social Democratic mechanism" with equal gusto and wit.

Travesties, however, actually has two endings, the inconclusive one just described and another that travesties it and is itself a travesty, in which the conflict between art as social critique and art for art's sake is mirrored and resolved in the mocking convolutions of Wilde's farce. Instead of Miss Prism leaving the baby in the handbag and putting her manuscript in the perambulator, we have Tzara and Carr mixing up the identical folders given them by Cecily and Gwendolen, one containing a chapter from Joyce's *Ulysses* and the other a chapter from Lenin's book on imperialism. When the heroes express their scorn for these texts, they alienate the heroines. Of course, the trivial mistake is soon discovered and the lovers reconciled, so that the play can end in the ancient comic way with a festive dance celebrating imminent marriages, betokening the smooth integration of dadaist and Marxist views into proper. society. Thus Stoppard lets us have our cake and eat it too.

Certainly, to a great extent, all Stoppard's plays play with ideas, raising questions without answering them. As he says:

> . . . There is very often *no* single, clear statement in my plays. What there is, is a series of conflicting statements made by conflicting characters, and they tend to play a sort of infinite leap-frog. You know, an argument, a refutation, then a counter rebuttal, so that there is never any point in this intellectual leap-frog at which I feel *that* is the speech to stop it on, *that* is the last word.[12]

But in *Travesties,* the medium of the debate is its message, part and parcel of what he means to say about art. The puns; the collages of historical, farcical, and fantastical action; the shifts of spokesmen, adversaries, contexts, and styles convey his central proposition that art must be uninhibited, speculative, purposeless play.

NOTES

1. The editors, "Tom Stoppard: Ambushes for the Audience: Towards a High Comedy of Ideas," *Theatre Quarterly,* May-July 1974, p. 7.
2. Eric Bentley, *The Playwright as Thinker* (New York: Harcourt Brace, 1946), p. 177.
3. "The Decay of Lying" from *Intentions* (1891), in *The Artist as Critic: Critical Writings of Oscar Wilde,* ed. Richard Ellmann (New York: Random House, 1968), pp. 299, 313.
4. "The Critic as Artist" from *Intentions* (1891), in Ellmann, pp. 380-381.
5. Johan Huizinga, *Homo Ludens: A Study of the Play Element in Culture* (Boston: Beacon Press, 1955). See especially pp. 1-13. In "Homo Ludens Revisited," Jacques Ehrmann criticizes Huizinga for assuming a given "reality" in relation to which he defines play. Ehrmann contends, "To define play is *at the same time and in the same movement* to define reality and to define culture" (*Game, Play, Literature,* ed. Jacques Ehrmann [Boston: Beacon Press, 1971], p. 55). He mounts a convincing and balanced critique of Huizinga, whose work I have cited as the *locus classicus* of thinking about play. Both Wilde and Stoppard, I believe, share Huizinga's assumption of a prior, given, external reality against which play is defined and appreciated.
6. Interview with Robert Ross, *St. James Gazette,* January 18, 1895; quoted in Hesketh Pearson, *Oscar Wilde: His Life and Wit* (Harmondsworth: Penguin, 1960), p. 178.
7. "The Decay of Lying," pp. 320, 305.
8. See the *OED* and C. Hugh Holman, *A Handbook to Literature,* 3rd ed. (New York: Odyssey Press, 1972).
9. This and all following quotations are taken from the Grove Press paperback edition of *Travesties* (New York, 1975).
10. In Ellmann, p. 362.
11. Huizinga, pp. 53, 65, but see Chapter Three, "Play and Contest as Civilizing Functions."
12. *Theatre Quarterly,* p. 7.

13

Clearings in the Jungle of Life: The Comedies of S. N. Behrman

CYRUS HOY

Critics of American drama of the 1920s and 1930s regularly pay tribute to Behrman's efforts to write high comedy in unpropitious times. His best plays were produced over a period of a dozen years, from *The Second Man* in 1927 to *No Time for Comedy* in 1939, and, true to their comic function, mirror the manners and the mores of a changing world, from the height of Coolidge prosperity through the Great Depression and increasing political tension both at home and abroad to the eve of World War II. No American dramatist has had a finer sense of comedy as "the ultimate civilizer" (in Meredith's phrase)[1] than Behrman, and he lived in times that tested its civilizing powers to the full. The four plays that he wrote in the mid-1930s—*Biography* (1932), *Rain from Heaven* (1934), *End of Summer* (1936), and *Wine of Choice* (1938)—are attempts to extend the range of social critique and commentary native to comedy into ever widening issues of contemporary political life, where the clase of individual freedom with totalitarian authority of both rightest and leftist varieties was fast coming to a head.

The quality of Behrman's achievement in these plays varies sharply, from the notable success of *Biography* to the conspicuous failure of *Wine of Choice;* and the record speaks for the problems that beset a dramatist seeking to affirm the civilizing power of comedy as the political situation in the late 1930s worsened. Nonetheless, before the end of the period, Behrman was to have one word more on the subject and in *No Time for Comedy* composed a brilliantly witty and cogent affirmation of the value of the comic spirit even in (indeed, most especially in) a time of world crisis, and on this note the period of his most creative work for the stage closed. What follows here is a survey of Behrman's plays during the twelve years that comprise this period. The plays are very much an *oeuvre,* the product of a single and distinctive dramatic vision; and each gains from being considered in the context of the others. They have long been absent from the stage, they are not much read today, but they deserve to be remembered for both the individual excellencies of single plays and their collective testimony to a humane and intelligent playwright's attempt to mirror the complexities and the anxieties of modern society in one of the most traditional of dramatic forms.

BEHRMAN AND THE 1920s

The Second Man (produced by the Theatre Guild in April 1927) was Behrman's first stage success, and it is very much a product of the prosperous, materialistic 1920s. Though it lays the groundwork for much that will come later in his work, he never wrote another play quite like it. It has for its central figure one Clark Storey, and its New York setting is his apartment in West Fifty-sixth street. He is a writer of sorts; he would like to marry the rich and immensely attractive Mrs. Kendall Frayne, a widow of thirty-five (he is thirty-one); and she is quite prepared to marry him. The play's principal complication comes from Monica Grey, age twenty and poor, who also wants to marry Storey, even though Storey's friend, a brilliant and quite rich young scientist named Austin Lowe, longs to marry her. Though he finds Monica attractive, Storey has no intention of marrying her because he finds Mrs. Frayne and her money more attractive. He is quite frank about this. Monica seeks to appeal to his better nature. "I want you to live up to the best that's in you," she tells him near the end of Act I, and she continues: "You ought to marry me for the sake of your art. If you marry Mrs. Frayne you'll be so comfortable you won't write a thing."[2]

This, in fact, is what Storey has freely admitted to Mrs. Frayne when she attempted to take a similar line with him earlier in the scene:

> KENDALL. Storey—outside of being in love with you—I'm
> very fond of you. I feel such fine things in you. If only you
> wouldn't waste yourself so, if only you'd make the effort to
> live up to the best in you— (p. 12)

But he has told her not to be fooled, that he is living up to the best in himself right now, that she is not to have illusions about his ability to do great work, that his talent is for pottering and he knows his limitations and has no craving for immortality: "When I'm rich—when I'm married to you—I probably shan't write at all. I'll be—what I've always wanted to be—a prosperous dilettante" (p. 12). Moreover, he assures her, when she wonders if he is joking, if this is a pose, that he is perfectly serious: "At least you can't say afterwards that I married you under false pretences. I tell you now I'm an adventurer—intellectually and morally—an *arriviste* with one virtue—honesty" (p. 13).

This last is not an artful claim: he is entirely honest, and the comedy's fineness resides in large part in the absolutely unblinking capacity for self-scrutiny with which Behrman has endowed this, his principal character. The dramatic metaphor for this capacity is contained in the title of the play, which Behrman found in a passage in the correspondence of the painter Lord Leighton and which he quotes at the head of the play's published text (and quoted as well in the program in the threater):

> For, together with, and as it were behind, so much pleasurable emotion, there is always that other strange second man in me, calm, critical, observant, unmoved, blasé, odious.

The title comes into prominence in the first scene of Act II when Monica, by now presumably engaged to Austin, comes to Storey. He is strongly tempted by her, he tells her he loves her, but he also tries to put her off:

> STOREY. I am old, dearest one.
> MONICA. Old! You're not.
> STOREY. I am. There's someone else inside me—a second man—a cynical, odious person, who keeps watching me, who keeps listening to what I say, grinning and sophisticated, horrid. He never lets me be—this other man.
> MONICA. Kill him.
> STOREY. I can't kill him. He'll outlive me.
> MONICA. (Nestling to him) I'll kill him for you.
> STOREY. You can't. Even now he's looking at me. He's mocking me. He's saying: "You damn fool, talking nonsense to this girl—pretending you want her above everything. You're making love to her because words come easily to you. But really you wouldn't get up early in the morning for her. You like to touch her because she's young and firm and lovely—"
> MONICA. Don't Storey.
> STOREY. "You wouldn't mind having her but after that—"
> MONICA. Storey, listen, darling. I know you're fine and decent.
> STOREY. He hears you say: "I'm fine and decent." And he says: "The illusion of an adolescent, of a love-struck girl—"

MONICA. I'll beat him, Storey—I'll beat him.

STOREY. I wish you could, honey.

MONICA. I just needed to know that you love me—tell me it again. Let me hear you say it again.

STOREY. I love you.

MONICA. The way you said it before.

STOREY. I'm afraid I can't now.

MONICA. Storey—

STOREY. You see how capricious I am.

MONICA. But you just said it. And when you did I knew it was true.

STOREY. It probably was—then. (pp. 47-48)

Monica persists in her delusion that marriage to her will be Storey's salvation as an artist and a man. Determined to snare him for his own good and her satisfaction, she announces to him, Austin, and Mrs. Frayne that he is the father of her unborn child. Storey's denial avails him nothing. Mrs. Frayne renounces him indignantly ("I did think, Storey, that you observed *some* code"—p. 65), and Austin is torn between fury at the betrayal by his friend and heartbreak at the loss of his beloved. Alone together at the end of Act II, Monica has a short-lived sense of triumph:

> I won't let you go, Storey, I'm going to fight for you—I'm going to bring you back—to what you were—to that youth you've let go. It's your one chance now, Storey—your last desperate chance —don't you see, Storey? (p. 66)

She refers to "the idealistic stage" through which, as he has told her earlier, he once passed:

> I used to sit in a garret and believe in Socialism, I used to commit realistic fiction and moonlit poetry. I dreamed— (p. 50)

But Storey does not want to go back to the way he was in a period that, as he has already made clear to Monica, he cannot contemplate without a shudder. Monica's rapt gaze is fixed on the vision of the "fine way" she and Storey might live, with him giving over his pampered ways and "standing up straight on [his] own feet" (p. 67), whereupon Storey proceeds to tear the scales from her eyes and present her with his own vision of their future:

> I can see us now—five years from now—in a cheap flat—you looking blowsy—with little wrinkles under your eyes—and I in cheap shirts and cracked shoes—brooding in a room over the corpse of my genius. (p. 67)

He has succeeded in disillusioning her by the end of Act II, and her disillusionment persists into the morrow of Act III.

> MONICA. I'll never be in love with you again, Storey. I'm sure. It's over. It's dead. . . . I see myself—all this time I've loved you—like a person looking from outside, a very old person. I see a little girl, a rather stupid little girl, reading a fairy-tale and believing it true—long after the other children knew it to be a lie.
> STOREY. I always told you your idea of me was an idealisation.
> MONICA. But I never believed it—till last night. Last night I saw you as you really are—mercenary and unadverturous and—practical. (p. 79)

Austin and his simplicity seem to Monica infinitely preferable to Storey and his emotional complexities, and fortunately Austin will still have her. They go off together, leaving Storey alone to reassemble his own future. Mrs. Frayne has earlier declined to believe Monica when she has confessed that her story about Storey and her unborn child has been a lie; Mrs. Frayne has announced her intention to forget Storey by taking a trip to Europe. Storey is talking with her on the telephone as the play ends:

> God, Ken, I've never known you so stubborn—in common justice you ought to take me back on probation until Austin and Monica—that's the very least you can do—and, Kendall, I promise you—I absolutely promise you—that if their baby—if their baby bears the *slightest* resemblance to me—thank God, Kendall, you're laughing—what?—no, why should you?—keep your passport and I'll get another—of course—I can write as well in Europe as I can here—even better—no, I've got a better idea—you cancel your passage and we'll go the Southern route—oh, yes, lovely this time of the year—land at Naples and motor to Nice—certainly—along the Riviera—beautiful trip—
> *(The descending curtain cuts short his itinerary)* (p. 84)

The situation is retrieved, and this is as it should be, for Storey does not deserve to have his prospects permanently undone. He is not a cad or a blackguard. Behrman has very deftly managed to show him as a civilized man who recognizes the need to pretend that life is more pleasant than it is, who sees a responsibility to contribute his small measure to its gaiety. Most suffering, he says, comes about as the result of "unintelligent people who want things beyond their limitations" (p. 78). Storey fully knows his limitations and is prepared to live with them. Nonetheless, just before the end, there is or can be "a terrible moment" when Storey suddenly realizes how much his acknowledgment of his limitations is costing him. Behrman has written of Alfred Lunt's performance in the original production.

> Just before the curtain fell I saw an element in the play which
> I had not written, certainly not consciously; the dramatization of
> a terrible moment, a watershed moment, when you face nullity.
> The nonhero has been abandoned by the older woman who loves
> him and by the young woman whom he, had he been less prac-
> tical, might have loved. He has just seen the younger woman
> out the door. My stage direction reads: "He leaves the door,
> goes to the telephone." That walk, that walk from the door to
> the telephone, shafted a light on the play and the character which
> I had not foreseen. It was a moment of self-confrontation, of
> complete awareness. Why hadn't he taken a chance? Why
> hadn't he tested himself? Perhaps he was better than the
> louse he knew himself to be? Alfred's eyes, when he picked up
> the telephone to get back what he didn't want, went insane.[3]

BIOGRAPHY AND A MELLOWED BEHRMAN

The Second Man is the most formally perfect play Behrman ever
wrote and the one that has the strongest ties with the classic tradition of
English comedy. The plays of the Behrman canon that immediately
followed it exhibit no advance on its technical mastery or any deepening
of its comic insights; in fact, they reveal a good deal of uncertainty as to
where the dramatist would proceed from his first stage success. *Meteor*
(1929) tells the implausible story of the rise and fall of a financial wizard.
Serena Blandish (1929) has a certain wispy charm but little dramatic
coherence. A dramatization of Enid Bagnold's novel, it appears, with
the knowledge of hindsight, an ominous foreshadowing of the later
stages of Behrman's career, when his powers of dramatic invention seem
to have run dry and he could only adapt other people's work to the stage.
Brief Moment (1931) is the real link between *The Second Man* and Behrman's plays of the 1930s. It tells of the marriage of an immensely rich,
cultivated but aimless young man to a vibrant, if slightly vulgar, nightclub singer and of her readiness to adapt herself to all that is most mere-
tricious in his social milieu. The subject is promising, but it cannot be
said that Behrman endows it with much dramatic life. It presents what
was clearly intended to be a varied cast of characters: the sybaritic friend
and confidant of the young man, conceived in the spirit of and acted in
the flesh by Alexander Woollcott; the young man's socialite sister; the
bootlegger with a criminal record but a heart of gold in whose speak-
easy the singer has come to fame and who continues to watch over her
like a father though he would marry her if she would have him; the polo-
playing cad who has once betrayed her and, now that she is prominently

married, appears in her life again. But Behrman can think of remarkably little for these characters to do, and *Brief Moment* amounts finally to nothing more than the kind of domestic comedy of marital misunderstanding referred to in its title: a brief moment of irritation between husband and wife that resolves itself with blissful ease. It hints hardly at all at Behrman's future efforts to widen and deepen the range of the social criticism in his comedies. From time to time, the hero of *Brief Moment* is heard expressing a sense of sophisticated malaise at the uselessness of the life he leads and voicing his desire to engage himself in purposeful activity; he considers going to Russia to view the social and political experiment there (thereby bearing witness to the general interest in the affairs of the Soviet Union that became ever more marked in the United States as the Great Depression deepened). But *Brief Moment* is, finally, a lightweight play that hardly prepares one for the rich gaiety and mellow wisdom of Behrman's next play, *Biography*.

The New York setting of *Biography*, like that of *The Second Man*, is an artist's studio in the West Fifties; but the artist of this later play, the painter Marion Froude, unlike dilettantish Clark Storey, is a celebrated, not to say slightly notorious, figure of world renown. She hails originally from Knoxville, Tennessee, but has long since left that place behind her and gone on to more stimulating regions. The half-formed intention to go to Russia, expressed by Roderick Dean in *Brief Moment*, is but one measure of the tentativeness of that play as compared with the purposefulness of *Biography* and its heroine. Marion has already been there, having gone "before the popular emigration set in" (p. 120); she has painted all the leaders of the revolution; and Russia has been only one stop in a busy itinerary that has also included a sojourn in Vienna, where she has had a tender affair with a now deceased composer. Early in the play there is a charming scene between Marion and the dead man's brother, also a composer, who stops off in New York to see her en route to Hollywood, whither he has been summoned by a movie mogul who has mistaken him for his more famous brother. This helps to establish something of Marion's cosomopolitan past, and the cause of dramatic exposition is furthered even more by her next visitor, Leander Nolan, known to her (once she recognizes him) as Bunny: a figure out of the Knoxville past, where they were childhood friends and adolescent lovers. Now a successful lawyer, he is about to run for election to the United States Senate and to marry the daughter of a powerful newspaper publisher who is also his strongest backer in his political race. Behrman's use of Nolan and of the Kinnicotts, father and daughter (who make a prominent appearance in the last act) contributes vitally to the play's comic effectiveness. They are the provincials who stumble incongruously into a society they do not understand and for which they feel a strong instinctive disapproval and yet which they find fascinating (in the last act, Behrman does a nice job of characterizing the daughter's response: to her, Marion is a revelation whose example she would like to emulate). Bunny Nolan's response to Marion, who terminated their teen-age affair with an abruptness he can never forget or entirely forgive and whose subsquent career he fears has been promiscous, is complicated by fear stemming from a new development. Marion has been commissioned to write her biography for publication in a popular weekly magazine, and Bunny is concerned lest her account of their past relationship compromise his political career. In a tone that Behrman's stage direction designates as "sepulchral," Nolan announces to Marion that she "must give this up" (p. 138).

> MARION. I've met distinguished men abroad—politicians, statesmen—a Prime Minister even—and this kind of "revelation"—as you so luridly call it, is no more to them than a theme for after-dinner banter. They take it in their stride. My God, Bunny, you take it so big!
> NOLAN. These people I'm depending on to elect me aren't sophisticated like you or me. (Marion looks at Nolan with some surprise) What I mean is—they're country people essentially—my future father-in-law is sympathetic to their point of view. (pp. 138–139)

And now we find that Behrman has a new detail for us concerning Kinnicott, the future father-in-law. "Is he," asks Marion innocently, "the man with the chest-expansion?"

> NOLAN. He's a fine sturdy man—as you perhaps know, he makes a fetish of exercise.
> MARION. You see his pictures in shorts in Health Magazines.
> NOLAN. There's no disgrace in that.
> MARION. It doesn't shock me, Bunny. I was just identifying him, that's all. (p. 139)

She is distressed at the moral prig Bunny has turned into. She strokes his arm in a gesture of sympathy; but he, all too vulnerable to her charms, recoils with a "Don't touch me!"

> MARION. You bewilder me—
> NOLAN. (Bitterly) I'm not surprised I bewilder you. You've spent your life among a lot of foreign counts. It's well known that foreigners are more immoral than we are. (pp. 139–140)

In the clash of cosmopolitanism with provincialism, the side of cosmopolitanism is aided, not altogether disinterestedly, by Richard Kurt, the editor who has originally approached Marion with the suggestion that she should write her biography. He is an intense young man of twenty-five, a left-wing radical who, in his way, disapproves of Marion as much as Bunny does. He finds her trivial, frivolous; in one particularly outspoken moment, he calls her "a second-rate artist who's acquired a reputation through vamping celebrities to sit for [her]" (p. 148). He finds her "superficial and casual and irresponsible," inclined to "take life, which is a tragic thing, as though it were a trivial, bedroom farce" (p. 148). Nonetheless, for all his assertions of contempt for Marion and her works, when Bunny Nolan's future father-in-law exerts his influence on the editor in chief of Kurt's magazine and word goes out to kill Marion's biography, Kurt is galvanized with an unholy zeal to see it published at all costs. Marion is calmly bemused at all the furor over her "poor little biography" (p. 148), whereas Kurt is spoiling for the chance to "make the Honorable Nolan the laughing stock of the country and his athletic father-in-law too" (p. 148). And in a superb scene at the end of Act II, Behrman, joining the issue between them, joins the issue between comedy and satire. Marion, the elder by some ten years, has been fascinated by Kurt from the outset and has tried to gain his confidence. She asks him now: "Why won't you tell me about yourself? What are you after?" (p. 150) He answers:

> My ambition is to be critic-at-large of things-as-they-are. I want to find out everything there is to know about the intimate structure of things. I want to reduce the whole system to absurdity. I want to laugh the powers that be out of existence in a great winnowing gale of laughter. (p. 150)

"An interesting research," says Marion, adding, however: "Of course it strikes me it's vitiated by one thing—you have a preconceived idea of what you will find. In a research biased like that from the start you are apt to overlook much that is noble and generous and gentle" (p. 151). Kurt replies that he has found little enough of these qualities in his life, and, at Marion's urging, he tells his story: it turns chiefly on his memory, as a child of fourteen, of a Sunday morning walk with his father, a coal miner: a strike is in progress; an organizer is making a speech; the militia arrive; a shot is fired, and the father is killed. Having now told his story, Kurt tries to make light of it. In a tone "hard and ironic" (according to Behrman's stage direction), he says to Marion:

> It's trivial really. People exaggerate the importance of human life. One has to die. The point is to have fun while you're alive, isn't it? Well, you've managed. I congratulate you! (p. 152)

Marion bids him be silent, and the second act ends in their embrace.

But they are not destined for each other. In Act III, Kurt, like some Alceste, is railing at Marion for her tolerance of Kinnicott during the visit from him that has just ended. She who has seemed so "fastidious and exacting" is suddenly found to be gross and indiscriminating (p. 173). This prompts Marion to a melancholy reflection on her lover:

You know, Dickie, I adore you and I'm touched by you and I love you but I'd hate to live in a country where you were Dictator. It would be all right while you loved me but when you stopped— (p. 173)

Kinnicott and Nolan and all that they represent drive Kurt to a fury; Marion merely finds them amusing. She has allowed them to believe that she will not publish her controversial biography because she has wanted to avoid a scene.

> KURT. You can't always avoid scenes. That's the trouble with you—you expect to go through life as if it were a beautifully lit drawing-room with modulated voices making polite chatter. Life isn't a drawing-room—!
> MARION. I have—once or twice—suspected it. (p. 174)

Left alone, Marion, a la Hedda Gabler, seats herself before the stove and burns the manuscript. When Kurt returns, she tells him what she has done and why and why their affair is over:

> Your hates frighten me, Dickie. These people—poor Bunny, that ridiculous fellow Kinnicott—to you these rather ineffectual, blundering people symbolize the forces that have hurt you and you hate them. But I don't hate them. I can't hate them. Without feeling it, I can understand your hate but I can't bring myself to foster it. To you, this book has become a crusade. It couldn't be to me. (p. 179)

Moreover, she confesses to him that there was nothing about Bunny in her book that anybody would ever have recognized. Kurt is delighted to hear it: "So much the better—! Think of the spectacle they'll make of themselves—destroyed by laughter" (p. 180). But Marion does not "believe in destructive campaigns": "outside of the shocking vulgarity of it all—I couldn't do it for the distress it would cause" (p. 180). Kurt denounces her weakness. He sees now why everything is the way it is:

> Why the injustice and the cruelty go on—year after year—century after century—without change—because—as they grow older—people become—*tolerant!* Things amuse them. I hate you and I hate your tolerance. (p. 180)

To this Marion can only reply: "You hate my essential quality." She would like to change him, but to change him would be to destroy what makes her love him. He leaves; Marion is left alone; she finds a telegram that has been delivered in her absence; it is from her Viennese friend, summoning her to Hollywood. He can get her a commission to paint the portraits of the motion picture academy award winners, and she is off as the curtain falls.

COMEDY IN THE FACE OF BARBARISM

Comedy, says Meredith in his essay on the subject, "is the fountain of sound sense," and "the higher the comedy, the more prominent the part [women] enjoy in it"; "comedy lifts women to a station offering them free play for their wit, as they usually show it, when they have it, on the side of sound sense."[4] *Biography* is the first of Behrman's plays to be built around the figure of a magnanimous, sensitive, and superbly civilized woman who presides over it like some incarnation of the mediating spirit of comedy. Such figures are the rational beings who must somehow find a way between the shrill and potentially destructive indignation of Alcestes like Kurt, and the bigots and the boors like Nolan and Kinnicott who incite that indigation. Derision is never part of the equipment of these figures; to laugh folly out of countenance is left to would-be satirists like Kurt. Women such as Marion Froude in *Biography* and Lady Lael Wyngrave in *Rain from Heaven* and Leonie Frothingham in *End of Summer* cope with the world's imperfections by means of their imaginative sympathies, their enlightened generosity of temperament and spirit. But as the world political situation deteriorates in the 1930s, Behrman the dramtist is faced with the problem of keeping the civilizing power of comedy operative in the face of an increasing barbarism. The problem is evident in his next play, *Rain from Heaven,* where the civilizing power of comedy is strained to its utmost limits.

What Bunny Nolan and his future father-in-law, Kinnicott, were to *Biography,* Hobart Eldridge and his younger brother, Rand, are to *Rain from Heaven:* in each play we are presented with a pair of provincials—one romantically attracted to the heroine, the other a man of powerful political influence—who make their incongruous way into the heroine's enlightened domain, which they do not understand and of which they profoundly disapprove. But the provincialism and the bigotry on exhibit in *Rain from Heaven* are far more sinister than anything apparent in *Biography* (though the roots were doubtless there), and this as much as anything else bears witness to the extent to which the prospects for human liberties had dimmed in the two years that separated the New York opening of *Biography* on December 12, 1932, and of *Rain from Heaven* on Christmas Eve in 1934. Hobart Eldridge is an American millionaire who would like to join forces with a lord of the British press in the formation of a Fascist league of Anglo-American youth. His brother, Rand, is an Antarctic explorer who has recently returned from an expedition to a hero's welcome in New York. From his ticker-tape parade up Fifth Avenue he has rushed to England to propose marriage to his friend, the widowed Lady Lael Wyngrave. It is her domain that the Americans enter: Rand comes to her country house for a visit, and Hobart follows to keep an anxious eye on his brother. He has plans for using his brother's heroic image in his crusade against communism and decadence; and he fears lest Rand, who is a political naïf, should fall under the influence of Lady Wyngrave, whose political sentiments are notoriously liberal. Hobart views her with dark suspicion, the darker because in his eyes she is a traitor to her class. Her late husband edited a left-wing newspaper "which her money supported and *still* supports":

> HOBART. It's communistic! That's what gets on *my* nerves—
> a woman of her class—whose fortune has been built up by a
> lot of hard-working manufacturers, supporting the *Clarion*—
> a Liberal weekly that's very dangerous—that wants to destroy
> the system that gives her her income. A woman of fine family
> whose father was knighted for war work, who might have her
> house full of the best people, surrounding herself with a lot
> of riff-raff.
> RAND. I don't see any riff-raff.
> HOBART. You will if you stay here— (p. 193)

For a man in Rand's position, with his reputation, to marry Lady Wyngrave, Hobart tells him portentously, "would be like Lindbergh marrying a young Emma Goldman!" (p. 197)

Rand at the moment is less concerned with Lady Wyngrave's politics, which he does not take seriously, then with her morals; like Bunny Nolan in the presence of a woman of acclaimed sophistication, Rand fears she may be promiscuous. Behrman interrupts a tender moment between the two near the end of Act I with a nice display of what a later generation would call male chauvinism. Lael tries to hint at the profoundly different ways of thinking that she fears will ultimately separate them.

> RAND. I'll never want anyone else but you.
> LAEL. If you thoroughly knew me, you'd be bewildered by
> me—you might even be horrified by me.
> RAND. You mean—darling, tell me—do you—
> LAEL. What?
> RAND. Do you have affairs with men?
> LAEL. *(Between annoyance and laughter)*. My dear!
> RAND. Do you? I must know.
> LAEL. Well, if it's any comfort to you, I may tell you that though
> I'm intellectually sympathetic to any indulgence, emotionally
> I'm fastidious and even puritanic.
> RAND *(Fervently)*. Thank God! (p. 216)

She laughs; she calls him "sex-ridden," says that she is ashamed of him, and tries to explain:

> I mean your assumption that as long as I'm sexually monogam-
> ous, no other foible I might have could matter to you. I might be
> nourishing an idea to destroy the universe. I might be the incar-
> nation of malice, a well, deep and poisonous; I might be anti-
> Christ, but so long as I didn't—well—you wouldn't mind, you
> wouldn't enquire. Your psyche, my dear Rand, is sex-ridden.
> It's obsessed. It's maggoty with possessive desire. (p. 216)

The sexual jealousy pointed to here is the complicating agent in the
plot of *Rain from Heaven* and produces the nasty scene at the end of
Act II that is the climax of the play and one of Behrman's most striking
coups de théâtre. Rain from Heaven is a play of ideological discussion
cast in the form of country-house-party comedy; Behrman had a precedent for the amalgam in such a play as Shaw's *Heartbreak House,* which
is referred to at one point in the text (p. 215); the form was nicely suited
to account for the assemblage of a varied cast of characters. The riffraff
with which, according to Hobart Eldridge, Lady Wyngrave surrounds
herself, turn out to be exiles from Communist Russia and Nazi Germany
who are her house guests. The latest to arrive is a former German music
and literary critic, Hugo Willens, whose Jewish blood and satiric pen
have been enough to land him in a concentration camp; he has managed
to escape to England—and a temporary refuge in Lady Wyngrave's house.
It is here that the machinery of sexual jealousy begins to direct the plot:
Lady Wyngrave finds herself sympathetically drawn to Willens; some
years before he has had an affair with Hobart Eldridge's wife, who now
appears on the scene; she still lusts after him, and when she suspects
that he is having an affair with Lady Wyngrave, she tells her husband,
who tells Rand. Act II ends as the American brothers denounce Willens;
and Lady Wyngrave, whose relationship with him is entirely innocent,
rises superbly to his support with a dazzling display of style:

> RAND. You dirty Jew!
> . . . .
> HOBART. You swine! Maybe those people over there are right.
> LAEL. Hobart, please remember—Herr Willens is not only my
> lover; he is also my guest. (p. 259)

In Act III, on the morrow, nothing has changed. Rand apologizes
to Hugo Willens, but confesses to Lady Wyngrave that he had to force
himself to do so. Hobart comes on. The British press lord has backed
out of the scheme for an Anglo-American Youth League, and the cup of
his bitterness is overflowing. He has been drinking all night, and Behrman gives him a maudlin scene of loud lamentation for the death of
world capitalism. "Who's going to pay for everything?" is the burden

of his song. Upstairs one of Lady Wyngrave's other house guests, an exiled Russian pianist, is playing Brahms.

> HOBART. Do you know, since the surtax, my income's shrunk to nothing. Do you know what I pay each year to the Government—State and Federal? *(He begins to weep. He becomes aware of the music and rushes to the foot of the stairs in the alcove, crying as he goes)* There's another one! Listen to him up there! *(At the foot of the stairs)* Who's going to pay for your God-damn concerts! (pp. 268–269)

He exits for the last time. However, it is not the demise of capitalism but the ruin of Hugo Willens's world of art that chiefly occupies Behrman at the end of *Rain from Heaven*. Years before, Hugo as a literary critic had been instrumental in establishing the reputation of one of Germany's greatest men of letters. (Behrman calls him Lehrmann; the episode is based on Gerhardt Hauptmann's rejection of his former friend, the critic Alfred Kerr.) When Hugo's satiric pamphlet came under attack, he turned to Lehrmann for support, and his literary hero denied him. The incident has been for him traumatic, and it figures prominently in the clarification he has arrived at when at the end of the play he announces that he will return to Germany. In his past career he sees himself "a public taster of the arts—a dilettante in everything, except that I was paid. Behind this decorative curtain I was forced to discover that there is a harsh reality. Well, I must investigate this reality further" (p. 271). In his power as a critic, he made and unmade reputations; he made a world in which Lehrmann was king but never tested the foundations on which that world rested. Now there is but one thing to do: "To destroy the inhuman—to discover humanity" (p. 271). Lady Wyngrave recoils from destructive campaigns as instinctively as Marion Froude has done. "The iron has entered into your soul, Hugo. You have crossed some frontier—into some region—where I cannot follow you," she tells him (p. 272). *Rain from Heaven*, like *Biography*, ends in a parting, but one shadowed with far darker and more portentous implications than anything in the earlier play. Hugo goes, determined at last to view himself and the world "completely without illusion." He will return if he can, and she assures him he will find her there. As she has acknowledged Hugo to have crossed into a region where she cannot follow, Rand now appears and confesses a comparable isolation:

> there's some awful fence in my mind and in my spirit, and you're on the other side, and no matter what I do I'll never be able to break through to you—never. (p. 273)

"We're all shut in behind our little fences," she replies, and the play is over. It is a long way from the sense of social community that the end of comedy traditionally affirms. What we have instead is a clear-eyed recognition of the forces that separate human kind, and it comes close to despair.

BEHRMAN'S CHEKHOVIAN *END OF SUMMER*

The poignant close of *Rain from Heaven* suggests the direction in which Behrman's comedy was tending. It would become more elegiac, more shadowed with uncertainty, more problematic. All these qualities are fully evident in *End of Summer* (produced in New York in February 1936), Behrman's most Chekhovian play, with its charming and feckless heroine and her identification with a social order that is coming to an end. The setting is a summer house on the coast of Maine, "a masculine Riviera" as it is called at one point (p. 313). At the center of the dramatis personae are the women of three generations of a family that has made its fortune in oil, and the play opens with a quiet conversation between old Mrs. Wyler and one of her grandaughter Paula's young suitors who is asking her about her girlhood in Oil City and Cleveland. The young man (his name is Will Dexter) is fascinated as he contemplates such dynastic families as this one, floating along "in luxurious Barges" in the golden stream that was "stumbled on so accidentally" and that continues to flow, quenchless (p. 280). The impression is strong that the house in Maine is a place of refuge in a world full of problems. Will and his friend Dennis McCarthey, seniors at Amherst, retreat to it periodically between turns at establishing careers in the depression-ridden world outside. They and Paula are the play's younger generation. At the center of the plot is Paula's mother, Leonie Frothingham; and the play turns on her relations with her daughter; with her husband from whom she has long lived apart and who now asks for a divorce so that he can marry again; with her Russian lover, Boris, who is attempting to write the life of the celebrated father whom he secretly hates; and chiefly with the new lover who replaces Boris, a vaguely sinister psychiatrist named Dr. Kenneth Rice. Dr. Rice, with his belief "in the individual career" (p. 301), in the power of the individual to "surmount statistics, violate the graphs," be a Superman (p. 302), is the enemy in this play; and his entrance into the heroine's domain threatens its status as a place of refuge against the troubled world outside. Dr. Rice soons wins considerable influence over Leonie. In accents reminiscent of Hobart Eldridge, he counsels her regarding her intentions in behalf of her daughter's friends:

> KENNETH. I gather you are about to endow a radical magazine for the *boys*—
> LEONIE. Will and Dennis! I thought it would be nice to give them something to do!

KENNETH. Yes. You are prepared to back them in a publication which, if it attained any influence, would undermine the
system which makes you and people like you possible.
LEONIE. But it never occurred to me anyone would read it.

(p. 321)

As the play progresses, it becomes clear that his real interest lies not
in Leonie but in Paula. In his efforts to alienate her from Will, whom
she loves, he dwells on the confused, muddled, contradictory condition
he notes in her. Her radicalism, for example: it is borrowed from her
friends and is unexamined and insincere.

KENNETH. You are rich and you are exquisite. Why are you
rich and exquisite? Because your forebears were not moralistic but ruthless. Had they been moralistic, had they been
concerned, as you pretend to be, with the "predatory system"
—this awful terminology—you'd be working in a store some
where wrapping packages or waiting on querulous housewives
with bad skins or teaching school. Your own origins won't
bear a moralistic investigation. You must know that. Your
sociology and economics must teach you that.
PAULA. Suppose I repudiate my origins?
KENNETH. That takes more courage than you have.
PAULA. Don't be so sure.
KENNETH. But why should you? If you had a special talent
or were a crusader there might be some sense in it. But you
have no special talent and you are not a crusader. Much
better to be decorative. Much better for a world starving
for beauty. Instead of repudiating your origins you should
exult in them and in that same predatory system that made
you possible. (pp. 340–341)

And he proceeds to tell her of his own origins: reared in a foundling
asylum, he put himself through medical school and practiced medicine
for a time, but "gave up tonsillectomy for the soul" because "only the
rich have souls" (p. 342). He glories in his success, and his success gives
him no sympathy for the underdog. "The herd bores me," he tells Paula.
"It interests me only as an indication of the distance I've traveled"
(p. 342).

PAULA. Will would say that you are a lucky individual who—
KENNETH. Yes, that is what Will would say. It always satis-
fies the mediocrity to call the exceptional individual lucky.
PAULA. You don't like Will?
KENNETH. I despise him.
PAULA. Why?

KENNETH. I detest these young firebrands whose incandescence will be extinguished by the first job! I detest radicals who lounge about in country-houses. (p. 342)

And he launches an extensive argument detailing the reasons why Paula ought not to marry Will, the sum of the argument being the demoralizing effect her wealth would have on the young man, who has no money in his own right. Will, when he hears Dr. Rice cast him in the role of a fortune hunter, is disconcerted because his conscience is uneasy on just that point; and the doctor's bland rationalization of the term does not help matters:

But my dear boy, that is no disgrace. We are all fortune-hunters — ... I see no difference at all between the man who makes a profession of being charming to rich ladies—or any other— specialist. (p. 344)

Alone with Paula, Will says: "While he was talking I felt like hitting him. At the same time a voice inside me said: Can you deny it?" (p. 344) He finds it appropriate that cynical, sneering Dr. Rice ("a marauder. The adventurer with the cure-all") should appear at just this moment and in just this place, and the sense of this informs his denunciation of the doctor in the presence of Leonie and her guests at the end of Act II:

Some men are born ahead of their time, some behind, but you are made pat for the instant. Now is the time for you—when people are unemployed and distrust their own capacities—when people suffer and may be tempted—when integrity yields to despair—now is the moment for you! (p. 348)

In the autumnal third act, the plot turns melodramatic. It is September; old Mrs. Wyler is dead; relations between Paula and Will are strained as a consequence of his jealousy of Rice's influence over her. In a high-pitched and rather lurid scene, Rice is made to declare his love to Paula. She confesses her fear of him, her sorrow for him, her belief that he may be insane. To this he responds:

Because I am ambitious, because I am forthright, because I deal scientifically with the human stuff around me—you think me insane. Because I am ruthless and romantic, you think me insane. This boy you think you love—who spends his time sniveling about a system he is not strong enough to dominate—is he sane? (p. 358)

And his tirade flows on:

When I hear the chatter of your friends, it makes me sick. While they and their kind prate of co-operative commonwealths, the strong man takes power, and rides over their backs—which is all their backs are fit for. Never has the opportunity for the individual career been so exalted, so infinite in its scope, so horizontal. House-painters and minor journalists become dictators of great nations. Imagine what a really clever man could do! See what he has done! And this I have done alone. From an impossible distance—I have come to you, so that when I speak, you can hear. What might we not do together, Paula—you and I—
(p. 358)

The upshot of all this is that Paula tricks Rice into telling Leonie that he wants to marry her daughter, whereupon the daughter announces her loathing for him. His miscalculation with the daughter costs him, of course, his chances with the mother, and he is sent packing. By the end of the play, Paula is off to persuade Will to have her in despite of her millions; and Leonie, alone on the darkening stage with fiery young Dennis McCarthey, is agreeing to finance his radical magazine. The closing bantering lines atone for much that is not first-rate Behrman in this final act. The world, says Dennis, "is middle-aged and tired. But we—"

> LEONIE. *(Wistfully)*. Can you refresh us, Dennis?
> DENNIS. Refresh you? Leonie, we can rejuvenate you!
> LEONIE. That's an awfully amusing idea. You make me laugh.
> DENNIS. In the youth of any country, there is an immense potentially—
> LEONIE. You're awfully serious about it, aren't you, Dennis?
> DENNIS. Where the magazine is concerned, Leonie, I am a fanatic.
> LEONIE. I suppose if it's really successful—it'll result in my losing everything I have—
> DENNIS. It'll be taken from you anyway. You'll only be anticipating the inevitable.
> LEONIE. Why—how clever of me!
> DENNIS. Not only clever but graceful.
> LEONIE. Will you leave me just a little to live on—?
> DENNIS. Don't worry about that—come the Revolution—you'll have a friend in high office.
> *(Leonie accepts gratefully this earnest of security. They touch glasses in a toast as the curtain falls)* (pp. 369–370)

The problem with *End of Summer* lies in the figue of the psychiatrist. As drawn by Behrman, the character is too slight to bear the burden of evil that seems designed for him; and when one hears him pay tribute to "house-painters and minor journalists" who have "become dictators of great nations," there cannot be much doubt what the nature of that evil is. In *End of Summer,* Behrman is flirting with allegory: the man of science, prophet of an unbridled individualism, "ruthless and romantic" and "endlessly realistic" in nature, makes a play for the daughter of the robber barons ("I am directly in the tradition of your own marauding ancestors," Rice tells Paula). The Fascist psychiatrist makes a bid—in a word—for the United States of America. He has duped its capitalistic middle generation in the person of Leonie, and now he is out to seduce the heiress to this generation in the person of Paula, though he might argue that, in doing so, he is saving her from her left-wing radical friends. And Paula and all that she represents, Behrman would have us understand, come perilously close to falling under Rice's spell until, by a prodigious effort of will, she rallies her strength and cleverly outwits him and joins in alliance with the ameliorative socialism of young Will Dexter. The principal effect of such a dramatization of the dynamics of politics and society on the design of Behrmanesque comedy is the virtual displacement of what in *Biography* and *Rain from Heaven* has been the presiding figure. Leonie Frothingham is, to be sure, the central figure in *End of Summer;* after all, the part was written for Ina Claire, who created the role; but it is only in a manner of speaking that she presides over the play; and it is not Leonie, but her daughter, Paula, who saves the plot's central situation; the day is passing when grace and wit and civilized humor and good sense can assure any degree of rational communication with the world. The play frankly discusses the fact that Leonie's era, her society, her style are ending; and some of its most affecting passages depict her sense of this and her affectionately bantering discussions of it with her daughter and her daughter's friends. The relation of Leonie with Paula (who tends to look on her mother as someone in need of her tenderest care) is especially well done, as moving in its way as the relation of Madame Ranevskaya to Anya in *The Cherry Orchard.* But none of this conceals the fact—which after all is essential to the play's principal dramatic point—that the Leonies of the world will no longer hold center stage; that their places are being taken by younger, more realistically minded, more hardheaded, and more practical types; and that the Marion Froudes and Lady Lael Wyngraves who ordered their own lives and the society around them with such enlightened authority are now represented by a charmingly impractical figure who is already regarded as slightly quaint, a survival from quieter, less violent, and less expensive times. Dennis, near the end of the play, speaks her epitaph: "Poore Leonie—she's the last of the lovely ladies. The inheritance taxes'll get 'em soon" (p. 355).

WINE OF CHOICE, AN INTERESTING FAILURE

Two years separate *End of Summer* from Behrman's next play,

Wine of Choice (in the interval, he had made his adaptation of Giraudoux's *Amphitryon 38,* produced in New York in November 1937). After a turbulent pre-Broadway tour (involving much rewriting and the departure of the leading lady, Miriam Hopkins, from the cast in Pittsburgh), *Wine of Choice* opened in New York on February 21, 1938, and was quickly, judged a failure (it closed after a run of forty-three performances). It is not hard to see why, but it is Behrman's most interesting failure, far more interesting than such earlier ones as *Meteor* and *Serena Blandish* or such later ones as *Dunnigan's Daughter* or *But for Whom Charlie.* *Wine of Choice* raises in acute form the problem concerning the future of those embodiments of the genius of comedy who had presided with such triumphant authority over *Biography* and *Rain from Heaven* and who continued to preside after a fasion over *End of Summer,* but whose day was clearly past. Behrman solved it by abandoning the presiding female figure altogether and substituting for it a startlingly different type (to be discussed later). The heroine of *Wine of Choice* (who by no means presides over the play) is of the breed and the generation, not of Leonie, but of her daughter, Paula (though without her millions). Behrman was right not to attempt another incarnation of Marion-Lael-Leonie in the altered political climate of this play, though, in abandoning the type, he was depriving himself of the opportunity to draw a kind of figure in which he excelled. Thus *Wine of Choice* seems deficient in just the department where Behrman's finest talents had come seemingly to reside: the creation of a central figure of Meredithian comic splendor.

The allegorical scheme discernible in *End of Summer* has its parallel in *Wine of Choice,* where again a young woman falls under the seductive powers of a man of sinister political persuasion. The difference is that in *Wine of Choice* the seduction is actually accomplished, and the political persuasion is frankly labeled Communist. The central character is a young woman named Wilda Doran: beautiful, talented, full of enthusiasm for life, of obscure parentage and so free of any burden of tradition to maintain, experienced (her own past is slightly shabby, but she possesses the capacity of youth to renew herself). Her slightly *déclassé* position in society is reminiscent of Abby Fane, the nightclub singer in *Brief Moment,* and so is the attraction she exerts on young gentlemen of the aristocracy. Hers is the choice of the play's title, and the action defines the options that are available to her. She can marry a wealthy young Long Island socialite named Laddy Sears and become a film star in the motion pictures he wants to make for her; she also has the option of marrying Laddy's cousin, Ryder Gerrard, who has left the East, gone to New Mexico, become an influential newspaper publisher, and is now a United States senator. The symmetry of these alternatives is interrupted by the arrival of a third party, a young Communist zealot and budding novelist named Dow Christophsen, with whom Wilda falls recklessly in love. Chris has briefly worked for Ryder in New Mexico. Ryder, whose political aim is "to divorce conservatism from reaction—to give back the term its proper meaning,"[5] would like to make Chris his protégé and take him to Washington, but Chris refuses the offer; he once entertained the hope that the future senator would become a convert to communism, but now realizes that Ryder will never break away from his class. Chris is completing a novel dealing with an unsuccessful strike and sharecroppers in the South. In the course of the play, the novel is accepted for publication. His future plans are uncertain. He may leave the country; he has nothing but contempt for the United States under its present political system. He is depicted as one who regularly rejects human overtures, keeping himself sternly free of commitments and obligations; he is almost frighteningly sufficient unto himself, informed with the power to move others though he himself is as stone. Wilda is fascinated by him and throws herself at him, and he proves sufficiently human to go to bed with her for an hour. But when their time together is past, he proceeds on his own undeflectable way. One of the most painful scenes Behrman ever wrote is the one in which Wilda pleads with him to take her with him wherever he goes, and he calmly refuses. Later he confesses to Ryder that he feels "a great deal" (p. 203) for her, but that he must be responsible only to himself:

> My life has got to be my own. I've got to be able to use it any way I like, sacrifice it any way I like—without thinking of anybody else. (p. 204)

This prompts Ryder's denunciation of him, which sparks the most spectacular scene in the play.

> RYDER. Nothing about you is so horrifying to me as your rejection of Wilda. You love her but you deny her because she won't fit into your scheme. You are locked deep in the cold fastness of theory—on that surface nothing can take hold, nothing can take root, nothing can flower—neither love nor friendship nor affection. I see now how people like you can condemn to death their best friends—because equally well you can condemn yourselves to lovelessness, to abnegation, to death.
> CHRIS. Yes. We can. (pp. 205-206)

In the Author's Note (dated March 1938) to the published text of *Wine of Choice*, Behrman speaks of Chris in words that echo those Marion Froude used of Kurt in *Biography:*

> The basis of Chris's indignation is only too valid. His objective, too, is admirable. (Would it were quickly attainable!) But if he had extreme power and you ventured to differ from him, you might find yourself in an awkward position. (p. xi)

But Chris is viewed with none of the tolerance that Behrman had managed for the left-wing radicals of *Biography* and *End of Summer*. *Wine of Choice* bears violent witness to the fear and the hate with which the dramatist now, in the aftermath of the Moscow trials, regards them. In his Author's Note, Behrman says:

> I did not in Chris attempt to do a factual portrait of an individual Communist. What interests me and fascinates me is a condition of mind so strained of any element of doubt that opposition or disagreement is converted automatically into either inanity or perversion.

And he continues:

> It is not a simple thing nor a casual thing to send a man to his death for a differing 'ideology.' You have to have a stranglehold on the truth to do it. Conviction carried to this point is dictatorship, and the casualties of such dictatorships are mounting sadly—unhappily even in Russia where so many had pinned their hopes. (p. xi)

Wine of Choice is presided over by the obese and epicene figure of Binkie Niebuhr, another of Behrman's characters modeled on Alexander Woollcott and played by him. Binkie is a sharp-tongued cherub, matchmaker, gossip columnist and social critic, intimate and confidant of all the smart world, adviser to its affairs and repository of its secrets. The son of Lithuanian emigrants, he is a staunch defender of American capitalism. He is installed in a guesthouse on Laddy Sears's estate, and it is in his living room that the action passes. He is a great arranger of other people's affairs: he puts Chris in touch with a publisher who takes his novel; he is the intermediary between Laddy and the motion picture director in charge of Wilda's film; chiefly he is the guardian and protector of Wilda, whom he has more or less discovered. It is he who arranges the plot that saves her from Chris, in so far as she is saved; he gambles on Chris's leaving her when word is given out (by Binkie) that the two will marry, and Chris does. She is still free to make her choices at the end, thanks in large part to Binkie.

Wine of Choice has the materials for a first-rate satire on efforts to re-create the world. "What is it in me that urges me to remold what is beyond my capacity even to touch?" Ryder asks, thinking simultaneously of his humanitarian political ideals, of his frustrated efforts to make Chris a disciple in his pursuit of these, and his equally frustrated efforts to possess Wilda, who as he now knows has given herself to Chris. "There is no vanity like the Pygmalion-vanity," says Binkie, who acknowledges his own efforts "to make a world in which instinct is subordinate to reason" (pp. 177–178). "With Wilda I seem to have chosen the most unpromising material," he adds (p. 178). But when confronted with one who has triumphantly managed to subordinate instinct to reason—Chris—Binkie and especially Ryder are revolted by the young man's inhumanity. When in the final confrontation, Ryder announces his determination to "struggle to keep alive a world in which choice will still be possible—without dictation" (pp. 207-208), Chris is quick to point to the chaos that freedom can produce:

> CHRIS. Look at Wilda. She has free choice. What does it bring her? Instinct rampant. Look at you—racked by a passion you despise—that takes you away from the work in which you believe—
> RYDER. It takes me away, but I return to it. We are weak, it is true. We suffer and succumb to our suffering. We are capricious, we are adolescent and fallible. But we emerge from our weakness and retain our dream.
> CHRIS. Well—good luck to you—and to the lady—and to the American dream. (p. 208)

And with these words, Chris leaves the play. "Why doesn't he want to live?" Wilda asks when he is gone. "I thought everybody wanted to live" (p. 209). And she confesses to feeling caught: "As if I'll always do again what I've done before. I feel caught in a pattern from which I'll never escape."

> RYDER. That's what Chris would say—he would seem to be right. Yet I don't believe it. I refuse to believe it.
> WILDA. I can break away then, you think?
> RYDER. We are pursued—we are caught—we break away. If we can't defeat the devil we must elude him. One day perhaps we may develop a technique superior to his.
> WILDA. Meantime—the struggle is painful. (pp. 209-210)

Dialogue such as this does not go very far toward dispelling the shadow that has been cast over the uses of freedom in this play. Those most accessible to the choices life makes available, the play seems to be saying, are ironically the most vulnerable to error and the most open to exploitation by the ruthless fanatic who is prepared to sacrifice everything human in the name of an inhuman ideal. There is about Chris the odor of death. Where he is concerned, individualism withers before the power of political and social abstraction, and choice gives way to a decreed inevitability; he conveys the sense of something mechanical encrusted on the living that makes *Wine of Choice* Behrman's most Bergsonian comedy. The program by means of which he would re-create the world is viewed by Behrman as profoundly inhuman, and the dialectic of the play brings Ryder's democratic tolerance into collision with Chris's inflexibility. Between the two is Wilda, whose freedom of choice Ryder with his gentlemanly and aristocratic code would never force and who gives herself to Chris only to be abandoned by him. Dimly perceivable in the design of the play is the conflict of forces that are accessible to all the vital variety of life with forces that have gathered themselves unnaturally into a single channel and, dismissing all else, touch life at but a single point. It would take a Ben Jonson to dramatize adequately the grim dynamics of such a struggle, and Behrman was no Jonson. Nonetheless, *Wine of Choice* is a fascinating minor witness to the confusions and anxieties of an era.

COMEDY IN AN AGE OF ANXIETY

The failure of *Wine of Choice* seems to have prompted Behrman to a direct attack on the problem of comedy's place in an age of anxiety, and the result was the most successful play he ever wrote. *No Time for Comedy* (produced in New York in April 1939) dramatizes the dilemma of a contemporary playwright, Gaylord Esterbrook by name, famous for the fashionable comedies he has written for his brilliant actress wife, Linda, who is suddenly overtaken with doubts concerning what a later generation would term the relevance of his work in the age of Guernica, the Munich pact, and the mass executions in Nanking. The *crise* that descends upon him is aided and abetted by one Amanda Smith, the wife of a wealthy financier who, according to her own husband, "has a passion for developing latent powers,"[6] real or fancied. Her first husband, we are told, "was a mediocre but amiable man whom she utterly ruined by persuading him he was first-rate" (p. 32).

Amanda is persuaded that Gay has a dramatic genius as yet unrealized in his work. She is very much of the Man's-reach-must-exceed-his-grasp way of thinking. "Expression should be not yourself but an extension of yourself. Not what you are but what you might be," she tells Gay (p. 72). "How else can you achieve anything except by going beyond what you can hope? That's the whole realm of imagination, isn't it—extension!" (p. 73) Gay is skeptical; he terms Amanda's program "living above your means artistically—inflation in the aesthetic realm—disastrous as it is in the economic" (p. 72); nonetheless, with her encouragement he undertakes a somber play on death and the illusion of immortality.

The intellectual, aesthetic, and ultimately moral issues on which *No Time for Comedy* turns are joined in a second act scene between Amanda and Linda, who has learned of her husband's involvement with the other woman.

> LINDA. Can one add a cubit to one's stature? Personally,
>   I agree with the authority that says you can't.
> AMANDA. Oh, but I disagree. I disagree profoundly. People

do it all the time. Great occasions make them, crises make them, love makes them. One is constantly called upon to extend oneself beyond one's capacities.

When Linda terms this "inflation," we know where her husband got the word.

> AMANDA. One must unearth one's latent powers—develop them.
> LINDA. How nice to believe in these psychic trapdoors!
> Snap them open, and lo and behold—hidden treasure! (p. 121)

In the course of the scene, Linda, a woman of formidable intelligence and wit, sets about demolishing the grounds of pretense on which Amanda has built her inspirational version of her relationship with Linda's husband. Linda is hurt to learn that he is working on a new play and has not told her of it. Amanda says he has not told her of it because he has thought that she will not be sympathetic to it.

> LINDA. But why shouldn't I be? I am really hurt.
> AMANDA. I'm sorry—I'm terribly sorry—I shouldn't have—
> LINDA. You aren't in the least sorry. You are very happy. You have probably never in your life been so ecstatically happy as you are at this moment.
> AMANDA. But, Mrs. Esterbrook, really—
> LINDA. *(Cheerfully)*. Call me Linda! Shall we be honest with each other? It's enormously difficult, I know. But shall we try? What harm can it do you possibly? You enjoy inspiring Gay. That is to say you enjoy sleeping with him. I can understand that perfectly.
> AMANDA. It's not true. I mean we haven't—It's not true.
> LINDA. If it's not true already then it's imminent. You'll inspire him into it. I hate it and I don't mind telling you I'm intensely jealous. Sleep with him if you like, but for pity's sake don't ruin his style. Immortality! What on earth's Gay doing writing about immortality! Why, when he can write about life and about love and can make people laugh in the theatre, do you push him off the deep end to write about immortality which, at best, is dubious and inhuman? Really, Mandy! (pp. 125-127)

And she hammers away at Amanda's pretense of high-minded dedication.

> LINDA. Come on, Mandy, let your hair down. It won't hurt you with Gay. You don't really believe this act of yours, do

you? You can't possibly. You've got Gay through this mystic
spray you shed about—this rainbow belief in the profundity
of his literary powers— . . . It's all in fun—come clean. I
wish you could teach me the technique, Mandy—all this
pastel theorizing—wonderful dim lighting for sex.
AMANDA. I understand now—I understand everything now?
LINDA. What do you understand?
AMANDA. He's always talking about your clairvoyance, your
critical faculty of which he's afraid, your pitiless clarity—
LINDA. My God, Mandy, you make me sound like an X-ray!
AMANDA. You are! You've shriveled him! . . . in his soul! You
can't understand anything but foolish, empty laughter.
You're destructive. You're merciless. If I have furnished
him with an oasis where he can escape to brood and dream,
I'm happy—do you hear—proud and happy! (pp. 132-133)

Earlier, Gay has described to Amanda his feelings about Linda:

I resent her lucidity, her clarity, the absence in her of—I find
myself becoming involved with another woman—I feel myself
settling into the worn grooves of seduction—and I never
fail—even when she is not there—even when she doesn't know.
I never fail to hear her silent laughter reducing my ardor to
platitude. (p. 94)

This sounds remarkably like Storey to Monica concerning the second
man: "a cynical, odious person, who keeps watching me, who keeps
listening to what I say, grinning and sophisticated, horrid." And
with this, Behrman's work in comedy may be said to have come full
circle, for the intellectual and emotional ambivalence at the heart of
No Time for Comedy recapitulates the central conceit of his first play.
Gaylord Esterbrook is a more successful Storey; Amanda (dedicated to
the work of aiding Gay to live up to the best in himself) is a more ambitious and more experienced Monica (both roles were originally
created by the same actress, Margalo Gillmore); and Linda is the voice
of critical self-consciousness, also the voice of a sternly demanding conscience, which had existed merely as a metaphor in Behrman's first
play and now at last, twelve years later, is made triumphantly incar-
nate in the most articulate of all the dramatist's embodiments of the
comic spirit.
    It is appropriate that the heroine of *No Time for Comedy* should be
both a brilliant actress and an intelligent and sympathetic woman (the
role of Linda was originally acted by Katharine Cornell, to the Gaylord Esterbrook of Laurence Olivier). She combines the wit and the
sound sense that, as Meredith has said, women can display in comedy;
and Behrman's apologia for comedy is fittingly entrusted to her. She

speaks it near the end of the play, when she and her husband discuss his effort at tragedy, which at last he has let her read:

> LINDA. I feel a revulsion from your play altogether because it is dominated by the idea of death—
> GAY. But we are living in an era of death. We are pervaded by death.
> LINDA. What if we are? Why should your play be? One should keep in one's own mind a little clearing in the jungle of life. One must laugh. . . . Is it more profound to write of death of which we know nothing than of life of which we may learn something, which we can illuminate, if only briefly, with gaiety, with understanding? (pp. 186-187)

Death "is an art that sooner or later Nature imposes on all of us":

> the difficult thing, the admirable thing is to live. That requires ingenuity, that requires skill, that requires imagination—that is the index of civilization—the ability to live, not the ability to die. (pp. 188-189)

It is now that Linda produces the resolution to the play's dilemma:

> Why don't you write a play about Mandy and me? Two opposite types of women in the life of a man, an artist, a writer—the builder-upper and the breaker-downer—the critical faculty versus the clinging vine— (p. 193)

In response to Gay's charge that she allocates for herself the superior role, she answers:

> Not at all. A lot to be said for Mandy. Great crises, she says, great occasions, great loves make people extend themselves—exceed their capacities—whereas the other woman—I—is skeptical, critical. Stay in your little street, I say, cultivate your garden—don't try to make a forest out of it—if you are a minaturist remain content with that and don't attempt the Michael Angelo frescoes—a playwright like you for instance caught between the upper and nether millstones of these two points of view.—Which wins out in the end? Whom does he stay with? (pp. 193-194)

The questions send the comedy orbiting into realms of artifice out of which a finale is born: an end that is also a beginning. Like *The Second Man*, *No Time for Comedy* closes with the hero on the telephone, talking this time, not to the woman he would marry (he is already married to her and she is by his side), but to the woman he needs to escape from: poor Amanda, downstairs in the cocktail lounge where she has been waiting while, above in their hotel apartment, Linda and Gay are reconciled. Linda's suggestion for a play has gotten hold of him; already he has a title for it *(No Time for Comedy);* and as the curtain falls on Behrman's play, Gay on the phone, searching for what to say to Amanda, is in the act of deciding the end of his. Behrman's stage direction (more elaborate than the comparable one at the end of *The Second Man* and influenced perhaps by the revelation that Lunt's performance had brought to the final minutes of that play) describes the process:

> He picks up the receiver. He prepares to speak. His face is twisted in agony. No words come from between his parched lips. Linda sits watching him, a knowing smile on her face. In the eternity of his inarticulateness, the curtain swiftly comes down. (pp. 215–216)

Behrman's art mirrors its own creation—is present, indeed, at its own birth—in this final scene of the highest, most sophisticated, most theatrically glamorous of all his plays. *No Time for Comedy* is one of the handsomest tributes ever paid to the art of comedy: a tribute that manages to embrace both the sense of comedy as a mode of dramatic vision and comedy as a humane attitude toward life—an attitude that, at once critical and sympathetic, realistic and compassionate, provides the coordinates for the only truly civilized design for living.

CONCLUSION

This survey of Behrman's work in comedy ends here with his greatest popular success, which also marks, ironically enough, the end of his creative work in the theater. He would live for many years (he died in 1973, age eighty), and he would long continue active in the theater, but thereafter he would be mainly concerned with adapting to the Broadway stage the works of other people. With the exception of *The Cold Wind and the Warm* (1958), the few original plays that he wrote after 1940 were ineffective things, and his best writing in his later years went into nondramatic works: volumes of autobiographical memoirs and biographical studies of Lord Duveen and Max Beerbohm. The plays he wrote during the twelve years surveyed here represent the most serious and dedicated effort of any dramatist of the period to make the civilized and civilizing virtues of comedy flourish on the stages of a world that had increasing need of them. It was an uphill battle, and individual plays met with varying degrees of success. In the end, in the spring of 1939, just before the world collapsed into the war that had been impending for nearly a decade, he made one last effort to sum up the case for comedy; and having done so, he must have recognized—with that fine awareness of limits so essential to the comic spirit—that he had said all he could say.

NOTES

1. In the Prelude to *The Egoist,* Riverside ed. (Boston: Houghton Mifflin Co., 1958), p. 7.

2. *The Second Man,* in *Four Plays by S. N. Behrman* (New York: Random House, 1952), p. 31. In the following discussion, all references to this play, *Biography, Rain from Heaven,* and *End of Summer* (referred to parenthetically by page number) are to this edition.

3. *People in a Diary, A Memoir by S. N. Behrman* (Boston, Little, Brown and Co., 1972), pp. 79–80.

4. In *Comedy,* ed. Wylie Sypher (New York: Doubleday Anchor Books, 1956), p. 14.

5. *Wine of Choice* (New York: Random House, 1938), p. 45. Subsequent parenthetical page references are to this edition.

6. *No Time for Comedy* (New York: Random House, 1939), p. 32. Subsequent parenthetical page references are to this edition.

Candy in Context

WILLIAM WALLING

The repressive activity of civilization brings it about that primary possibilities of enjoyment, which have now, however, been repudiated by the censorship in us, are lost to us. But to the human psyche all renunciation is exceedingly difficult and so we find that [certain kinds of] jokes provide a means of undoing the renunciation and retrieving what was lost.

Freud, Jokes and Their Relation to the Unconscious
(1905)

In Chapter 4 of *Candy,* our heroine is lying in bed with the family gardener, locked in his passionate embrace and on the very point (to recall the punning in *Shamela*) of being deflowered, when the sound of approaching footsteps is heard out in the hall. "Good Grief," Candy cries, "it's Daddy!"

And true enough, the door burst open at that instant and Mr. Christian appeared, looking like some kind of giant insane lobsterman. At the sight of them he reeled, his face going purple, then hatefully black, as he crashed sideways against the wall, smashed back by the sheer impact of the spectacle itself. It was not as though he couldn't believe his eyes, for it was a scene that had formed a part of many many of his most lively and hideous dreams—dreams which began with Candy being *ravished,* first by Mephesto, then by foreigners, then by Negroes, then gorillas, then bulldogs, then donkeys, horses, mules, kangaroos, elephants, rhinos, and finally, in the grand finale, by all of them at once, grouped around different parts of her, though it was (in the finale) *she* who was the aggressor, *she* who was voraciously ravishing *them,* frantically forcing the bunched and spurting organs into every orifice—vagina, anus, mouth, ears, nose, etc. He had even dreamed once that she asked him if it were true that there was a small un- covered opening in the *pupil of the eye,* because if it were, she had said, she would have room there (during the finale) for a miniscule organ, like that of a praying mantis to enter her as well! So that now, actually confronted by the scene, one would think he was not unprepared, yet as dreams of death do not prepare a young man for the firing squad, but perhaps only build to the terrible intensity of it, so Mr. Christian appeared now to be actually strangling with shock![1]

No doubt, we could make something sufficiently portentous of this if we chose to invoke the sort of critical mode that is always pressing towards "ultimate" readings. Ludwig Jekels, for example, in his "On the Psychology of the Comic" of 1926, offers us a more than adequate clue (the italics are Jekels's own): *"The feeling of guilt which, in tragedy, rests upon the son, appears in comedy displaced on the father;* [in comedy] *it is the father who is guilty."* For what reader of *Candy* has entirely forgotten the way the novel ends? Our heroine, after a long series of misadventures, has arrived in Tibet; she is in a Zen tem- ple one day, diligently meditating on the Buddha. Lightning strikes the roof of the temple, the statue of the Buddha topples over with a great crash, and in the ensuing wreckage Candy finds herself tightly sandwiched between the intimate pressure of the statue beneath her and the even more intimate pressure of a mud-caked holy man on the top. As the rain continues to fall through the gaping hole in the tem- ple roof, washing over the mud-caked face of the holy man who has been thrown upon her (and who, indeed, has virtually been thrown *inside* her as well), our heroine suddenly realizes that he is someone she knows all too thoroughly, from an earlier stage of her life. "GOOD GRIEF," she cries in the novel's final line, as the now recognizable "holy man" writhes in the beginning throes of his climax, "IT'S DADDY!"

The outline, in short, for a psychoanalytic reading of the comedy in *Candy* seems obvious enough. The *"guilty father"* of Jekels's formulation appears in the earlier part of the novel as a comic send-up of the very idea of parental authority and of the superego. Accordingly, in Chapter 4, we have the parody of the dynamics of repression I have already glanced at: a furious "Daddy" bursts into his daughter's bedroom to interrupt her lovemaking; but his own dream life in connection with her is so energetically obscene that it threatens to engulf whatever conscious pretensions to sexual morality he has. By the end of the novel, as we have seen, "Daddy" is ludicrously revealed in the act of fulfilling those long-repressed desires for his daughter that his conscious will had earlier been restraining under only the most precarious of controls.[2]

The problem with an interpretation like this, of course, is that it turns *Candy* much too starkly into something it patently is not. The dynamics of repression may well have a good deal to do with our laughter while reading the novel (I believe that they do). But the apparent persuasiveness of the model suggested by Jekels collapses at once if we consider how inappropriate the inevitable seriousness of such a model is for reflecting the kind of knockabout farce in which so much of *Candy* is written. The critical issue I want to raise, then, is one that rather closely resembles the difficulty many of us have experienced when attempting to address ourselves responsibly to a work of popular culture. As Geoffrey Hartman has recently remarked in *The Fate of Reading* (1975), the impulse to "read" the nonliterary products of a culture "may be as perverse an activity as westernizing China. Reading is not a neutral technique; it is shaped by classics it in turn supports."

By this, I should add, I don't mean at all to imply some rigid hierarchy that would make a book like *Candy* "nonliterary." But I do think it worth stressing the peculiar tact necessary for the genuine criticism of works that seem themselves to subvert most serious efforts to come to grips with them. Consider, for example, the facile comparison with *Candide* that is often invoked during the discussions of *Candy*. The later novel, to be sure, begins with an epigraph from Voltaire; and it is easy enough to see that both *Candy* and *Candide* describe the comic misadventures of an absurdly naïve protagonist. But the very resonances set in motion by the comparison to Voltaire's moral fable—most particularly, perhaps, the resonances associated with *Candide*'s more than two centuries of critical reputation—suggest precisely that misshaping through the "classics" about which Hartman wants us to be wary.[3]

VERBAL CONVENTION AND COMIC EFFECTS

But what may be a good deal less distorting, I suspect, is our closer exploration of the verbal conventions out of which so much of the parodic style of *Candy* grows. Rather clearly those verbal conventions are, first of all, "American." Yet I would argue that their "Americanness" can be defined even further as belonging most naturally to a particular context and to a particular time—to the kind of fiction that flourished in certain American magazines for roughly forty years, from the period soon after the World War I to the opening years of the Kennedy era. It was a fiction, we can assume, whose audience had already sharply declined by the time *Candy* got itself written in the second half of the 1950s. We can assume this because most of the magazines that favored it are no longer with us, casualties of the enormous transformation in public taste after World War II, for which television still serves as the most convenient counter. But the striking relationship between verbal convention and social form in this fiction offers a suggestive model for many of the comic effects in *Candy*.

Two illustrations may help to make this point. Both are drawn from stories that were published in the 1950s, the same decade that saw the composition of *Candy;* and both appeared in *The Saturday Evening Post,* the magazine that was perhaps most representative over the years for the kind of fiction I have in mind. In the first, "This Time It's a Blonde" by Richard McKelvey (March 24, 1956), a group of young men are in a restaurant, intending to strike up an acquaintance with the attractive young waitress who works there. As she approaches their table, the shiest of the group, Juan,

> smiled nervously and ducked his head toward the floor when he felt the sharp, sweet pain shoot from her eyes directly into his.

A second young man named Casey, however, is a good deal more self-assured, and, "looking up with muscular casualness into her eyes, said 'Hi, kid!' " The effect of this effrontery on the first young man is rather surprising, even if we grant the premises of the story that he is a student from Latin America, still untutored in the great social freedoms possible in the United States: "Juan gasped as if seeing his mother crowded by a freight train." But the young waitress is hardly nonplussed:

> The girl looked at Casey with gentle tolerance which yet had in it something of the steely reproach of a Sherman tank. She smiled, her silken lips parting smoothly. And for the first time since he had pitched a no-hitter in prep-school, Casey blushed.
> "Sorry," he said.

In the second story, "Caught in the Act" by Steve McNeil (January

21, 1956), Jerry, the young man who serves as romantic lead, is judged by his father Horace to be "tanned and rugged and as full of energy as a diesel engine." Unfortunately, Jerry is also engaged to marry a pushy young woman who is certain to make him unhappy—or so his father feels. Determined to break the engagement, Horace is encouraged one evening by a conversation he has with his son at the bar of their country club. For what Jerry tells him is that the older woman who is one of their guests for dinner that night (her name is Gwen) has given him second thoughts about the kind of wife his fiancee is going to make: it seems that Gwen, in her loud middle-aged pushiness, suggests unpleasantly what his own wife will be like in twenty years if he does go ahead with the marriage. Father and son then return to the dining room where the women are waiting—and where Gwen soon reveals another aspect of her pushiness:

> Eventually they were served dinner. Mr. and Mrs. David Blackstone graced the dining room with their presence.
> Gwen screamed, "Blacky!"
> The Blackstones came to their table. "Well, Horace," the Earl of Multnomah Heights said, "nice to see you. We must get together for lunch."
> "Certainly," Horace said. "Any time."

After this interruption, Horace proceeds with his plan to free his son from the undesirable engagement. Visible from the dining room through long windows is the club's swimming pool. Because Horace knows that Molly O'Brien, the girl his son really cares for, will be using the pool that evening, he sends his son outside when he sees Molly on the diving board. Then he leaves the table himself and goes into a back room where the club has its electrical switches:

> Someone turned on the outside lights. Suddenly the entire pool and surrounding areas were illuminated. Standing on the springboard were Jerry Cooper and Molly O'Brien. She was engaged in getting Jerry's suit wet, but he didn't seem to notice, since he was currently engaged in smearing Molly's lipstick.
> Everyone, including the personnel of the club, was as stunned as a man hit in the head with a wild pitch. Jerry pulled himself away from Molly, blinked into the glare, took a step and fell ungracefully into the pool. The lights went off.

Perhaps the most noticeable quality of these two excerpts is the extraordinary degree of social constraint they suggest. In the first, a brash young man is quickly reduced to abject apology by the reproachful glance of a young waitress. In the second, a middle-aged woman further condemns herself for the intended reader by crudely calling to the community's leading citizen across a sedate dining room. Indeed, in that second excerpt, the entire community itself is "as stunned as a man hit in the head with a wild pitch" by the spectacle of an unmarried young man in street clothing kissing an unmarried young woman in a bathing suit.

To be sure, the dramatic strategy of such fiction—the excerpts I've chosen could be multiplied almost endlessly—is to focus upon characters who are in some way outsiders or "rebels." Thus in the first story the central figure is a foreign student, whereas in the second we are meant to sympathize with the breakup of a socially advantageous engagement. But the degree of otherness and the dimensions of rebellion are invariably on a scale so unthreateningly compatible with the established order that the implications of social restraint are finally reinforced rather than challenged.

Furthermore, the style of these stories appears as the perfect instrument for reflecting the exact process of accommodation I've sketched. For if both authors make repeated gestures towards an imagery of violence and of unmanageable force (mothers are "crowded" by imaginary freight trains; reproachful glances take on the quality of "a Sherman tank"; a young man is "as full of energy as a diesel engine"; public kissing has the impact on others of getting "hit in the head with a wild pitch"), the attempts really add up to nothing more than strained and pointless departures from an overall convention of language thoroughly devitalized by cliché (Juan feels "the sharp, sweet pain shoot from her eyes"; "her silken lips" parted "smoothly" in a smile; a distinguished couple "graced the dining room with their presence"; Jerry "was currently engaged in smearing Molly's lipstick"). Evidently by this point, in the 1950s, the authors of such fiction were capable of exhibiting wryness and even self-irony at their own employment of the clichés. But the overall effect still remains pointless, like the play of prisoners caught in a self-conscious game with an inflexible jailer.

Consider now the scene in Chapter 5 of *Candy* where Candy herself, Aunt Livia, and Uncle Jack are on their way to dinner at "a luxury roadhouse." As Jack parks the car, he tries to apologize to Candy for the bawdy speech of his wife:

> "Liv's in one of her moods," Uncle Jack explained to Candy as he helped her out of the car.
> "I'll say!" said Candy.
> "I'm in the mood for cock and plenty of it!" cried Liv gaily. "About ten pounds, please, thick and fast!"
> "Now, Liv, this won't do," said Uncle Jack firmly, as, with a gracious sweep, he bade them through the wide portals of

Halfway House.

They were a handsome party and, to all appearances, as wholesome a representation of middle-class innocence as had ever been in Halfway House; the *maître d'hôtel* came forward with a flourish and secured them a choice table.

"What about a bite to eat, as well, girls?" asked Uncle Jack, genially looking over the menu while the waiter hovered at hand.

"Yes, a bit of giant Male Organ—piping hot!" quipped Liv, scrutinizing the menu with a frown.

"Now, Liv," said Uncle Jack, laying down his menu gently, "you *will go too far.*"

"Who's talking about 'go'?" demanded Liv.

"The girls want to *come!* Am I right, Can?"

Candy blushed crimson, and Uncle Jack sighed and shrugged a look of bemused patience at the waiter, who, though fidgeting about, managed to smile uneasily.

Admittedly, much of the comedy arises from the fundamentals of the situation itself—on the one hand, there is the "luxury" restaurant with its maître d'hôtel and its officious waiters; on the other, there is the unrestrained bawdiness of Aunt Livia. And if we laugh, it may be that we are simply responding to some long-forgotten experience of our own, some still subliminally rankling moment when we ourselves were distressingly unable to behave with anything like the absolute lack of inhibition Aunt Livia shows, in a setting of potential intimidation not so very different from the Halfway House. Yet as I have already suggested, there remains another aspect to the comedy of *Candy* that takes its point from the particular context of language out of which so much of Aunt Livia's bawdiness seems to emerge.

The overall effect of the passage is the odd one of a style that both parodies and invigorates—or at least, in the process of its duality, *appears* to point in the only direction that its already devitalized model could follow (if, that is, the possibility of invigoration were actually to exist). For what we encounter here is the unmistakable evidence of the same deadened formulas of language we saw earlier in the two excerpts from *The Saturday Evening Post.* Indeed, the parodic effect of the passage resides most centrally in the very showiness with which the deadened formulas are displayed: Aunt Livia *cries gaily* and *quips* and *demands,* Uncle Jack speaks *firmly* and approaches menus both *genially* and *gently,* the *portals* of Halfway House are *wide,* Jack's *sweeps* are *gracious,* the three of them add up to *a handsome party,* and the *maître d'hôtel* greets them *with a flourish,* before leading them to a table that is *choice.* Yet at the same time, as we can hardly help seeing, the deadened formulas are counterpointed by the outrageous bawdiness of Aunt Livia's conversation, a conversation replete with words and conceptions more deeply insulated against the conventions of the printed page (at least until the 1950s) than any other code of language in actual existence.

THE COMPLEXITY OF THE COMEDY OF REPRESSION

The comedy of repression, in short, is not nearly so simple as it might appear. For the striking point we have arrived at is this: that the curiously free-floating images of violent energy in the magazine fiction we looked at earlier—those Sherman tanks and diesel engines and threatening freight trains—seem to find their no longer repressed correlative in the obscenities of Aunt Livia's conversation. Against the backdrop of a long, weary tradition of formulaic conventions, *Candy* absurdly reminds us—by the display of a sexual boldness unthinkable within the models it parodies—of the problematic loss we have endured, in exchange for whatever social codes are ours.

But even more. For the formulaic conventions themselves can be seen to provide a reassuring base of homely reference to the "real" world, with its inevitable social codes and repressions. In other words, the reader of *Candy* is hardly asked to participate in a fictional universe that actually suggests the dissolution of repression.[4] Indeed, in the strategy that *Candy* generally employs, we can perceive an almost radical demonstration of the conservatism at the heart of parody: however deadly the aim, the parodic impulse also preserves, conferring upon the corpse it seems to inter the paradox of reanimation.

It may be, then, that the reassuring presence of formulaic conventions explains as well as anything can the widespread popularity *Candy* enjoyed when it first appeared in this country in 1964. (In that year alone the book went through thirteen different impressions in hardcover.) Certainly, at any rate, its comedy has continued to prove accessible to a good many more readers than that of any other of the "shocking" books that began to be openly published about that time. Indeed, within that context, William Burroughs's *Naked Lunch* seems an especially illuminating case in point. For, like *Candy, Naked Lunch* was written in the 1950s; and, like *Candy* again, *Naked Lunch* had to wait until the following decade before it could be published openly in the United States. But perhaps the illustrations drawn from a single scene will be enough to make clear how sharply different from *Candy* are the dynamics of repression to be found in Burroughs's novel.

The scene I have in mind (it can be found on p. 148 of the Grove Press paperback edition of *Naked Lunch*) is set in *Chez Roberts*, the most exclusive of exclusive gourmet restaurants. It is, in fact, so grandly intimidating a place that, as Burroughs tells us, many a customer

> has rolled on the floor and pissed all over himself in convulsive attempts to ingratiate.

There is, however, one customer who is wholly irrepressible—a man named A. J. And one evening, as Robert himself approaches his table, A. J. shouts out a demand for a bottle of ketchup, calling Robert "Boy." The consequences are somewhat extreme:

> Thirty gourmets shop chewing at once. You could have heard a *soufflé* drop. As for Robert, he lets out a bellow of rage like a wounded elephant, runs to the kitchen and arms himself with a meat cleaver. . . . The Sommelier snarls hideously, his face turning a strange iridescent purple. . . . He breaks off a bottle of Brut Champagne. . . . '26 . . . . Pierre, the Head Waiter, snatches up a boning knife. All three chase A. J. through the restaurant with mangled inhuman cries of rage. . . . Tables overturn, vintage wines and matchless food crash to the floor. . . . Cries of "Lynch him!" ring through the air. An elderly gourmet with the insane bloodshot eyes of a mandril, is fashioning a hangman's knot with a red velvet curtain cord.

Doubtless this is a fiercely brilliant comic style in its own right. And there are touches that depend on nothing more extreme than an exquisite sense of timing (perhaps the finest of these is the wonderful pause before the vintage of the champagne is announced). But the overall effect of the passage finally suggests a sensibility of anarchic recklessness, one for whom even the initial comic premise—the impossibly pretentious restaurant that is crying out to be deflated—is swiftly transformed into something much more serious (or absurd). For it is the murderous implications of social restrictions themselves that become the true subject of the scene: quite literally, people are willing to *kill* to maintain the integrity of the social codes they share.

Of course, if we wish, we can readily conclude that the suggestion of anarchic recklessness is illusory: the language of the passage is, after all, under remarkable control. But further attention would seem to lead to the ancillary conclusion that the control is itself at the service of an anarchic recklessness. Nor is the argument at all persuasive that proceeds from this to discover that the violence in Burroughs's restaurant scene functions in much the same manner as Aunt Livia's bawdiness does in *Candy*. For the language in the passage from *Naked Lunch* simply remains too consistent in the extremity of its notation—from the servile customers who are known to have "pissed" all over themselves in order to "ingratiate" to the elderly gourmet "with the insane bloodshot eyes of a mandril"—to convey anything other than a bleakly threatening indifference to the conventional dynamics of repression. *Candy,* on the other hand, makes no such threat felt, the reflex of its parody "devouring" (as Blake might say) at least something of the dangerous "prolific" of its sexual energy.

And yet to bring *Candy* into juxtaposition with another book of the

1950s (whatever the book) is to remind ourselves of the decade in which the particular form of parody in *Candy* took shape. Morris Dickstein has recently remarked, of the prevailing tone of the decade (in his *Gates of Eden,* 1977), that it was "another Old Regime whose convenient symbol was Eisenhower . . . and whose stability was grounded in a suppression of grievances and new energies" (p. 26). But although Dickstein goes on to chart the emergence in the latter half of the fifties of a "new sensibility"—one whose sharply revised Freudianism was to promise a "liberation" from "repression" (pp. 54, 52)—he chooses to ignore *Candy* entirely. In this, I think, he surrendered the opportunity to refine even further upon some of the provocative discriminations he makes in his text.

For as one of Dickstein's heroes of the "new sensibility" was to make clear in 1960, at the beginning of the new decade, even recent American history was no longer exempt from the subversion of Oedipal visions. "Came the Korean War," we find Norman Mailer writing in his extraordinary "Superman Comes to the Supermarket," the essay Mailer himself likes to believe swung the 1960 presidential election to Kennedy,

> Came the Korean War, the shadow of the H-bomb, and we were ready for the General. Uncle Harry gave way to Father, and security, regularity, order, and the life of no imagination were the command of the day.

It is this notion of Eisenhower as the "Father," presiding over a deeply repressed national life, that offers a particularly amusing and illuminating point of departure. We have already seen, for example, how *Candy* ends: with "Daddy" in the actual process of absurdly breaking the most formidable of social taboos. Yet to reach that point, Daddy has had to be lobotomized, the gardener having driven his trowel through Daddy's forehead at the end of the bedroom scene in Chapter 4. Moreover, just before the trowel descends, Daddy is allowed to give utterance to the supreme insult at his command, the crystallization into a single word of all the thwarted energy of his repressed sexual desires: "*You . . . you . . . you* COMMUNIST!" he shouts at the gardener.

It is this comic identification of sexual repression with political paranoia, then, that places the parody of *Candy* a little more clearly within the social and cultural milieu of the decade in which it was written. And in the following chapter, when we see the now lobotomized Daddy "smiling benevolently" above the naked bodies of his daughter, Candy, and his twin brother, Jack, as they writhe together on the hospital floor (p. 63), it may not be entirely perverse to be reminded of the ubiquitous images of a smiling Eisenhower (good old Ike!) that did so much to serve for visual punctuation in our newsreels and the interiors of our public buildings during the 1950s.

A specific intent to have us identify Daddy with Eisenhower, I should add, is not at all a crucial element in our ability to enjoy the parody of *Candy*. Much more important is our recognition of the implication of a lobotomized father figure who smiles "benevolently" above a comic theater of sexual release—and who, indeed, becomes a participant in that same release by the end of the novel. It is an implication that helps us to see more clearly the kind of book *Candy* actually is: one that both looks ahead to the "liberation" of the 1960s (Dickstein's "new sensibility") and behind to the "repression" of an entrenched culture, whose internal logic seemed almost to be approaching the idea that lobotomy was the one safe route to fulfillment.

Finally, in this divided aspect of *Candy,* we can discern an uncannily comic relationship to the poem that perhaps best defined the 1950s to itself, Robert Lowell's "Memories of West Street and Lepke." In Lowell's poem, the peculiar moral vapidity of "the tranquilized fifties" is first presented to us; then, after a series of recollections drawn from Lowell's imprisonment in the 1940s as a conscientious objector, the poem ends with one last, sustained impression of a fellow prisoner, a once murderous thug named Lepke, the former "Czar" of Murder Incorporated:

> Flabby, bald, lobotomized,
> he drifted in a sheepish calm,
> where no agonizing reappraisal
> jarred his concentration on the electric chair—
> hanging like an oasis in his air
> of lost connexions.

The "agonizing reappraisal" in Lowell's poem is a phrase from the speeches of John Foster Dulles, Eisenhower's secretary of state during so much of the long period of cold-war anxieties. From the allusion we are surely meant to draw some unflattering conclusions of our own concerning the real nature of the energies beneath the postures of our foreign policy at that time. But it is in the comedy of *Candy* that we can also see an illusory reestablishment of the "lost connexions" between energy and repression, private fantasy and public speech. It is, I think, an especially apt "connexion" to argue for, in the light of the quotation from Freud that serves as epigraph to this paper—and in the light of the comedy of repression that takes place in *Candy*.

NOTES

1. Terry Southern and Mason Hoffenberg, *Candy* (1964; rptd. New York: Putnam, 1968), pp. 41–42. All quotations are from this edition.

2. To be sure, the "Daddy" at the end of the novel is lobotomized, but the presence of this lobotomized "Daddy" suggests, among other things, an amusing variation on one of the recurrent themes of "serious" pornography: the inclusion in the erotic plot of a permissive parental figure whose real function is to serve as a kind of Lord (or Lady) of Erotic Misrule.

3. The point that *Candide* itself was often dismissed as frivolous when it first appeared in the eighteenth century is not quite apposite. Any work that has remained a part of our literary tradition for more than two centuries carries with it an inevitable seriousness almost impossible to bring into genuine relationship with a book like *Candy*.

4. Merely to *suggest* such a dissolution is, of course, the farthest reach to which language can bring us—which may explain the proverbial sadness of written pornography.

PART 5

COMIC NOSTALGIA:
SILENT MOVIES,
RADIO,
AND
A. J. LIEBLING

15

A Pratfall Can Be a Beautiful Thing

B. H. FUSSELL

. . . if somebody laughs. In analyzing the aesthetics of the pratfall in *My Wonderful World of Slapstick,* Buster Keaton names three ingredients for comedy: pratfalls, custard pies, and laughter. It takes the same three to make a visual joke as it takes to make a verbal joke: a comic butt, a joker, and an audience. The butt is so named because that is what he falls on. He may fall by his own agency or someone else's. Some joker may have planted a banana peel or may wait in the wings with a custard pie. In any event, the audience will laugh only if the victim's pratfall or face smear *appears* to be unintended.

Mack Sennett did not hire professional acrobats for his Keystone comedies, Keaton says, because their falls did not get laughs. Although Keaton could do acrobatic tricks like the "flip-flap," a back somersault in which the hands touch the ground, he insists that his "flip-flap" was not professional. If it were, it would not be funny. At the same time, the comic must know how to take a fall to avoid getting hurt. To take a fall properly, Keaton warns, one must protect both ends of the spine, the spine that connects a man's head to his bottom (see Figure 1). The

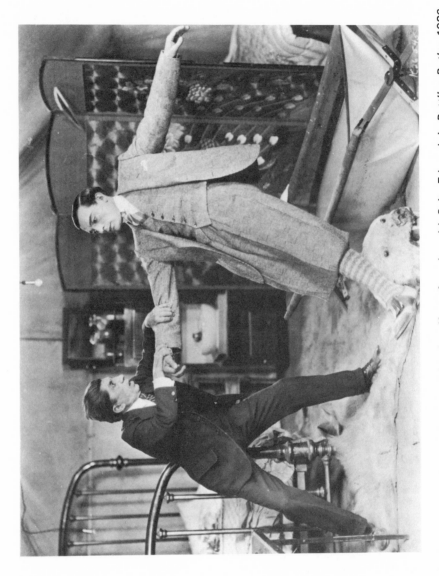

Figure 1. Buster Keaton demonstrating the effect of gravity with Snitz Edwards in *Battling Butler*, 1926. (The Museum of Modern Art/Film Stills Archive)

fact that man has two spheroids connected by a rod, like the ends of a dumbbell, connects the fall on the prat with the pie in the face and suggests the root of comic action.

Fall as a noun means, "a dropping from a high . . . position by the force of gravity." *To fall* as a verb means, "to lose the erect position (primarily with suddenness)." *Pratt* joined to *fall* adds both result and cause. The common meaning of *pratt,* according to the *OED,* derives from rogues' cant for *buttocks,* as in, "First set me down here on both my pratts" (1641). Originally, however, *pratt* meant, "a trick, prank, or frolic," as in ". . . the perte and pernicious pratt thay playd to thair Bischop" (1596). The linking of prank to buttocks suggests some intervention in nature's course that would help gravity to exert its force—primarily with suddenness. The pratfall provides an "unintended discovery" of the sort Freud mentions in describing the way comedy unmasks something hidden or invisible. The pratfall makes gravity visible and unmasks its force as a secret weapon. If the fall is unintended, the faller will get laughs from an audience because the discovery is also unintended.

What the audience discovers or is forcibly reminded of is that the natural position of man is horizontal. In comedy, gravity is the given; all bodies are earthbound. Any attempt of man to erect himself from his natural position in the mud or from his natural condition as "thinking mud" makes him an upstart, a fellow who—literally—puts on airs. When man is an infant, "he thinks as his mouth does," Auden writes in *Mundus et Infans,* and praises his Creator at the top of his voice and with the motion of his bowels. When man with infinite daring wills himself into an upright position that turns one end up and the other down, he assumes that position is his rightful one, forgetting that he is as subject to gravity as any stone or clod and that he will fall at the same rate of acceleration. In comedy, gravity is the custard pie that makes fall guys of us all.

When we laugh at a baby who tumbles, we laugh at our common feet of clay and our own attempts to rise above them. When we laugh at a grown-up who tumbles in his effort to become more erect than we are, we laugh because he has forgotten our common feet of clay. (The clown's slapshoes keep those feet visible, just as his baggy pants keep his bottom visible.) We laugh, of course, at any reminder of man's earthy parts, of his fundament and its functions, as in the phallus, turd, or fart. We laugh because all men, thinking or not, are the same at bottom. Our first great comic writer, Aristophanes, remains great because he places man's center of gravity not in the head but in the red leather thong, the stuffed bum and belly, and the unintended crap, for which the mere breaking of wind was perhaps a more dramatically practicable substitute. In *The Clouds,* for example, Aristophanes makes the fart a topos of human destiny and creates an entire cosmology by its means, from "the tootle of the flatulent gnat" to the "infinite farting of the heavens" in thunder (William Arrowsmith, translator).

When a fart is added to a fall, sound doubles the pleasure of sight. A philosopher, king, father, grandmother—any figure of authority—who falls from a high position in the pecking order of the tribe, becomes a comic butt if he or she falls suddenly enough and makes enough noise in the falling. Aristophanes makes the falling of Socrates, Euripides, Cleon and such like noisy indeed. The medieval dramatists of the mystery plays make the falling of Satan, Herod, and similar riffraff similarly thunderous. Like the Keystone Kops, Satan's minions are comic villains whose dramatic function is to take pratfalls as often and as loudly as possible. Herod outlines the job nicely in these exit lines from the *Ludus Coventriae:*

> I ffalle down here a ffowle freke
> ffor þis ffalle I gynne to qweke
> with a ffart my brech I breke
> my sorwe comyth ful sone.

His use of the word *breech* may remind us of its Indo-European stem meaning either "to smell" or "to make a crackling noise." *Breeches* meaning "trousers" reveals in the word what the thing means to conceal—a bad smell or noise threatening at any moment unintended discovery.

Socrates and Herod take the kind of pratfalls performed centuries later, with and without sound, by the comedians of vaudeville, burlesque, and silent movies. Mack Sennett defined comedy as whaling the daylights out of Pretension or Authority. "The whacking of Fat Lady's backside," he wrote, "is the basis of all true comedy—from the paradoxes of Bernard Shaw (who was one of the best bed-slat wielders of his time) to the Keystone Kops." Comedy poses the question, "Is nothing sacred?" and answers with a fart.

For Sennett there are only two comic actions: the fall of dignity and the mistaking of identities. Whacking the backside of Pretension and Authority with a bed slat makes the fall fast and noisy. If a comedian substitutes for a bed slat or rubber bladder a slapstick, he need not whack an actual backside to simulate the sound of that action. The slapstick is composed of two flat pieces of wood that slap together loudly when hit against something, but it is the sound that counts, not what is hit. The sound becomes a trope for the sound a backside would make were it falling or farting or getting whacked. The slapstick is a synecdoche, we might say, for the pratfall as the pratfall is a synecdoche for the fall of dignity. The custard or breakaway pie is, in turn, a cinematic refinement of the stage slapstick that turns its auditory effects into visual ones and makes the face of the comic butt equivalent to his bottom. The joker with the pie causes the comic butt to lose dignity by losing face.

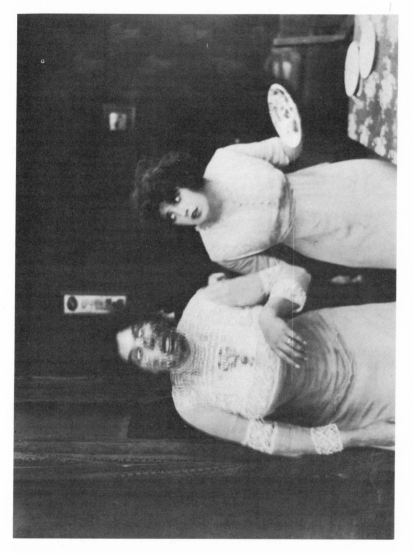

Figure 2. Mabel Normand, reputedly the first pie thrower, executes "the shot putt" on Minta Durfee in *A Misplaced Foot*, also known as *Revenge with a Pie*, 1913. (The Museum of Modern Art/Film Stills Archive)

THE ROLE OF THE PIE IN COMIC ACTION

In anatomizing the breakaway pie, Keaton explains that there are two types of pie and four types of thow. Black and white film demanded black and white pies: therefore, a blackberry filling was used for blonds, lemon meringue for brunettes. Throws were categorized according to length and type of trajectory. Keaton names "the shot putt" of three to five feet (see Figure 2); "the walking thrust," which entails a light twist at the moment of push; "the Roman discus," the most artistic trajectory for a middle distance; and "the overhand throw" for a long-distance throw such as a catcher would make to second base from behind the plate.

In the breakaway pie, silent movie comedians found a way of making the fall of dignity visible without necessitating an actual fall. The pie suited close-up camera shots. Although many claim to be the first pie thrower, Sennett states authoritatively that the first pie recipient was Fatty Arbuckle (in *A Noise from the Deep*, July 17, 1913). "Fat faces and pies seem to have a peculiar affinity," Sennett notes. Pies seem to attract fat faces the way bed slats attract backsides and the ground attracts pratts. The pie resembles gravity as a force that is seemingly innocent of malice until suddenly unmasked as a weapon to lay the mighty low. In Sennett's world of comedy, the humble and innocent pie became the weapon of the rube against the snobs and plutocrats. When silent comedy grew more genteel, the pies faded, and the movie comedian began to internalize the idea of the pie in a comic character. The comedian whacked Pretension and Authority not by attacking it with pie or slat but by imitating its clothes or gestures—badly. Harry Langdon, sucking his thumb in his diapered pants, whacks the pretensions of childish men to be adult. Chaplin, in his bowler and cane, whacks the pretensions of rich men to be cultured and just. Keaton, in his porkpie hat and deadpan face (see Figure 3), whacks the pretensions of thinking men to conquer nature. Each makes the fall of dignity visible in his costume.

SILENCE AND WORDS IN COMEDY

Silent movies by their silence make us aware of how much ordinarily we use words as weapons, their sounds and their meanings. Words, of course, can complement or substitute for costumes, gestures, pies, bed slats. And like the silent joker, the verbal joker will make his most effective whacks by imitating the pretensions of the particular backside under attack. Puns, paradoxes, and riddles do to language what pies do to faces and pratfalls to bottoms—destroy its dignity. R. P. Blackmur has called punning "the onomatopoeia of meaning," or we might say that punning is sound whacking sense. The Marx Brothers, for example, adding

Figure 3. Buster Keaton falling apart in *The Three Ages*, 1923. (The Museum of Modern Art/ Film Stills Archive)

verbal to visual comedy, whack language and its pretensions to authority by a self-destruct universe of puns. In one of the many chain reactions of *Duck Soup,* Harpo lights his cigar with a telephone, plays ball with Trentino's cigar, hands Trentino a phonograph disk when asked for Groucho's "record," shoots the disk when Trentino hurls it away, and is awarded Trentino's cigar by Chico as a prize. A whole system of unlikely correspondences is suddenly uncovered. The audience is jolted into laughter by an unintended discovery of the uniformity of matter.

Purely verbal puns do their work with similar economy, especially when the jokers adopt the stance, as they do in *Duck Soup,* of the big wigs attacked.

> SECRETARY OF WAR. How about taking up the tax?
> GROUCHO. How about taking up the carpet?
> . . . .
> MINISTER OF FINANCE. No, I'm talking about taxes—money, dollars.
> CHICO. Dollas! There's a where my uncle lives. Dollas, Taxes.

Riddles make a bigger sound than puns by making sense take a pratfall in slow motion and by planting the banana peel for all to see in the initial question proposed. The Marx Brothers do "flip-flaps" with riddles, as in the following exchange:

> GROUCHO. Now, what is it that has four pair of pants, lives in Philadelphia, and it never rains but it pours?
> CHICO. Atsa good one. I give you three guesses.
> GROUCHO. Has four pair of pants, lives in Philadelphia. . . . Is it male or female?

The biggest sound of all is made by Harpo the mute. The blonk of his taxi horn demolishes the sound of both sense and non-sense alike; he whacks the daylights out of all acoustic images by a rude noise resembling the fart.

What the pun does to the word, the paradox does to the sentence. The paradox whacks the backside of syntax by imitating its structures, its pretensions to order and meaning. As an instrument of greater refinement and more delicate calibration than the pun, the paradox finds its analogue in the pie throw rather than in the bed slat. The paradox achieves its particular effects by setting up its own fall guy in the first part of the sentence to receive the pie in the second part. The greater the distance between the two parts, the more difficult the throw, but the lovelier the trajectory. In the hands of a master such as Oscar Wilde, the weapon can ascend to the variety and beauty of effect ascribed by Keaton to the master pie thrower.

"The walking thrust," for example, characterizes Wilde's technique in the following sentence: "The only way to get rid of a temptation is to yield to it." Here the sentence is brief but affords no clue to the on-coming pie until the fatal "yield" is thrust with a slight twist into the face of the sentence. "The Roman discus" increases the arc of the trajectory, as in this Roman or Latinate construction of Lady Bracknell's: "You can hardly imagine that I and Lord Bracknell would dream of allowing our only daughter—a girl brought up with the utmost care—to marry into a cloak-room, and form an alliance with a parcel." Here the discovery of the pie is delayed and even deliberately waylaid by a parenthetical phrase until the squish of "cloak-room" and the additional splat of "parcel."

"The long distance throw" increases the trajectory to such an extent that no more than a "poof" is audible when the pie finally hits its target. Such is the effect of Lord Illingworth's utterance in *A Woman of No Importance:* "Sentiment is all very well for the button-hole. But the essential thing for a necktie is style. A well-tied tie is the first serious step in life." Here the pie must traverse a complete syllogism of two statements and a conclusion. Although the pie may be glimpsed in the first statement when "sentiment" is coupled with "button-hole," the spectator must wait in suspense while the second statement delays the action as a straight man would. Only in the third statement does the equation of "well-tied tie" with "serious step in life" bring pie and face together at last.

PARADOX IN COMEDY

What the paradox can do in small, the form of the play or film as a whole can do in large. Like the Marx Brothers, Wilde in *The Importance of Being Earnest* imitates the Newtonian universe by setting up a complete system of false equations. Wilde's primary device is to make mere equivalence between signifier and signified the same thing as mathematical equation: muffins = repentance, babies = manuscripts, a man's name = his person. Form as a whole is made to serve as a weapon to whack the pretensions of reason and logic.

In his comedies, Shakespeare's use of parodic form is less overt at the same time his objects of attack are more comprehensive. Shakespeare whacks the pretensions of man to any form of perception or understanding whatsoever. In *Two Gentlemen of Verona,* the clown Launce calls Speed a blockhead because he understands Launce less than the staff Launce holds in his hand. "My staff understands me," Launce tells him because to stand-under and to under-stand is all one. In his punning, Launce undercuts the basis of symbolic transformation on which any kind of understanding depends by making his shoe, with the hole in it, stand for his mother; by making his hat stand for Nan the maid; by making his dog Crab stand for himself; and by making himself stand for the dog. If to stand-under and to stand-for is all one with to under-stand, man's attempt to maintain an erect position of understanding is laughable.

OTHER KINDS OF FALLS

In Shakespeare the fall of dignity occurs through a universal mistaking of identities. The form and action of his comic plays jolt his audience into laughter by an unintended discovery of a relation between stage plots of mistaken identities and our everyday mistakings and misunderstandings in the actual world. Bottom the weaver in *A Midsummer Night's Dream* mistakes his identity when he believes himself to be a mighty fellow instead of an ass. Bottom "translated" equals ass, and by wearing his ass on his head, Bottom is a walking pun. Bottom in his person as in his name makes visible the breech between what is said and what is meant, between what is seen and what is understood to be seen.

Shakespeare's lovers no less than his clowns suffer "translation" from man to ass simply by mistaking their identities as creatures of reason and common sense. In *Two Gentlemen of Verona*, Valentine does not need to wear an ass's head to make his asshood apparent. His servant Speed tells him that he is so "metamorphized with a mistress" that his follies shine through him "like the water in an urinal." Valentine, who thought himself to be a young gentleman from Verona, is actually a walking urine specimen. To be young is to fall in love, and to fall in love is to fall on one's pratt. No custard pies required.

Love and its characteristics are all described by falls of one kind or another. Love's food is music, which has a dying fall. Love's god is blind, which causes blindness in his victims so that they trip and fall. Love is blind not only to reason but to all constructs of the human mind by which it orders time and space, so that to fall in love is to fall in love at first sight and head over heels. The silent movie comedian at first sight of his girl falls into a manhole or off a steamboat or over a cliff (for the unromantic version see Figure 4). Shakespeare's lovers describe the same parabola within the space of a sentence: "no sooner met but they looked; no sooner looked but they loved; no sooner loved but they sighed; no sooner sighed but they asked one another the reason; no sooner knew the reason but they sought the remedy. . . ." (*As You Like It*, 5.2.32–36) Contrary to the sonnet, Love *is* Time's fool because lovers more than the rest of us are victims of the time warp in which time ambles, trots, gallops, or stands still withal.

Falling in love makes time visible the way falling on one's pratt makes gravity visible. Simply to be born, however, is to fall into time and hence into folly, as Lear remarks—"When we are born we cry that we are come to this great stage of fools." Is there any difference then between a comic fall and a tragic fall except that one evokes laughter

Figure 4. Roscoe "Fatty" Arbuckle and a pushy friend in *A Bath-House Beauty*, 1914. (The Museum of Modern Art/Film Stills Archive)

and the other evokes tears? The question is moot with Shakespeare when Hamlet can say, "There's a special providence in the fall of a sparrow" and when tragic events can provoke the comment, "Some falls are means the happier to arise." Tragic and comic falls alike suggest a dropping from a high or an erect position, and in both the fall must appear to be unintended (see Figure 5). Professional martyrs do not get tears any more than professional acrobats get laughs. What differs is the speed of the fall and the resilience of the object falling. Comedy speeds up time, whereas tragedy slows it down. If Richard II fell from his throne in a matter of minutes instead of dwindling by degrees for five acts, his fall might bring laughter. Or if he fell from his throne and then bounced back, like a rubber ball on the end of a string, we might think his fall comic. By speeding up time, comedy makes the rhythm of falling and rising, the rhythm of death and life, visible. As Groucho says of comedy, "We want a real old lady crashing downhill into a wall in her wheel chair—only to walk away unharmed."

Staged comedy as well as staged tragedy resigns us to the fact that golden lads and girls must come to dust, along with chimney sweepers and sparrows and Bowery bums and suburbanites. Samuel Beckett's characters lie in a giant dust bowl somewhere between comedy and tragedy, and they begin where other comic and tragic fallers end—on bum or belly in the dust, immured in ash cans, buried in mounds, entombed in vases. Barely distinguishable from the dust from which they have, during a lifetime's struggle, failed to erect themselves, they, nonetheless, still "fall," though there is no place to fall from or to. The double negatives of *Waiting for Godot* make an ironic positive. The rope that is no good for hanging because it breaks permits Estragon and Vladimir to continue "falling." Falling, while remaining still, is Beckett's metaphor for living. The four characters of *Godot* choreograph the fall of man while waiting motionless in a heap. "Who farted?" Estragon asks. "Pozzo," Vladimir answers. Beckett makes man all bum, an obscene noise or a bad smell, a fart in the face of the universe. "My work," Beckett once said to an interviewer, "is a matter of fundamental sounds (no joke intended)." The fart in Beckett is the sound time makes while bodies fall.

In his radio play *All That Fall,* Beckett orchestrates the sound effects of falling in a universe in which falling is impossible because there is no up or down. To go forwards is the same as to go backwards; faces are the same as bums. "Or you forwards and I backwards," says old and blind Mr. Rooney to old and fat Mrs. Rooney, "the perfect pair. Like Dante's damned, with their faces arsy-versy. Our tears will water our bottoms." Faces and bottoms coalesce in mingled tears and laughter. When Mrs. Rooney announces the text of the Sunday preacher, "the Lord upholdeth all that fall and raiseth up all those that be bowed down," the stage directions read, *"Silence. They join in wild laughter."* In Beckett's *Footfalls,* he has refined the sound of falling and the action it represents

Figure 5. Buster Keaton falling in love with Katherine McGuire in *The Navigator*, 1924. (The Museum of Modern Art/Film Stills Archive)

Figure 6. "Buster Keaton, The Human Mop," at age six in 1901.
(British National Film Archive/Stills Library)

COMEDY: NEW PERSPECTIVES

to the "audible rhythmic pad" of footsteps on a darkened stage. "Footfalls" is a synecdoche for "it all," that which the daughter May revolves in her mind. The voice of her mother tells us what May has said: "The motion alone is not enough, I must hear the feet, however faint they fall." Only the sound of feet falling gives evidence of existing rather than not existing or of existing as May and her mother do only within each other's mind.

As the youngest member of The Three Keatons, when he played vaudeville with his parents, Buster was billed as "The Human Mop" (see Figure 6). He was an object that his father threw into the scenery or the wings, onto the bass drum in the orchestra pit or once, at Yale, straight at some heckling students. The audience, Buster says, was amazed that he didn't cry, but he didn't cry because he wasn't hurt: "Little kids when they fall haven't far to go." When he grew up, he had farther to fall and was often hurt, but still he did not cry—or laugh either. He found he got bigger laughs when he took his falls by making his pan dead, by wearing a mask of gravity. His is the look of an old artificer become engineer who observes, coolly, the appalling convolutions of his fall. He is kinetic man, Hugh Kenner has said, played by himself and watched by himself, trapped in the wrong universe. But for the critic, Keaton the craftsman has a final pie: "I never realized I was doing anything but trying to make people laugh when I threw my custard pies and took pratfalls."

16

Superheterodyne: Radio Comedy of the Thirties

DON WIENER

My Rosebud was a secondhand table-model Crosley radio that my oldest sister, Mildred, gave me when I was eleven years old. It had a burled metal case and a separate speaker that would fit under my pillow for muffled, late-night listening—Sherlock Holmes, Will Rogers, Eddie Cantor, Ed Wynn, and all the radio comics. Through it I knew the joys of independence because I could listen to what I wanted. Mother liked the Goldbergs, my sister Ruth insisted on Mert and Marge, and I could have Amos and Andy without a struggle. Wherever that old Crosley is today, in my memory it's still in tune with all my old favorites.

Mother and I had seen many of the radio comics when they were on the vaudeville stage: Burns and Allen, Ed Wynn, Eddie Cantor. We had seen Joe Penner wanting to sell his duck, and ve vas dare, Charley, when Jack Pearl played Baron Munchausen. We had seen Fred Allen and Portland Hoffa.

Fred Allen had not been a big vaudeville headliner. As he said himself, he was too good for the small time and not good enough for the big time. But he was great on radio. Allen's verbal wit was ideal for radio. His act died on television, and the few movies he made were complete disasters. Milton Berle, on the other hand, went from stealing jokes in vaudeville, through radio, without leaving a trace, and into television, where he and Ed Sullivan owned the sets for ten years or better. It has always been of more than passing interest and no minor coincidence to me that Texaco sponsored Berle on television when they had underwritten Ed Wynn, a truly great burlesque and vaudevillian comic, on radio. Wynn and Berle offered Texaco a kind of continuity of comic representation that they tried to find again with an aging Jack Benny that did not play.

Many of these comic spirits who grew out of the vaudeville tradition did not change their acts at all for radio. Some retained their dance routines and the same sight gags with sound effects—jokes punctuated with tap dancing—and I, as a listener, had little trouble putting the whole improbable act together. Radio was never the nonvisual medium it was supposed to be. Between the sound effects and the live audience reaction, I could see it all—could see the McGee closet disgorging trash saved from before the Waters, could see Jack Benny descending to his vault, and could see Amos's fresh air taxi. Because radio was in some mysterious way a visual medium, one of its most successful comedy acts was a ventriloquist and his dummy—unreconstructed vaudeville.

The burlesque vaudevillian cleaned his shtick for radio. He continued to dance but left out the bumps and grinds and rarely dropped his pants. In TV, blue material has come back in the worst taste—originally through the late show, adult audience, and club-date ambience. The pastoral and innocent world of radio comedy, maybe because of sensitive sponsors or network censors, was smut-free. And this innocence was carefully guarded. When Mae West and Charlie McCarthy launched a gently racy routine about Adam and Eve—about as suggestive as the Bobbsey twins—the heavy curtain came down, and Mae's guest spots on the Bergen-McCarthy Show were over, with due apologies to the clergy. Maybe the country was innocent in those days, too innocent for dirty jokes as family entertainment. Bob Burns's rural routines at the expense of his kinfolks had no hint of Chick Sales's earthiness, nor did Will Rogers's folksy wisdom.

SITUATION COMEDY AND ONE-LINER ROUTINES IN RADIO

Radio humor, like TV, offered its audience both the situation comedy and the stand-up, wisecracking comedian with one-liners. Bob Hope was the apotheosis of the one-line comedian stringing his routine together in what seemed like an endless monologue of non sequiturs that was punctuated with laughter and applause. It did not necessarily build to anything, but just stopped as abruptly as it began when that segment of the show's format had been filled. There is no dramatic structure to the monologue, and it may or may not refer to current events. The opening monologue was frequently followed by a dialogue between Hope and a guest star, where more one-liners were exchanged in the form of insults. This act has gone on and on. Hope and his one-line writers may just be eternal.

Some shows, like those of Fred Allen and Jack Benny, combined the situation comedy and the one-liner routines. These shows were formulated with stand-up monologues right out of vaudeville and burlesque and then went into skits. The "Fred Allen Show" offered somewhat more variety—the opening monologue, the opinion survey, Allen's Alley. The show concluded with a playlet performed by the Mighty Allen Art Players. The tone of the "Fred Allen Show" was gentle satire directed at topical events through Senator Claghorne, the Southern stereotype; Titus Moody, the Down East rube; and the New York Jewish humor of Mrs. Nussbaum. Ethnic humor was another part of the innocence allowed radio with the Goldbergs, Amos and Andy, and Pick and Pat—the minstrel-show blacks free of threat. TV has turned on the black comedian and black humor as an astringent comment about the plight of blacks in society—the laughter is embarrassed and not just a little nervous.

Fred Allen was touted as cerebral and of a more intellectual bent than the competition. This feeling may still be held by those who have not heard his shows for forty years—heard them only in the inner ear the way they would like to remember. Maybe it was even then the difference between New York and Hollywood humor: Allen was not the clown of his show the way Benny was of his. Allen always seemed to be above and outside his material, a very gentle precursor of Lenny Bruce. Much of the humor on the "Jack Benny Show" turned on Jack's foibles and character—his vanity, his inept violin playing, and his parsimony.

COMEDY OF CHARACTERS AND SITUATIONS IN RADIO

All radio comedy, as much of TV comedy, created characters and situations that could be the focus of recurrent jokes week after week. The wheel did not have to be reinvented each week, and the laughter built and grew louder week after week as Mrs. Nussbaum said, "You were expecting, maybe Hedda Gabler?" Or Fibber McGee, ignoring Molly's warning, opened the closet. Jack Benny would celebrate again his thirty-eighth birthday. Gracie Allen would read a letter from her mother, and George would repeat her inanities with an upbeat inflection. The writers developed a format they could live with week after week, and if no show was as perfect as *The Importance of Being Earnest,* at least they got on and off the air, brought laughter to millions, and created myths that many of us still believe in.

Somewhere in all the comic mythmaking of forty years ago, one program stands out in my faulty memory as a perfect jewel of the comic radio pastoral: Vic and Sade, with their small house halfway up the next block, came out of Chicago, the home of the soaps, and had the quality of affectionate humor of the comic strip *Peanuts.* "Vic and Sade" was written in the depth of the Great Depression by Paul Rhymer. There were four characters that comprised the Gook family, and they were the complete live cast of the show five days a week for fifteen minutes a day, a little vignette each day that formed a perfectly rounded world. The Gook family: Father Vic; Mother Sade; Rush, the preteen-aged son; and Sade's pleasantly senile Uncle Fletcher. Love and warm humor seemed the qualities of this pastoral bit of small-town Middle America, with none of its ugliness or threat. Unlike the other soaps, each episode of "Vic and Sade" was a complete playlet unto itself, a model of Aristotelian unity, having a beginning, middle, and payoff. You did not have to tune in tomorrow to see how it would come out. You did not live from month to month with the perpetual miseries of Helen Trent or Our Gal Sunday.

A "Vic and Sade" episode might involve Vic's working out elaborate parade formations in the living room for his lodge, the Sacred Stars of the Milky Way—this at about the time when the Ku Klux Klan was marching in Washington or the Shriners were holding one of their water-bagging conventions in Chicago. Or Rush's wanting to help his friend Rooster Davis get a better job at the barber shop by having his age changed; the suggested procedure was writing to the Secretary of the Navy—Nazi Germany then was organizing the Hitler Youth Bund. Or Sade's being as angry as she could be when her neighbor was in arrears in the fifteen cents' monthly rent for keeping his bicycle in her shed—this when the dustbowl winds were moving farmers from Oklahoma to California.

The listener doing the family ironing may have been able to relate what was going on outside the pastoral frame to the tribulations of the Gooks, but it didn't matter. The mythic world of Rushville Center, Illinois, and the Gooks' friend, Richigan Fishigan from Sishigan, Michigan, were as completely drawn as Faulkner's Yoknapatawpha County, as unashamedly mid-American as Booth Tarkington or Mark Twain. "Vic and Sade" seems to me the purest kind of radio comedy—Chicago style, like early Dave Garroway and TV—without an audience in the studio laughing or applauding on cue. Bob Hope's audiences being cued to applaud instead of using natural laughter has always seemed contrived, unlike the warm smile evoked by Vic and Sade.

Although the actual cast included only the four characters, whose voices you heard five days a week, you quickly came to know and smile with all the people in Rushville Center. You got acquainted with Fred and Ruthie Stembottom, who lived next door and with whom Vic and Sade played a perpetual game of 500 rummy. You knew about Fred's driving habits and his inability to assert his preference for a given ice-cream flavor. You knew that Mr. Gumpox, the garbage collector, had a horse named Howard, and you knew that it was one of the major events of the day when Mr. Gumpox came down the alley on his appointed rounds. It was an extra special treat when Rush got to go downtown and watch the fat men play handball at the Y. Uncle Fletcher would send Rush down the cellar when he wanted to discuss some adults-only problem, such as why his numskull landlady, Mrs. Keller, put ten numskull meals around the numskull house for him before going to visit her brother, Charlie, who was an armed guard at the Ohio State Home for the Agreeable, residing in Dismal Seepage, Ohio. (He had previously been an armed guard at the Wisconsin Home for the Obstinate, residing in Sweet Esther, Wisconsin.) Rush never went down the cellar. He participated at great length in the family's most adult problems. If interrupted, Uncle Fletcher was just as likely to suggest that Sade and Vic, too, go down the cellar. Mr. Rush Gook was never the subject of discrimination.

If Mr. Rush Gook was preoccupied with the adventures of 3rd Lt. Clinton Stanley, about whom he would read to his father at any opportunity, Vic was equally concerned with the doings of his lodge and the lodge rituals delivered in fractured Latin. Sade, who was usually indifferent to the lodge activities, did get somewhat exercised when Vic proposed to have Robert and Slobert Hink and their wives, Bessy and Messy, stop by Rushville Center for a weekend of parade practice. But then Sade, too, had affiliations, and her Thimble Ladies were a force in the community. When Vic called his son "razor strap," "inner sole," "overshoe," "Willie," and an endless stream of other nicknames, you recognized it all as affectionate and loving humor.

World War II, Korea, Vietnam, and, finally, Linda Lovelace and *Deep Throat* may have made the world in that little house halfway up the next block unrecapturable; and I suppose that nostalgia is the personal fantasy of remembering it the way it was without all the intervening historical disturbance. Radio comedy was a comedy of character and not of plot, had a kind of finite life, and now seems a carefree interlude between vaudeville and television. Radio grew a star system that was sustaining rather than consuming, the way television is. Nostalgically, radio's limitations now seem like virtues. The comic spirits of radio seem to me bigger than life, much bigger than anything yet produced by television.

17

The Reporter as Comic Writer:
A. J. Liebling

ELMER M. BLISTEIN

The multifaceted sanity that is comedy can be found in many forms and in many places. It can be as ethereal as George Meredith's Comic Spirit floating in the empyrean and as knockabout and slapstick as Joe Keaton's hurling his five-year-old son Buster into the wings or high against the painted canvas, forest-scene backdrop of Bill Dockstader's Wonderland Theatre in Wilmington, Delaware. It can be as subtle as a Cole Porter lyric and as obvious as a Mike Sachs monologue. It can be found in Shakespearean tragedy (even *Othello* has a clown) and in a Woody Allen film, in a Byronic rhyme and in a Groucho Marx one-liner.

Connoisseurs, collectors, and anthologists of comedy seem to have neglected one form of comic writing that provides laughter and enjoyment on a daily, weekly, or monthly basis: the news story. In the Preface to *A Subtreasury of American Humor,* edited in 1941 by E. B. White and Katharine S. White, E. B. White attempts to explain the neglect and attempts to offer a solution. He argues that timeliness makes a news story: "Even the perfect newspaper story, by the most expert and gifted reporter, dies like a snake with the setting of the sun. The news goes out of it (although some humor may remain), and when the news goes out of it the heart goes out of it." So the Whites eliminated all of the pieces written for the daily press from their anthology and included "only the magazine stuff, including a few pieces from 'The Talk of the Town' in *The New Yorker*." They did so because "the 'Talk of the Town' pieces . . . stood up a little better, we found, than the daily paper pieces, probably because the prime purpose of a daily story is to acquaint you with the facts, whereas the prime purpose of a *New Yorker* story is to entertain you with the facts."

Here it becomes a matter of emphasis, or which is the adverb and which is the verb. Do we instruct delightfully or do we delight instructively? The returns have been coming in for over two thousand years and from many scattered precincts. From Aristotle and Horace to E. B. and Katharine White is not a major quantum leap. It may be argued that the Whites were guilty of special pleading because their relationship with *The New Yorker* was a long and fruitful one, but their solution to the problem of selections seems to have held up—for me, at least. And even the Whites hedged their bet. Every example of reportage that they chose was written by a person who at some time had worked on a daily newspaper, for they knew that "the best reporting (including the best humorous reporting) is to be found in newspapers, not in magazines." One of the writers they chose for their florilegium was Abbott Joseph Liebling.

It was a happy choice. A. J. Liebling had served his apprenticeship on daily newspapers. He loved them and had a lot of them to love. The day of the one-newspaper town was barely a gleam in news syndicates' eyes. The first thing he remembered reading (not, of course, the first thing he read) "was a newspaper story about a fighter called Carl Morris, the Sapulpa (Okla.) Giant." As the article touted Morris as a "White Hope" who would certainly cause Jack Johnson, then heavyweight champion of the world, no end of difficulties, and as Morris was beaten easily a day or two later by Jim Flynn, "a fighter of ordinary dimensions and accomplishments," Liebling learned early not to believe everything he read. It was a salutary element in his education.

Yet he continued to read newspapers and continued to learn much from them: ". . . many of my early impressions of the world, correct and opposite, came to me through newspapers. Homicide, adultery, no-hit pitching, and Balkanism were concepts that, left to my own devices, I would have encountered much later in life." The phrase "correct and opposite" points to a healthy skepticism so necessary to a good reporter; so, too, does the explanatory—by no means the parenthetical—remark in this sentence: "Through newspapers I acquired a vicarious knowledge, or perhaps more accurately an illusion of knowledge, of just about everything in the world."

Ten years of avid newspaper reading followed his experience with the "Sapulpa Giant" before he entered Dartmouth in 1920, shortly before he turned sixteen. In his freshman year he heard a lecture by a professor of sociology named Mecklin on the great steel strike of 1919. Mecklin's comment that the Pittsburgh newspapers were so untrustworthy that he had to read Philadelphia and New York papers to find out what was going on in the strike "continued the journalistic education that Carl Morris's downfall had begun." Of all the newspapers in Pittsburgh, Philadelphia, and New York, only the New York *World* "told the truth about the strike"; so Liebling naturally wanted to work on the *World*.

He finally did, but the way to the *World* was not short and was not straight. He was thrown out of Dartmouth twice for cutting chapel on cold mornings ("Every morning from October to May is cold in New Hampshire"). When he was thrown out the second time, this time "definitively," he decided to go to the Pulitzer School of Journalism at Columbia. He was soon disillusioned with the Pulitzer School, particularly its course in "newswriting," which "had all the intellectual status of a training school for future employees of the A & P." Excused from a course in "just straight writing" because he already wrote "well enough," he quite properly wondered "well enough for what? The aim of a serious professional school should have been to teach every journalist to write as well as Tom Paine or William Cobbett." It may be worthy of note that he never heard Cobbett's name mentioned in his two years at Pulitzer.

Because he didn't have to take the course in "just straight writing," he was permitted to choose another course from the university catalog and "picked Old French, under Raymond Weeks . . . who occupied the chair of Romance philology. This proves that, if the way to learn about journalism is in a class in sociology, the way to learn about Tristan and Iseult is to attend a school of journalism." Here is a case where disillusion led to happiness, for Professor Weeks became one of a select group of five persons in Liebling's pantheon. The other four were Max Fischel, a police reporter for the *Evening World;* Sam Langford, the prizefighter who raised counterpunching to a fine art; Beatrice Lillie, who could always make him laugh; and Harold Ross, the first editor of *The New Yorker.* The inclusion of Ross in this exalted group is strange, for "it is hard for a writer to call an editor great, because it is natural for him to think of the editor as a writer *manqué.* It is like asking a thief to approve a fence, or a fighter to speak highly of a manager."

If ability, natural or acquired, permitted Liebling to substitute Old French for "just plain writing" and, hence, introduced him to Raymond Weeks and the pleasures and intricacies of the Middle Ages, then plain stubbornness and intellectual honesty gave him the opportunity to meet and learn from Max Fischel, "the best head-and-legman I ever saw. The head helps the legs when it knows its way around." Liebling detested the formal instruction in reporting that the school required.

The students were provided with press cards of a sort and were sent out to interview people in the news. "There were two ways to get such interviews, by impersonating a real reporter or by throwing yourself on the mercy of the victim and implying you would flunk if he didn't talk to you. The whole business seemed to me an imposition on the subject." One of the two professors in the course had the effect on Liebling of "a glass of warm water and mustard"; so he went to C. P. Cooper, the other professor, with his problem. Cooper was discreetly sympathetic and sent him to Max Fischel at the newspaper shacks behind Police Headquarters for two days a week. Liebling brought in police items, and Cooper arranged a passing grade.

On the police beat, Liebling learned how to cover a story, how to use his head and his legs, and "that most people are eager to talk about their troubles. . . . Women, in particular, are never so friendly as when something has happened to their husbands. Petronius' story of The Widow of Ephesus should be assigned reading in any practical course on reporting."

From the Pulitzer School, Liebling, recommended by Professor Cooper, went to the *Times* as a copyreader in the sports department. He lasted eight months on the job. His early departure was occasioned by a combination of boredom, a waggish disposition, and a knowledge of Italian. The *Times* did not print basketball stories without knowing and printing the name of the official. School and college games had one official in those days. Frequently, the stringers who called in the stories to the copy desk didn't know the referee's name and were probably low on nickels. A man called Ignoto refereed a lot of basketball games in the New York area that winter, at least according to the *Times*. The sports editor, finally discovering Liebling's peccadillo, fired him one "bitter night in March. 'You are irresponsible. Not a *Times* type. Go.' "

Except for a few weeks when he was between engagements (Liebling never seemed to get a new job while he still had an old one) and except for about fifteen months he spent in France (ostensibly reading medieval literature at the Sorbonne, but actually learning how to eat, learning how to drink, learning how to speak idiomatic French—all esoteric subjects), he worked for daily newspapers from September 1925 until May 1935, when he negotiated a steady job on *The New Yorker*. He had done what he wanted to do. He had even worked for the *World* until it was sold out from under him and almost three thousand other employees. He had established his *bona fides* as a newspaper man. Perhaps "man" is the wrong word, for Liebling once wrote, "newspaper people speak of a police reporter, a City Hall man, and a Washington correspondent, but always of a sports *writer*." On another occasion he extended his taxonomy of newspaper people:

There are three kinds of writers of news in our generation. In

inverse order of worldly consideration, they are:
1. The reporter, who writes what he sees.
2. The interpretive reporter, who writes what he sees and what he construes to be its meaning.
3. The expert, who writes what he construes to be the meaning of what he hasn't seen.

LIEBLING THE CLASSIFIER

He was interested in classification, as these quotations indicate, but he did not confine himself to newspapers and publishing (although I should mention that in *The Wayward Pressman* and *Mink and Red Herring* he insisted that a distinction could and should be made between a Sevellon Brown and a Roy Howard, between a Col. Robert Rutherford McCormick and a Capt. Joseph Medill Patterson; publishers should be classified, too). Classification helped him explain politics in *The Earl of Louisiana;* helped his readers to understand the fine art of "getting by" in *The Telephone Booth Indian* (Indians, Heels, Tenants—there *is* a difference) and *The Honest Rainmaker* (one must learn to distinguish between a plain thief and a "grand old thief"); *Chicago* is *The Second City.*

Liebling, the great taxonomer, worked through genus, through species, through epithet. In *The Sweet Science,* for example, Pierce Egan is, at various times, the Herodotus, the Thucydides, the Froissart, the Holinshed, the Arnold Toynbee, the Edward Gibbon, the Sir Thomas Malory, the Sire de Joinville, the Philippe de Commines of the London prize ring. All these I could understand. But when he referred to Egan as the Blind Raftery of the London prize ring, I went to my reference books. Yes, Virginia, there is a Blind Raftery. He is the title character in a novel written by Brian Oswald Donn-Byrne. Liebling had won again: he had educated while he entertained.

Even war, ineffable war, is subject to classification. *The Road Back to Paris, Mollie, Republic of Silence,* and *Normandy Revisited* give us genus, subgenus, and species. Taxonomy lives and, perhaps, reaches its apotheosis in *Between Meals,* a delightful book that has the alluring subtitle, "An Appetite for Paris." At one point in the book he has something to say about distinctive tastes and sensitive palates:

> Personally, I like tastes that know their own minds. The reason that people who detest fish often tolerate sole is that sole doesn't taste very much like fish, and even this degree of resemblance disappears when it is submerged in the kind of sauce that patrons of Piedmontese restaurants in London and New York think characteristically French. People with the same apathy toward decided flavor relish "South African

lobster" tails—frozen as long as the Siberian mammoth—because they don't taste lobstery. ("South African lobsters" are a kind of sea crayfish, or *langouste,* but that would be nothing against them if they were fresh.) They prefer processed cheese because it isn't cheesy, and synthetic vanilla extract because it isn't vanillary. They have made a triumph of the Delicious apple because it doesn't taste like an apple, and of the Golden Delicious because it doesn't taste like anything. In a related field, "dry" (non-beery) beer and "light" (non-Scotchlike) Scotch are more of the same. The standard of perfection for vodka (no color, no taste, no smell) was expounded to me long ago by the then Estonian consul-general in New York, and it accounts for the drink's rising popularity with those who like their alcohol in conjunction with the reassuring tastes of infancy—tomato juice, orange juice, chicken broth. It is the ideal intoxicant for the drinker who wants no reminder of how hurt Mother would be if she knew what he was doing.

All this is the big picture, A. J. Liebling as gourmand (he would be outraged to be called a gourmet), philosopher, taxonomer, reporter, correspondent, boxing aficionado, critic of the press. But my thesis is that he was a comic writer, and the adjective is more important than the noun. What was his technique? What was his method?

LIEBLING'S COMIC TECHNIQUE

He dealt primarily with farfetched simile and elaborate metaphor. His frame of reference (when he did, and only on occasion, use that phrase, he would frequently modify it by the clause, "as the boys on the literary quarterlies say") was so extremely large that it could encompass such disparate times, places, and cultures as Sisyphus and Rocky Marciano in the same sentence. He probably chuckled as he wrote that pun. He could not resist—and although I find it amusing, I recognize the weakness—such a simile as "an inhibition is a challenge to a psychiatrist, like a leaky faucet to an amateur plumber." Only the adjective, "amateur," redeems it.

And he frequently reaches for the *outré* comparison as in his description of the stagnation of Chicago around 1930: ". . . it stopped as suddenly as a front-running horse at the head of the stretch with a poor man's last two dollars on its nose. What stopped it is a mystery, like what happened to Angkor Vat." A *truite au bleu* he once ate "was served up doused with enough melted butter to thrombose a regiment of Paul Dudley Whites." Lillian Russell "was a butterscotch sundae of a woman, as beautiful as a tulip of beer with a high white collar." Of an extremely thin boxer he wrote, "His torso was so narrow that his heart had standing room only."

Liebling seems to demand a literate reader, one with wide-ranging interests, one who reads and remembers fillers in newspapers. He does not need a profound thinker; he needs someone more important: a reader who can smile; who can chuckle; who can laugh at the adroit juxtaposition of words, sentences, and ideas. "I have always found the New England accent endearing in women. There is a suggestion of primness about it that is as aphrodisiac as a starched gingham dress." Two sentences like that can make an afternoon for me.

Although he devoted a great amount of time to criticism of the press, he was by no means a raw hand at literary criticism. Indeed, he was the author of the most cogent analysis of a great American novel that I have ever read. He was writing on the Marciano-Moore heavyweight championship fight; and he was pointing out, sadly but accurately, that Moore had no chance, when he tossed off this gem, nay this apothegm of literary criticism: "What would *Moby Dick* be if Ahab had succeeded? Just another fish story." In that piece, Moore was both Sisyphus and Ahab; Marciano was the Rock and the white whale; the reader was lucky and laughing.

He was occasionally guilty of a solecism that only a purist would notice, but he rarely misused a noun or a verb. It was an article of faith with him that "the misuse of words should be punished as severely as the misappropriation of funds, and can have far more serious consequences."

The word on the page was important to him, to be sure, but the sound of the word and the sound of the sentence were equally important. He met Wendell Willkie for the first time in January 1941, after Willkie had lost the presidential election to Franklin Delano Roosevelt's third-term bid. Liebling wanted to dislike him, but he could have only compassion for him: "I had imagined him a knave. I found him a naif." Admittedly his ear was not always perfect: "A retroussé nose, for example, looked better under a cloche. The cloche made a girl with an aquiline nose look like the familiar portrait of Savonarola in his hood. It gave her the profile of that bigot or a spigot."

When he first met James Stuart Aloysius Macdonald, a/k/a Colonel John R. Stingo, he was stunned by the colonel's youthful appearance; the colonel was astonished by Liebling's maturity: " 'From your voice,' he [the colonel] said, 'I judged you to be a young neophyte. But I see before me a man with the outward aspect of a Russian heavyweight wrestler.' " Liebling's comment on the colonel's encomium contains almost all the devices found in the sound-effects section of a handbook of poetic analysis and in only eighteen words: "Nothing flatters a fat man more than the suggestion that he is in fact a mass of muscle." Assonance, consonance, alliteration, internal rhyme: what more can you ask of a prose sentence?

Liebling died young (he had just turned fifty-nine), but his collected works fill some fourteen volumes. I keep the seven that I have been able to find (most of them are now out of print; and one of them, *Back Where I Came From,* is available in only one library in the state where I live and Liebling once worked) on a handy shelf next to my easy chair. When I want to smile, chuckle, or laugh, I choose one of the volumes at random. He has never disappointed me. Although he had his serious side and a fine capacity for anger, he could always see the ludicrous in the pretentious.

He is good on everything he writes about, but he is best, I think, when he writes of older people, Colonel Stingo, Madame Hamel, Ned Brown, Al Mayer, Yves Mirande. Perhaps because he wrote so well about old age, he did not have to live it. Although that is a sentimental notion, I am comforted by it. I am also comforted by a memory of two statements that Liebling, as he so often did, translated literally from the French idiom to the English nonidiom. The first was from a young waitress who consoled him when he had drunk himself into melancholy on the first night of his return to Paris as it was liberated. She said, "A chagrin of love never forgets itself . . . You must not make bile about it." The second was from Madame Hamel after he had told her that Sainte-Lô had fallen to the Allied forces. She said, "Perhaps monsieur would like a glass of Calvados? The day must have made you some emotion."

PART 6

TEXTS
AND
DOCUMENTS

Georges Feydeau's
Hortense Said, "No Skin Off My Ass!"

NORMAN R. SHAPIRO

TRANSLATED WITH AN INTRODUCTION

INTRODUCTION

Hortense a dit: "Je m'en fous!" has the sad distinction of being
Georges Feydeau's last completed play, produced in 1916, some five
years before his death at age fifty-eight.[1] Capping—or crowning—his
illustrious career, it has the less sad distinction of being one of the
few comedies ever written about a dentist. (Pun intended. With Feydeau no apologies necessary.) But Follbraguet the dentist is, obviously
enough, only a convenient excuse for Follbraguet the long-suffering
husband, enmeshed in the web of his wife's extravagant behavior.
And it doesn't take too daring an interpretation to go one step further and see Follbraguet the husband as only a flesh-and-blood embodiment of Man, abstract sufferer and victim, trapped in an indifferent,
if not outright hostile, universe.

To some extent all farce portrays its characters as victims, from
Pathelin to Ionesco and beyond, with Chaplin and the Keystone Kops
thrown in—victims of something or someone, whether brickbats or

bullies, one's adversaries or oneself, comic quid pro quos or cosmic misadventures. Feydeau's theater, from beginning to end, is no exception. From his earliest farces—a term that, by the way, to the best of my knowledge, he never applied to his comedies himself—it presents an array of hapless victims whose suffering—sometimes deserved, more often gratuitous—runs the gamut from mere embarrassing misunderstanding to physical discomfort, panic, and unbridled, unspeakable frustration.

It is especially this frustration that harries the antiheroes of the group of five late one-act plays of conjugal discord, originally to be entitled *Du mariage au divorce*.[2] Unlike the jack-in-the-box *vaudevilles*, the door-slamming extravaganzas that had made Feydeau famous—complex, intricately crafted bedroom farces like *Champignol malgré lui* (1892), *Un Fil à la patte* (1894), *La Dame de chez Maxim* (1899)—these semiserious comedies, tracing the vicissitudes and gradual disintegration of a marriage, portray the prototypic *mal mariés*, each time with different names and in different circumstances, but clearly the same couple behind the veil of theatrical fiction. They even seem to imply, ironically, that Feydeau, the uncontested master of the Boulevard for so many years, was far from being master of his own ménage. In fact, Jean-Louis Barrault takes this assumption as a given: "Madame Feydeau was in a sense his muse . . . [for] these one-act masterpieces"[3]—and a plausible assumption too, considering the couple's divorce in 1916, the very year in which *Hortense* was produced. But such details are hardly essential. Truistically, the play's the thing, and the circumstances behind it are only petty gossip.

Why Feydeau decided, after so many successes, virtually to abandon the comedy of frenetic imbroglio that had been his stock-in-trade in favor of these more modestly dimensioned (but no less frenetic) comedies need not be a subject for lengthy speculation in this brief introduction. He was, to be sure, no stranger to short plays. But the jovial one-acters written at the beginning of his career and those that dotted it sporadically throughout were a far cry from the late tableaux of marital bedlam and breakup. Do these latter, indeed, represent something of a sublimation, a therapeutic working-out of his own domestic problems? Or are they, perhaps, the result of a kind of artistic menopause, a change in the rhythm of his creative life and sign of a need for renewal? More simply, are they, as I have suggested elsewhere, an evidence of the turn-of-the-century decline of the prestige of the *vaudeville*? Or even of Feydeau's legendary laziness?[4]

Be that as it may, these late plays, though hailed by critics of the time as a new departure for Feydeau's comic talent, don't really depart all that much from the Feydeau of the nineties. The quintessential element remains constant throughout, namely, that hallmark of his technique, the Bergsonian buildup of minute cause into gigantic effect. Because of the reduced dimensions, the intensity is, in a sense, all the greater. Thus, for example, in *On purge Bébé,* young Toto's debatable case of constipation will result, through a chain of absurdly logical links, in his father's professional, social, and marital debacle. Likewise in the other plays of the group. In the present comedy, readers will see for themselves how Hortense's cat (allegedly) sets off a string of events that lead the innocent Follbraguet over the concrete threshold of home to the abstract threshold of utter emotional collapse.

Here, too, is another important similarity between the late comedies and the more flamboyant, hilarious nightmares so long synonymous with Feydeau's name. Realistic as they are, in the tradition of *fin de siècle* stagecraft, they are nonetheless interpretable, as I have implied, as dramatizations of Man's fate, with a capital *M.* If earlier heroes—victims?—like a Champignol, a Bouzin, a Petypon—look like so many helpless puppets caught up in frenzied attempts to resist seemingly arbitrary and larger-than-life destinies, surely our poor dentist friend seems no less so, despite the more down-to-earth proportions of his plight. And if Follbraguet is symbolic of innocent suffering, what should we say about his patients Leboucq and Vildamour, physical victims-once-removed of the rage and frustration that have snowballed within him at each of Madame's infuriating attacks?

* * *

Such, of course, is only one interpretation, and I have put it forward myself on more than one occasion.[5] Others may choose to see this comedy in terms of its social implications: the age-old battle of the sexes; the conflict of the classes, embodied in the venerable antagonism between master (or, in this case, mistress) and servant; the power of the word in human interaction. Still others may even plow through the text to unearth a structuralist interpretation or labor in the sacrosanct vineyards of semiotics... But just to keep everything in proper perspective, let us not forget—my own interpretive prejudices notwithstanding—that we need not really look for "deep meanings" in Feydeau in order to enjoy him. (Some might even suggest that it is counterproductive to do so.) No doubt he considered himself more a craftsman than a commentator. And no shame in that. He was, after all, a playwright, not a philosopher or sociologist, and he would probably be the first to guffaw at metaphysical or social interpretations, however defensible. His intention, quite simply—"intentional fallacy" aside—was to make his audiences laugh; and at this he was, and is, a consummate master, doubling them up—then and now—when well performed. In an often-quoted passage he gives us his recipe:

> When I am arranging all that madness that unleashes the

spectators' glee, I am not amused by it. I keep the cool, calm
poise of the chemist measuring out his medicine. I put into
my pill a gram of imbroglio, a gram of licentiousness, a gram
of observation. As well as I can, I grind them all into a pow-
der. And I can tell, almost without fail, what effect they will
produce.[6]

His comic genius lay, precisely, in knowing how to dose each ingredient to produce exactly the proper amalgam.

But Feydeau, in this formula, barely scratches the surface, leaving
out, it seems, much more than he puts in. No mention here of the
many devices that a reading of *Hortense* alone will reveal—devices of
low and high comedy alike: the off-color anatomical allusion (cat pee
indeed!), the evocative name, the wordplay and pun, the cajoling
manipulation of one character by another, the *faux pas,* the affecta-
tion... Readers will discover each, one and more, without my guidance.

And, above all, that tearing of hair and that gnashing of teeth.
That grinding of relentless, implacable gears that we find so irresis-
tibly, almost perversely, amusing—as Baudelaire and Freud were
to tell us, each in his own way—only because we're not caught in them
ourselves. Only because we can watch, on page or stage, from the
comfort of our armchairs.

* * *

Not long ago I brought the manuscript of *Hortense Said, "No
Skin Off My Ass!"* to be xeroxed. When I went to pick it up, the clerk
handed it to me with a wry smile and quipped: "Catchy title! I bet
it'll sell!" I'm sure he had no idea how much of a problem that title
had posed. (Only the first of many. Like most translations, this one
presented its share and demanded a corresponding number of liberties.) At first casual glance, Hortense's vulgar outburst, triggering the
reverse-Ibsenian—Ibscene?—denouement of sorts, would not appear
to offer the translator any special challenge. *Je m'en fous!* is a common enough exclamation, and it springs to a Frenchman's lips as
readily and in roughly the same circumstances as "I don't give a damn!"
to an American's. Indeed, dictionaries usually translate it that way.
But here a kind of linguistic generation gap yawns open before us:
at the time Feydeau was writing, *je m'en fous!* was a much more scan-
dalous curse than "I don't give a damn!" would be to audiences today.
Clearly something stronger had to be found to preserve Feydeau's
intent and something, by the way, that would let Madame Follbraguet
display no less vulgarity than her maid, when, moments later, in her
own lapse of verbal decorum, she uses the same then-taboo verb to

order her husband: *"Fous-la dehors!"*

But problems, as I have parenthetically suggested, seldom end with titles. Even something as seemingly straightforward as names can often raise roadblocks. Where most practical to do so, I have left them as is, despite temptation. "Follbraguet" and "Laboucq," for example. The former evokes vaguely lascivious associations—"Wild-pants," or something in that general area—funny but not essential. The latter might well have been translated to imply the character's innocent suffering—as in *bouc émissaire,* "scapegoat"—but *bouc* has so many other connotations that Feydeau's intent wasn't really clear enough to justify a change. Other names, however, have had to be altered for obvious reasons. What spectators or readers today, for instance—even in France, let alone the United States—would appreciate an allusion to La Belle Otéro? Rather few, at most. Hence, in this version, she becomes another foreign theatrical beauty of the day, but one whose fame has better weathered the years: the celebrated Pavlova. A minor point, to be sure, for she is only referred to in passing and never appears on stage. Like Monsieur Grosbourgeois, whose name—"Monsieur Bienassis" in the original—should, in translation, conjure up visions of a prosperous, even pompous, well-established burgher, while remaining French (and comprehensible French at that). More important, because the characters play a functional role onstage, are the names of Albert and Madame Bizarre, rebaptized from Feydeau's originals, "Adrien" and "Madame Dingue." Practical acting considerations dictated the first change. "Albert" is more common to American ears; and, even more to the point, it is easier for an American actor to pronounce with a reasonable French accent than is "Adrien," with its Gallic *r* and its nasal ending, too likely to slip into its English equivalent. As for Madame Dingue, her name is too explicit to leave unchanged. The slang term *dingue* translates roughly as "dingbat." A counterpart had to be found in English that got across the meaning, yet still sounded French. Fortunately, "Madame Bizarre" is as bizarre a name in both—with a little help from "Zsa-Zsa" as icing on the cake.

But titles and names, however thorny, take a backseat to the pun as the translator's bugbear, especially in Feydeau. And no less so in this, his final play, then in all its predecessors. Without my troubling to enumerate them in detail, suffice it to say that Hortense's outrageous malapropisms and other examples of verbal banter throughout only represent attempts at equivalent wordplay. The same tune in a different key, as it were. No one, I hope, will take them for literal translations. Literally translatable puns are rare birds indeed. And perhaps just as well. Wrestling with the challenge is, after all, half the fun...

So much, in sum, for the problems faced and the liberties taken. Speaking of these, let us not forget that the greatest liberty of all is translating a text of a master in the first place. But translation, to its adepts, is a curious kind of pleasure. (Masochistic, in a sense. How else can we explain the translator's devotion to a discipline where one flaw stands out above a myriad successes?) And so, I beg Feydeau the master's posthumous indulgence for taking that liberty and reaping that pleasure. If others enjoy the results as well, so much the better.

NOTES

1. Two comedies dating from the last years of his life remained unfinished: *Cent millions qui tombent* and *On va faire la cocotte.* (The first was eventually finished by Yves Mirande.)

2. The other plays are *Feu la mère de Madame* (1908), *On purge Bébé* (1910), *Mais n'te promène donc pas toute nue!* (1911), and *Léonie est en avance (ou Le Mal joli)* (1911).

3. *Une Troupe et ses auteurs* (Paris: Vautrain, 1950), p. 52. (Translation my own.)

4. See my *Four Farces by Georges Feydeau* (Chicago: University of Chicago Press, 1970), pp. xli–xliii.

5. Ibid., pp. xliii ff.

6. Quoted in Adolphe Brisson, *Portraits intimes* (Paris: Armand Colin, 1901), Vol. 5, pp. 15–16. (Translation my own.)

Georges Feydeau's
Hortense a dit: "Je m'en fous!"
translated by
Norman R. Shapiro as
Hortense Said, "No Skin Off My Ass!"

Characters

Follbraguet   Marcelle Follbraguet
Monsieur Jean   Hortense
Vildamour   Madame Bizarre
Leboucq   Yvette
Albert

FOLLBRAGUET'S *office. Upstage, a wall with two doors: one far left, leading to the waiting room; the other far right, leading to the hall. Between the two, a sink. In the wall midstage left, a drape-covered doorway. Next to it, downstage, a small table with an autoclave. In the wall midstage right, the door to* MADAME FOLLBRAGUET'S *room. Next to it, downstage, a fireplace. Downstage left, a desk, perpendicular to the footlights, with an armchair between it and the wall. Upstage, a coatrack with* FOLLBRAGUET'S *hat and coat. Center stage, facing the audience, the dentist's chair, drill, and appropriate apparatus: bowl, saliva-pump, and so on. Close by, stage right, a small instrument cabinet with a number of drawers. Other incidental furniture ad lib.*

At rise, VILDAMOUR *is sitting in the dentist's chair, a napkin around his neck. A rubber gag is strapped tightly over his mouth, leaving only the crucial tooth exposed. The saliva-pump is hanging from one corner. He is obviously in agony.* FOLLBRAGUET, *in his long smock, is busily drilling.*

VILDAMOUR. Aaaay! Aaa-aaa-aaaay!
FOLLBRAGUET. It's all right. All right... Just a little more now. Open wide.
VILDAMOUR. Aaa-aaa-aaaay!
FOLLBRAGUET. *(drilling away)* Don't even think about it. Try and think of something pleasant.
VILDAMOUR. *(grunting through the gag, just barely comprehensible)*

Gakf ee-vee fuh oo kuh fay! ["That's easy for you to say!"]

FOLLBRAGUET. Keep your head still. Please... Now open wide... It doesn't hurt a bit. Believe me.

VILDAMOUR. *(louder)* Aaaaaaaay!

FOLLBRAGUET. You'll see. When it's going to hurt, I'll tell you. Don't worry.

(He stops and changes the burr on the drill)

VILDAMOUR. *(as before)* Fankf uh waw! A kahnk waik! ["Thanks a lot! I can't wait!"]

FOLLBRAGUET. All right now. Open wide... Good. Now just relax. This time it's going to hurt a little.

VILDAMOUR. *(terrified)* Haaa?

FOLLBRAGUET. See? I'm not trying to fool you... *(VILDAMOUR desperately shakes his head from side to side)* Please! Keep your head still! I told you...

VILDAMOUR. *(worn out)* Ho gik... Ho gik uh ngi-ik! Fuh gaw fake, ho gik! ["Hold it... Hold it a minute! For God's sake, hold it!"]

FOLLBRAGUET. Just a little more now. We're almost finished. It's nothing... Nothing at all...

VILDAMOUR. Aw ngaw! Ngaw fuh oo! Oo kahnk fee ik, gang ik! ["Oh no! Not for you! You can't feel it, damn it!"]

FOLLBRAGUET. *(mechanically agreeing)* Yes, that's right... I know...

VILDAMOUR. Ik feev ngike oor gri-i froo ngy graign! Froo ngy haw gaw-gi! ["It feels like you're drilling through my brain! Through my whole body!"]

FOLLBRAGUET. I know... I know...

VILDAMOUR. Gaw-ga koo-fake! A ngike kuh gek ngy hangv aw guh fung-uv-uh-gikf hoo ing-veng-kug ik! ["Goddamn toothache! I'd like to get my hands on the son-of-a-bitch who invented it!"]

FOLLBRAGUET. I know...

VILDAMOUR. A hag wung uh kuh-koo uh eev uh-gaw, guh ik wuv nguh-fing ike gif! ["I had one a couple of years ago, but it was nothing like this!"]

FOLLBRAGUET. Yes, I know... *(About to begin drilling again)* All right now, open wide.

VILDAMOUR. Fuh gaw fake! Ngaw guh gri uh-geng! ["For God's sake! Not the drill again!"]

FOLLBRAGUET. Just once more. A little touch for good measure. *(Drilling)* See? You can hardly feel it. Now can you? ·

VILDAMOUR. Aaaaaay!

FOLLBRAGUET. *(Still drilling over VILDAMOUR'S groans)* It's got to be done if you want to save the tooth... Open... Open wide... There! That's not so terrible, is it? Every day like this for a week, and I bet you'd get to like it.

VILDAMOUR. *(with a desperate look, even louder)* Aaaaay! Aaaaay! Aaaaay!

FOLLBRAGUET. Don't worry, I'm only joking!... All right, there we are. All finished... *(He keeps on drilling)* All finished...

VILDAMOUR. Aaaaay!

FOLLBRAGUET. There! *(He finally stops)*

VILDAMOUR. *(starting to get up, sighing)* Ah!

FOLLBRAGUET. *(pushing him back down)* Not yet. I'm not through. *(He lights a little alcohol burner)*

VILDAMOUR. *(aghast)* Oo keek fay-ing, "Aw fi-if, aw fi-if," guh oo ngo fkok! ["You keep saying 'All finished, all finished,' but you don't stop!"]

FOLLBRAGUET. *(heating a rubber bulb over the flame)* This won't hurt. Just a little hot air... Now open up nice and wide. *(VILDAMOUR winces with each jet)* See?

VILDAMOUR. Ugh! Af aw-fl! ["That's awful!"] *(He begins to close his mouth)*

FOLLBRAGUET. *(quickly)* No, no! Open! Open! Don't close until I tell you! *(He prepares a cotton swab, dips it into a vial of liquid, and plugs it up into the tooth)* Fine! That wasn't so bad now, was it? *(He undoes the rubber gag, removes the saliva-pump, and hands VILDAMOUR a small glass of mouthwash)* Spit out!

VILDAMOUR. *(rinsing his mouth a few times)* Whew! I wouldn't want to go through that again!

FOLLBRAGUET. *(moving to his desk)* Don't be silly. It's all in the mind. It only hurts if you let yourself think so... Well now, we'll leave the medication in for a day or two. Then you'll come back and we'll put in the filling. *(Flipping through his appointment book)* Let's see what my appointments look like... Hmmm... How about the day after tomorrow? Say five o'clock? Are you free?

VILDAMOUR. Day after tomorrow? Five o'clock?... No... No, there's this man I have to see...

FOLLBRAGUET. Well then... *(About to look for another time)* How about...

VILDAMOUR. Never mind. That's all right... He's coming to collect a bill. He can go whistle for it!

FOLLBRAGUET. Oh? If you're sure... *(Jotting down the appointment)* February the eleventh, five o'clock, Monsieur Vildamour. There! You won't forget...

VILDAMOUR. Me? Forget an appointment? Never!... Look, if I remember when somebody's coming to collect a bill... *(He pauses)* Five o'clock, the eleventh... *(He pauses again, putting his hand to his cheek)* You know, doctor, this tooth is still killing me.

FOLLBRAGUET. *(waiting for him to leave, indifferently)* Right, right...

VILDAMOUR. I mean, it hurts like the devil.

FOLLBRAGUET. *(nodding)* Right...

VILDAMOUR. It really does.

FOLLBRAGUET. Right, right...

VILDAMOUR. *(a little piqued at* FOLLBRAGUET'S *apparent lack of concern)* But it's killing me, doctor. Is that all you can say?

FOLLBRAGUET. That's all I can say because it's perfectly normal. After all that drilling... It takes time to settle. Give it about fifteen minutes. It should start to let up.

VILDAMOUR. Aha?

FOLLBRAGUET. *(ringing for the butler as he speaks)* Of course, if you keep having trouble, don't hesitate to come back. I'll manage to fit you in.

VILDAMOUR. Thank you, doctor. I appreciate that. There aren't many like you, believe me. It's like I always tell my friends: "My dentist is a prince! He's one of a kind!... And painless? Absolutely painless!"

FOLLBRAGUET. *(flattered)* And what do your friends say to that?

VILDAMOUR. They usually say: "So is mine."

FOLLBRAGUET. *(taken aback)* Oh? Well...

(ALBERT enters from the hall, up right)

ALBERT. Monsieur rang?

FOLLBRAGUET. Yes, Albert. Show Monsieur Vildamour out, will you please? *(ALBERT and VILDAMOUR move to leave)* And while you're at it... *(Pointing off, left)* ...step around and send in Monsieur Jean. *(Calling after* VILDAMOUR*)* Day after tomorrow, then?

VILDAMOUR. *(nodding)* Five o'clock.

FOLLBRAGUET. And be sure to keep your mouth covered. We don't want you catching a cold in that tooth. *(Suddenly noticing that* VILDAMOUR *still has the napkin around his neck)* Just a minute! My napkin!

VILDAMOUR. Oh, sorry! *(He takes it off and drapes it over the back of the dentist's chair. ALBERT has already opened the door, up right. MARCELLE can be seen in the hall, arguing with HORTENSE, who keeps trying to get a word in edgewise)*

MARCELLE. No, no, no! I've had all I'm going to take! When I tell you something, young lady, you can keep your mouth shut!

FOLLBRAGUET. What in the name... What's the matter?

(VILDAMOUR goes out the door with ALBERT close behind)

VILDAMOUR. *(squeezing by MARCELLE)* Madame!

MARCELLE. *(curtly)* Monsieur!

FOLLBRAGUET. For heaven's sake, Marcelle! The hall is no place to be arguing with the help. Especially during office hours!

(MARCELLE stamps into the office, brandishing a fur muff. She heads straight for FOLLBRAGUET and holds it out to him)

MARCELLE. Here! Feel this!

FOLLBRAGUET. I'm telling you, the hall is no place—

MARCELLE. Well, I'm not in the hall! I'm in your office! Now just feel this!

FOLLBRAGUET. *(mechanically complying)* Why on earth... What is it? It's all wet.

MARCELLE. *(triumphant)* Aha! *(Toward HORTENSE, still in the hall)* See? *(To FOLLBRAGUET)* You can feel how wet it is, can't you?

HORTENSE. *(at the threshold)* So? I never said it wasn't.

FOLLBRAGUET. *(instinctively sniffing his fingers)* A little water or something...

MARCELLE. Water? You really think it's water?

FOLLBRAGUET. Well? It's wet, isn't it?

HORTENSE. *(to MARCELLE)* See!

MARCELLE. It's cat pee, that's what it is!

FOLLBRAGUET. *(furious, holding up his hand)* It's what?

MARCELLE. That shows how much you know!

FOLLBRAGUET. *(going to the sink and washing)* Then why the hell did you make me stick my fingers in it? What kind of a disgusting—

HORTENSE. Don't blame me, Monsieur. It's Madame... She's got this idea that my cat went and did a job on her muff. But it couldn't be my cat, Monsieur. Everybody knows she never does it in the apartment. It just couldn't be...

MARCELLE. Good God, all you've got to do is smell it! *(Thrusting the muff under FOLLBRAGUET'S nose)* Here!

FOLLBRAGUET. *(recoiling)* No, damn it!

(MONSIEUR JEAN enters through the draped doorway, stage left, in a long smock)

MONSIEUR JEAN. You wanted to see me, Monsieur Follbraguet?

FOLLBRAGUET. *(wiping his hands)* Yes... Yes, I did.

MARCELLE. *(holding out the muff)* Here, Monsieur Jean. Please smell this and tell me what you think it is.

FOLLBRAGUET. Oh no, for heaven's sake! You're not going to—

MARCELLE. *(to FOLLBRAGUET)* Please! Don't say a word. Let him make up his own mind.

MONSIEUR JEAN. *(taking a few polite whiffs)* Hmmm! I can't say I care much for it...

MARCELLE. That's not what I asked you. What do you think it is?

(FOLLBRAGUET grits his teeth)

MONSIEUR JEAN. *(inhaling deeply, scratching his head)* Eucalyptus oil?

MARCELLE. *(brandishing the muff in his face, categorically)* No, Monsieur! It's cat pee!

MONSIEUR JEAN. *(wiping his nose)* Hmmm! I can't say I care much for it at all...

MARCELLE. *(to HORTENSE)* You see? Everyone says so. Now that ought to shut you up!

FOLLBRAGUET. *(trying to push them into the hall)* Listen, I don't care what it is. Cat pee or not. Go argue somewhere else. I'll be damned if I want my patients to have to hear your nonsense!

MARCELLE. *(as FOLLBRAGUET pushes her out, to HORTENSE)*
Now maybe you'll admit that that cat of yours—
HORTENSE. *(still at the threshold)* What? Admit what? Why
should I go and admit some stupid lie?
MARCELLE. Oh! Don't you dare... Don't you dare speak to me that
way! When I tell you something—
FOLLBRAGUET. *(finally pushing them out)* Damn it, you two! Get
out and let me work in peace! *(He slams the door on them and
grumbles to himself, as the argument, muffled, can be heard trailing
off)* Incredible! Always something... Not a day goes by... *(To
MONSIEUR JEAN)* Now then, what did I want to ask you?... Oh
yes... *(Pointing to the draped doorway)* Are you working on any-
one in there?
MONSIEUR JEAN. Not anymore, Monsieur. Madame Pavlova was
here a few minutes ago...
FOLLBRAGUET. Madame Pavlova?
MONSIEUR JEAN. Yes, Monsieur.
FOLLBRAGUET. *The* Madame Pavlova?
MONSIEUR JEAN. Yes, Monsieur. A little trouble with a wisdom
tooth...
FOLLBRAGUET. Oh?
MONSIEUR JEAN. I incised the gum for her. No problem.
FOLLBRAGUET. Aha! *(Muttering under his breath, impressed)*
Madame Pavlova! *(To MONSIEUR JEAN)* What does she look
like? Is she as pretty as her pictures?
MONSIEUR JEAN. Is she? I'll say!
FOLLBRAGUET. Then why on earth didn't you call me in? I'd give
anything to see her.
MONSIEUR JEAN. Well, you were busy with a patient... And I knew
I could handle her myself...
FOLLBRAGUET. *(with a knowing wink)* I'll bet!
MONSIEUR JEAN. So...
FOLLBRAGUET. *(facetiously)* Never miss a chance, do you, Monsieur
Jean! Especially when they're pretty!
MONSIEUR JEAN. *(suddenly understanding his veiled allusions,
naïvely)* Oh, Monsieur Follbraguet! Really! Me? With Madame
Pavlova?... I wouldn't dream... She wouldn't... We never even gave
it a thought!
FOLLBRAGUET. *(slyly)* Oh?
MONSIEUR JEAN. *(solemnly)* Never! I swear!
FOLLBRAGUET. Well, if you say so... *(Getting back to business,
after a few chuckles at MONSIEUR JEAN'S expense)* Look, I'd like
you to run over to What's-His-Name... The supplier...
MONSIEUR JEAN. Bringuet.
FOLLBRAGUET. Right, Bringuet... And tell him that last batch of
amalgam he sent us wasn't worth a damn. Every filling I use it for

breaks up and falls out. I'm not complaining, tell him. I just want him to exchange it.

MONSIEUR JEAN. Yes, Monsieur. Anything else?

FOLLBRAGUET. No, that's all.

(MONSIEUR JEAN *nods and is about to leave. Before he has a chance,* MARCELLE *bursts in, up right)*

MARCELLE. Look, will you please—

FOLLBRAGUET. Oh no! Not again!

MARCELLE. *(looking around, pointing to the empty dentist's chair)* What's the matter? You're not busy...

FOLLBRAGUET. I beg your pardon! *(Gesturing up left)* There are people out there waiting.

MARCELLE. Well, let them wait! When you've got a toothache, you expect to have to wait. This is more important. I want you to tell that girl she's fired. And I mean this very minute!

FOLLBRAGUET. What? What now?

MARCELLE. What now? I'll tell you "what now"! I was standing there giving her a piece of my mind, and you know what she comes out with? "No skin off my ass!" *(Hands on hips)* Now how do you like that?

FOLLBRAGUET. Well... Tell her it's no skin off yours either, damn it!

MARCELLE. *(furious)* Tell her... You mean you're going to let her talk to your wife—

FOLLBRAGUET. *(sarcastically)* She's lucky! She lets things roll off her back!

(MONSIEUR JEAN *tries to stifle a little laugh)*

MARCELLE. *(to* MONSIEUR JEAN*)* I suppose you think that's funny!

MONSIEUR JEAN. Me, Madame?

MARCELLE. *(to* FOLLBRAGUET*)* Oh yes, very clever! Of course, I'm not surprised. A lot you care how people insult me! You let them walk all over me... Say anything they please... Everybody knows. That's why nobody thinks twice...

FOLLBRAGUET. What are you talking about? Walk all over you... If you'd just leave that poor child alone... Stop picking on her all the time...

MARCELLE. Oh, of course! Now it's my fault! Now I'm picking on her! Really!

MONSIEUR JEAN. *(to* FOLLBRAGUET*)* Should I go now, Monsieur?

FOLLBRAGUET. Yes, please, Monsieur Jean. I'm sure you don't want to have to listen to this.

MONSIEUR JEAN. Oh no, it's not that... I just thought...

FOLLBRAGUET. I know, I know... I understand... *(He motions him off with several waves of the hand.* MONSIEUR JEAN *exits through the draped doorway)*

MARCELLE. There! That's typical! Even someone like him can insult me! Just typical!

FOLLBRAGUET. What?

MARCELLE. And why not, when he sees the way you make fun of me yourself...

FOLLBRAGUET. What are you talking about? In the first place, he didn't insult you...

MARCELLE. No, but give him time. You'll see... The idea! Standing up for that... that tramp! Taking her side...

FOLLBRAGUET. Whose side? I'm not taking her side...

MARCELLE. Oh, forget it! I've learned my lesson. *(Sarcastically)* From now on I'll remember that a fur muff is something for my maid's cat to pee on!

FOLLBRAGUET. *(moving upstage)* Now look, I've had it up to here with that cat! You can grind her up into mincemeat for all I care, only let me have some peace!

MARCELLE. *(after a brief pause)* Well?

FOLLBRAGUET. Well what?

MARCELLE. Are you going to fire her, or aren't you?

FOLLBRAGUET. Marcelle, you're... you're impossible!

MARCELLE. *(going to the door, up right, calling)* Hortense!... Hortense!

FOLLBRAGUET. Listen, that's enough!

MARCELLE. Hortense! Come here this minute!

HORTENSE'S VOICE. I'm coming!

(FOLLBRAGUET throws up his hands. The door, up right, opens and HORTENSE appears at the threshold)

MARCELLE. *(pointing)* Inside! Monsieur has something to tell you. *(HORTENSE enters)*

FOLLBRAGUET *(babbling)* What?... No... I mean...

MARCELLE. He wants to tell you that you're fired. *(Glowering at FOLLBRAGUET)* Doesn't he?

FOLLBRAGUET. I mean...

MARCELLE. I just told him the lovely way you answered me back, and he's perfectly furious.

FOLLBRAGUET. *(losing patience)* Damn it! It's incredible!

MARCELLE. *(to HORTENSE)* There! You see? He thinks it's incredible.

HORTENSE. *(to FOLLBRAGUET)* Did Monsieur mean me when he said that, Monsieur?

MARCELLE. *(to HORTENSE)* I suppose you have the nerve to suggest he meant me?

HORTENSE. Who can tell?

MARCELLE. *(to FOLLBRAGUET)* There! You hear that? You hear the way she answers me back?

FOLLBRAGUET. Well...

MARCELLE. Go on. Tell her. Be man enough to say what you think
   for once.
FOLLBRAGUET. Like what, for instance?
MARCELLE. Like what? Like... She tells your wife, "No skin off my
   ass!" and you think that's right? You're just going to stand there and
   let her get away with it?
FOLLBRAGUET. *(without much conviction)* No...
MARCELLE. Well, prove it then. Tell her she's fired. *(Long pause)*
   Well?
FOLLBRAGUET. What's the hurry?
HORTENSE. *(to* FOLLBRAGUET*)* I'm sure Monsieur knows how
   much I'd hate to leave. He's always been so nice to me, I mean. But
   if Monsieur says I have to...
FOLLBRAGUET. Look, Hortense. Why don't you show me exactly
   how you said it...
MARCELLE. *(angrily)* Show you how... "No skin off my ass!" That's
   how! How many ways can you say a thing like that?
FOLLBRAGUET. Well...
MARCELLE. Well nothing! No maid is going to swear like a trooper
   at me. Not at me, understand?
FOLLBRAGUET. But—
MARCELLE. Shoot off her filthy mouth in my face, will she?
FOLLBRAGUET. But—
MARCELLE. *(losing control)* Now kick her out, damn it! Kick her out
   on her ass! Once and for all!
FOLLBRAGUET. *(to* HORTENSE, *resigned)* I'm afraid Madame has
   her mind made up, Hortense. You heard what she said.
HORTENSE. *(to* FOLLBRAGUET*)* Yes, Monsieur. I understand.
   (Long, uneasy pause) You know, I'm really going to miss Monsieur.
   He's always been so good to the help, I mean, and—
MARCELLE. *(sharply)* That's enough! Go on! Go get your account
   book, and Monsieur will figure up what he still owes you. Go on!
(HORTENSE exits, up right)
FOLLBRAGUET. *(standing by his desk)* Did you have to bite the poor
   child's head off just because she was trying to say something nice to
   me?
MARCELLE. Nice, my foot! How can you be so blind? That was just
   another one of her nasty pokes at me.
FOLLBRAGUET. Oh yes! That's you! That's you all over! Always
   looking for those deep, dark motives...
MARCELLE. Well, that's better than being a... a jellyfish, for heaven's
   sake!
FOLLBRAGUET. Of course! Dare disagree, and you're a jellyfish!
   What else! *(There is a knock at the door, up left)* Come in!
(ALBERT enters)
ALBERT. Monsieur won't forget. He has a lady in the waiting room.

FOLLBRAGUET. I know. If Madame here would get off my neck for one minute...

MARCELLE. Now that's really what I call tact!

FOLLBRAGUET. Well, it's true. *(to ALBERT)* Show her in.

MARCELLE. *(exiting to her room, stage right)* Jellyfish!

FOLLBRAGUET. *(calling after her as she leaves)* Of course! You're right!

ALBERT. *(opening the door, up left)* This way, Madame.

(MADAME BIZARRE enters, carrying a handbag and a muff)

FOLLBRAGUET. Please, Madame. Come right in.

MADAME BIZARRE. *(to ALBERT, as he steps aside)* Excuse me...

(ALBERT exits by the same door)

FOLLBRAGUET. *(consulting his appointment book)* Did you have an appointment, Madame?

MADAME BIZARRE. *(leaving her muff on the desk)* No, Doctor. This is my first visit. I hope you don't mind. You see, my regular dentist passed away...

FOLLBRAGUET. Oh, I'm sorry...

MADAME BIZARRE. Yes, I really have terrible luck when it comes to dentists. He's the third one I've lost already.

FOLLBRAGUET. The third... *(Half-seriously)* Thanks for telling me!

MADAME BIZARRE. *(realizing her gaffe)* Oh no, Doctor. That doesn't mean that... Well, besides, only time will tell.

FOLLBRAGUET. Much obliged!

MADAME BIZARRE. Anyway, Doctor, one of your patients is a very dear friend of mine, and I thought it would be all right. Monsieur Grosbourgeois...

FOLLBRAGUET. *(nodding)* Aha...

MADAME BIZARRE. You do know the one I mean?

FOLLBRAGUET. Monsieur Grosbourgeois? Of course I know him. I've got a lawsuit going with Monsieur Grosbourgeois...

MADAME BIZARRE. *(taken aback)* Oh! He didn't tell me...

FOLLBRAGUET. Yes. Nonpayment of bills.

MADAME BIZARRE. *(relieved)* Oh, nothing serious then. Only money...

FOLLBRAGUET. *(echoing)* Only money...

MADAME BIZARRE. Money isn't everything, after all.

FOLLBRAGUET. No...

MADAME BIZARRE. Like I always say, it can't buy happiness!

FOLLBRAGUET. It's a wonder the rich are so damned attached to theirs!

MADAME BIZARRE. Isn't it the truth!... *(FOLLBRAGUET nods)* But I really shouldn't take your time chatting this way, Doctor. Let me tell you my problem. My little accident.

FOLLBRAGUET. Yes... Please...

MADAME BIZARRE. It happened while I was eating some lentils, and... Well, you know how careless the help can be these days... Anyway, Doctor, to make a long story short, I bit into a little stone and broke a tooth.

FOLLBRAGUET. My, my! That's a shame! Let's have a look. *(Pointing to the dentist's chair.)* Here, make yourself comfortable.

MADAME BIZARRE. With pleasure. *(She sits down)*

FOLLBRAGUET. *(ready to examine her mouth)* Now then, which tooth is it? *(He raises the chair with several pumps of the pedal)*

MADAME BIZARRE. Just a second. I'll show you. *(Taking a denture out of her handbag.)* See?

FOLLBRAGUET. *(surprised)* Oh, you mean... I thought...

MADAME BIZARRE. *(a little embarrassed)* It goes without saying, I'd rather no one knew.

FOLLBRAGUET. Of course, my dear lady. Medical ethics... I wouldn't dream...

MADAME BIZARRE. *(handing him the denture, admiringly)* Really a lovely job, don't you think?

FOLLBRAGUET. *(nodding approval)* Hmmm... Very nice...

MADAME BIZARRE. They were the last ones he ever made. Just before he died.

FOLLBRAGUET. Your last dentist, you mean? Before me, that is...

MADAME BIZARRE. Yes, poor thing. I asked him to make me something really special. Something... Well, I don't know if you feel the way I do, Doctor, but I've always thought the first thing a woman should have is beautiful teeth.

FOLLBRAGUET. *(nodding)* As long as she can afford them.

MADAME BIZARRE. Exactly.

FOLLBRAGUET. You won't find a dentist in the world who'll disagree. *(He lets the chair down)*

MADAME BIZARRE. *(amused)* Wheeee!

FOLLBRAGUET. *(laughing)* Last stop. Everybody out!

MADAME BIZARRE. Oh, that was fun! *(She stands up)*

FOLLBRAGUET. *(gradually getting back to business, examining the denture)* Well now, this doesn't look so bad. We'll have to replace one tooth, that's all. The only thing is, it's going to take a few days. I hope you don't need them right away.

MADAME BIZARRE. Oh no! Take your time. I'll just use my everyday set...

FOLLBRAGUET. Oh, you mean these are your Sunday best?

MADAME BIZARRE. Heavens no, Doctor! Nothing that pretentious! It's just that, when I go to a party or a dinner... You know... But I have no parties or dinners in the offing.

FOLLBRAGUET. Fine! No problem then. *(Going to the draped doorway, calling)* Monsieur Jean! Could you come in here, please? *(He absentmindedly puts the denture in his pocket)*

MONSIEUR JEAN'S VOICE. One moment, Monsieur.

FOLLBRAGUET. *(behind his desk, opening his appointment book, about to write)* Now then, if you'll just give me your name and address...

MADAME BIZARRE. Madame Bizarre. 8 Rue Bugeaud.

FOLLBRAGUET. Bizarre? B–I–Z... *(He pauses, uncertain)*

MADAME BIZARRE. *(continuing)* A–R–R–E. Madame Zsa-Zsa Bizarre.

FOLLBRAGUET. *(shrugging his shoulders)* Bizarre! *(Speaking as he writes)* "Madame Zsa-Zsa Bizarre, 8 Rue Bugeaud, repair upper munch-munch..."

MADAME BIZARRE. What? "Repair upper munch-munch"?

FOLLBRAGUET. Yes. That's my code. After all, you wouldn't want someone to open my book, by mistake, and read: "Madame Zsa-Zsa Bizarre, repair upper denture..."

MADAME BIZARRE. Certainly not!

FOLLBRAGUET. That's why I write "munch-munch." I know what it means. But anyone who isn't in on the secret...

MADAME BIZARRE. I see! Very clever!

FOLLBRAGUET. I always do it in cases like this. You know... Where it could be embarrassing.

MADAME BIZARRE. Of course.

FOLLBRAGUET. The same with all my patients. You're not the only one... *(Leafing through his book)* See? Here's one. "Madame Rethel-Pajon: munch-munch..." *(Musing)* Lower left incisor, if I remember...

MADAME BIZARRE. Madame Armand Rethel-Pajon?

FOLLBRAGUET. That's right.

MADAME BIZARRE. Why, she's one of my dearest friends. Don't tell me *she* has false teeth, Doctor!

FOLLBRAGUET. *(trying to cover his blunder)* Who? Madame Rethel... Why no! No! Not Madame Rethel-Pajon...

MADAME BIZARRE. But what about her "munch-munch"? You said—

FOLLBRAGUET. It was a mistake! I meant someone else!

MADAME BIZARRE. *(unconvinced)* Come now, Doctor. You can trust me. I won't breathe a word...

FOLLBRAGUET. *(resigned to his gaffe, sighing)* Please, Madame Bizarre... I... Really, I hope you'll be discreet.

MADAME BIZARRE. My lips are sealed.

FOLLBRAGUET. Besides, you're in no position... If you see what I mean...

MADAME BIZARRE. *(reflecting)* Madame Rethel-Pajon! I never would have dreamed... I always thought she had such beautiful teeth. *(FOLLBRAGUET nods, smiling)* Simply exquisite!

FOLLBRAGUET. *(bowing slightly)* Thank you. You're much too kind.

MADAME BIZARRE. You mean they're yours?

FOLLBRAGUET. Yes, they're mine.

MADAME BIZARRE. *(admiringly)* Oh, Doctor! You're an artist! An absolute artist!

(MONSIEUR JEAN enters through the draped doorway)

MONSIEUR JEAN. You wanted to see me, Monsieur?

FOLLBRAGUET. *(ringing for ALBERT the butler)* Yes, Monsieur Jean. Madame Bizarre is going to leave us her... *(Looking around for the denture)* Where on earth are they?

MADAME BIZARRE. What?

FOLLBRAGUET. Your teeth... Where did I put them? *(Looking all over, and finally feeling in his pocket)* Ah! Here they are. *(Handing the denture to MONSIEUR JEAN)* Single replacement, second molar, upper left.

MONSIEUR JEAN. Very good, Monsieur.

FOLLBRAGUET. And let's make it really extra fine. These are her special occasion teeth.

MONSIEUR JEAN. Of course, Monsieur. *(To MADAME BIZARRE)* Was Madame thinking of a particular day for her bridge?

MADAME BIZARRE. Bridge? What bridge?... I don't even know how to play...

MONSIEUR JEAN. No, I mean Madame's... *(Holding up the denture)* ...Madame's...

FOLLBRAGUET. *(to MADAME BIZARRE)* Yes, we call that type a "bridge."

MADAME BIZARRE. Oh, I didn't know...

FOLLBRAGUET. *(to MONSIEUR JEAN)* That's fine, Monsieur Jean. You can go. I'll arrange a time...

(MONSIEUR JEAN exits through the draped doorway, just as ALBERT enters, up right)

ALBERT. Monsieur rang?

FOLLBRAGUET. Yes. Show Madame out, will you please?

ALBERT. Certainly, Monsieur.

MADAME BIZARRE. Thank you so much, Doctor. You've been very kind. *(She goes to the desk and picks up her muff)*

FOLLBRAGUET. *(to ALBERT)* Do I have anybody waiting, Albert?

ALBERT. No, Monsieur. Only Hortense. She'd like a word with Monsieur as soon as he has a minute.

FOLLBRAGUET. *(grimacing)* Oh? *(Controlling his obvious impatience in front of MADAME BIZARRE)* Fine. First show Madame out, then I'll see what she wants.

(ALBERT moves to comply. MADAME BIZARRE hesitates, reluctant to leave)

MADAME BIZARRE. Well, Doctor?

FOLLBRAGUET. *(preoccupied)* Madame?

MADAME BIZARRE. When will it be ready?

FOLLBRAGUET. When will what be ready?

MADAME BIZARRE. My... *(Inhibited by ALBERT'S presence, giv-*

ing FOLLBRAGUET *a knowing glance)* My "munch-munch"...
(ALBERT stifles a little guffaw)

FOLLBRAGUET. Oh yes... Your... Well, I'd say about a week... But that's all right. I'll send it. I have your address.

MADAME BIZARRE. Oh? Why, thank you!

FOLLBRAGUET. *(anxious to be rid of her)* Not at all! My pleasure!

MADAME BIZARRE. *(exiting, up right, with ALBERT at her heels)* Bye-bye, Doctor. And thank you again...

FOLLBRAGUET. *(at the door, nodding)* Madame... *(To HORTENSE, as soon as MADAME BIZARRE is out of earshot)* All right, come on in!

HORTENSE. *(entering)* I'm bringing Monsieur my book, like Madame told me.

FOLLBRAGUET. Good. Let's have it. *(He takes the account book to his desk and sits down)*

HORTENSE. Monsieur can see for himself. It only goes to the end of January. And today's the ninth of February, so that means expenses for... *(Counting on her fingers)* ...for nine more days.

FOLLBRAGUET. *(scanning the pages)* Right... Right...

HORTENSE. Plus my wages... Monsieur knows they go from the fifteenth of the month. So if this is the ninth, that adds up to a month, minus... *(Laboring)* ...minus six days. But Monsieur has to give me a whole week's notice. So that makes... That makes a month and one day altogether. And its sixty francs for a month, and... *(More complicated calculations)* ...and two francs for the extra day... So that makes sixty-two francs...

FOLLBRAGUET. *(hardly listening, more absorbed in his wife's expenses)* Look at this! Day after day, all this useless junk! Ribbons, lace, ribbons, lace, ribbons, ribbons, ribbons...

HORTENSE. *(quick to defend herself)* Oh, Monsieur! Madame insisted...

FOLLBRAGUET. Yes, I'm sure she did! I know only too well...

HORTENSE. Thank you, Monsieur. I knew Monsieur knew.

FOLLBRAGUET. But why so much, for goodness' sake?

HORTENSE *(sarcastically)* Madame loves pretty things, Monsieur!

(FOLLBRAGUET shakes his head in resignation, still scanning the book.)

FOLLBRAGUET. *(stopping at another item)* What on earth is this?

HORTENSE. *(looking over his shoulder)* I'm sorry I write so bad, Monsieur. I never had a chance—

FOLLBRAGUET. That's not the problem. I can read it all right. I just don't know what it means: "Ingredients for poultry, 80 centimes."

HORTENSE. Oh, that was one night when Monsieur was away, and Madame had the grippe. She sent me to the druggist's so she could make a poultry to put on her chest.

FOLLBRAGUET. A what?

HORTENSE. A poultry, Monsieur. You know, a kind of plaster.

FOLLBRAGUET. *(smiling in spite of himself)* Aha!

HORTENSE. The druggist had everything except for the mouse turd...

FOLLBRAGUET. Except for the what?

HORTENSE. The mouse turd. Madame said it had to be a mouse turd plaster... I don't know how she managed...

FOLLBRAGUET. *(trying to keep a straight face, figuring)* Well now, that gives us eighty-six francs, twenty centimes in expenses. Plus your sixty-two francs. Or a total of one hundred forty-eight francs and twenty centimes. *(Putting the book on the desk and handing her a piece of paper)* Here... Just write what I tell you: "Received in full payment of all indebtedness heretofore incurred, the sum of one hundred forty-eight francs, twenty centimes." Then date it and sign your name.

HORTENSE. Oh, Monsieur... If it's all the same, I wish Monsieur would write it himself. With all those foreign words, I mean...

FOLLBRAGUET. *(indulgent)* If you'd rather... *(He begins writing)*

HORTENSE. And Monsieur won't forget my reference, I hope!

FOLLBRAGUET. *(writing)* Not today. You can send for it tomorrow. *(Finishing the receipt)* "...the sum of one hundred forty-eight francs, twenty centimes. February 9, 1915." There! Now you sign it.

HORTENSE. *(taking the pen)* Thank you, Monsieur. I was never too good at spelling.

FOLLBRAGUET. That's all right...

HORTENSE. Or puncturation *[sic—she mispronounces the word]* either.

FOLLBRAGUET. I know... Just sign the receipt.

HORTENSE. I never knew where the commas and semaphores went, and all those things...

FOLLBRAGUET. Please, Hortense. Just sign it.

HORTENSE. *(finally complying, laboriously)* There you are, Monsieur.

FOLLBRAGUET. *(standing up)* Good! Now I'll go get your money.

HORTENSE. *(sheepishly)* I hope Monsieur isn't angry with me, Monsieur.

FOLLBRAGUET. Angry? Why should I be angry? *(Sarcastically)* I'm having a fine time, thanks to you!

HORTENSE. But it's not my fault, Monsieur. If only... I mean...

FOLLBRAGUET. If only what?

HORTENSE. Well, if only Madame didn't say what she did. You know... About my cat... Going on her muff...

FOLLBRAGUET. So what? Who cares? Why get so insulted? It's only your cat, after all. You'd think it was your sister or your mother, the way you're carrying on! You're blowing the whole thing up into a national crisis, for heaven's sake!

HORTENSE. I'm sorry, Monsieur. But just because a girl is somebody's maid, that doesn't mean she should let somebody talk to her any way they please!

FOLLBRAGUET. What's the difference? Let her rave all she wants!...
(HORTENSE *bows her head*) No! Instead, you've always got to
answer her back!

HORTENSE. I know, Monsieur. I try, but I just can't help it. Monsieur knows how Madame can be... How she talks to people, I mean...

FOLLBRAGUET. All right, but still...

HORTENSE. You'd think Monsieur never noticed it himself. And
after the awful way she treats Monsieur, too!

FOLLBRAGUET. Oh? Well, I... Really, I don't think—

HORTENSE. And in front of the help! It's so embarrassing, Monsieur!

FOLLBRAGUET. *(beginning to squirm)* Yes, I'm sure... I... Really...

HORTENSE. We were talking about it in the pantry, just the other day.
Albert was simply furious...

FOLLBRAGUET. He was?

HORTENSE. And he said... Well, Monsieur knows it takes a lot to get
Albert to talk, but he's nobody's fool. And he said: "You know, I
really admire Monsieur. I wouldn't put up with a woman like that
for even one day."

FOLLBRAGUET. Well, I do my best...

HORTENSE. Take yesterday, for instance... While we were serving
dinner... All the nasty things she screamed at Monsieur. Like his
"belly's full of jelly!", and he's "nothing but a unit..."

FOLLBRAGUET. *(correcting)* K... k...

HORTENSE. Monsieur?

FOLLBRAGUET. "Eunuch..." The word was "eunuch..."

HORTENSE. Well, I knew what she meant.

FOLLBRAGUET. And besides, it's not true!

HORTENSE. True or not, Monsieur. I don't care. That's none of my
business.

FOLLBRAGUET. No, but I don't want you to think—

HORTENSE. *(incensed at the thought)* Really! Is that any way to
talk in front of the help?

FOLLBRAGUET. I know...

HORTENSE. I mean, how are we supposed to respect Monsieur when
she says such things?

FOLLBRAGUET. You're right...

HORTENSE. Your kind don't realize how something like that can hurt
them. I mean, would the help ever talk that way in front of them?
We wouldn't be caught dead...

FOLLBRAGUET. You're right. I only wish you could tell that to her!

HORTENSE. Oh, that'll be the day!

FOLLBRAGUET. *(waxing confidential)* I don't know how many times
I've tried to stop her. But you know, she just can't help it. The minute she's got an audience... Heaven help me if I say something that
rubs her the wrong way... If I find fault with her dress or her hair or

whatever... That's enough to get her started. Me... My family...
(Imitating) "Oh, of course! You'd rather see me dress up like some
slut, I suppose. Like that sister of yours!"

HORTENSE. *(feigning outrage)* Oh! Not Monsieur's sister!

FOLLBRAGUET. You were here the other day, when she made that
scene... *(Very matter-of-fact)* Please, sit down... Sit down... *(HOR-
TENSE takes the seat behind the desk)* You remember... About her
clothes... How I never give her enough money, and she doesn't have
a thing to wear... You remember...

HORTENSE. *(shaking her head, as if to say, "Incredible!")* Tsk, tsk,
tsk!

FOLLBRAGUET. And if anyone knows it's not true, I'm sure you do.
You know how much I pay, day in day out. *(Picking up the account
book from the desk and brandishing it)* Bills, bills, bills! And what
for? For foolishness!

HORTENSE. *(nodding)* Ribbons, lace, ribbons, lace...

FOLLBRAGUET. Exactly! Ribbons, ribbons, ribbons!

HORTENSE. But... Then why doesn't Monsieur put his foot down for
a change?

FOLLBRAGUET. How? I've tried everything.

HORTENSE. Monsieur should just tell Madame, once and for all:
"That's it! That's enough! So much for clothes, and not one centime
more!"

FOLLBRAGUET. That's easy to say. But when the bills come in, the
clothes are all bought!

HORTENSE. Then Monsieur should say: "Too bad! I'm sorry, I just
won't pay it!" The next time Madame will know better!

FOLLBRAGUET. *(pondering)* I suppose so...

HORTENSE. Monsieur is too good. He lets people walk all over him.
That's his trouble.

FOLLBRAGUET. Well, what can I do? It's better to give in sometimes for a little peace and quiet.

HORTENSE. Maybe Monsieur thinks so...

FOLLBRAGUET. And it wouldn't have done you any harm either,
frankly. Instead of talking back like that and picking a fight.

HORTENSE. Well, I guess I've just got a worse temper than Monsieur.

FOLLBRAGUET. Besides, you know Madame... You know how she
blows up at the least little thing. But it's over in no time, if you just
let it pass. Why, tomorrow... I'll bet when she sees you here, same
as always, she won't even remember that she wanted to fire you.

HORTENSE. Well, I don't know... I hope Monsieur sees my point...
But I just don't see how I can stay. Not the way things are...

FOLLBRAGUET. Oh, come now, Hortense! Now who's being stubborn?

HORTENSE. It's not that, Monsieur. It's just that... Well, when you
know that somebody doesn't appreciate your work... For example,

Monsieur, when I first took this job, I asked Madame for seventy francs. And she told me: "No, sixty. And after six months, if I'm pleased with your work, I'll give you ten more." Well, I didn't want to argue, so I said all right.

FOLLBRAGUET. *(waiting for her to make her point)* So?

HORTENSE. So? It's been eight months already, Monsieur, and I still haven't had my raise.

FOLLBRAGUET. Oh? Madame must have forgotten...

HORTENSE. No, Monsieur. She couldn't have. I reminded her about it. All she said was: "Not now. We can talk about it later!"

FOLLBRAGUET. Just for ten measly francs?

HORTENSE. *(wheedling)* I'm sure Monsieur wouldn't tell me no. I'm sure...

FOLLBRAGUET. Of course not! What's ten francs?

HORTENSE. Oh, thank you, Monsieur! Thank you! Thank you!

FOLLBRAGUET. For what?

HORTENSE. For my raise, Monsieur!

FOLLBRAGUET. For your... *(Clearing his throat)* Don't mention it!... Just be sure you behave from now on. I don't want any more scenes, you understand? They get on my nerves, and that's one thing I don't need!

HORTENSE. Oh yes, Monsieur!

FOLLBRAGUET. *(noticing the account book, still in his hand)* Now I'll get you your money, as long as your book is up to date...

HORTENSE. If Monsieur thinks he should...

(FOLLBRAGUET moves toward the draped doorway. A knock is heard)

FOLLBRAGUET. *(stopping in his tracks)* Come in!

(YVETTE the cook enters, up right, appropriately dressed)

YVETTE. It's me, Monsieur.

FOLLBRAGUET. *(looking at her in surprise)* What are you doing here? Why aren't you in the kitchen, where you belong?

YVETTE. Because I just got through helping Madame get dressed, Monsieur, since she doesn't have anyone else to do it now, and she told me to come in...

FOLLBRAGUET. *(with several impatient gestures)* Fine! That's fine! *(He exits)*

YVETTE. *(as soon as he has left, to HORTENSE)* Well?

HORTENSE. Well what?

YVETTE. How come you're still here?

HORTENSE. Why not?

YVETTE. I thought you got fired.

HORTENSE. I did.

YVETTE. For talking dirty to Madame.

HORTENSE. That's right.

YVETTE. So?

HORTENSE. So Monsieur just gave me a raise. Ten francs!

YVETTE. *(astonished)* He didn't!

(FOLLBRAGUET returns with the money)

FOLLBRAGUET. *(to YVETTE)* Are you still here?

YVETTE. Like I was telling Monsieur... Madame told me to come in...

FOLLBRAGUET. *(shrugging)* What now?

YVETTE. ...and ask Monsieur if... *(Trying to remember verbatim)* ...if "it's all taken care of."

(FOLLBRAGUET gives HORTENSE a knowing glance)

FOLLBRAGUET. *(to YVETTE)* Thank you! That's fine! Go tell Madame I'll speak to her myself.

YVETTE. Yes, Monsieur. *(She exits, up right)*

FOLLBRAGUET. *(gritting his teeth)* She just can't leave me alone!

HORTENSE. *(with a gesture as if to say, "What did you expect?")* No, Monsieur.

FOLLBRAGUET. *(sighing)* Anyway... Here you are, Hortense. We said one hundred forty-eight francs, twenty centimes.

HORTENSE. Yes, Monsieur.

FOLLBRAGUET. *(paying her piecemeal)* First the twenty centimes... Then the one hundred francs... And... Three twenties make sixty. Do you have change from sixty?

HORTENSE. Yes, Monsieur. *(Taking some coins from her purse)* There you are, Monsieur. Two francs.

FOLLBRAGUET. Two? No, no. Twelve... Forty-eight from sixty leaves twelve. Twelve francs.

HORTENSE. But Monsieur... My raise... Ten francs, remember?

FOLLBRAGUET. Your... Oh yes... Yes, of course...

HORTENSE. Thank you, Monsieur.

(Suddenly MARCELLE bursts onstage from her room, midstage right. She is obviously shocked to see HORTENSE sitting at FOLLBRAGUET'S desk.)

MARCELLE. *(to HORTENSE, sarcastically)* Well, well! Aren't we making ourselves right at home! *(HORTENSE jumps up)* No, please! Don't mind me! *(Glowering at FOLLBRAGUET)* I didn't know you had a guest!

FOLLBRAGUET. Please, Marcelle! I was talking to the child...

MARCELLE. And we let the help sit down now, do we? Just so we can talk?

FOLLBRAGUET. Well for goodness' sake, I couldn't keep her standing. It was going to take time.

MARCELLE. Yes, I'm sure.

FOLLBRAGUET. Besides, Marcelle, I wish you wouldn't be so hard on her. Down deep, she's got a heart of gold... Believe me, she... Really, she... *(He pauses, groping for more convincing arguments)*

MARCELLE. *(archly)* Are you through? *(FOLLBRAGUET sighs and throws up his hands)* Now then, did you give her her money?

FOLLBRAGUET. *(hesitant)* Yes... Yes, I did... I gave her her money. *(To* HORTENSE*)* Didn't I, Hortense?

HORTENSE. Yes, Monsieur.

MARCELLE. Then what is she waiting for? Why doesn't she get out?

FOLLBRAGUET. Why doesn't she... Well, as a matter of fact... The two of us were talking just now, and... Actually, you know, she thinks the world of you, Marcelle... A real lady, I mean... That's what she thinks...

MARCELLE. *(coldly)* Very touching, I'm sure. Who asked for her opinion?

FOLLBRAGUET. That's not the point. What she meant was... Well, sometimes... Even you'll admit, sometimes you can blow up at people...

MARCELLE. What?

FOLLBRAGUET. Even at me, sometimes. I know you don't mean it... But it's like Hortense was saying. There are some things you just shouldn't say in front of the help.

MARCELLE. *(scandalized)* Oh? And since when do you ask the help to pass judgment on your wife?

FOLLBRAGUET. No, no. It's not that. We were talking, that's all. Just one of those things. Like... like the raise you promised her when she first came to work... The ten-franc raise...

MARCELLE. What about it?

FOLLBRAGUET. Well, I mean... You did promise, after all. So I thought it was only right, and...

MARCELLE. And?

FOLLBRAGUET. And I told her she could have it.

MARCELLE. *(with a start)* You what?

FOLLBRAGUET. I'm sure you see my point...

MARCELLE. *(furious)* Now isn't that lovely! I tell you to fire her, and you give her a raise!

FOLLBRAGUET. But—

MARCELLE. No! That's the last straw! That's just the last straw!

FOLLBRAGUET. But Marcelle—

MARCELLE. Don't "But Marcelle" me! I know what I've got to do!

FOLLBRAGUET. But—

MARCELLE. Never mind! I see how much I count in this house! *(Pointing to* HORTENSE*)* I see whose word you take instead of mine!

FOLLBRAGUET. Marcelle—

MARCELLE. I see who's running things around here now!

FOLLBRAGUET. For heaven's sake, calm down! Don't go flying off the handle!

MARCELLE. Oh, I'm calm! I'm calm! I just know what I've got to do, that's all... The same as any self-respecting woman in my place... I'm leaving! Understand?

FOLLBRAGUET. Marcelle! For heaven's sake—

MARCELLE. No! My mind is made up!

FOLLBRAGUET. But—

MARCELLE. I'm leaving! That's final!

FOLLBRAGUET. *(fed up)* All right, damn it! Leave! Go ahead! I'm not holding you back!

MARCELLE. *(going toward her room)* Don't worry, you won't have to tell me twice!

FOLLBRAGUET. *(to HORTENSE)* What a temper! My goodness!

(HORTENSE looks up at the ceiling and raises her eyebrows, as if to say, "You're telling me!")

HORTENSE. I always said Monsieur has the patience of a saint.

MARCELLE. *(returning, looking FOLLBRAGUET straight in the eye)* And you can have my room too... For your precious Hortense! That way you won't have so far to go when you take your maid to bed!

FOLLBRAGUET. *(scandalized)* What?

HORTENSE. *(unable to believe her ears)* What did she say?

(MARCELLE stalks off into her room and slams the door)

FOLLBRAGUET. She's out of her mind! That's all there is to it!

HORTENSE. *(incensed)* Well, I never, Monsieur! Never in all my born days!...

FOLLBRAGUET. Please, Hortense...

HORTENSE. I don't have to let anyone talk to me that way!

FOLLBRAGUET. Please... Don't listen to her...

HORTENSE. *(on the verge of tears)* I mean, just because someone's a maid, Monsieur, that doesn't mean people can say anything they like!

FOLLBRAGUET. Of course not... But you know Madame. You know what I've had to put up with all these years.

HORTENSE. Well, maybe Monsieur has to put up with it, but I don't! Not me, Monsieur! I'm sorry, but I'm leaving! I won't stay in this house another minute!

FOLLBRAGUET. Hortense, please...

HORTENSE. *(sobbing)* No, Monsieur! I'm leaving!

FOLLBRAGUET. *(distraught)* Good God, what a mess! *(A knock is heard at the door, up left)* Come in!

(ALBERT enters, leaving the door open)

ALBERT. Monsieur Leboucq would like to see Monsieur. He thinks he has an abscess.

FOLLBRAGUET. Damn him and his abscess!

(HORTENSE moves to leave, up right)

ALBERT. *(to HORTENSE, seeing her whimpering)* What's the matter with you?

HORTENSE. *(petulantly brushing him aside as she exits)* Nothing! Leave me alone!

ALBERT. *(following her out)* What is it? What's the matter?

HORTENSE'S VOICE. Nothing, I told you...

FOLLBRAGUET. *(pacing)* Goddamn!... Oh!... Goddamn!... *(Brusquely, to LEBOUCQ, appearing at the open door, up left, a bandage around his swollen jaw)* What do you want?

LEBOUCQ. My jaw, Doctor... It's killing me! It's swollen up twice the size! I must have an abscess.

FOLLBRAGUET. *(still fuming)* You don't have to tell me! I can see for myself! *(Pointing to the dentist's chair)* Here, sit down! Take off the bandage!

(LEBOUCQ complies. FOLLBRAGUET goes to the sink and fills a little glass with mouthwash)

LEBOUCQ. I think I must have caught it last night, at the theater. I was sitting in a terrible draft, and—

FOLLBRAGUET. That has nothing to do with it! Absolutely nothing!

LEBOUCQ. *(sheepishly, taken aback)* Oh?... I thought...

FOLLBRAGUET. *(placing the glass on his instrument cabinet)* Open your mouth! *(Grumbling, as LEBOUCQ obeys)* Enough is enough, damn it! I've had it up to here! *(He joins the gesture to the expression)*

LEBOUCQ. *(quizzically)* Doctor?

FOLLBRAGUET. Nothing, nothing!... Open your mouth!

LEBOUCQ. *(pointing to the offending tooth)* It's this one...

FOLLBRAGUET. I can see! *(After a cursory glance at the tooth, very matter-of-fact)* It'll have to come out.

LEBOUCQ. What?

FOLLBRAQUET. It's too far gone...

LEBOUCQ. But...

FOLLBRAGUET. It'll have to come out!

LEBOUCQ. But Doctor, can't you save it?

FOLLBRAGUET. Save it? Why in hell should I save it? You think I collect them?

LEBOUCQ. No, I mean... *(Emphasizing)* ...save it... For me...

FOLLBRAGUET. Look, if you want the damn thing that much, you can keep it!

LEBOUCQ. *(timidly)* Really, Doctor... You don't have to growl...

FOLLBRAGUET. *(taking the forceps from his instrument cabinet)* Oh? If you'd been through what I've been through... Open your mouth! *(He plunges the forceps into LEBOUCQ'S mouth and begins to pull the tooth)*

LEBOUCQ. *(caught unawares, screaming)* Ayyyyyy!

FOLLBRAGUET. *(tugging)* Not so loud, damn it! I've had all I can take for one day, thank you!

(The tooth finally gives)

LEBOUCQ. Ohhhhh!

FOLLBRAGUET. *(over LEBOUCQ'S protracted moans and groans)* There! Very pretty!... *(Sarcastically)* I think you ought to keep it!

(He puts the tooth into a little pillbox, then takes the glass of mouth-
wash and hands it to LEBOUCQ)

LEBOUCQ. *(panting)* Good God in heaven!

FOLLBRAGUET. Here, rinse your mouth. (LEBOUCQ, *ready to faint,*
takes the glass and gulps down the contents, as FOLLBRAGUET
tries in vain to stop him) What are you doing? You're not supposed
to drink it!

LEBOUCQ. *(feebly)* No... Leave me alone... *(He gets up from the*
chair, totters, almost collapses)

FOLLBRAGUET. Hold on! You're not going to get sick on me, I hope!
That's all I need!

LEBOUCQ. I... I think I'm going to faint...

FOLLBRAGUET. No, no!... Hold on! Don't faint!... Not in here...
(Running to the draped doorway and calling) Monsieur Jean!...
Monsieur Jean! *(He runs back to* LEBOUCQ, *trying to hold him up.*
MONSIEUR JEAN *appears at the door)*

MONSIEUR JEAN. Monsieur?

FOLLBRAGUET. *(pointing off, left)* Here, take Monsieur out and
have him lie down. *(He passes* LEBOUCQ, *reeling, over to* MON-
SIEUR JEAN)

MONSIEUR JEAN. *(nodding)* Of course... *(to* LEBOUCQ) Please...
This way...

FOLLBRAGUET. *(stopping* LEBOUCQ *as they reach the doorway)*
Oh, just a minute...

LEBOUCQ. *(barely audible)* Doctor?

FOLLBRAGUET. *(handing him the little pillbox)* You're forgetting
your tooth! You wanted to save it, remember?

LEBOUCQ. *(taking it halfheartedly)* Who needs it now? *(Putting the*
box in his pocket) I... I think I'm going to faint...

FOLLBRAGUET. Yes... Well, just don't faint in here.

MONSIEUR JEAN. *(leading* LEBOUCQ *off)* This way, Monsieur...
(They exit)

FOLLBRAGUET. *(sitting down at his desk, sighing)* Good God, what
a day! *(There is a knock at the door, up right)* Come in!

*(*ALBERT *opens the door and appears at the threshold)*

ALBERT. It's me, Monsieur.

FOLLBRAGUET. *(after a quizzical pause)* So?

ALBERT. *(very stiff and proper)* There's a matter I'd like to discuss
with Monsieur.

FOLLBRAGUET. What? What now?

ALBERT. I waited for Monsieur to finish with his patient. When I
heard him call for Monsieur Jean to take him out, I knocked at the
door.

FOLLBRAGUET. All right, go ahead. I'm listening.

ALBERT. Very good, Monsieur... *(Stepping into the office, moving*
downstage) Certainly Monsieur is aware that Madame has insulted

Mademoiselle Hortense... Cut her to the quick, I might add...

FOLLBRAGUET. Oh no! Please! Not you too! Not another earful!

ALBERT. *(still very correct)* I'm sorry to be giving Monsieur another earful. It's not something I enjoy. But Monsieur must know that Mademoiselle Hortense and I have been seeing one another.

FOLLBRAGUET. Oh?

ALBERT. I can go so far as to tell Monsieur that we haven't seen fit to resist temptation.

FOLLBRAGUET. I see...

ALBERT. Even so, Monsieur can rest assured that I still have every intention of making her my wife.

FOLLBRAGUET. Of course! Of course!... *(Waiting for ALBERT'S conclusion)* So what?

ALBERT. Well, Monsieur, as Mademoiselle's husband, so to speak, I can't stand by and let Madame say that my wife, as it were, goes to bed with Monsieur! It's outrageous!

FOLLBRAGUET. Damn right it's outrageous! I hope you don't believe it!

ALBERT. Of course not, Monsieur. I know Mademoiselle Hortense too well.

FOLLBRAGUET. *(wryly)* Much obliged, I'm sure!

ALBERT. Besides, wasn't it just yesterday that Madame informed Monsieur that he was nothing but a eunuch?

FOLLBRAGUET. *(with a start)* Now you wait just one minute!...

ALBERT. Nothing personal, Monsieur. I only bring the matter up to point out to Monsieur how illogical women can be.

FOLLBRAGUET. Maybe so, but—

ALBERT. At any rate, Monsieur, given the present state of affairs, I'm afraid I have to tell Monsieur that I have no choice but to leave Monsieur's employ.

FOLLBRAGUET. Well, leave it then! What do you expect me to say?

ALBERT. Very good, Monsieur. *(Drawing himself up to his full height)* And now, since I'm no longer Monsieur's social unequal, we can speak man to man.

FOLLBRAGUET. *(cocking his head, incredulously)* I beg your pardon!

ALBERT. I'm just another husband, Monsieur, defending his wife's honor.

FOLLBRAGUET. Of course!

ALBERT. Now, either Madame takes back what she said and apologizes to Mademoiselle Hortense...

FOLLBRAGUET. *(with a nervous little laugh)* Ha! That I'd like to see!

ALBERT. ...or else... Well, Monsieur, I haven't forgotten my regimental days... *(Another quizzical cock of the head from FOLLBRAGUET)* As assistant fencing master, Monsieur...

FOLLBRAGUET. Oh?

ALBERT. And I beg to inform Monsieur that my seconds will be paying him a visit in the morning.

FOLLBRAGUET. Your seconds? Your... *(Standing up)* What kind of a joke... You really expect me to fight a duel with my butler?

ALBERT. Excuse me, Monsieur. I've stopped being Monsieur's butler.

FOLLBRAGUET. *(striding up to him)* Too bad! I'll toss your seconds right out on their ears!

ALBERT. In that case, Monsieur will be publicly disgraced. It will have to be reported—officially, Monsieur—that Monsieur provokes people, then refuses to duel. He'll lose by default.

FOLLBRAGUET. *(convulsed)* Default? Default, my... Fine! Let it be reported! You think I give a damn?

ALBERT. *(very calmly)* That's up to Monsieur, I'm sure.

FOLLBRAGUET. *(ready to tear his hair)* Good God! Why me? What on earth have I done? Why is everyone on my neck?

ALBERT. Oh, it's not Monsieur's fault. I know he's not to blame. It's just that a husband has to answer for his wife, and, that being the case... Well, I'll wait until tonight for Monsieur to decide. Either Madame takes back what she said...

FOLLBRAGUET. You can't really believe—

ALBERT. ...or two of my friends will come by in the morning.

FOLLBRAGUET. Look, if you imagine for one moment that she would even dream—

ALBERT. Well, it's not for me to say, but perhaps if Monsieur started putting his foot down... Perhaps if he stopped giving in to her, I mean... After all, the law says a wife is supposed to obey her husband. Perhaps if Monsieur told Madame, once and for all: "That's enough! I'm the boss, and what I say goes!"...

FOLLBRAGUET. Ha! That's easier said than done.

ALBERT. Well anyway, Monsieur, as I was saying... Monsieur has until this evening. After that, I send my seconds.

(HORTENSE has appeared at the door, up right, still ajar since AL-BERT'S entrance, and has apparently overheard the last exchange)

HORTENSE. *(running in, flinging her arms around ALBERT'S neck)* Seconds? What seconds? Don't tell me you've got a duel?

ALBERT. *(breaking away, sharply)* Who asked you, woman? This is man to man. Now quiet!

HORTENSE. But Albert... Not a duel... Not with the likes of them!

ALBERT. That's enough! I'm the boss, and what I say goes!

HORTENSE. *(meekly)* Yes, Albert...

(The doorbell rings offstage)

ALBERT. *(changing his tone, to FOLLBRAGUET)* I'll remain in Monsieur's employ until this evening. If Monsieur will excuse me, I'll go see who's at the door. *(He moves off, up right, taking HORTENSE with him. Before they reach the door, MARCELLE comes bursting out of her room)*

MARCELLE. Here's the key...

FOLLBRAGUET. *(startled)* Marcelle!

(At the sight of HORTENSE, MARCELLE *stops in her tracks. She looks her up and down with obvious contempt, until the pair, never losing their aplomb, are out the door)*

MARCELLE. *(throwing the key onto* FOLLBRAGUET'S *desk)* Here's the key to my room. Now you two can use my bed to your heart's content!

FOLLBRAGUET. Your key? Your... *(Picking it up)* Here's what I'll do with your goddamn key! *(He hurls it across the room, into the fireplace)*

MARCELLE. *(utterly indifferent)* You can do what you please...

FOLLBRAGUET. *(fuming)* Do you know what your foolishness has gotten me into?

MARCELLE. I don't know, and I don't care.

FOLLBRAGUET. Oh no? Well I'll tell you! I've got myself a duel, that's what! And with my butler, no less!

MARCELLE. *(sarcastically)* My, my! Fancy that!

FOLLBRAGUET. *(mimicking)* "Fancy that! Fancy that!..." What do you expect? Hortense is practically married to Albert. You insult Hortense. So he challenges me to a duel. What else?

MARCELLE. Of course! Some men stand up for their women when someone insults them. At least Albert has blood in his veins! Good for him!

FOLLBRAGUET. Yes, well in the meantime I'll thank you to tell Hortense you're sorry, and you take back what you said...

MARCELLE. *(incredulous)* Tell her what?

FOLLBRAGUET. And right this minute!

MARCELLE. *(needling him)* Well, well! Don't tell me we're afraid of our butler!

FOLLBRAGUET. What kind of talk... *(Summoning up all his authority)* Besides, that's enough! I'm the boss, and what I say goes!

(ALBERT appears at the door, up left. He stops short at the threshold)

MARCELLE. *(to FOLLBRAGUET)* Oh, really? You don't say! *(She gives him a resounding slap across the face)* I'll try to remember. *(She strides off, up right)*

FOLLBRAGUET. *(agape, rubbing his cheek, to ALBERT)* There! You see what happens when I put my foot down!

ALBERT. Monsieur has an uphill struggle, if I may say so.

FOLLBRAGUET. Goddamn!

ALBERT. But he does have the rest of the day... Until tonight... After that...

FOLLBRAGUET. *(exasperated)* I know! I know!... Now what did you want to tell me?

ALBERT. That gentleman is back, Monsieur.

FOLLBRAGUET. Who? What gentleman?

ALBERT. The one who was here just before the lady, Monsieur... The lady with the "munch-munch"...

FOLLBRAGUET. Oh?

ALBERT. He says his tooth still hurts, Monsieur.

FOLLBRAGUET. So? It hurts! Too bad!

(MARCELLE enters, up right. YVETTE is close behind, stopping at the threshold)

MARCELLE. *(to FOLLBRAGUET)* Here, I brought you the cook. She's all yours, too!

FOLLBRAGUET. What? What now?

MARCELLE. *(to YVETTE)* Don't just stand there, Yvette. Come in, come in! *(To FOLLBRAGUET, as YVETTE enters)* Since I don't seem to count in this house anymore...

FOLLBRAGUET. *(gnashing his teeth)* Marcelle!

MARCELLE. Since you seem to think more of the help than your wife...

FOLLBRAGUET. Marcelle!

MARCELLE. Oh no, don't try to deny it!

FOLLBRAGUET. Marcelle!

MARCELLE. Well, they're all yours. I'm through! Here, you can run the house, buy the food, plan the meals... *(To YVETTE)* From now on Monsieur will be giving you your orders. *(To FOLLBRAGUET)* I quit!

FOLLBRAGUET. But, for heaven's sake—

MARCELLE. *Q-U-I-T,* quit! Understand? *(She storms out the open door, up right)*

FOLLBRAGUET. *(running to the door)* Marcelle!

MARCELLE'S VOICE. And that's that!

YVETTE. *(after a brief, embarrassed pause)* Monsieur?

FOLLBRAGUET. What is it?

YVETTE. I have no idea what to make Monsieur for dinner.

FOLLBRAGUET. *(beside himself)* Well, that's no skin off my ass, damn it!

YVETTE. *(snippily, giving him tit for tat)* Well, it's certainly no skin off mine, Monsieur!

FOLLBRAGUET. *(exploding)* What? What did you say?

YVETTE. I said—

FOLLBRAGUET. You dare talk to me like that? You dare...

YVETTE. *(suddenly losing her composure)* But Monsieur—

FOLLBRAGUET. Never mind! Go pack your bags and get out of here. You're fired!

YVETTE. But I didn't mean any offense, Monsieur. I just thought—

FOLLBRAGUET. Too bad! You're still fired! *(Pointing to the open door, up right)* You heard me! Get out!

YVETTE. *(beginning to whimper)* But I thought Monsieur would give me a raise. Like Hortense, I mean—

FOLLBRAGUET. Out, I said! Out! Out! *(Pushing her bodily out the door and slamming it behind her)* What in hell do they take me for? What kind of an idiot...

ALBERT. *(still standing discreetly in the corner, up left)* Shall I show the gentleman in, Monsieur?

FOLLBRAGUET. Yes!... No!... Yes, yes, goddammit!

ALBERT. *(opening the door, up left, calling out)* Monsieur, the doctor can see you now.

(VILDAMOUR enters, obviously in pain)

VILDAMOUR. Oh, thank heaven! *(To FOLLBRAGUET, as ALBERT exits, up right)* Doctor, I'm sorry to bother you like this, but I just can't stand it. It's worse than before.

FOLLBRAGUET. *(pointing to the dentist's chair)* Fine... Sit down!

VILDAMOUR. *(sitting)* Thank you...

FOLLBRAGUET. *(visibly distraught, shaking his clenched fists in an uncontrollable outburst, under his breath)* Damn! Damn! Damn! Damn!

VILDAMOUR. Please?

FOLLBRAGUET. Nothing! I wasn't talking to you!... Sit still! *(He attaches the napkin around VILDAMOUR'S neck, catching his chin)*

VILDAMOUR. *(pointing to his chin)* Doctor...

FOLLBRAGUET. *(brusquely pulling the napkin into the proper position)* Watch what you're doing! *(He picks up the rubber gag)*

VILDAMOUR. Do you have to put all that stuff back in my mouth?

FOLLBRAGUET. If I have to, I have to!

VILDAMOUR. Good God, what a pain! It's killing me, Doctor!

FOLLBRAGUET. *(thinking of his own situation)* Some people have worse, believe me!

VILDAMOUR. Well, mine's bad enough! I can't worry about theirs!

FOLLBRAGUET. Of course not! Why should you give a damn?... Open your mouth!

VILDAMOUR. It's not going to hurt, is it?

FOLLBRAGUET. *(impatient)* No, no, no! Come on, open up! *(He arranges the rubber gag and the saliva-pump. Then he goes to the sink and fills a glass with mouthwash)*

VILDAMOUR. *(grunting, as before)* A foo uhv ag gif koof fikfk wong uh-gaw, guh a faw a koo waik, av wong av ik wawv-nk gawvuh-ing ngee. ["I should have had this tooth fixed long ago, but I thought I could wait, as long as it wasn't bothering me."]

FOLLBRAGUET. *(coming back with the glass, placing it on the instrument cabinet)* Fine! Fine!

VILDAMOUR. Guh wak ngyk ik wuv faw gag, a faw a wuv gaw-nguh ngy! ["But last night it was so bad, I thought I was going to die!"]

FOLLBRAGUET. Fine! Open your mouth!

(VILDAMOUR complies. FOLLBRAGUET pulls out the cotton swab left in the tooth and throws it aside)

VILDAMOUR. A gi-gnk fweek uh wink. A faw ngy heg wuv gaw-nguh gurfk! ["I didn't sleep a wink. I thought my head was going to burst!"]

FOLLBRAGUET. *(on edge)* Please! Shut up! I can't do anything if you keep on blabbing!

VILDAMOUR. *(cowed)* Aaaah...

FOLLBRAGUET. *(musing aloud as he works on the tooth)* Go get married and see what it gets you, goddammit! *(VILDAMOUR stares at him quizzically)* Open your mouth! *(He takes the drill and sets it in motion)*

VILDAMOUR. *(grimacing, trying in vain to close his mouth)* Ngaw! Ngaw! ["No! No!"]

FOLLBRAGUET. I said open your mouth! *(He begins drilling the tooth, over VILDAMOUR'S groans. After a moment, MARCELLE bursts in, up right)*

MARCELLE. Now what's this all about? Yvette says you fired her...

FOLLBRAGUET. *(jumping at the sudden intrusion)* Marcelle!... Please! *(He inadvertently lets the drill slip)*

VILDAMOUR. *(in agony)* Ayyyyy!

FOLLBRAGUET. *(to VILDAMOUR, realizing that he is drilling his cheek)* Sorry! *(To MARCELLE)* Leave me alone. Can't you see I'm busy?

MARCELLE. That's too bad! You're not firing Yvette, understand? I've never had even the slightest bit of trouble—

FOLLBRAGUET. Listen, when a cook talks dirty to me, I throw her out! That's that! Now I'm busy! This is no time—

MARCELLE. I see! *(To VILDAMOUR, still groaning)* I'm sure Monsieur will excuse me... *(To FOLLBRAGUET)* You haven't heard the end of this! Not by a long shot! *(She exits, up right, leaving the door open)*

FOLLBRAGUET. Incredible! Just incredible! The whole damn day... *(To VILDAMOUR)* Open your mouth! *(He hangs up the drill and begins poking away at the tooth with another instrument)*

MARCELLE'S VOICE. *(just outside the door)* Don't you worry, Yvette. Monsieur Follbraguet just isn't himself. You mustn't listen to a thing he says. *(FOLLBRAGUET bites his lip and struggles to hold back his rage)* It's all right when somebody insults his wife, but say one word to him... *(Appearing at the threshold)* Besides, I don't care what he told you. I give the orders here, and I say you're staying! *(Obviously aiming the remark at FOLLBRAGUET)* I hope that's clear!

(FOLLBRAGUET flings down the instrument and dashes out into the hall, closing the door behind him)

FOLLBRAGUET'S VOICE. Over my dead body!

MARCELLE'S VOICE. *(snickering)* Don't make me laugh!

FOLLBRAGUET'S VOICE. You can laugh your damn head off! You give the orders when I let you give the orders! That's when you give the orders! And don't you forget it! And in case you don't believe me, I just fired your cook, and I'll thank her to get the hell out of my house!

YVETTE'S VOICE. But Monsieur, it's not my fault...

FOLLBRAGUET'S VOICE. Too bad! Out of my house!

MARCELLE'S VOICE. I told you, Yvette. Don't listen. He's out of his mind.

FOLLBRAGUET'S VOICE. Maybe so. But she'll do what I tell her, understand? *(He returns, grumbling, and slams the door)* Of all the goddamn... Who does she think she is? *(To VILDAMOUR)* Open your mouth! *(Handing him the glass of mouthwash)* Here!

YVETTE'S VOICE. *(whimpering)* But Madame...

MARCELLE'S VOICE. Now, now... Don't you worry... Don't pay any attention. Just leave everything to me.

(FOLLBRAGUET makes another dash for the door, opens it, and sticks his head out)

FOLLBRAGUET. *(at the top of his voice)* I said, Leave me alone! I'm sick of the two of you standing out here yapping. Enough is enough! .

MARCELLE'S VOICE. I beg your pardon!

FOLLBRAGUET. You heard me, woman! Go do as you're told! *(He returns again, slamming the door behind him)* Why me, for God's sake? Why in hell... *(To VILDAMOUR)* Spit out!

(VILDAMOUR obeys)

MARCELLE'S VOICE. *(furious)* Now that's the last straw! I won't stay in this house! I won't stay here another minute!...

FOLLBRAGUET. *(opening the door)* Fine! Get out! Who's stopping you? *(Mimicking)* "I won't stay in this house! I won't stay in this house!" That's all you ever say! But you're still here, goddamnit!

MARCELLE'S VOICE. Oh? Well this time I mean it!

FOLLBRAGUET. That suits me just fine! *(Slamming the door)* Nagging bitch!

MARCELLE. *(flinging the door open)* What was that?

FOLLBRAGUET. *(turning her around bodily and giving her a push)* Out! Out! Out! *(He closes the door and this time bolts it shut. MARCELLE, outside, pounds in vain to get it open)*

MARCELLE'S VOICE. Let me in! Let me in!

(FOLLBRAGUET heaves a disgusted sigh)

FOLLBRAGUET. *(to VILDAMOUR)* I hope you'll excuse this ludicrous display...

(VILDAMOUR replies with an indulgent wave of the hand. Just at that moment, MARCELLE bursts in through the other door, up left, and heads straight for VILDAMOUR)

MARCELLE. *(to VILDAMOUR)* You heard him, Monsieur! You heard what he called me! *(VILDAMOUR tries to give a noncommittal shrug)* You heard him order me out of this house. You heard...

You heard...

FOLLBRAGUET. Yes! He heard, he heard, he heard!

MARCELLE. *(arms akimbo)* Well, that's just too bad! I'm not budging one inch! This is *my* house, remember? It's in *my* name, not yours!... You and your fancy little legal tricks!... So if anyone gets out, it's going to be you!

FOLLBRAGUET. Then it's going to be me! Damn right I'll get out! If you think I'm working my fingers to the bone... For what? For you?... You want to run the show? Well, that's fine with me! It's yours! Lock, stock, and barrel! Patients and all! I'm through, damn it! Here! *(He scoops up a bunch of instruments and plants them squarely in* MARCELLE'S *hands)*

MARCELLE. Me? *(*VILDAMOUR *grimaces in horror at the prospect)* Me? Stick my fingers in all those filthy, repulsive mouths? *(Wincing)* That's all right for you, but...

FOLLBRAGUET. *(ripping off his smock and going to the coatrack to put on his hat and coat)* Yes, well just don't forget... You can thank those filthy, repulsive mouths that I stick my fingers in, day in day out... *(Pointing unthinkingly to* VILDAMOUR*)* You can thank them for all your fancy clothes... And your goddamn lace! And your ribbons, ribbons, ribbons! From now on, you can earn them yourself! I quit!

MARCELLE. Go ahead! Only don't be surprised when you come home tonight and I'm gone!

FOLLBRAGUET. Same here! Good-bye! *(He storms out, up right)*

MARCELLE. Good-bye! *(She throws the instruments down on the cabinet and exits to her room.* VILDAMOUR, *having followed the last few exchanges with mounting concern, sits up straight, appalled at being left all alone with a mouthful of apparatus)*

VILDAMOUR. *(not knowing which way to turn)* Wuh a-gou ngee?... Wuh a-gou ngee?... ["What about me?... What about me?..."]

CURTAIN

About the Authors

RALPH BERRY is Professor of English at York University in Canada. His publications include *The Art of John Webster* and *Shakespeare's Comedies: Explorations in Form.* His latest book is *On Directing Shakespeare: Interviews with Contemporary Directors,* published by Barnes & Noble in the United States. He divides his life between Canada and his home in Dingley Dell, Higher Trewhiddle, St. Austell, Cornwall.

ELMER M. BLISTEIN teaches Shakespeare, Comedy, and Poetry at Brown University. He is the author of *Comedy in Action* and various works on Renaissance drama and popular culture, as well as original poetry. To him, the increasing number of one-newspaper towns is a more serious problem than the decline of the franc, the pound, or even the dollar.

MAURICE CHARNEY, Professor of English at Rutgers University, is better known as a critic of Shakespeare (*Shakespeare's Roman Plays, Style in "Hamlet," How to Read Shakespeare),* but he has recently been indulging an adolescent fascination with comedy. His new book, *Comedy High and Low: An Introduction to the Experience of Comedy,* is currently being published by Oxford University Press.

CHARLES FREY, Professor of English at the University of Washington, has a Harvard Law degree and practiced in Philadelphia from 1961–1967. He has published widely on Shakespeare and related subjects,and his book *Shakespeare's Romances Reconsidered* is in press at the University of Nebraska. He has also published poems in literary reviews.

B. H. FUSSELL, who teaches courses on movies and the drama at The New School for Social Research, has written on figures as diverse as T. S. Eliot, M. F. K. Fisher, and Margaret Dumont. As a free-lance writer, she has published articles on food, travel, movies, and drama in *The New York Times, Holiday, 1,000 Eyes,* and *The Hudson* and *Sewanee Reviews.* She is currently working on a biography of silent film star Mabel Normand.

MARGARET GANZ, Professor of English at Brooklyn College of the City University of New York, has previously written on humor in her critical study *Elizabeth Gaskell: The Artist in Conflict* and in essays and reviews on Dickens in *Dickens Studies Annual, Dickens Studies News-letter,* and *Mosaic.*

DANIEL GEROULD has written plays (among others, *Candaules Commissioner,* produced by the Theatre Company of Boston, Stanford Repertory Theatre, Chelsea Theatre, and in France and Germany); translated several volumes of Witkiewicz as well as Gałczyński's *The Little Theatre of the Goose* and comedies by Olyesha and Aksyonov; and done articles on drama and theater (Shaw, Shakespeare, Chekhov). Recently completed are a new volume of Witkiewicz plays called *The Beelzebub Sonata* and a critical study of the Polish author's life and works. In progress is a book dealing with the revolt of the battleship *Potemkin* (including several plays about the mutiny) and a modern version of Monk Lewis's *The Castle Specter.*

MORTON GUREWITCH teaches English at State University of New York at Cortland and is the author of *Comedy: The Irrational Vision.* His essay on irony condenses certain themes that will be expanded in a book he is writing on the ironic imagination.

CYRUS HOY is John B. Trevor Professor of English at the University of Rochester, where he teaches courses in Shakespeare and non-dramatic Elizabethan literature. His study of comedy, tragedy, and tragicomedy titled *The Hyacinth Room* was published in 1964 by Knopf. He is one of the editors of the new Cambridge edition of the plays of Beaumont and Fletcher and is the author of "Comedy" in the *Encyclopaedia Britannica.* His commentary on the Cambridge edition of Thomas Dekker's *Dramatic Works* will be published in four volumes by the Cambridge University Press in 1978.

COPPÉLIA KAHN teaches English at Wesleyan University. She is currently engaged in a psychoanalytically oriented study of masculine identity in Shakespeare, parts of which have been published as articles. An avid snowshoer and Buxtehude fan, she is also the mother of an eight-year-old southpaw.

MALCOLM KINIRY is a Cape Codder who has spent his summers lobstering and looking for pickup basketball games. He is writing a book on comic aspects of the collaborated plays of Beaumont and Fletcher.

HERBERT J. LEVOWITZ is director of the Adolescent Psychiatric Day Hospital of the Long Island Jewish-Hillside Medical Center and Assistant Clinical Professor of Child Psychiatry of the Stony Brook Medical School of the State University of New York. He has a long-range interest in integrating the work of Piaget and Freud. For recreation, he attends international psychoanalytic conferences like the one described in *Fear of Flying* and gains intermittent ablution from water-skiing in New Hampshire.

JOHN J. O'CONNOR, who is Professor of English at Rutgers University, has published a book on *Amadis de Gaule* and its influence on Elizabethan literature as well as several articles on medieval and Renaissance themes. His current enthusiasm is for chivalric and pastoral romances of the sixteenth century.

ANNE PAOLUCCI is executive director of the Council on National Literatures and editor of *Review of National Literatures*. She has written extensively on ancient tragedy, Shakespeare, Dante, Machiavelli, contemporary theater of the "absurd," Pirandello, Hegel, aesthetics; she has translated works from Italian and French; and she has published poetry, fiction, and plays. Her one-act *Minions of the Race* won the drama award of the Medieval and Renaissance Conference (Western Michigan University) in 1972. She has been University Research Professor and is currently Professor of English at St. John's University.

NORMAN R. SHAPIRO is Professor of Romance Languages and Literatures at Wesleyan University. He is best known for his brilliant translations of Feydeau, especially the widely used *Four Farces of Georges Feydeau,* published by the University of Chicago Press. He is currently working on further translations of Feydeau, old French fables, and critical studies of Black French literature.

WILLIAM WALLING is Professor of English at University College, Rutgers University. Most recently, he has written on literature and art (for a collection of essays to be published under his name by Yale in 1978). He is now at work on a novel he hopes no one will find either parodic or especially comic.

DON WIENER, an alumnus of the Kenyon School of English (1950), began his career as a producer for WBKB in Chicago and is now a part-time Catskill beekeeper who remembers a different kind of buzzing.

MATHEW WINSTON teaches English and comparative literature at Columbia University and has published essays on comedy and Renaissance literature. He has recently returned from a two-year stint at the Freie Universität Berlin. His *New Concepts of Comedy* will be published by Methuen in 1979.

Bibliography

FIFTY TITLES ON COMEDY
by Maurice Charney

As an introductory reading list on comedy, I have selected a group of fifty titles that may prove useful to readers. These titles include books on the theory of comedy, jokes, laughter, irony, the fool, and on such major comic writers as Aristophanes, Plautus, Rabelais, Shakespeare, Jonson, and Molière. For a detailed account of psychological and psychoanalytic studies, see the bibliography in Goldstein and McGhee, *The Psychology of Humor.* There is also a running account of the literature on comedy in my book *Comedy High and Low.*

Bakhtin, Mikhail. *Rabelais and His World,* tr. Helene Iswolsky (Cambridge, Mass.: Massachusetts Institute of Technology, 1968).

Barber, C. L. *Shakespeare's Festive Comedy: A Study of Dramatic Form in Its Relation to Social Custom* (Princeton: Princeton University Press, 1959).

Barish, Jonas A. *Ben Jonson and the Language of Prose Comedy* (New York: Norton, 1970).

Bergson, Henri. *Laughter* (1900), in *Comedy,* ed. Wylie Sypher (Garden City, N.Y.: Doubleday, Anchor Press, 1956).

Berry, Ralph. *Shakespeare's Comedies: Explorations in Form* (Princeton: Princeton University Press, 1972).

Blistein, Elmer M. *Comedy in Action* (Durham, N.C.: Duke University Press, 1964).

Charney, Maurice. *Comedy High and Low: An Introduction to the Experience of Comedy* (New York: Oxford University Press, 1978).

Cook, Albert. *The Dark Voyage and the Golden Mean* (Cambridge, Mass.: Harvard University Press, 1949).

Cooper, Lane. *An Aristotelian Theory of Comedy* (New York: Kraus, 1969).

Cornford, Francis M. *The Origin of Attic Comedy* (Cambridge: Cambridge University Press, 1934).

Dobrée, Bonamy. *Restoration Comedy, 1660–1720* (London: Oxford University Press, 1966).

Donaldson, Ian. *The World Upside-Down: Comedy from Jonson to Fielding*

(Oxford: Clarendon Press, 1970).

Duchartre, Pierre Louis. *The Italian Comedy,* tr. Randolph T. Weaver (New York: Dover, 1966).

Duckworth, George. *The Nature of Roman Comedy: A Study in Popular Entertainment* (Princeton: Princeton University Press, 1952).

Durgnat, Raymond. *The Crazy Mirror: Hollywood Comedy and the American Image* (London: Faber & Faber, 1969).

Eastman, Max. *Enjoyment of Laughter* (New York: Simon & Schuster, 1936).

——. *The Sense of Humor* (New York: Scribner, 1922).

Esslin, Martin. *The Theatre of the Absurd* (Garden City, N.Y.: Doubleday, Anchor Press, 1961).

Freud, Sigmund. *Jokes and Their Relation to the Unconscious* (1905), tr. James Strachey (New York: Norton, 1960).

Frye, Northrop. *Anatomy of Criticism* (Princeton: Princeton University Press, 1957).

Fujimura, Thomas H. *The Restoration Comedy of Wit* (Princeton: Princeton University Press, 1952).

Goldstein, Jeffrey H., and McGhee, Paul E., eds., *The Psychology of Humor: Theoretical Perspectives and Empirical Issues* (New York: Academic Press, 1972).

Gregory, J. C. *The Nature of Laughter* (London: Kegan Paul, 1924).

Greig, J. Y. T. *The Psychology of Laughter and Comedy* (New York: Dodd Mead, 1923).

Grotjahn, Martin. *Beyond Laughter* (New York: McGraw-Hill, 1957).

Gurewitch, Morton. *Comedy: The Irrational Vision* (Ithaca, N.Y.: Cornell University Press, 1975).

Hoy, Cyrus. *The Hyacinth Room* (New York: Knopf, 1964).

Hubert, Judd D. *Molière and the Comedy of Intellect* (Berkeley: University of California Press, 1962).

Huizinga, Johan. *Homo Ludens: A Study of the Play-Element in Culture* (Boston: Beacon Press, 1955).

Kernan, Alvin. *The Cankered Muse* (New Haven: Yale University Press, 1959).

Kerr, Walter. *Tragedy and Comedy* (New York: Simon & Schuster, 1967).

Legman, Gershon. *Rationale of the Dirty Joke: An Analysis of Sexual Humor, First Series* (New York: Grove Press, 1971). Second Series published as *No Laughing Matter* (New York: Bell, 1975).

Levin, Harry, ed. *Veins of Humor* (Cambridge, Mass.: Harvard University Press, 1972).

Levine, Jacob, ed. *Motivation in Humor* (New York: Atherton Press, 1969).

Lynch, Kathleen M. *The Social Mode of Restoration Comedy* (New York: Octagon Books, 1965).

Mast, Gerald. *The Comic Mind: Comedy and the Movies* (Indianapolis, Ind.: Bobbs-Merrill, 1973).

Montgomery, John. *Comedy Films 1894-1954,* 2 ed. (London: Allen & Unwin, 1968).

Moore, W. G. *Molière: A New Criticism* (Oxford: Clarendon Press, 1969).

Olson, Elder. *The Theory of Comedy* (Bloomington, Ind.: Indiana University Press, 1968).

Palmer, John. *Comedy* (London: Secker, 1914).

Piddington, Ralph. *The Psychology of Laughter: A Study in Social Adaptation* (New York: Gamut Press, 1963).

Salingar, Leo. *Shakespeare and the Traditions of Comedy* (Cambridge: Cambridge University Press, 1976).

Sedgewick, G. G. *Of Irony, Especially in Drama* (Toronto: University of Toronto Press, 1934).

Segal, Erich. *Roman Laughter: The Comedy of Plautus* (Cambridge, Mass.: Harvard University Press, 1968).

Thompson, Alan Reynolds. *The Dry Mock: A Study of Irony in Drama* (Berkeley: University of California Press, 1948).

Welsford, Enid. *The Fool* (Garden City, N.Y.: Doubleday, Anchor Press, 1961).

Whitman, Cedric. *Aristophanes and the Comic Hero* (Cambridge, Mass.: Harvard University Press, 1964).

Willeford, William. *The Fool and His Scepter: A Study in Clowns and Jesters and Their Audience* (Evanston, Ill.: Northwestern University Press, 1969).

Wolfenstein, Martha. *Children's Humor: A Psychological Analysis* (Glencoe, Ill.: Free Press, 1954).

Worcester, David. *The Art of Satire* (Cambridge, Mass.: Harvard University Press, 1940).

Index

Editorial and Graphic Services

Comedy High and Low

An Introduction to the Experience of Comedy

MAURICE CHARNEY, Rutgers University. In a lively and broad-ranging exploration of the nature of comedy, Maurice Charney poses a number of basic questions: "Why is something comic?" "What are the comic conventions?" "How does the author elicit laughter, and to what purpose?" *Comedy High and Low* bridges the gap between literature—especially stage comedy—and the popular comedy of jokes, graffiti, and grotesque daily happenings. It is richly illustrated with examples, from Aristophanes and Plautus through Shakespeare and Jonson, up to Dürrenmatt and Stoppard.

May 1978   200 pp.; 20 photos   paper $4.00

Price and publication date are subject to change.

OXFORD
UNIVERSITY
PRESS

1478
1978

Publishers of
Fine Books for
Five Centuries

200 Madison Avenue, New York, New York 10016

Menander to Marivaux: The History of a Comic Structure

E.J.H. Greene
An exuberant examination of comedies built round a three-tiered distribution of characters—the Old, the Young, and the Slaves or Servants—a structure first used by Menander in the 4th Century, B.C., and brought to its most precise formulation and brilliance in France between 1660 and 1760, especially in the comedies of Molière and Marivaux. Over 700 plays are considered and many of them critically examined both for their intrinsic dramatic merit and their adherence to the structure, which Dr. Greene has christened "F".
*208 pages, 9 x 6, illustrated chapter openings, notes, bibliography, list of plays considered, index.
Soft cover, $10.00.
ISBN 0-88864-018-8.*

The University of Alberta Press
Room 450   Athabasca Hall
Edmonton   Alberta   T6G 2E8
Canada

Vol. 1 COMEDY: NEW PERSPECTIVES, Maurice Charney, Editor

LC 77-18626   ISSN 0149-1040   ISBN 0-931196-00-0   336 pages   Spring 1978

$7.50 ☐

Vol. 2 INTERTEXTUALITY, Hanna Charney and Jeanine P. Plottel, Editors

LC 77-18628   ISSN 0149-1040   ISBN 0-931196-01-9   224 pages   Winter 1978

$7.50 ☐

Vols.
1 & 2   **$13.00** ☐

Vol. 3 ANDRÉ MALRAUX: METAMORPHOSIS AND IMAGINATION,
Françoise Dorenlot and Micheline Tison-Braun, Editors

LC 77-18629   ISSN 0149-1040   ISBN 0-931196-02-7 Spring 1979

$7.50 ☐

Vol. 4 THE OCCULT IN LANGUAGE AND LITERATURE, Hermine
Riffaterre, Editor

LC 77-18630   ISSN 0149-1040   ISBN 0-931196-03-5   Winter 1979

$7.50 ☐

Vols.
3 & 4   **$13.00** ☐

Each volume includes an Index and Bibliography and is Illustrated.

Above prices are for individual orders; libraries, $9.50 per volume; adoptions for courses, prices upon
request. Outside the United States, add $2.00 per volume except in Canada, add $1.00 only per volume.
Prices subject to change.

Enclosed please find check for $ _____ .

Send publication to _____

Name

_____

Address

_____

City   State   Zip